Taking a Common Concern Approach to Economic Inequality

World Trade Institute Advanced Studies

VOLUME 6

The titles published in this series are listed at *brill.com/wtia*

Taking a Common Concern Approach to Economic Inequality

Implications for (Cooperative) Sovereignty over Corporate Taxation

By

Alexander D. Beyleveld

BRILL
NIJHOFF

LEIDEN | BOSTON

Open access publication of this book has been made possible by the Swiss National Science Foundation.

The Library of Congress Cataloging-in-Publication Data is available online at https://catalog.loc.gov
LC record available at https://lccn.loc.gov/2021059523

Typeface for the Latin, Greek, and Cyrillic scripts: "Brill". See and download: brill.com/brill-typeface.

ISSN 2405-9331
ISBN 978-90-04-51174-3 (hardback)
ISBN 978-90-04-51175-0 (e-book)

This book is printed on acid-free paper and produced in a sustainable manner.

Contents

Acknowledgements

This book is a revised version of my PhD monograph of the same title. At the time that I submitted that monograph for evaluation, I wrote a note of acknowledgement, which, owing to its words applying with equal if not more force today, I repeat below with only slight modifications.

Economic inequality is easy to get engrossed in as a topic. There have been countless tangents and rabbit holes in getting to this point. There have been obsessive streaks, during which I wanted to think about little else. There have also been lengthy spells of procrastination and depression. For their endless patience and indulgences, therefore, during times that have been quite tumultuous (even before the onset of the COVID-19 pandemic), I would like to thank my family and my friends who have had to live with me during the completion of my PhD and this monograph. Above all, I owe an extraordinary debt to my wife Aisuluu and to my mother Juanita. Without their love, laughter and unwavering support I would be in all kinds of trouble.

I also owe my supervisors, Professors Michael Hahn and Thomas Cottier, a great big 'thank you'—I am especially indebted to Professor Cottier. I have written about a rather peculiar subject, I have taken numerous detours and I have missed deadlines—Professor Cottier has given me the necessary licence to pursue what I am interested in, he has encouraged my explorations and he has shown endless patience with me. For all of this I am truly grateful.

This monograph could also not have been completed without the tireless hours spent by my colleagues at the World Trade Institute (WTI) on providing me with their insights and support. To the Common Concern team and all my WTI colleagues, thank you. I am especially grateful to Zaker Ahmad and Iryna Bogdanova with whom I spent countless hours in the 'trenches': Zaker and Ira, thank you for keeping the caffeine and the good ideas flowing for all these years.

For its invaluable financial support and making my PhD studies possible, I would like to thank the Swiss State Secretariat for Economic Affairs. I would also like to thank Professor Tumai Murombo, former director of the Mandela Institute at the University of the Witwatersrand, for always being encouraging and supportive. Without SECO and Prof Murombo I would not be where I am today.

'I would also be remiss if I did not make two modifications to the original note of acknowledgements. First, to the team at Brill, and the editorial board of the World Trade Institute Advanced Studies series, I say thank you; thank you not only for making the publication of this work a possibility, but also for making it effortless. It really has been a pleasure working with you all. Secondly, I would like to extend my sincere gratitude to the Swiss National Science Foundation for providing the necessary funding to allow for this work to be published open access.'

ADB
Bishkek
7 January 2022

Figures

Abbreviations

BEPS	base erosion and profit shifting
BIT	bilateral investment treaty
CUP	Cambridge University Press
DTT	double taxation treaty
FDI	foreign direct investment
GATT	General Agreement on Tariffs and Trade
GVC	global value chain
HMA	hybrid mismatch arrangement
HUP	Harvard University Press
ICT	information and communication technology
ILC	International Law Commission
ILO	International Labour Organization
IMF	International Monetary Fund
NBER	National Bureau of Economic Research
OECD	Organisation for Economic Co-operation and Development
OUP	Oxford University Press
PUP	Princeton University Press
SDGs	Sustainable Development Goals
TPM	transfer pricing manipulation
UN	United Nations
UN Charter	Charter of the United Nations
UNGA	United Nations General Assembly
UNCED	United Nations Conference on Environment and Development
UNEP	United Nations Environment Programme
UNFCCC	United Nations Framework Convention on Climate Change
WID.world	World Inequality Database
WTID	World Top Incomes Database
WTO	World Trade Organization

Abbreviations

CHAPTER 1

General Introduction

> Wealth exists only for the benefit of mankind. It cannot be measured adequately in yards or in tons, nor as equivalent as so many ounces of gold; its true measure lies only in the contribution it makes to human well-being. Now, when bricks and sand and lime and wood are built up into a house, they constitute a greater aggregate of wealth than they did before; even though their aggregate volume is the same as before; and, if the house is overthrown by an earthquake, there is indeed no destruction of matter; but there is a real destruction of wealth, because the matter is distributed in a manner less conducive to human well-being. Similarly, when wealth is very unevenly distributed, some have more of it than they can turn to any very great account in promoting their own well-being; while many others lack the material conditions of a healthy, clean, vigorous and effective family life. That is to say the wealth is distributed in a manner less conducive to the well-being of mankind than it would be if the rich were somewhat less rich, and the poor were somewhat less poor; and real wealth would be greatly increased, even though there were no change in the aggregate of bricks and houses and clothes and other material things, if only it were possible to effect that change without danger to freedom and to social order.
>
> ALFRED MARSHALL (1842–1924), 'Fragments'[1]

Distributional concerns are as old as humankind itself. The 'recent' interest in the distribution of income and wealth that is frequently referred to in contemporary literature is but the next episode in a lengthy series, the origin of

1 See Alfred Marshall, 'Fragments' in A C Pigou (ed), *Memorials of Alfred Marshall* (MacMillan, London 1925) 366.

© ALEXANDER D. BEYLEVELD, 2022 | DOI:10.1163/9789004511750_002

which predates our own existence by millennia.[2] What makes the current episode interesting is the extent to which technology has evolved and the extent to which the globe is economically integrated compared to times past.[3] The contemporary state of economic globalization has prompted a range of questions that are largely novel in the history of thought; one of these is the extent to which the distribution of income and wealth *within* nations is, could and should be something that falls within the scope of *international* law. This monograph is an attempt at filling part of the apparent void in this area of scholarship.[4]

It should be noted, however, that little *empirical* interest, in the sense that we today understand the term, had been shown in distributional concerns within nations at the level of the individual as unit of measure prior to the Second World War, even within the economics profession;[5] this was primarily, it appears, due to methodological constraints with respect to data collection and processing.[6] It was only really in the 1950s with the work of Simon Kuznets that the distribution of income as between all the individuals within a nation began to receive proper empirical attention.[7] Kuznets came to the conclusion, essentially, based on a ground-breaking methodological approach

2 Plato, for instance, had already written with clear interest and in great depth about the distribution of income and wealth by the fourth century BCE. See, for example, Plato, *Laws, Volume I: Books 1–6* (William Heinemann, London 1926) 323–92.

3 The contemporary state of global economic integration is addressed in Chapter 3 of this monograph. See also Richard Baldwin, *The Great Convergence: Information Technology and the New Globalization* (HUP, Cambridge, MA 2016) for a simple yet compelling overview of the history of global economic integration.

4 Prior works have more frequently focused, directly or indirectly, on distributional concerns as *between* states. For a good recent example, see Oisin Suttle, *Distributive Justice and World Trade Law: A Political Theory of International Trade Regulation* (CUP, Cambridge 2018).

5 The study of income had previously been limited to its distribution between factors of production, such as capital and labour. On this point, Hugh Dalton noted in 1920 that 'most "theories of distribution" were almost wholly concerned with distribution as between "factors of production". Distribution as between persons, a problem of more direct and obvious interest, was either left out of the textbooks altogether, or treated so briefly, as to suggest that it raised no question, which could not be answered either by generalisations about the factors of production, or by plodding statistical investigations, which professors of economic theory were content to leave to lesser men'. See Hugh Dalton, *Some Aspects of the Inequality of Incomes in Modern Communities* (George Routledge & Sons, London 1920) vii.

6 For an overview of the historical development of the use of data in the measurement of the distribution of income, see Thomas Piketty, *Capital in the Twenty-First Century* (HUP, London 2014), translated by Arthur Goldhammer, 2–15.

7 See Simon Kuznets (assisted by Elizabeth Jenks), *Shares of Upper Income Groups in Income and Savings* (NBER, New York 1953) and Simon Kuznets, 'Economic Growth and Income Inequality' (1955) 45 *American Economic Review* 1. See also the discussion in Piketty (n 6) 11–6.

and what was very meticulous data work, that income would tend to become increasingly concentrated—income inequality would rise—as a society was developing, but that after a certain level of development had been reached it would become ever less concentrated with the passage of time—inequality of incomes would fall. Interest in the distribution of income within countries accordingly started to wane as it was not perceived to be much of a problem at the time: rising inequality of income was a necessary side-effect of economic development but would subside once a particular level of development had been reached, an implication being that there should simply be a focus on aggregate economic development without giving consideration to distributional matters which would take care of themselves in due course.[8]

During the late 1970s Anthony Atkinson and Allan Harrison developed a methodology similar to that of Kuznets, but in respect of the distribution of wealth.[9] The study of the distribution of income and wealth within nations now had a good methodological foundation from an empirical point of view, but distributional concerns such as these had been pushed to the fringes of the economics field.[10] Also by the late 1970s, income inequality had steadily been on the decline in virtually all of the wealthier nations (and quite likely in less wealthy nations as well) for many decades.[11] This would soon enough begin to change: as would the interest of economists in issues of distribution. As a general trend towards greater inequality of income within these same states began to take off between the late 1970s and early 1980s, the distribution of income—but not yet wealth—slowly started receiving attention.[12]

---

8 See Piketty (n 6) 13–5.

9 See Anthony B Atkinson and Allan J Harrison, *Distribution of Personal Wealth in Britain* (CUP, Cambridge 1978).

10 See Anthony B Atkinson, 'Bringing Income Distribution in From the Cold' (1997) 107 *Economic Journal* 297. See also Agnar Sandmo, 'The Principal Problem in Political Economy: Income Distribution in the History of Thought' in Anthony B Atkinson and François Bourguignon (eds), *Handbook of Income Distribution* (*Volume 2A*) (Elsevier, Amsterdam 2015) 4–5.

11 On the trends in the distribution of income see Chapter 2 of this monograph.

12 See also Henry Phelps Brown, *The Inequality of Pay* (OUP, Oxford 1979), particularly 1–10, where Phelps Brown explains why by that point—that is, by 1979—such an interest had developed in the subject of income distribution. One particularly interesting example of someone showing interest is the work of Jan Pen, who made use of an imaginary parade as a device to depict the distribution of income in a given society. Each person in a given society would be part of the parade, which would be made up of a line, with the people arranged from shortest to tallest. Instead of their actual height, however, Pen imagined what the parade would look like if each person's height was proportional to their income. Parade observers—themselves the height of the average person in the parade—see the members of the society pass by, starting with persons a mere few inches tall and

Full-scale interest, however, only manifested itself in the 1990s as the trend towards greater inequality of income continued on its path.[13]

In his 1996 address to the Royal Economic Society, Atkinson sought to 'highlight the way in which the subject of income distribution has in the past been marginalised', noting that '[f]or much of this century [that is, the twentieth century], it has been very much out in the cold'.[14] His address was accordingly titled 'Bringing Income Distribution in from the Cold'.[15] Whilst noting that '[t]here [were] signs that in the 1990s it [was] being welcomed back' he sought to use the address 'to give further impetus to the re-incorporation of income distribution into the main body of economic analysis'.[16] With the trend towards greater inequality of income continuing around the world since the 1990s, his call has certainly been heeded by a broad set of economists from a variety of institutional settings.[17]

It was only really with Thomas Piketty's *Capital in the Twenty-First Century*, however, that distribution of wealth, which had for many decades been treated as being a more or less fixed characteristic of an economy, was brought back into focus.[18] Importantly, he also brought into question—most obviously with his now famous or perhaps infamous r > g—the relationship between the distribution of income and the distribution of wealth.[19] An upshot of these

---

ending with a few persons hundreds of feet tall. See further Jan Pen, *The Distribution of Income: Facts, Theories, Policies* (Praeger, New York 1971).

13 On the trends in the distribution of income see Chapter 2 of this monograph.

14 Atkinson (n 10) 297.

15 Atkinson (n 10) 297.

16 Atkinson (n 10) 297.

17 Providing a comprehensive list of all the research is unnecessary—if not impracticable or impossible—for current purposes. A recent example of institutional economists tilting their research in a more distribution-oriented direction is that of the staff of the International Monetary Fund (IMF), particularly on the relationship between the distribution of income, economic growth and its sustainability over time. See, for example, Andrew G Berg and Jonathan D Ostry, 'Inequality and Unsustainable Growth: Two Sides of the Same Coin?' (2017) 65 *IMF Economic Review* 792; Francesco Grigoli and Adrian Robles, 'Inequality Overhang' (IMF Working Paper WP/17/76, 28 March 2017).

18 See Piketty (n 6) 216–22.

19 Piketty's r > g stands for the proposition that when 'r'—the rate of return on capital (as defined by Piketty)—exceeds 'g'—the growth rate of an economy—capital becomes relatively more important within that economy vis-à-vis other factors. Since wealth has historically tended to be more unequally distributed than income, it therefore follows that when r > g, and capital is accordingly becoming more important, the distribution of income will become more unequal. See further Piketty (n 6) 336–76. Piketty's r > g has of course been subject to a substantial amount of criticism. For a quick review of these critiques, see Marshall Steinbaum, 'Why Are Economists Giving Piketty the Cold Shoulder?' (*Boston Review (online)*, 12 May 2017) <https://bostonreview.net/class-inequality/marshall-steinbaum-why-are-economists-giving-piketty-cold-shoulder> accessed 30

developments is that to date there has been a much broader effort to collect and analyse data pertaining to the distribution of income and wealth in a systematic fashion for a large number of countries around the globe.[20]

Partially as a result there has been greatly increased academic attention—across a wide range of disciplines—to issues related to economic distributions. Scholars across these various disciplines have begun to more precisely identify the consequences—most of which are seen as harmful—that follow as a result of observable changes in the various distributions of income and wealth around the world. The list of areas where the distribution of income and/or wealth conceivably play a causal role has become increasingly lengthy: climate change,[21] civil war,[22] crime,[23] population health,[24] economic growth and its effect of poverty reduction,[25] intergenerational mobility,[26] societal cooperation, collective action and public goods provisioning,[27] and financial crises make up what is a truncated list of these areas.[28]

September 2021. As Steinbaum points out, scholars appear largely to have ignored this part of Piketty's work.

20 See further Chapter 2 of this monograph.

21 See, for example, Nicole Grunewald et al, 'The Trade-off between Income Inequality and Carbon Dioxide Emissions' (2017) 142 *Ecological Economics* 249 and Andrew K Jorgenson et al, 'Domestic Inequality and Carbon Emissions in Comparative Perspective' (2016) 31 *Sociological Forum* 770.

22 See, for example, Lars-Erik Cederman, Nils B Weidmann and Nils-Christian Bormann, 'Triangulating horizontal inequality: Toward improved conflict analysis' (2015) 52 *Journal of Peace Research* 806 and Gudrun Østby, 'Polarization, Horizontal Inequalities and Violent Civil Conflict' (2008) 45 *Journal of Peace Research* 123.

23 See, for example, Pablo Fajnzyber, Daniel Lederman and Norman Loayza, 'Inequality and Violent Crime' (2002) 45 *Journal of Law and Economics* 1 and Neil Metz and Mariya Burdina, 'Neighbourhood income inequality and property crime' (2018) 55 *Urban Studies* 130.

24 See, for example, Angus Deaton 'Health, Inequality, and Economic Development' (2003) 41 *Journal of Economic Literature* 113 and Kate E Pickett and Richard G Wilkinson, 'Income Inequality and Health: A Causal Review' (2015) 128 *Social Science & Medicine* 316.

25 See generally, for example, Research Department, Agence Française de Développement, (ed) *Poverty, Inequality and Growth: Proceedings of the AFD-EUDN Conference*, 2003 (Maggelan & Cie, Paris 2004) and Giovanni Andrea Cornia (ed) *Inequality, Growth, and Poverty in an Era of Liberalization and Globalization* (OUP, Oxford 2004).

26 See, for example, Raj Chetty et al, 'The Fading American Dream: Trends in Absolute Income Mobility since 1940' (2017) 356 *Science* 398 and Miles Corak, 'Income Inequality, Equality of Opportunity, and Intergenerational Mobility' (2013) 27 *Journal of Economic Perspectives* 79.

27 See, for example, Lisa R Anderson, Jennifer M Mellor and Jeffrey Milyo, 'Inequality and Public Good Provision: An Experimental Analysis' (2008) 37 *The Journal of Socio-Economics* 1010 and Stephen Mark Rosenbaum et al, 'Income Inequality and Cooperative Propensities in Developing Economies: Summarizing the Preliminary Experimental Evidence' (2016) 43 *International Journal of Social Economics* 1460.

28 On financial crises, see for example Michael D Bordo and Christopher M Meissner, 'Does Inequality Lead to a Financial Crisis?' (2012) 31 *Journal of International Money and Finance* 2147 and Raghuram Rajan, *Fault Lines* (PUP, Princeton 2010).

These consequences have led to an increasing amount of concern being expressed beyond the academic world about rising concentration of income and wealth within states: by globally well-known figures, such as Pope Francis and Bill Gates for example,[29] who have expressed their concerns on issues of economic distributions; but also increasingly from more overtly political figures, some of whom have increasingly been referring to some of the actual consequences—as opposed to appealing purely to a certain brand of justice or morality—that accompany the rising inequality of economic distributions.[30] These concerns about the consequences of changing economic distributions are also reflected in policy goals at various levels of governance: as part of the Sustainable Development Goals (SDGs), for example, the international community has set itself the target of 'progressively [achieving] … and [sustaining] … income growth of the bottom 40 percent of the population at a rate higher than the national average' by 2030.[31]

The distribution of income and wealth within nations, however, has largely escaped the attention of lawyers, especially *international* lawyers;[32] this despite the fact that many of the areas listed above that are affected by the distribution of income or wealth within states—such as climate change and its effects, for example—are also issues that are dealt with explicitly and as matters of urgency by international law. This fact is easily understood when viewed through the lens of particular (mis)understandings of state sovereignty: the distribution of income and wealth within a state would appear to be a matter for that state to address at the national level without external interference from other states.[33] It is accordingly quite difficult, at least at first blush, to see how or why changing economic distributions *within* states

29 See, for example, Pope Francis, *The Joy of the Gospel:* Evangelii Gaudiuum (Veritas Publications, Dublin 2013) 35–9 and Bill Gates, 'Why Inequality Matters' (13 October 2014) <https://www.gatesnotes.com/Books/Why-Inequality-Matters-Capital-in-21st-Century-Review> accessed 30 September 2021.

30 The most commonly cited example, it would appear, is that of a speech made by then President of the United States Barack Obama, wherein he decried the practical economic consequences of rising economic inequality and reduced mobility. See Barack Obama, 'Remarks at the Town Hall Education Arts Recreation Campus' (speech delivered by Barack Obama on 4 December 2013) <http://www.presidency.ucsb.edu/ws/index.php?pid=104522&st=&st1=> accessed 30 September 2021.

31 United Nations General Assembly Resolution A/RES/70/1 (21 October 2015) with the title 'Transforming our World: the 2030 Agenda for Sustainable Development'.

32 There are, of course, some notable exceptions to this general state of affairs. A good example is the work of Greg Shaffer. See, for example, Gregory Shaffer, 'Retooling Trade Agreements for Social Inclusion' (2019) 1 *Illinois Law Review* 1.

33 See further Chapter 3 of this monograph.

should be considered as potential candidates for forming part of the law *between* nations.[34]

The continued trend towards greater inequality of income and wealth within states, however, starts to beg the question: why is it that such a large number of states—many of whom care a great as deal about distributional matters—are experiencing the same distributional changes despite the numerous deleterious consequences of such changes? One plausible explanation is that the traditional mechanisms that kept distributions within states more equal in the past are no longer effective; this applies to distributions before and after taxation and transfers are accounted for. The justifications for this explanation pertain in large part to the nature, pace and scale of technological and economic change in the contemporary world economy: distributional 'shocks' that occur today are different in nature, far larger than in past times and they occur far more quickly since the advent of the so-called Information Age.[35]

One of the motivations for this monograph is therefore a question about the extent to which the realities of contemporary economic globalization have made it challenging for states acting on their own to halt the near-global trend towards greater inequality of income and wealth within states.[36] As an answer to this question, it will be argued that in order for states to succeed in this endeavour certain forms of international cooperation are necessary. Portions of the chapters that follow seek to justify this central premise, which—if

34 It is worth noting that there exists a lengthy tradition of nations seeking to reduce inequality of incomes and wealth *between* states and that the goals associated with such movements have sometimes been read as implying that there should be less economic inequality within states. For example, as Giorgio Sacerdoti explains about the New International Economic Order (NIEO) movement, there existed a push in the 1970s towards 'participatory equality of developing countries in international economic relations, *and the broadest cooperation of all States so that the prevailing disparities in the world be banished*' (see Giorgio Sacerdoti, 'New International Economic Order (NIEO)' in *Max Planck Encyclopaedia of International Law* (OUP online, September 2015, emphasis added). Similarly, the Millennium Development Goals (MDGs), although being less explicit than the SDGs on distributional issues, can be read as implying that internal distributions should be more equitable. For an overview of the MDGs, see Gunter Pleuger 'United Nations, Millennium Declaration' in *Max Planck Encyclopaedia of International Law* (OUP online, March 2007). See also Thomas Cottier, *Equitable Principles of Maritime Boundary Delimitation* (CUP, Cambridge 2015) 21–8 for an overview of these developments from the perspective of distributive justice. See also Thomas Cottier, 'Equity in International Law' in Thomas Cottier, Shaheeza Lalani and Clarence Siziba, *Intergenerational Equity: Environmental and Cultural Concerns* (Brill | Nijhoff, Leiden 2019).

35 On this point, see Chapter 3 of this monograph.

36 Again, see Chapter 2 of this monograph on the development of these trends over time.

accepted—potentially necessitates a new conceptualisation of certain concepts and areas of international law such that they can play their proper role in connection to the distribution of income and wealth within states.

The first area in which new concepts are necessary is that of sovereignty. The concept is accordingly interrogated throughout this monograph, with the view taken that sovereignty entails both positive and normative components, all of which need redefinition given the contemporary state of technological change and economic globalization. In this regard the base concept of sovereignty proposed for adoption in this monograph is that of 'cooperative sovereignty',[37] acceptance of which it will be argued should result in enhancing the capability of states to address distributional concerns—both positive and normative—within their own territories. One way in which this can be achieved is through recognising the changes in the distribution of income and wealth within states and the adverse effects that stem from such changes as a 'common concern of humankind'.[38]

The common concern of humankind concept is currently applied in the fields of climate change and biodiversity.[39] The recognition of a common concern of humankind implies that a particular issue cannot be addressed by individual states in isolation; one of its central implications being that international cooperation is required to solve certain global problems. One of the core arguments of this contribution is that the common concern of humankind concept should essentially be employed in pursuit of redefining sovereignty

---

37 I use the term as it has been described by Samantha Besson and applied by others such as Claus Zimmermann. See Samantha Besson, 'Sovereignty in Conflict' (2004) 8 *European Integration online Papers (EIoP)* 1, 7 and Claus D Zimmermann, *A Contemporary Concept of Monetary Sovereignty* (OUP, Oxford 2013).

38 I readily accept that there are various other ways in which one might approach this task and it is quite possible that this might not be the best out of all the available options. For the reasons given later in this monograph, however, contemplation of the recognition of what will often be referred to as a 'distributional common concern'—that is, recognition of the changing distribution of income and wealth within states and the adverse effects associated therewith as a common concern of humankind—could, in conjunction with other steps, be a good start.

39 Some authors argue that it is also applied, at least in kind, in other fields such as natural and cultural heritage. See, for example, Thomas Cottier, 'The Principles of Common Concern of Humankind' in Thomas Cottier (ed), *The Prospects of Common Concern of Humankind in International Law* (CUP, Cambridge 2021) and Jutta Brunnée, 'Common Areas, Common Heritage, and Common Concern' in Daniel Bodansky, Jutta Brunnée and Ellen Hey (eds), *The Oxford Handbook of International Environmental Law* (OUP, New York 2007) 565. See also the discussion in Chapter 3 of this monograph where some of the other arguments in favour of common concerns of humankind existing in particular fields are reviewed.

in such a way that problems that are of common and imminent concern to humankind, or a substantial portion thereof, are rendered capable of being solved as a matter of urgency. Seen this way, the common concern of humankind concept could act as a helpful basis for the formation of more concrete international rules relating to the distribution of income and wealth within states. This would essentially entail placing certain well-defined limits on unilateral action—including particular types of inaction—taken by states in respect of economic policy goals but which result in the imposition of distributional externalities on other states.

While arguing for the recognition of a new common concern of humankind, the causal drivers of changing distributions of income and wealth will be explored; what will be made clear through these discussions, amongst other things, is that there are a vast number of causes of changing economic distributions. Many of these are tied to existing international legal regimes, for example to existing international rules on foreign investment and the law of international taxation. The point of recognising a new common concern of humankind, at least in part, would be for it to serve as a mechanism that ties different legal regimes that have an impact on the same factual issue—that of the distribution of income and wealth within states—together. At the very least, the interactions between these regimes should be properly considered in order to give proper effect to the recognition of a distributional common concern.

Simultaneously, the recognition of a distributional common concern of humankind would imply reorienting existing international rules that affect the distribution of income and wealth within states and should lead to the creation of new ones where necessary in order to solve the problem captured by such recognition.

Dealing with each and every causal driver of distributional change within states, however, is well beyond the scope of this work.[40] Having made the general case for the recognition of a new common concern of humankind, then, select causes will be identified and examined in greater depth. These relate predominantly to the 'de-nationalization' of production made possible through technological advances in the form of information and communication technology (ICT), the concomitant rise of the global-value-chain (GVC), the effects of ever-increasing capital mobility and the process of transmutation

40 This is in part because there are a large number of these that can be appropriately addressed without recourse to international cooperation and in part to ensure that the causal drivers that are taken up might be discussed in sufficient detail in order to make the overarching points this monograph seeks to make.

undergone by multinational enterprises (multinationals), the main actor involved in taking advantage of ICT, GVCs and mobile capital. Multinationals by definition pose problems for traditional conceptions of sovereignty—and can by definition only be subjected to consistent laws in the event that states cooperate with one another—but are simultaneously important, yet underexplored, actors affecting the distribution of income and wealth within states. In this monograph, their role in this regard is explored—through the lens of the corporate responsibility of multinationals, broadly construed—in the context of the international legal regime pertaining to taxation.

In light of the above, the remainder of this monograph is structured as follows. Chapter 2 serves predominantly as a factual primer on the distribution of income and wealth within states, how these distributions have changed over the course of time and some of the effects these changes bring about. The principal aim of this chapter is to provide definitional clarity with respects to the various distributional concepts referred to throughout this monograph and to foster a common understanding of the myriad different effects associated with changes in the distribution of income and wealth over time. This chapter should act as a base factual foundation for the chapters that follow, which is where the causes—a more controversial topic than the effects themselves—of the various types of distributional change are discussed.

In Chapter 3, the changes in the distribution of income and wealth within states and the effects that follow as a consequence of these changes are contemplated as a potential common concern of humankind. This assessment first entails examining what is different about contemporary technological change and economic globalization and what this implies for sovereignty, particularly as it relates to the distribution of income and wealth amongst the people within those states.

Next, the common concern of humankind concept is introduced, and a particular understanding of the concept is posited with a particular focus on when and how common concerns of humankind are recognised in international law and what the legal implications of such recognition might be. Finally, the two prior discussions are brought together in order to contemplate whether a new common concern of humankind could be recognised.

Chapter 4 turns to contemplating the recognition of a distributional common concern as described in Chapter 3 in the realm of international corporate taxation as it applies to multinational enterprises. Before getting to this, however, it first attempts to thoroughly lay the necessary groundwork for having a proper discussion on this topic. It thus begins by discussing the extent to which multinationals drive the distribution of income and wealth within countries with a view to more generally situating the role of multinationals in causing—and, indeed, solving—problems of a global nature. More specifically, it explores the problematic issue of *responsibility* for solving the problems that sit as the heart of the various common concerns of humankind, including the distributional common concern described in Chapter 3.

This discussion, starts from the premise that it is states—and not multinationals or other actors—that are ultimately responsible, at least *most directly*, for taking steps to overcome common concerns of humankind. Given that multinationals are the institutional actors that *contribute most directly* to the problems animating common concerns it is implicit that an *effective* Doctrine of Common Concern of Humankind must necessarily entail an understanding of how state responsibility is parsed into helpful actions—whether proactive or reactive—on the part of multinationals. A 'responsibility-action' framework for thinking about this process is thus devised and applied in the context of the distributional common concern.

Next, the chapter looks at the issue of taxing multinationals in a time of record high profits and during which multinationals avoid taxes at unprecedented rates. It then argues for a more cooperative understanding of tax sovereignty and applies the 'responsibility-action' framework devised earlier in the chapter in order to illustrate *how* common concerns of humankind should be recognised in order for the concept to be useful. In essence, states must not merely recognise common concerns without acting appropriately and states must likewise not act decisively in respect of matters that are not directly related to the common concern at issue. The chapter ends with some thoughts on the potential implications and utility of recognising a distributional common concern in the area of international corporate taxation.

The monograph wraps up with Chapter 5, which provides concluding remarks and some ideas on possible future research directions.

CHAPTER 2

The Distribution of Income and Wealth within States Since the Beginning of the Twentieth Century

Changes and Effects

> [M]uch of the world has entered what could become the next long stretch—a return to persistent capital accumulation and income concentration. If history is anything to go by, peaceful policy reform may well prove unequal to the growing challenges ahead. But what of the alternatives? All of us who prize greater economic equality would do well to remember that with the rarest exceptions, it was only ever brought forth in sorrow. Be careful what you wish for.
>
> WALTER SCHEIDEL, *The Great Leveler*[1]

1 Introduction

Issues pertaining to the distribution of economic resources are currently hotly debated, although this has probably been the case for most of human history. Nothing new to see here. What is fairly new, however, is the precision with which we represent economic distributions and accordingly so is the manner in and precision with which we study the empirical effects of changing economic distributions over time. In a 1971 article, Lester Thurow posed the following question: 'What are the empirical effects of the income distribution on crime, social stability, political stability, or any other characteristic of society?'[2] His answer acknowledged what appears then to have been the reality: '[p]erhaps

1 Walter Scheidel, *The Great Leveler: Violence and the History of Inequality from the Stone Age to the Twenty-First Century* (PUP, Princeton 2017) 444.

2 Lester C Thurow, 'The Income Distribution as a Pure Public Good' (1971) 85 *Quarterly Journal of Economics* 327, 335–6.

 | DOI:10.1163/9789004511750_003

the impact is significant; perhaps it is insignificant', acknowledging that at that time '[w]e [just did] not know'.[3]

At the time that Thurow wrote his article, the reason for his conclusion was essentially that there were a paucity of data. Better data would be needed in order for these topics to be studied systematically. As a greater amount of data became available—were collected, often by tireless scholars—the empirical effects stemming from the distribution of income and wealth began to be investigated systematically; today, studies abound. Historians, sociologists, medical doctors, psychologists, economists, biologists, anthropologists and climatologists, amongst many others, use recently constructed datasets on economic distributions to study the effects of distributional changes over time.

While there are still many unanswered questions, it is no longer the case that 'we just do not know' what the empirical effects are. The primary aim of this chapter is to illustrate this through providing a sense of how the distribution of income and wealth has changed within different countries around the globe since the beginning of the twentieth century and by reviewing a subset of the literature on the empirical effects of these changes. The idea is not to be exhaustive or even to give a complete summary of what has become an extremely vast literature but rather to set the scene in anticipation of the discussions in the following chapters, the main purpose of which is to examine whether the distribution of income and wealth within states and the adverse effects that stem therefrom could be deemed a common concern of humankind from the viewpoint of international law, what this would imply and why it might be useful.

In this regard, the work done by this chapter pertains predominantly to what 'distributions of income and wealth' are, how they have changed—particularly over the last four decades—and what effects such changes have produced and may produce in the future. On the idea of 'effects', it should be emphasised that the point of this chapter is not to judge whether they are 'bad' or 'good': this issue is taken up in the next chapters.

The primary motivation of this chapter is a task most lawyers are faced with at some point—attempting to establish a shared understanding of certain facts. To the extent possible, then, this chapter will essentially consist of a string of statements such as 'the distribution of income has changed in G way and accordingly H has happened' or 'the distribution of wealth is changing in Q way and therefore we can be fairly sure that U will happen' without labelling

3 Thurow (n 2) 336.

'G', 'Q', 'H' or 'U' in terms of any value system. The aim is to refrain from judgement to the extent possible.

The chapter is accordingly structured into two parts. First, a concise and fairly representative illustration of how the distribution of income and wealth within the countries of the world has changed since the start of the twentieth century is provided (*Part I*). The latter part of the chapter examines some of the empirical effects that have resulted as the changes described in Part I have occurred, with a particular focus on some of the types of effects deemed broadly relevant for the discussions in the chapters that follow (*Part II*).

2 Changes to the Distribution of Income and Wealth within States Since 1900

Prior to describing the actual changes, definitions are warranted. What is 'income'? What is 'wealth'? Amongst *whom* are they distributed? All adults? All people? Different racial groups? Different people within a given racial group? Sexes? Genders? Religions? Moreover, given a set of definitions, questions remain about methodology: how are distributions measured? Questions of a definitional or methodological nature are addressed first in this part of the chapter (*Section 2.1*). With this out of the way, a *snapshot*—more is beyond the scope of this monograph—of the distributional changes within states since the early twentieth century is provided (*Section 2.2*).

2.1 *Definitions and Methodologies*

2.1.1 Definitions

'Income' may be defined as '[t]hat which comes in as the periodical produce of one's work, business, lands, or investments (considered in reference to its amount, and commonly expressed in terms of money); annual or periodical receipts accruing to a person or corporation; revenue'.[4] For the purposes of this monograph, income generally refers to an annual amount of money accruing to a person or other unit of measurement, such as a tax unit or a family. It may from time to time be qualified by certain modifiers. For the most part, these

4 See 'income, *n.1*' in John Simpson (ed), 'Oxford English Dictionary Online' (OUP online version) <http://www.oed.com.innopac.wits.ac.za/view/Entry/93645?rskey=w233Ga&result=1&isAdvanced=false#eid> accessed 30 September 2021.

are used here to reflect the definitions used by the *World Inequality Database* (*WID.world*).[5]

'Fiscal income', as used by *WID.world*, refers to an individual's 'total income that is or should be reported on income tax declarations'.[6] The term 'fiscal income' is broader than the term 'taxable income'. Fiscal income refers to income before any deductions allowed for under a country's fiscal laws are taken into account.

'Pre-tax income' refers to all income flows accruing to the individual owners of the production factors before taking into account the operation of a country's tax and/or transfer system, but after taking into account the operation of its pension system.[7]

'Pre-tax factor income' or 'factor income' refers to the same income as pre-tax income but before taking into account the operation of a particular country's pension system.[8]

'Post-tax disposable income' refers to pre-tax income less all taxes on production, income and wealth, plus social assistance benefits afforded by the particular country in question in a cash amount.[9]

As for 'post-tax income', 'social transfers in kind' are added.[10] This includes transfers at the individual level such as education and healthcare spending, as well as 'collective consumption expenditure' which includes things that are consumed collectively (public goods broadly speaking) such as national defence.[11]

'Wealth' is a more contested term than 'income'. In its economics sense, 'wealth' as a term has resulted in 'much controversy among economists as to the precise extent of meaning in which the term should be used'.[12] The Oxford English Dictionary asserts that '[t]he definition that has been most widely accepted is that of Mill', who asserted that '[m]oney, being the instrument of an important public and private purpose, is rightly regarded as wealth; but everything else

5 See Facundo Alvaredo et al, 'Distributional National Accounts Guidelines: Methods and Concepts Used in WID.world' (*WID.world* methodological document published on its website, 7 September 2020) <https://wid.world/document/distributional-national-accounts-guidelines-2020-concepts-and-methods-used-in-the-world-inequality-database/> accessed 30 September 2021.

6 Alvaredo et al (n 5) 35.

7 See generally Alvaredo et al (n 5) 35–68.

8 See generally Alvaredo et al (n 5) 35–68.

9 See generally Alvaredo et al (n 5) 35–68.

10 See generally Alvaredo et al (n 5) 35–68.

11 See generally Alvaredo et al (n 5) 35–68.

12 See 'wealth, *n*'. in John Simpson (ed), 'Oxford English Dictionary Online' (OUP online version) <http://0-www.oed.com.innopac.wits.ac.za/view/Entry/226575?redirectedFrom=wealth#eid> accessed 30 September 2021.

which serves any human purpose, and which nature does not afford gratuitously, is wealth also'.[13] As a result, the economics entry in the Dictionary explains 'wealth' as being '[a] collective term for those things the abundant possession of which (by a person or a community) constitutes riches, or "wealth" in the popular sense'.[14] In an ordinary, non-specialised sense the Dictionary contains the following entry: 'Prosperity consisting in abundance of possessions; "worldly goods", valuable possessions, esp. in great abundance: riches, affluence'.[15]

From the above definitions, it is easy to see how a best definition of 'wealth' is something difficult to define in anything resembling an objective sense. Many thousands of arguments have been made over the course of time pertaining to how 'wealth' *should* be defined.[16] These are not of much relevance here. For current purposes, 'wealth' is, as with 'income', simply defined to reflect the definitions used by *WID.world*. 'Wealth' therefore essentially amounts to the 'assets' less the 'liabilities' of its holder.[17] 'Assets' can be further divided into 'housing', 'business' and 'financial'.[18] As with income, *WID.world* employs certain modifiers when it comes to wealth. For example, 'personal wealth' refers to the wealth held by the household sector, whereas 'private wealth' is the sum of 'personal wealth' and 'non-profit' wealth'.[19] Thus far, the database consists largely of data

---

13 See Simpson (n 12).

14 See Simpson (n 12).

15 See Simpson (n 12).

16 A fairly recent example of a debate on this point comes from the late 1970s and early 1980s. In 1979, a Richard Posner article was published in *The Journal of Legal Studies* (see Richard A Posner, 'Utilitarianism, Economics, and Legal Theory' (1979) 8 *Journal of Legal Studies* 103). In this Article, Posner laid out his theory that the purpose of law, essentially, was to maximize wealth. This theory was met by criticism based on, amongst other things—both explicitly and implicitly—what it is that is meant by the term 'wealth'. Some of these criticisms were published in the same journal in 1980 alongside Posner's response to them (see Ronald M Dworkin, 'Is Wealth a Value?' (1980) 9 *Journal of Legal Studies* 119; Anthony T Kronman, 'Wealth Maximization as a Normative Principle' (1980) 9 *Journal of Legal Studies* 227; Richard A Posner, 'The Value of Wealth: A Comment on Dworkin and Kronman' (1980) 9 *Journal of Legal Studies* 243). Another set of articles on the topic were published in the *Hofstra Law Review* in the same year, again alongside an article by Posner (see Richard A Posner, 'The Ethical and Political Basis of the Efficiency Norm in Common Law Adjudication' (1980) 8 *Hofstra Law Review* 487; Ronald M Dworkin, 'Why Efficiency?' (1980) 8 *Hofstra Law Review* 563; Jules L Coleman, 'Efficiency, Utility and Wealth Maximization' (1980) 8 *Hofstra Law Review* 509; Guido Calabresi, 'About Law and Economics: A Letter to Ronald Dworkin' (1980) 8 *Hofstra Law Review* 553; and Mario J Rizzo, 'The Mirage of Efficiency' (1980) 8 *Hofstra Law Review* 641). Many additional articles have also been written since 1980 on this exact debate (see, for example, D Bruce Johnson, 'Wealth is Value' (1986) 15 *Journal of Legal Studies* 263).

17 See generally Alvaredo et al (n 5) 69–82.

18 See generally Alvaredo et al (n 5) 69–82.

19 See generally Alvaredo et al (n 5) 69–82.

pertaining to personal wealth and for this reason the term 'wealth' as used in this monograph generally refers to personal wealth unless otherwise stated.

The phrases 'distribution of income' and 'distribution of wealth' raise an additional question: amongst whom is the income or wealth in question distributed? The aim of *WID.world* has thus far generally been to be able to describe the distribution of income and wealth between all adult individuals where an adult individual is any individual that is 20 years old or older.[20] This kind of general snapshot of the distribution of income and wealth within states around the world is for the most part sufficient for the discussions in *this* monograph. For current purposes, then, references to the distribution of economic resources, whether income or wealth, refers to how these resources are distributed amongst adults within a given state unless otherwise specified. Additionally, it is generally assumed that income and wealth within a given tax unit is split equally amongst the adults in that tax unit.[21]

2.1.2 Methodologies

In the event that the above definitions are taken as given, many ways of measuring and representing income and wealth distributions remain. The most common way for some time now of representing distributions—an industry standard of sorts—has been to use the 'Gini coefficient' (sometimes represented as an index).[22] Sometimes the 'Theil index' is used;[23] on other occasions the 'Palma ratio'.[24] As for this monograph, distributions are generally

20 See Alvaredo et al (n 5) 21.

21 Some of the critiques of taking such a simple approach are examined below in this chapter.

22 The Gini coefficient measures how far a given distribution is from perfect equality of distribution. The result is a figure between 0 and 1, with 0 representing a perfectly equal numerical distribution and 1 representing a situation where one person has everything while all others have nothing. The Gini index is simply the coefficient represented as a percentage. The concept and how it is calculated finds its origins in Corrado Gini, *Variabilità e Mutabilità* (Tipografia di Cuppini, Bologna 1912). See also Lidia Ceriani and Paolo Verme, 'The origins of the Gini index: extracts from Variabilità e Mutabilità (1912) by Corrado Gini' (2012) 10 *Journal of Economic Inequality* 421 for an excellent summary of the key insights from Gini's original work (in English).

23 See further Henri Theil, *Economics and Information Theory* (North-Holland, Amsterdam 1967).

24 The Palma ratio starts from the supposedly empirical premise that the share of deciles five to nine in actual income distributions remains more or less fixed at 50%. The ratio accordingly compares the share of income of the top decile with that of the bottom four deciles as a way to represent how income or wealth is distributed. See José Gabriel Palma, 'Homogeneous Middles vs. Heterogeneous Tails, and the End of the "Inverted-U": It's All About the Share of the Rich' (2011) 42 *Development and Change* 87. See also José Gabriel Palma, 'Has the Income Share of the Middle and Upper-middle Been Stable around the

represented by the income or wealth shares of the following economically defined groups of the overall populace in a given state: the percentage of income received by the top 1 percent of recipients (T1), the top percent (T10), the 'middle' percent (M40) and the bottom 50 percent (B50).[25] This is the preferred methodology of *WID.world*.

Prior to the founding of *WID.world*, its authors together with dozens of other collaborators worked on the *World Top Incomes Database* (WTID), a repository created in January 2011 that pertained only to income distributions.[26] After the WTID had been developed quite extensively, it was subsumed into *WID.world* in 2015, *WID.world* having been created as a new version of WTID with a focus on income *and* wealth distributions.[27] Taking their lead from earlier work by Kuznets on income, as well as work done on wealth by Atkinson and Harrison, the authors of *WID.world* combine fiscal data, survey data and national accounts in a systematic way in order to achieve the aims of the database.[28]

To simplify, *WID.world* collects information related to the income and wealth of each person in a given country over time, mostly using data from tax returns. They then represent the data for each year that they have information for using the T1, T10, M40 and B50 metrics. So, if X country were to have a population of 100 adults, they would collect information on the income and wealth of each of these adults for a particular year. They would then rank the entire population in terms of income and wealth respectively. One adult could, and likely would, be assigned a different position in each of the two rankings. In this country, the person receiving the most income or wealth would constitute the entire T1 for the given economic concept. Therefore, if the entire income of X as a country in 2018 were 1000 units of X's currency and the highest income recipient received 190 out of 1000 then T1 would amount to 19 percent for 2018.

Similarly, if the entire wealth stock of X were 1 000 000 in 2018 and the person with the most wealth owned 300 000 out of that 1 000 000, then the T1 for wealth would be 30 percent. T10 for income in 2018 would be calculated

"50/50 Rule", or Has it Converged towards that Level? The "Palma Ratio" Revisited' (2014) 45 *Development and Change* 1416.

25 The M40 share refers to the cumulative share of the persons that sit above the B50 but below the T10.

26 Alvaredo et al (n 5) 11–3.

27 Alvaredo et al (n 5) 11–3.

28 See Simon Kuznets (assisted by Elizabeth Jenks), *Shares of Upper Income Groups in Income and Savings* (NBER, New York 1953); A B Atkinson and A J Harrison, *Distribution of Personal Wealth in Britain* (Cambridge University Press, New York 1978). The *WID.world* authors follow the same general methodology, extending Kuznets' thinking and applying it to far longer periods of time for many more countries. See Alvaredo et al (n 5) 13–4.

by summing the incomes of the 10 people ranked highest for income and dividing that number by 1 000, whereas T10 for wealth would be calculated by summing the wealth of the 10 people ranked highest for wealth and dividing that number by 1 000 000. For M40, the same process would be repeated using the incomes and wealth of the persons ranked 51–90 respectively. For B50, the same process would be repeated using the incomes and wealth of the persons ranked 1–50 respectively. This would make up the data points for one year, 2018, which could then be plotted on a graph with the data for as many years before 2018 for which data is available. This is essentially what *WID.world* does, which allows them to construct graphs that look something like Figure 1 below.

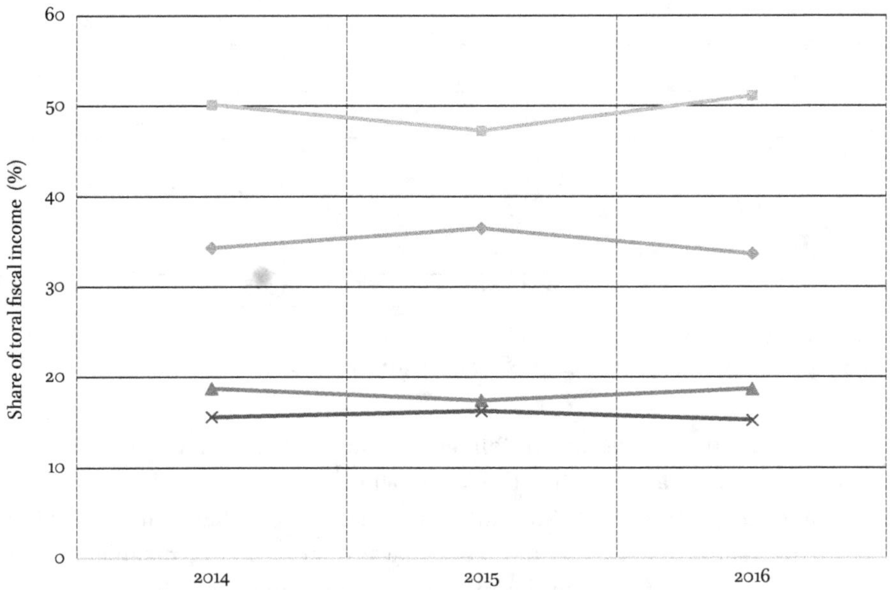

FIGURE 1 T1, T10, M40 and B50 income shares for Thailand, 2014–2016
FIGURE PRODUCED USING DATA FROM *WID.WORLD*

This is not a graph for the imagined country X, but rather a graph showing the T1, T10, M40 and B50 for fiscal income in Thailand for the years 2014, 2015 and 2016. For the most part, the T1 share in Thailand seems to hover a bit below the 20 percent line, which indicates that income accruing to the top 1 percent in Thailand in 2014 and 2016 was proportionally similar to that of the T1 in X in 2018. Note also that what is represented in the above graph is fiscal income, which is the amount of income declared on a Thai tax return before deciding how much of that income is, in fact, taxable. The various curves for the same period look slightly different when constructed for pre-tax—that is taxable—income. Figure 2 shows Thailand's T1 curve only for the same period, but illustrating both fiscal and pre-tax income:

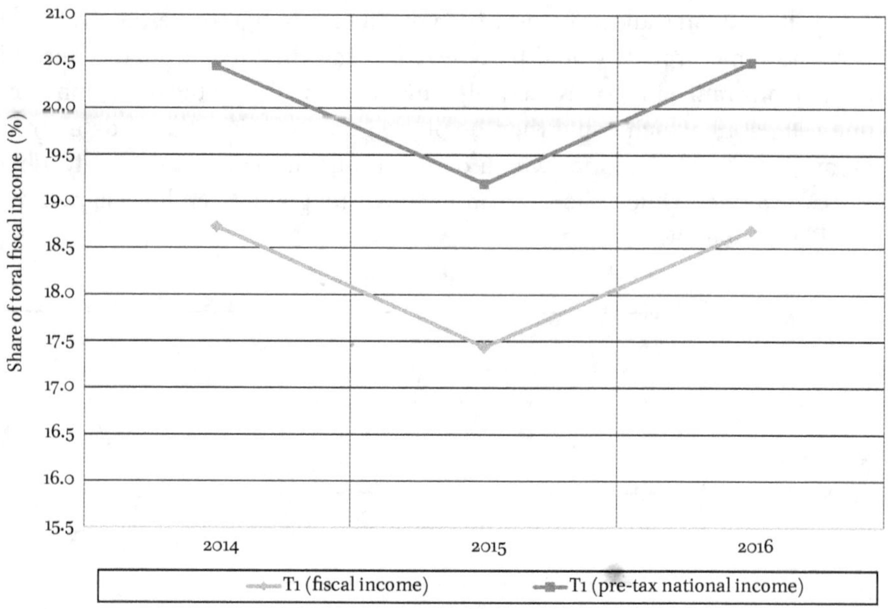

FIGURE 2 T1 income shares for Thailand, 2014–2016
FIGURE PRODUCED USING DATA FROM *WID.WORLD*

While the two curves above follow the same trend—they have the same shape—it would appear that the T1 in Thailand for the period 2014–2016 received a disproportionate amount of all the income—that is disproportionate to their share of fiscal income—which was not considered taxable in terms of the laws of Thailand. At this point one may also want to examine the post-tax income distribution for Thailand during the same period in order to examine what differences taxes and transfers made to the distribution. Unfortunately, however, *WID.world*, for various reasons, does not yet contain all the data its creators would like for it to contain. For Thailand, as of the time of writing, *WID.world* contained data for Thailand from 2001–2016 for the T1, T10, M40 and B50 shares in terms of fiscal and pre-tax income.[29] It contained no data, however, on other types of income, such as post-tax income or factor income. It also contained no data on wealth.

For other countries, more complete data exists. Currently, one of the most complete sets of data is the one for the United States, the T1 curves for

29 It did, however, also contain estimations and projections for earlier periods through to 2019.

which—in respect of both income and wealth—can be illustrated as follows using the various types of data available for that country:

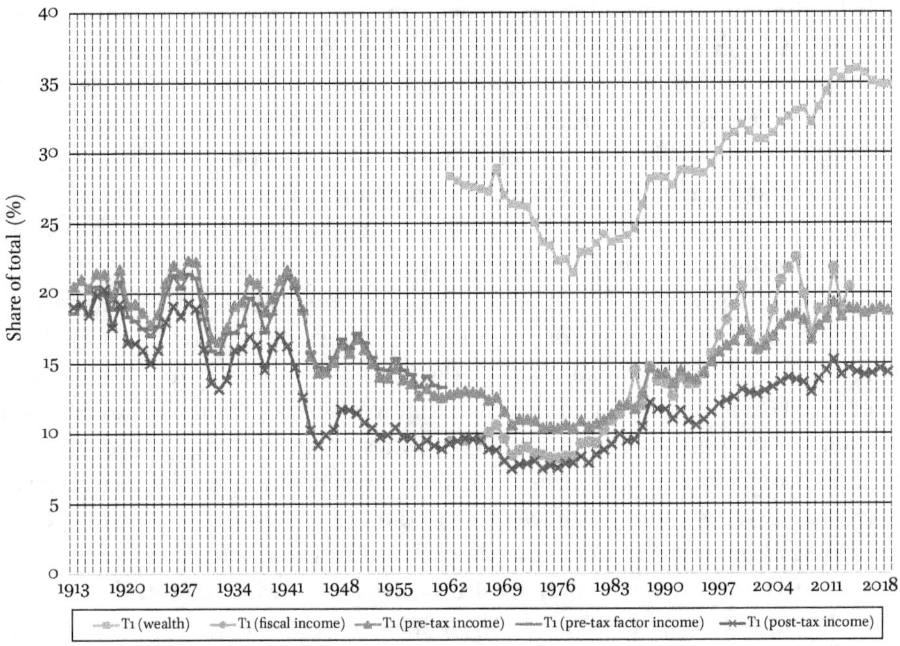

FIGURE 3 T1 income and wealth shares for the United States, 1913–2019
FIGURE PRODUCED USING DATA FROM *WID.WORLD*

Figure 3 shows five curves: four are income curves for the T1 in the United States over a period spanning a bit more than a century, with the fifth curve illustrating the T1 for wealth over the same period of time. This allows for a more complete picture of how income is distributed given different assumptions. It also shows what has been happening in the United States for T1 in terms of wealth. The graph shows, for example, that the T1—which could theoretically be the same group of people for both income and wealth, but in practice were not, despite some overlaps—for wealth in the United States was at similar levels during parts of the 1960s as it was in the above-imagined country X in 2018.

2.1.3 Clarifications and Critiques

Having set out appropriate definitions and summarised the methodology of *WID.world*, it is worth clarifying in what ways the database is still some way from perfection. As a general proposition, the authors of *WID.world* rely on official national accounts statistics.[30] They are quick to acknowledge, however, that these data are imperfect and can be improved on for future iterations of

30 See generally Alvaredo et al (n 5).

WID.world.[31] An upshot of recognising the distribution of income and wealth within states and the adverse effects stemming therefrom as a common concern of humankind may well be that data collection in some or all of the areas below improves.[32] Indeed, the systematic and detailed collection of income and wealth data should be seen as priority and therefore as an important part of the utility of potentially recognising a common concern of humankind as described in this monograph.[33] In order to get a better sense of what information may be helpful, some clarifications and critiques of *WID.world* are set out below.

The first clarification, perhaps, should be on the subject of how the distributions of income and wealth relate to one another systematically. The reason this relationship is of importance is simple and forms the basis for the first critique: errors pertaining to either distribution may result in errors being made with respect to the other. For example, it is quite well known that throughout the course of history wealth has for the largest part been more unevenly distributed than income.[34] It is also clear that wealth—and not only other factors such as the application of labour—generates income. If, then, there is a large correlation between who earns (relatively) large labour incomes and who owns (relatively) large amounts of wealth—and therefore generate (relatively) large incomes from wealth—one can expect that the over- or under-representation, respectively, of how unevenly wealth is distributed will result in the over- or under-representation, respectively, of how unevenly income is distributed. There appears to be some evidence suggesting that such a relationship exists, at least in some parts of the world.[35]

In the United States, for example, a positive correlation exists between (relatively) high labour incomes and (relatively) large incomes derived from wealth and this correlation has steadily increased since 1980, with the correlation coefficient having seen an increase from being less than one percent in 1980 to being consistently around 10–12 percent since 1995.[36] Moreover, the likelihood

---

31 See, for example, Alvaredo et al (n 5) 36 where the authors state that their choice of using national accounts income and wealth concepts for distributional analysis certainly does not mean that they believe that these concepts are perfectly satisfactory or appropriate. Quite the contrary: their view is that official national accounts statistics are insufficient and need to be improved.

32 On this point, see further Chapter 3 of this monograph.

33 See further Chapter 3 of this monograph.

34 See Thomas Piketty, *Capital in the Twenty-First Century*, translated into English by Arthur Goldhammer (HUP, Cambridge, MA 2014) 305–8.

35 Here the phrase 'some parts of the world' is not meant to suggest that the same sort of pattern does not exist is other parts of the world, but rather that there is currently an insufficient level of research on this topic for conclusions to be drawn with respect to the situation elsewhere in the world.

36 See B Milanovic, *Global Inequality: A New Approach for the Age of Globalization* (HUP, Cambridge, MA 2016) 187.

of being in the T10 of the US wealth income distribution has increased once it is a given that a particular individual is in the T1 of the labour income distribution.[37] The reverse is also true: the likelihood of being in the T10 of the labour income increases once it is a given that a particular individual is in the T1 of the wealth income distribution.[38] Milanovic, based on data from Lakner and Atkinson, represents this graphically as follows (Figure 4):[39]

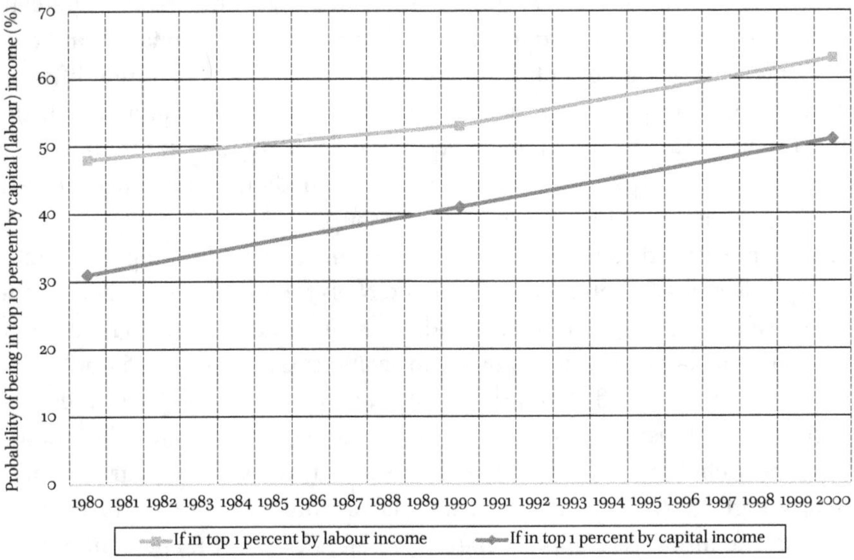

FIGURE 4 Probability (in percent) of being in the T10 by capital (labour) income if a person is in T1 by labour (capital) income, 1980–2000
REPRODUCED FROM MILANOVIC (N 36) 185

If the distribution of wealth is incorrectly represented, then, it is quite possible (and probably highly likely) that the distribution of income is also incorrectly represented. This logic is perhaps most clear when considering it in the context of another critique of *WID.world*, which stems from its own authors: that of the impact of tax avoidance and evasion on its estimates. Gabriel Zucman has done a fair amount of work on this point, usually in collaboration with other authors. For example, in his book, *The Hidden Wealth of Nations*, Zucman estimates that approximately eight percent of global household financial wealth is

37 Milanovic (n 36) 185.
38 Milanovic (n 36) 185.
39 Milanovic (n 36) 185 relying on data from Anthony B Atkinson and Christoph Lakner, 'Wages, Capital and Top Incomes: The Factor Income Composition of Top Incomes in the USA, 1960–2005' (2014), unpublished manuscript <http://www.ecineq.org/ecineq_lux15/FILESx2015/CR2/p196.pdf> accessed 30 September 2021.

held offshore.[40] This amounts to an estimated 10 percent of global GDP.[41] Such findings, even if one disputes the exact figures, have important implications for the measurement and representations of income and wealth distributions.

Breaking Zucman's figures down, one sees a large variance in different countries with respect to how much financial wealth is held offshore. In the United States, for example, it is estimated that four percent of financial wealth is held off shore.[42] His estimated figure for 'Europe' is 10 percent.[43] For Russia and 'Gulf countries', his estimations are much higher at 52 percent and 57 percent respectively.[44] It follows therefore that the impact of tax avoidance and evasion (or wealth being held offshore for other reasons) can be quite different depending on the particular country or countries being examined. All the same, the fact remains that financial wealth held offshore poses problems for databases such as *WID.world* where tax data is relied on to construct the various shares of different income and wealth groups.

This is particularly so if one considers the more recent finding of Zucman and his colleagues Annette Alstadsæter and Niels Johannesen that those at the very top of the wealth distribution tend to be much more likely to hold financial wealth offshore in order to avoid or evade taxes.[45] This study only covers Norway, Sweden and Denmark but shows how tax evasion may affect the measurement of distributions: at about 1.9 percent of total wealth, the amount of total household wealth held offshore in Norway does not appear to be particularly high.[46] However, if one extrapolates from sample data taken from tax leaks and amnesties, approximately 77 percent of that 1.9 percent of total wealth belongs to the top 0.1 percent of Norwegian households.[47] Therefore the inclusion of offshore wealth in distribution calculations is likely to end in substantially different results, even in countries like Norway where relatively low amounts of wealth are held offshore.[48] In fact, for the period 2000–2009,

40 Gabriel Zucman, *The Hidden Wealth of Nations: The Scourge of Tax Havens*, translated into English by Teresa Lavender Fagan (University of Chicago Press, Chicago 2015) 35.

41 See Annette Alstadsæter, Niels Johannesen and Gabriel Zucman, 'Who Owns the Wealth in Tax Havens? Macro Evidence and Implications for Global Inequality' (2018) 162 *Journal of Public Economics* 89, 89.

42 See Zucman (n 40) 53.

43 See Zucman (n 40) 53.

44 See Zucman (n 40) 53.

45 See generally Annette Alstadsæter, Niels Johannesen and Gabriel Zucman, 'Tax Evasion and Inequality' (2019) 109 *American Economic Review* 2073.

46 See Alstadsæter, Johannesen and Zucman (n 45) Table 2.

47 See Table B4 in the Online Appendix to Alstadsæter, Johannesen and Zucman (n 45) <http://gabriel-zucman.eu/files/AJZ2017Appendix.pdf> accessed 30 September 2021.

48 It is worth recalling that in Russia and 'Gulf' countries there is evidence to suggest that more than *half* of total wealth is held offshore.

it appears that the share of wealth held by the top 0.1 percent of Norwegians (the T10 of the T1) was not the 8.4 percent estimated without accounting for offshore wealth but 9.8 percent.[49] As for the top 0.01 percent of Norwegians (the T1 of the T1), their wealth was found, for example, to be under-valued by approximately 25 percent in 2010.[50]

In a different paper, Alstadsæter, Johannesen and Zucman pose a broader question: what would wealth distributions look like if offshore financial wealth were accounted for in a larger sample of countries? Using ten countries with comparable statistics, the authors study the household wealth share of the top 0.01 percent in each of the country's respective wealth distributions for the 2000–2009 period.[51] They emphasise that the effects of holding wealth offshore depends largely on the particular country one looks at, but come to the overall conclusion that the household wealth share of the top 0.01 percent in each of the ten countries is substantially understated if offshore wealth is not accounted for. Figure 5 captures this finding quite succinctly:[52]

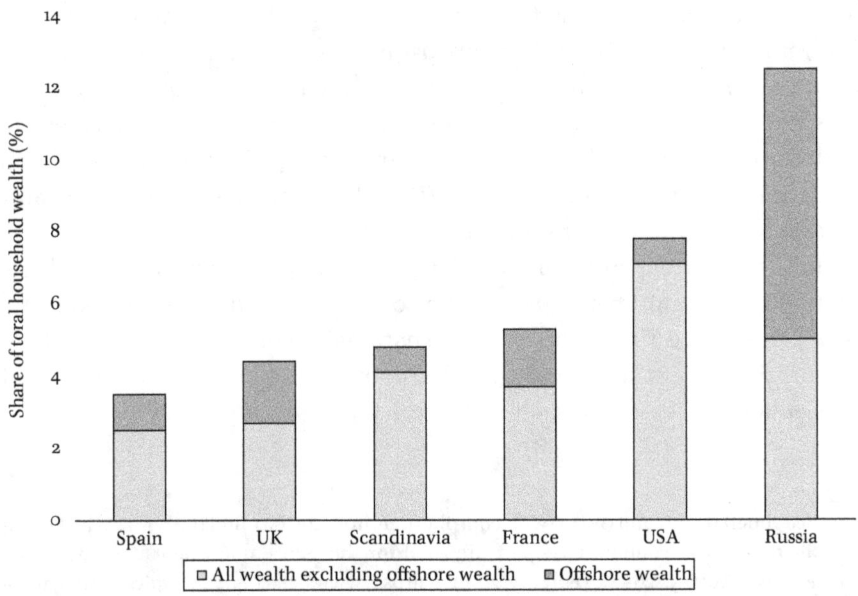

FIGURE 5 Probability T0.01 wealth shares in various countries, 2000–2009 (average) Scandinavia, for purposes of this figure, comprises Denmark, Norway and Sweden
REPRODUCED FROM ALSTADSÆTER, JOHANNESEN AND ZUCMAN (N 41) 98

49 Alstadsæter, Johannesen and Zucman (n 45) 19.
50 Alstadsæter, Johannesen and Zucman (n 45) 19.
51 See generally Alstadsæter, Johannesen and Zucman (n 41).
52 Alstadsæter, Johannesen and Zucman (n 41) 98.

If we accept that the top of the wealth and labour income distributions are becoming more intertwined (or correlated) at the top end of both distributions, then it follows that the understatement of the wealth income share at the top is also more likely to impact the overall income distribution through an understatement of the top of the income distribution. This is especially likely during periods when a smaller portion of overall income accrues to labour over time, which appears to be the case for a significant number of countries over the course of the last few decades.[53] While this is a serious simplification of a fairly complex topic, the point is simply to illustrate that without accounting for how much wealth is held offshore, which national accounts statistics usually do not account for, it may be incorrectly stated how both wealth and income are distributed, with a substantial likelihood of an understatement of how unequally they are distributed. In other words, not accounting for offshore wealth and/or tax avoidance and evasion is highly likely to lead to a situation whereby the true level of income and wealth inequality in a given state is masked.

A second set of clarifications essentially constitute the second critique. This set of clarifications pertains to the manner in which national accounts are kept, with the critique being that the existing ways are wrong. For example, as the authors of *WID.world* note, one of the central limitations of GDP accounting is the fact that it does not provide 'any information about the extent to which the different social groups benefit from growth'.[54] From the description of the concepts and methods used in *WID.world*, it is not particularly clear how the term 'social groups' is or should be defined.[55]

A final accounting problem is that 'official national accounts are often fairly rudimentary in a number of developing countries and some developed countries'.[56] This means that on occasion the national account statistics of particular countries are not sufficiently detailed in order to allow for construction of series entailing the concepts defined by the *WID.world* authors.

53 See generally ILO and OECD (with contributions from the IMF and the WBG), 'The Labour Share in G20 Economies' (Report prepared for the G20 Employment Working Group Antalya, Turkey, 26–27 February 2015) <https://www.oecd.org/g20/topics/employment-and-social-policy/The-Labour-Share-in-G20-Economies.pdf> accessed 30 September 2021.

54 Alvaredo et al (n 5) 36.

55 One could imagine social group filters to account for race, ethnicity, region within a particular country, and whether a person is from a rural or urban area. As definitionally problematic and difficult as this may be, it may be a worthwhile undertaking, particularly given the deleterious impacts of 'horizontal' or group-level inequalities as discussed later at various stages in this monograph.

56 Alvaredo et al (n 5) 42.

A third clarification pertains to the tax records themselves from which the *WID.world* authors extract their data. Income taxes are filed by tax units and these units are usually not homogenous between or within countries. The unit used also depends on the peculiarities of a given countries laws and on data collection methods. In many countries a range of different tax units exist. For example, some people file taxes as a married couple while others file them as a single individual.

While the database accounts for this to a degree,[57] certain problems still remain and lend themselves to critique, the main one being that the authors should not work off the assumption, as they mostly do, that income and/or wealth within a given tax unit is split equally amongst the adults in that unit. This sort of egalitarian distribution within the tax unit is unlikely to reflect reality,[58] so the authors initially created a separate filter labelled 'individuals' as an attempt to account for this.[59] When applied, the filter would represent the various shares accruing to different parts of the income and wealth distribution as if tax units were broken into individual income recipients or owners of wealth.[60] This too may be problematic because while it is unlikely that income and/or wealth are split equally among the adults in various types of tax units, it is also probably not the case that individuals within the same tax unit operate purely individualistically.[61]

57 Previously all units were treated as if they were the same, which lead to certain biases. For example, married couples appeared richer than single individuals. This was because married couples' incomes were not divided by two in order to account for the fact that their tax unit consisted of two people. See further Alvaredo et al (n 5) 9–10.

58 For an overview on the economics of intra-household income inequality, see Sophie Ponthieux and Dominique Meurs 'Gender Inequality' in Anthony B Atkinson and François Bourguignon (eds), *Handbook of Income Distribution* (*Volume 2A*) (Elsevier, Amsterdam 2015) 982, 983–1004 and Pierre-André Chiappori and Costas Meghir, 'Intrahousehold Inequality' in Anthony B Atkinson and François Bourguignon (eds), *Handbook of Income Distribution* (*Volume 2B*) (Elsevier, Amsterdam 2015) 1369. See also Sara Arber, 'Unequal Partners: Inequality in Earnings and Independent Income within Marriage' in Linda McKie, Sophia Bowlby and Susan Gregory (eds), *Gender, Power and the Household* (Palgrave Macmillan, Basingstoke 1999) 175; Carrie Yodanis and Sean Lauer, 'Economic Inequality in and outside of Marriage: Individual Resources and Institutional Context' (2007) 5 *European Sociological Review* 573.

59 See Alvaredo et al (n 5) 9.

60 The authors of *WID.world* stress that they view these different views as equally valuable because they offer 'two interesting and complementary perspectives on different dimensions of inequality'. See Alvaredo et al (n 5) 10.

61 See n 58. See also Rense Nieuwenhuis, Henk van der Kolk and Ariana Need, 'Women's Earnings and Household Inequality in OECD Countries, 1973–2013' (2017) 60 *Acta Sociologica* 3 for an illustration of the income-inequality-reducing impact of women's earnings accounting for a greater share of total earnings over time.

A fourth, and for current purposes final, clarification is simply the confirmation of the focus of *WID.world* as well as this monograph: that is, the distribution of income and wealth *within* states. The discussions in this monograph are well served, however, by a brief sketch of distributions at other levels too: first, because it will help to distinguish the various types of distributions from one another and assist in providing definitional clarity for later chapters; and secondly, because it is useful to situate within-country distributions in a broader context given the global nature and potential impact of the common concern of humankind concept. This will allow for a more informed discussion of the potential interlinkages between different types of distributions and the implications of these interlinkages for solving some of the problems posed in this monograph.[62]

As a starting point, it is perhaps necessary to distinguish three types of income and wealth distributions: (1) the global interpersonal distribution; (2) distributions between states; and (3) distributions within states, which is the focus of this monograph and *WID.world*. Perhaps the simplest way of thinking of the global interpersonal distribution of income or wealth is to imagine that there are no countries.[63] Imagine also that there is capacity to line them all up in a row according to how much income or wealth

62 Authors have frequently noted that—broadly speaking—the distribution of income between countries of the world has become more equal in the twenty-first century and that within-country distributions have concomitantly risen. As a result, one often gets the sense that certain zero-sum assumptions are made about one's views pertaining to within-country distributions. For example, it is often assumed that if one is for decreasing economic inequality within countries, it must follow that one is also against the supposed decrease in economic inequality between countries that is currently occurring. As the discussion below hopefully reveals, this is an overly simplistic view of what is in fact happening at the between-country level. It is also incorrect to assume that a form of zero-sum logic applies insofar as the within-country-between-country levels are concerned. It is quite possible for one to be in favour of a reduction of economic inequality between countries and within countries. It is also not true *a priori* that economic inequality cannot simultaneously decrease between countries and within countries. For a thoughtful take on these issues, see Dani Rodrik, 'Is Global Equality the Enemy of National Equality?' (online working paper, January 2017) <https://drodrik.scholar.harvard.edu/files/dani-rodrik/files/is_global_equality_the_enemy_of_national_equality.pdf> accessed 30 September 2021.

63 This idea is taken from Surjit S Bhalla, *Imagine There's No Country* (Institute for International Economics, Washington, DC 2002). The use of the word 'interpersonal' is taken from Branko Milanovic, 'Global Income Inequality in Numbers: in History and Now' (2013) 4 *Global Policy* 198. I have used this phrasing as it makes it fairly clear that we are referring to the income and wealth distributions amongst the citizens of the globe. In their paper, the authors only address the global income distribution; in this work the same notion is applied to wealth.

they receive or have. This data could then be collected, and representations could then be made concerning the economic distributions amongst all the constituent human beings that make up humankind as a whole. As François Bourguignon puts it:

> Global inequality is defined as the level of inequality between all inhabitants of the world, thus combining rich and poor people in Latin America as well as in Europe or in the United States. Although this topic has not received much attention, it presents a rather complex combination of inequality between nations and inequality within nations.[64]

Constructed this way—and given that the world as it currently stands is organised into states—the global interpersonal distribution, as Bourguignon suggests, consists of two components: the distributions between or among these states and the distributions within each state. A distribution within a state is the sort of thing examined thus far in this chapter and refers to the manner—the T1, the T10, the M40 and the B50 within a given state for current purposes—in which income or wealth is distributed among all the residents of that state. Thus far we have defined distributions in terms of individual people, with the globe and the state acting as boundaries within which to measure economic inequality levels. The next concept—the distribution of income and wealth between countries—however, requires that distributions be defined not in terms of people but, instead, in terms of states. This is, at least conceptually, a more complex concept and hence requires some unpacking.

The most obvious challenge or complexity, perhaps, is that states are not all made up of the same number of people. This makes it difficult to directly compare different states. Consider, for example, if the world were made up of only three states: State X, which has a population of 1000 people; State Y, which has a population of 100 000 people; and State Z, which has a population of 10 000 000 people. If each person in this world received the exact same income, then a conclusion could still be reached that income is very unevenly distributed between states because State Y, in aggregate, would have 100 times as much income as State X and State Z would have 100 times as much income as State Y and 10 000 times as much income as State X. If this were the way income

64 François Bourguignon, *The Globalization of Inequality* (Princeton University Press, Princeton 2015) 9.

distribution between states was to be measured, the entire emphasis would clearly be on the population size of states.

If it were desired for population size to play less of a role in distributional measurements of this sort, each state might be reduced to a single person generally representative of the income level of that state; the mean or the median income in each state might be used. If this were the case, the conclusion that would follow is that there is perfect equality between states in terms of incomes because the mean and the median income in all three countries would be the same. The role of population size would have become entirely insignificant. Alternative approaches may also emphasise population size less than in the first example but more than in the second. Ultimately, irrespective of which approach is taken, a value judgment must be made, the central question in this regard being what weight should be given to the sizes of different states.

Branko Milanovic captures the tensions of this debate quite well. He uses three concepts to describe inequality beyond the borders of a single state, usually referred to as 'inequality 1', 'inequality 2' and 'inequality 3'.[65] Inequality 1 and 2 both describe how income is distributed between states.[66] Inequality 1 represents the distribution of total global income between all states in the world on the basis of GDP per capita or mean income without giving weight to population size.[67] Inequality 2 does the same thing as inequality 1, but also gives weight to population size.[68] Inequality 3 refers to the global interpersonal distribution as it is described above.

Milanovic has labelled a decision between which of these three concepts should be preferred as a measure the global state of inequality as the 'mother of all inequality disputes'.[69] It is fairly easy to see why. Each concept, if calculated for the world as a whole, essentially accounts for all the people in the world, but in a fundamentally different manner. The first concept predominantly focuses on states. It presumes that all states matter equally irrespective of the size of their population. The state concept also plays a role in inequality 2, but each state plays a role that is proportionate to its population size. The third concept, as alluded to above, looks at the world as if there were no states at all.

65 See Milanovic (n 63) 198–202.
66 See Milanovic (n 63) 198–9.
67 See Milanovic (n 63) 198–9.
68 See Milanovic (n 63) 199–202.
69 See Milanovic (n 63) 200.

As Milanovic has tried to illustrate using Gini coefficients, with respect to income, the observable trend for each concept has been quite different over time: Inequality 1 has rose steadily over time until around 2000 and has been declining steadily since then; inequality 2—largely due to the growth of the two most populous countries, China and India—has been steadily declining since around 1950 if one takes into account the size of the world's different countries (inequality 2); and global interpersonal inequality—inequality 3—had remained fairly constant but has begun to fall slightly since around 2000.[70]

The *WID.world* authors, however, have illustrated the same trends in a different manner. As far as inequality 1 is concerned, they have shown the unevenness of economic growth for the average adult in an array of countries during the period 1980–2016.[71] The average growth of mean adult income for the world as a whole grew 54 percent.[72] However, in 2016 the average adult in China made 831 percent more than she did in 1980 and the average Indian adult made 223 percent more than he did.[73] Mean income in 2016 was 45 percent higher in the European Union, 58 percent higher in Australia and New Zealand, 56 percent higher in Japan and 71 percent higher in the United States and Canada.[74]

What this implies, on the one hand, is that certain poorer countries in the world caught up substantially with the richest countries in inequality 1 terms during the last three and a half decades. With the mean adult income growth for the world on average being 54 percent, however, it is also implied, on the other hand, that a substantial number of poor countries are falling further behind on average income terms or are staying more or less where they were before. During the same 1980–2016 period, Latin American countries saw average adult income growth of only 12 percent and African countries saw mean adult income grow by a (comparatively) meagre 20 percent. Similar trends took place during the 1950–1980 period.[75] The *WID.world* authors have illustrated a comparison between the one hand and the other using the information depicted in Figures 6 and 7:

70 See Milanovic (n 63) 200. The figure depicted there has since been updated by Milanovic, with the same trends persisting, i.e. inequality 1, inequality 2 and inequality 3 have all continued to fall post 2010.

71 Facundo Alvaredo et al (eds), *World Inequality Report 2018* (HUP, Massachusetts, MA 2018) 64.

72 Alvaredo et al (n 71) 64.

73 Alvaredo et al (n 71) 64.

74 Alvaredo et al (n 71) 64.

75 See Alvaredo et al (n 71) 64.

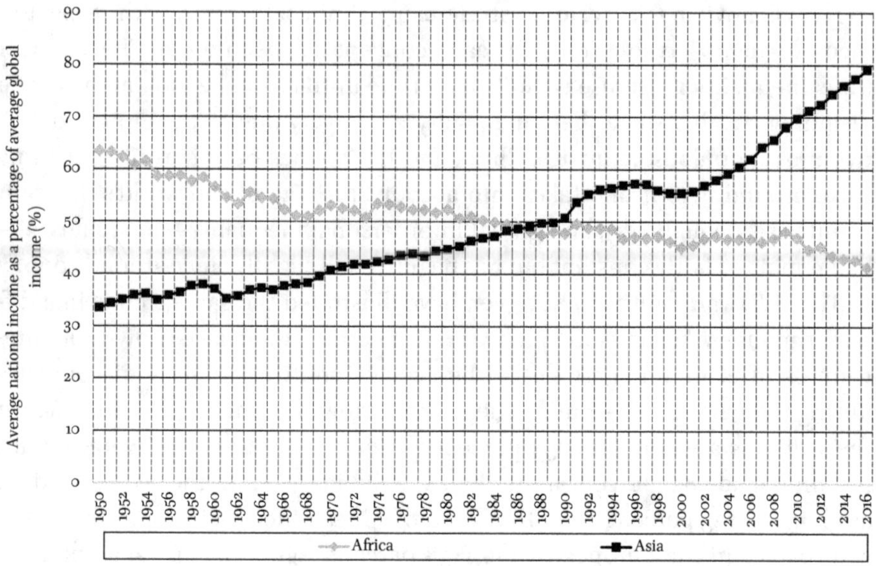

FIGURE 6 Average income in Africa and Asia relative to the global average, 1950–2016
REPRODUCED FROM THE DATA UNDERLYING THE FIGURE IN ALVAREDO ET AL (N 71) 65

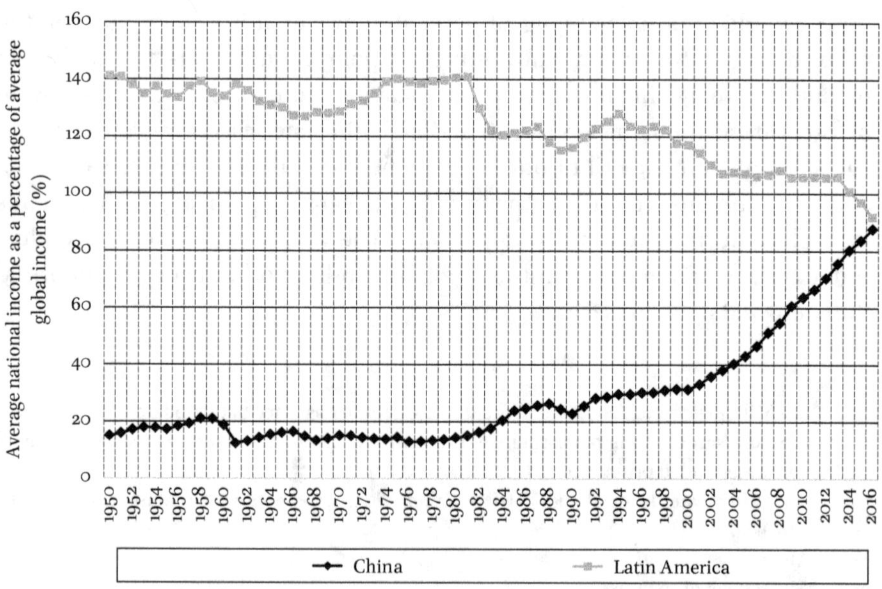

FIGURE 7 Average income in China and Latin America relative to the global average, 1950–2016
REPRODUCED FROM THE DATA UNDERLYING THE FIGURE IN ALVAREDO ET AL (N 71) 66

What these graphs illustrate, essentially, is how using inequality 1 as a measure results in the view that between-country inequality has been rising substantially since 1950. Population size is given substantial, perhaps disproportionate, weight. Consider, for example, that Asia consists of approximately three times more people than Africa, but that Africa consists of slightly more countries. Therefore, of the two areas Africa has slightly more weight in the measurement of inequality 1 because it consists of a few more countries. Similarly, China consists of roughly twice as many people as does the entire Latin America, but Latin America influences an inequality 1 measurement much more heavily because it consists of 20 different countries.

In essence, inequality 1 has been rising because two areas that are made of a relatively large number of countries—Africa and Latin America—have been growing relatively slowly whereas another area with a large number of countries—Asia—has been growing relatively (very) rapidly while most other parts of the world have been growing close to the average pace. Once population size is taken into account, the same reasons result in a substantial decrease since 1950 of inequality between countries from an inequality 2 viewpoint because instead of Africa and Latin America counting as 74 countries against Asia's 48 countries, they count for around 2 billion people against Asia's 4.5 billion people.

As for inequality 3, the authors of *WID.world*, have made use of income shares to illustrate their data, but this time they did so in order to represent global intertemporal inequality of income. As a starting point, they presented the information depicted in Figures 8 and 9:

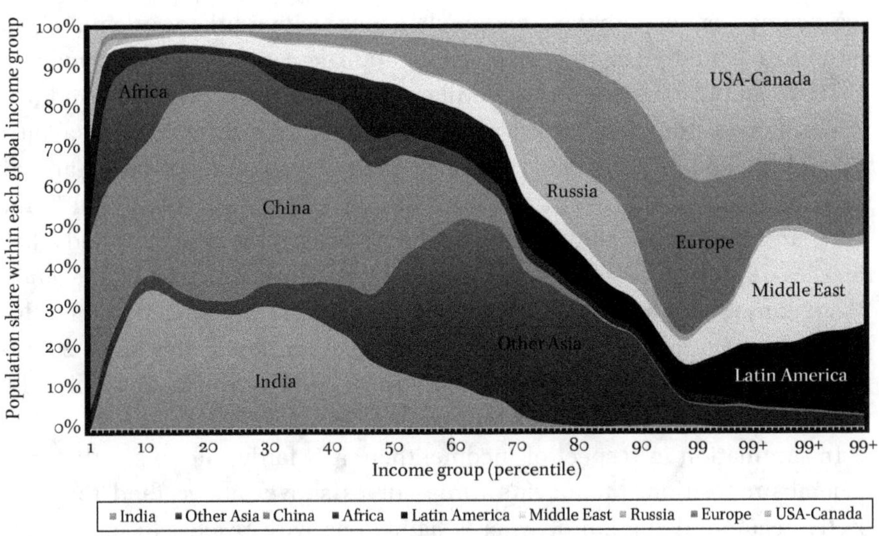

FIGURE 8 Geographic breakdown of global income groups in 1990
REPRODUCED FROM THE DATA UNDERLYING THE FIGURE IN ALVAREDO ET AL (N 71) 52

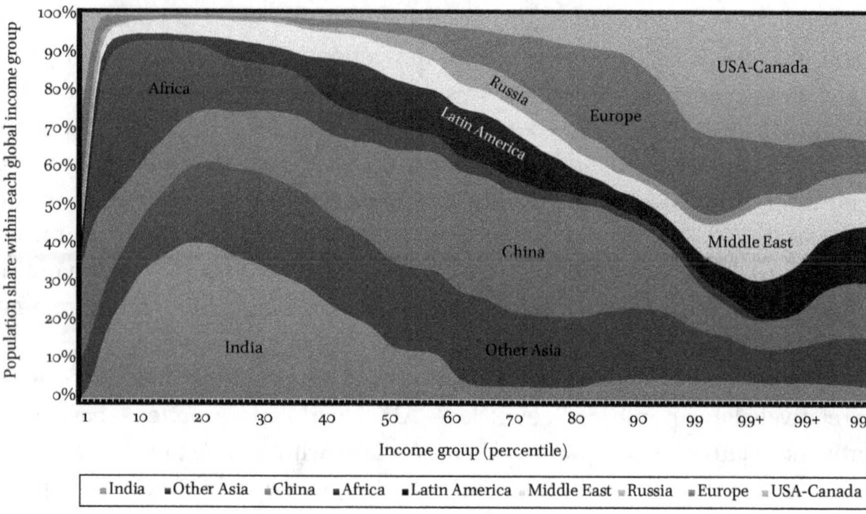

FIGURE 9 Geographic breakdown of global income groups in 2016
REPRODUCED FROM THE DATA UNDERLYING THE FIGURE IN ALVAREDO ET AL (N 71) 53

The larger part of the change from the first graph to the second is explained through the growth patterns discussed above that resulted in rising inequality 1 and falling inequality 2. The change, however, also reflects within country distributions of income, which, for example, explains why substantial portions of the world's lowest income recipients are still in countries, such as China and India, that have far outpaced the rest of the world during the 1990–2016 period in average income growth. With these two graphs acting as appropriate background, the authors then proceed to present the information depicted in Figures 10 and 11.

These graphs tend to illustrate Milanovic's inequality 3 curve reproduced above in greater detail but also appear to be consistent with it its general intuition: although it is perhaps on the early side to tell, it appears that in around 2005 the global income distribution hit a turning point, with the global T1 and T10 shares declining steadily in the next decade after (at least) two and a half decades of both these shares having risen significantly. Since 2005, the global B50 income share has also risen slightly. As a result, Milanovic's finding that global intertemporal inequality has in fact been on the decline since 2005 is therefore perfectly plausible; the *World Inequality Report* of 2018 simply adds more detail to the picture.

In summation in respect of income, then, it is fairly safe to say that, as a general proposition, Milanovic's three curves shown above tend to give a pretty accurate depiction of what is happening with respect to inequality 1 (average income between-country inequality without population weighting), inequality 2 (average income between-country inequality with population weighting) and inequality 3 (global intertemporal inequality). Since the 1950s,

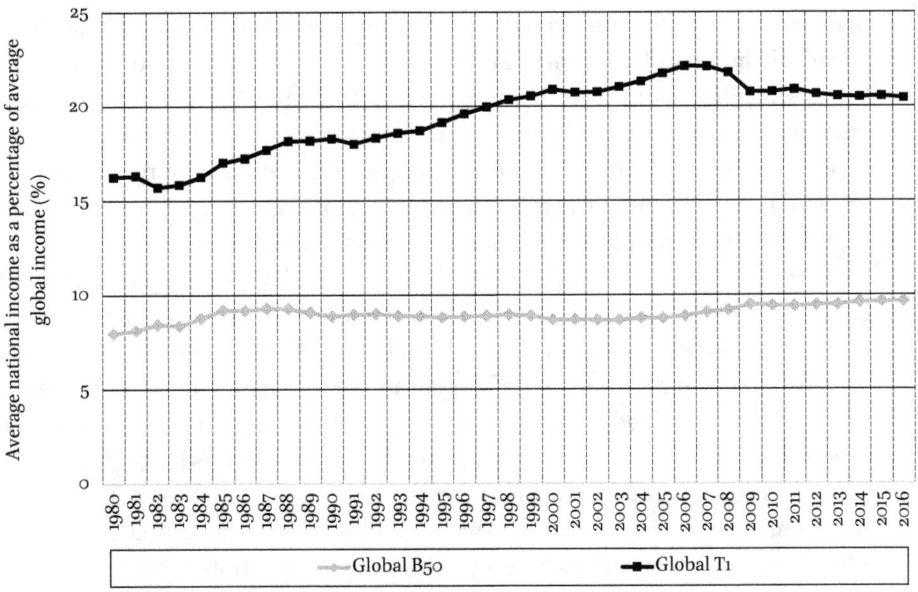

FIGURE 10 Global B50 and T1 income shares, 1980–2016
REPRODUCED FROM THE DATA UNDERLYING THE FIGURE IN ALVAREDO ET AL (N 71) 54

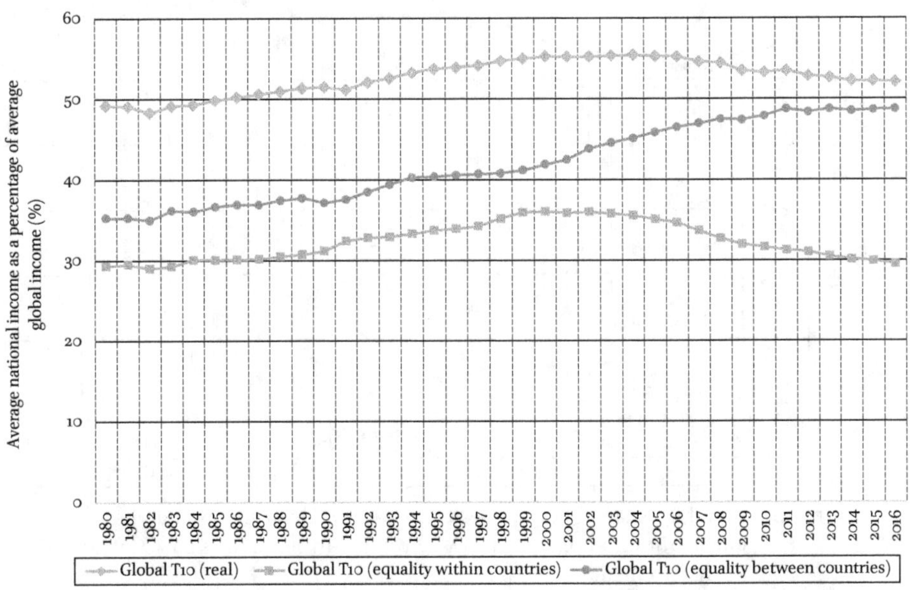

FIGURE 11 Global T10 income share, 1980–2016: between- versus within-country inequality
REPRODUCED FROM THE DATA UNDERLYING THE FIGURE IN ALVAREDO ET AL (N 71) 55

Latin America and Africa have fallen increasingly behind the rest of the world insofar as average income growth is concerned, with Asia pulling substantially ahead of the rest of the world and the rest of the world sustaining more or less average levels of mean income growth, thus resulting in ever higher inequality 1 but in ever lower inequality 2. Once within-country distributions are taken into account, however, the resulting trend becomes more ambiguous. From 1990 until (seemingly) reaching a turning point in 2005, inequality 3 rose slightly before declining somewhat in the 2005–2016 period.

As for wealth, the authors of the *World Inequality Report* have made the claim that 'the available data on wealth inequality is much sparser than for income inequality, especially at the global level'.[76] They continue that '[i]t is therefore more difficult to provide a complete picture of how global wealth inequality has evolved over the past few decades' and strongly stress their intent that 'available data sources make it impossible at this stage to properly estimate the level and evolution of the global distribution of wealth'.[77] For the time being, then, the best the authors could do was to construct T1 and B75 'global' income shares for 1980–2017 using data from Forbes and Credit Suisse, but only with data for China, the European Union and the United States.[78] This allowed them to present the information depicted in Figure 12:

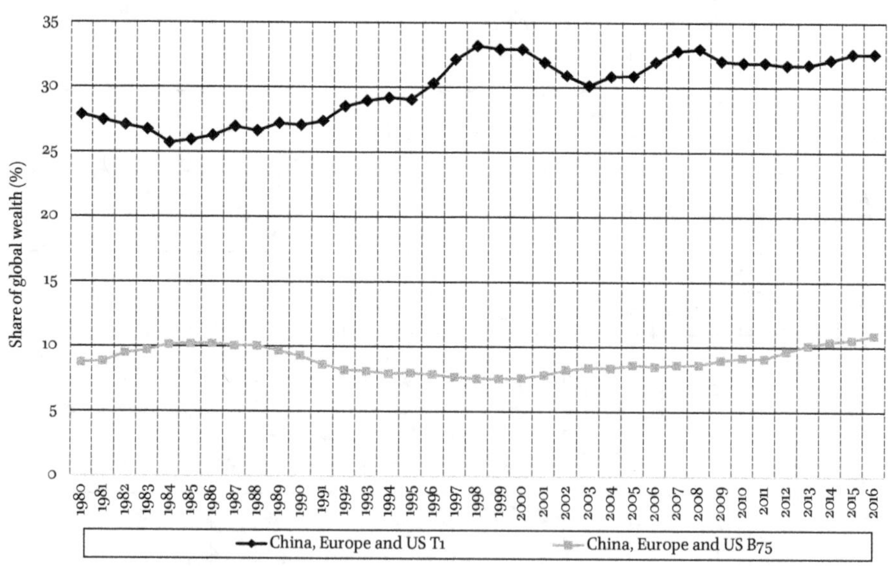

FIGURE 12 T1 and B75 shares of global wealth, 1980–2017: China, Europe and the US
REPRODUCED FROM THE DATA UNDERLYING THE FIGURE IN ALVAREDO ET AL (N 71) 200

76 See Alvaredo et al (n 71) 199.
77 See Alvaredo et al (n 71) 199.
78 See Alvaredo et al (n 71) 200.

While the world consists of more than the European Union, the United States and China, it is also true that these three countries account for a majority of the wealthiest persons on the planet and do not account for the majority of the B75.[79] The above estimate therefore appears to be a fairly conservative one.[80] Indeed, the Credit Suisse Research Institute estimated the global T1 wealth share to be 50.1 percent in 2017.[81] Moreover, current data is likely to substantially underestimate wealth inequality because taxation is disproportionately avoided and evaded by those at the very top of national wealth distributions.[82] Given the paucity of systematic research on the global distribution of wealth, however, the matter is not taken up any further here, save to conclude that it is highly probable that the global distribution of wealth is substantially more unequal than the global distribution of income.

This clarification—that is, on economic distributions between countries or at a global level—provides necessary context for the discussions that follow in this monograph. Context of this kind is necessary because declining global inequality, especially of income, is often used as a critique of those who focus on distributions within states. As is the global poverty rate, which has declined substantially over the last three to four decades. These points should, of course, be acknowledged and taken into account where appropriate. At the same time, it should not be assumed *a priori* that a reduction in global or international economic inequality is an aim that is at odds with a reduction in economic inequality within states.[83]

2.2 *A (Very) Brief Overview of Distributional Changes within the States Since 1900*

Having started with a section on definitions and methodology (*Section 2.1*), this section shifts to the trends in income and wealth distribution within the states of the world since the beginning of the twentieth century, with a particular focus on what has happened since 1980. Given the fairly immense scope of the topic at hand, the discussion that follows will of necessity be a truncated one. An overview of economic distributions within states for present purposes is

79 See Alvaredo et al (n 71) 200. See also Gabriel Zucman, 'Global Wealth Inequality' (2019) 11 *Annual Review of Economics* 109.

80 See Alvaredo et al (n 71) 200.

81 Credit Suisse Research Institute, 'Global Wealth Report 2017' (November 2017) 16 <https://www.credit-suisse.com/corporate/en/research/research-institute/global-wealth-report.html> accessed 30 September 2021.

82 See further Zucman (n 79).

83 See n 62.

presented from a regional perspective. The approach adopted below entails looking at a number of economies in a given region, with economies within each region being chosen primarily on the basis of the completeness of *WID.world* data available for different countries in that region as at the time of writing.

2.2.1 North America

For current purposes, 'North America' refers to the United States and Canada. Collectively, these two states make up approximately five percent of the global population. As for the distribution of income and wealth within each of these states, *WID.world* contains especially complete data for the United States. Figure 13 through 20 provide a fairly decent snapshot of how economic distributions have changed over time in the United States, especially since 1962:

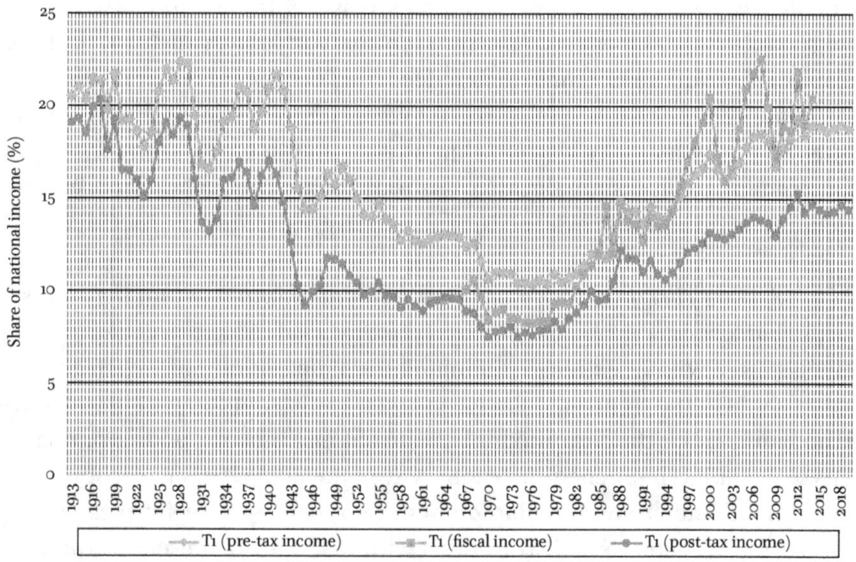

FIGURE 13 T1 income share in the US, 1913–2019
FIGURE PRODUCED USING DATA FROM *WID.WORLD*

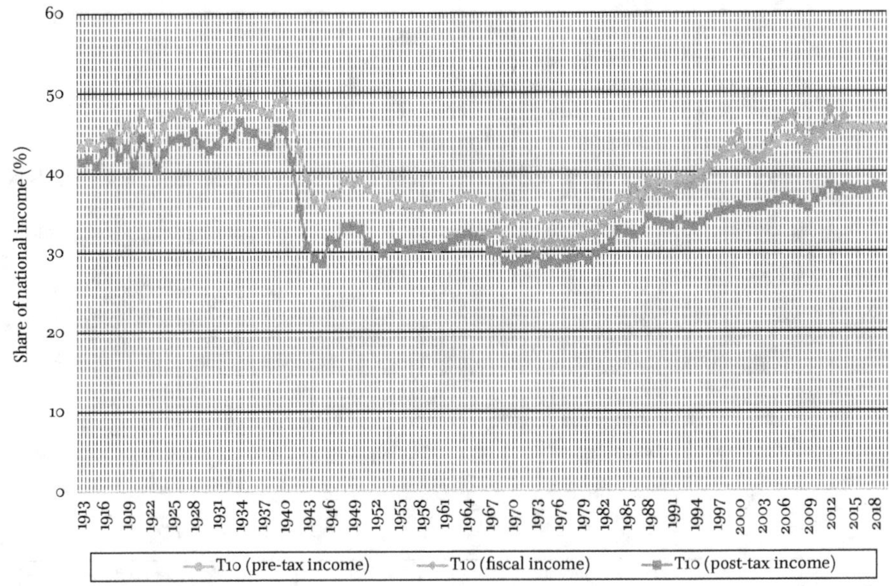

FIGURE 14 T10 income share in the US, 1913–2019
FIGURE PRODUCED USING DATA FROM *WID.WORLD*

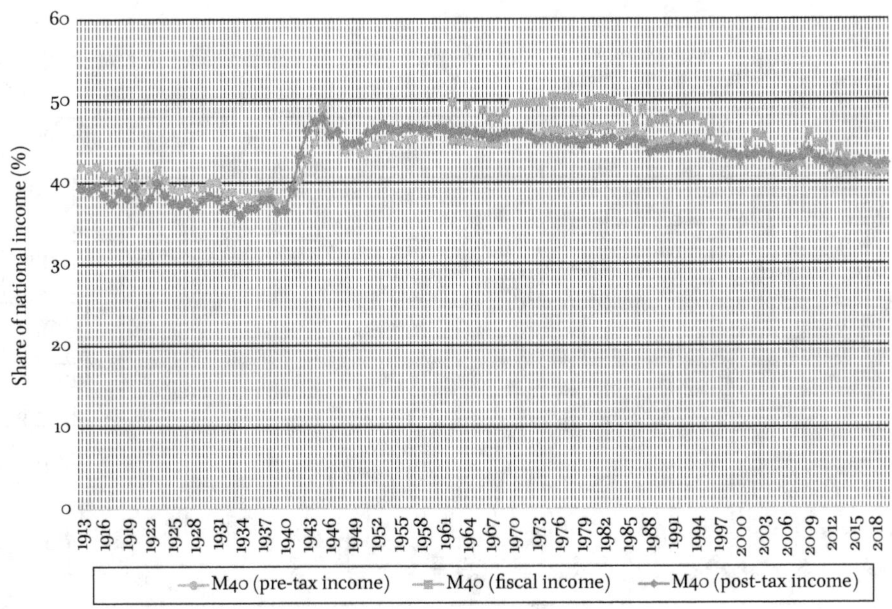

FIGURE 15 M40 income share in the US, 1913–2019
FIGURE PRODUCED USING DATA FROM *WID.WORLD*

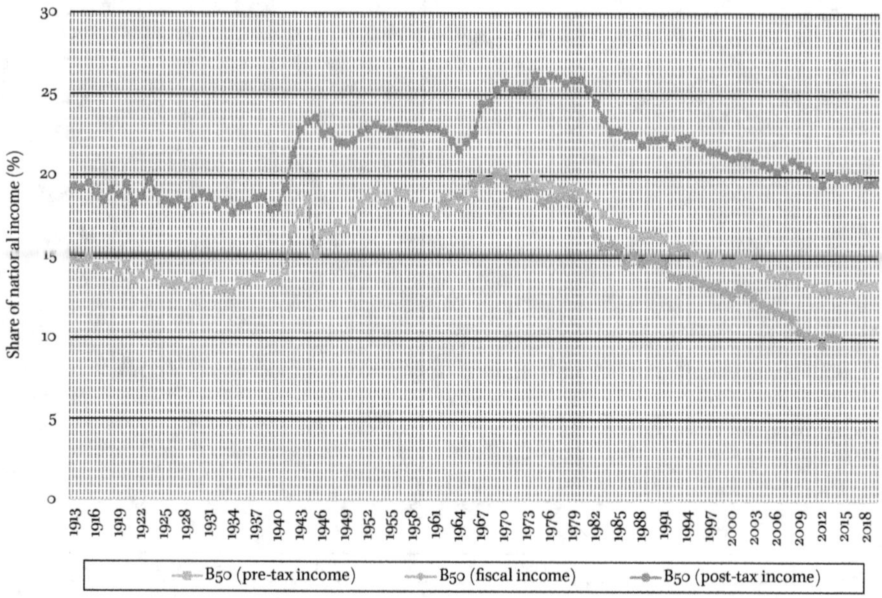

FIGURE 16 B50 income share in the US, 1913–2019
FIGURE PRODUCED USING DATA FROM *WID.WORLD*

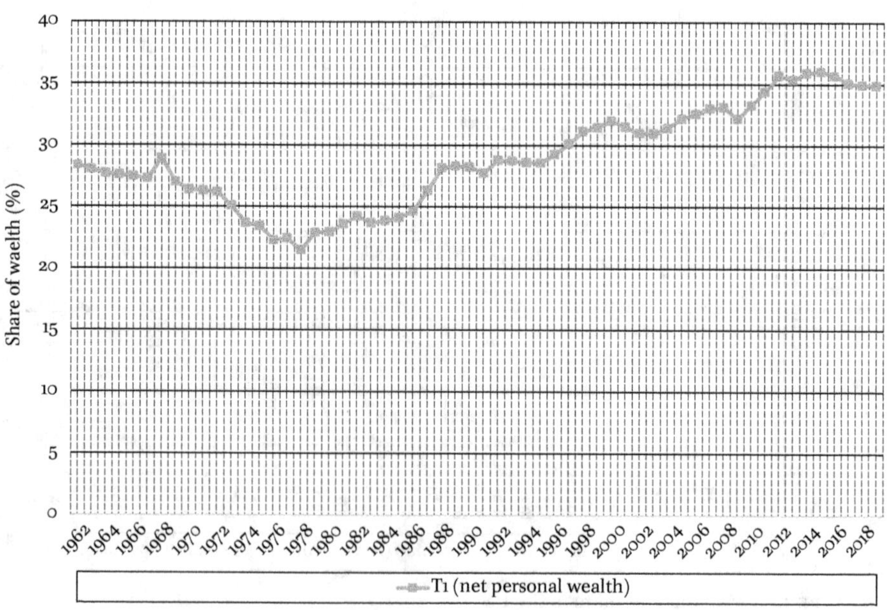

FIGURE 17 T1 wealth share in the US, 1962–2019
FIGURE PRODUCED USING DATA FROM *WID.WORLD*

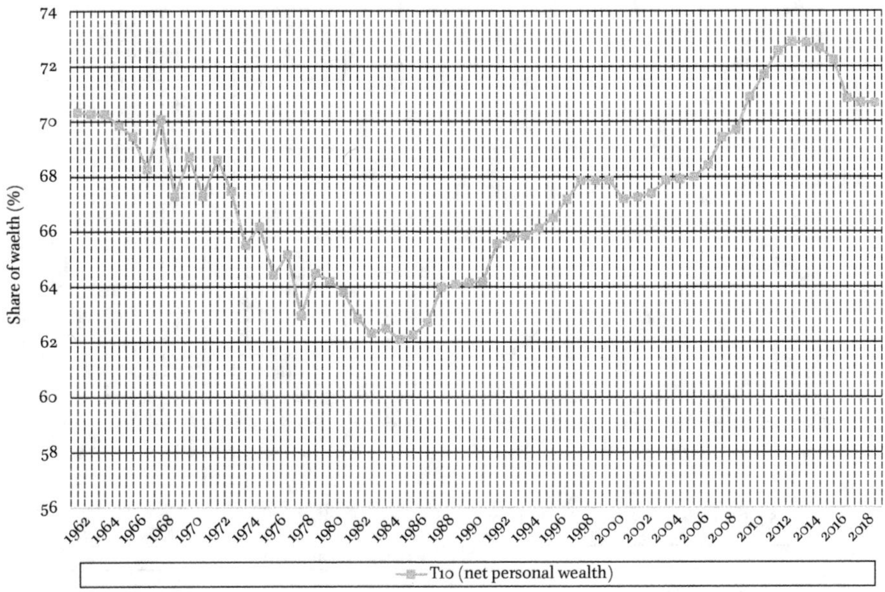

FIGURE 18 T10 wealth share in the US, 1962–2019
FIGURE PRODUCED USING DATA FROM *WID.WORLD*

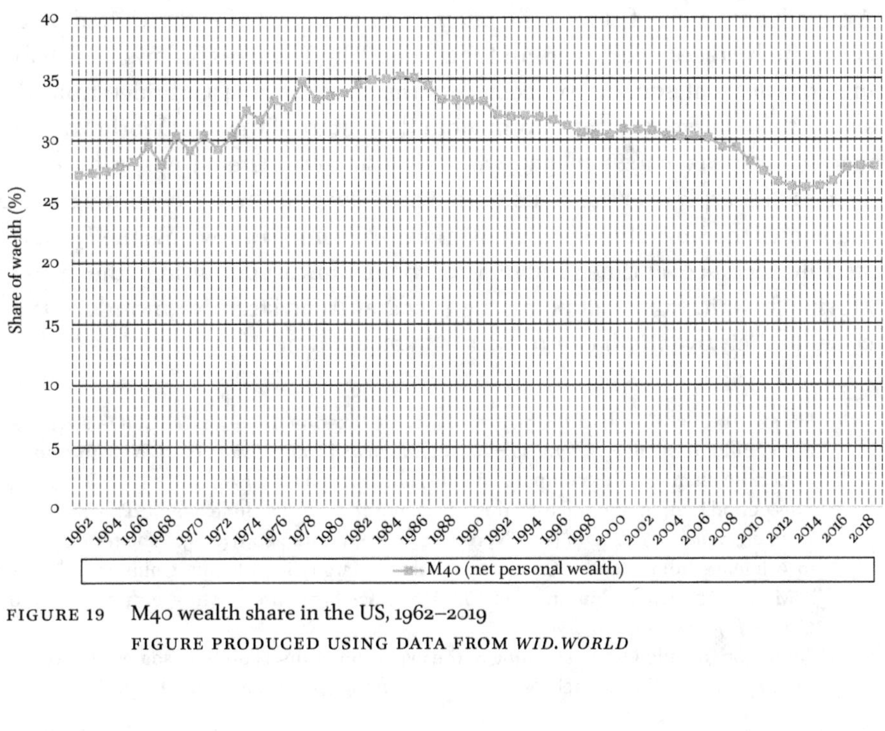

FIGURE 19 M40 wealth share in the US, 1962–2019
FIGURE PRODUCED USING DATA FROM *WID.WORLD*

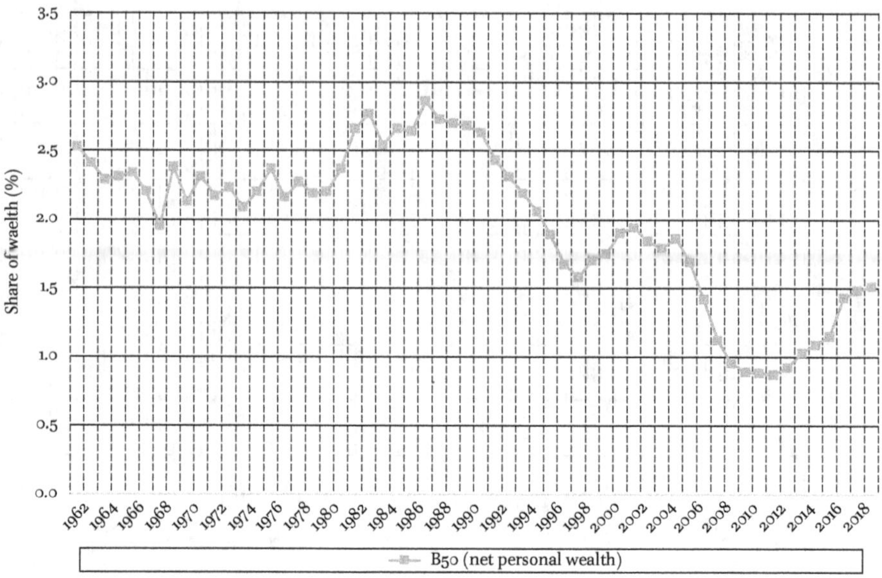

FIGURE 20 B50 wealth share in the US, 1962–2019
FIGURE PRODUCED USING DATA FROM *WID.WORLD*

The first permanent income tax was instituted in the United States in 1913.[84] A significant share of the data contained in *WID.world* for the United States accordingly traces back to around that time. The T1 curves follows a 'u-shape' of sorts, or what some have likened to the shape of a large bridge from the side:[85] these curves start at a point around the start of the First World War and reach a first peak in 1928. In 1929, with the onset of the Great Depression, the T1 shares fall sharply over the course of the next few years before beginning to rise again until the start of the Second World War. From 1939 onwards the T1 shares steadily decline over time until they reach their lowest points in in the 1970s.[86] Moving forward from that point, the T1 shares trend steadily upwards, getting closer to their twentieth century peaks in recent times.[87]

---

84 For an excellent sketch of the history of income taxation in the United States, see generally W Elliot Brownlee, *Federal Taxation in America: A Short History* (CUP, New York 2004).

85 Robert Reich makes this comparison in his film 'Inequality for All'.

86 This period is often referred to as the 'great compression'. See, for example, Paul Krugman, *The Conscience of a Liberal* (WW Norton & Co, New York 2009) 37–56. The term appears to originate from Claudia Goldin and Robert Margo. See Claudia Goldin and Robert A Margo, 'The Great Compression: The U.S. Wage Structure at Mid-Century' (1992) 107 *Quarterly Journal of Economics* 1.

87 For a more detailed understanding of the evolution of the T1 and T10 shares, the work of Thomas Piketty, Emmanuel Saez and their various co-authors is helpful. A summary of

T10 income shares trend consistently upwards until the onset of the Second World War, this despite the First World War and the Great Depression. Thereafter, the T10 shares plumet, reaching, much like the T1 curves, what are presumably historical lows in the 1970s. Also as in the case of the T1 curves, the T10 curves trend steadily upwards thereafter, gradually approaching their twentieth century peaks in recent times.

As for the M40 curves, they trend consistently downwards until the onset of the Second World, before leaping up to what was presumably their historical peak during the War. Ever since, the M40 curves have trended downwards, slowly approaching their pre-Second-World-War lows, albeit that the M40 shares have remained fairly stable for the last 80 years or so.

The B50 income curves exhibit a similar pattern to the M40 curves prior to the onset of the Second World War, also spiking quite dramatically as the War gets going. After the conclusion of the War, however, the B50 share increases quite precipitously until 1980 before dropping almost as precipitously in the next four decades thereafter.

The wealth picture appears to look similar directionally, albeit that the curves generally appear to be shifted to the right by a number of years. From the early 1960s until the 1980s, the T1 and T10 wealth shares drop, while the M40 and B50 wealth shares concomitantly rise. Thereafter, the trends reverse direction: the T1 and T10 shares increase handsomely as the M40 and B50 shares decline.

As it turns out, the general directional trends with respect to income were similar in Canada in many respects during roughly the same periods of time.[88] Consider Figures 21 through 24:

---

how their thoughts on this subject have progressed over time can be gleaned from reading the following three papers: Thomas Piketty and Emmanuel Saez, 'Income Inequality in the United States, 1913–1918' (2003) 118 *Quarterly Journal of Economics* 1; Facundo Alvaredo, Anthony B Atkinson, Thomas Piketty and Emmanuel Saez, 'The Top 1 Percent in International and Historical Perspective' (2013) 27 *Journal of Economic Perspectives* 3 and Thomas Piketty, Emmanuel Saez and Gabriel Zucman, 'Distributional National Accounts: Methods and Estimates for the United States' (2018) 133 *Quarterly Journal of Economics* 553.

88 This is not say that the magnitude of the changes were the same or even largely similar. For a sense of how income inequality has been changing in Canada and how the changes in Canada compare to those in the United States, see generally Charles M Beach, 'Changing Income Inequality: A Distributional Paradigm for Canada' (2016) 49 *Canadian Journal of Economics* 1229.

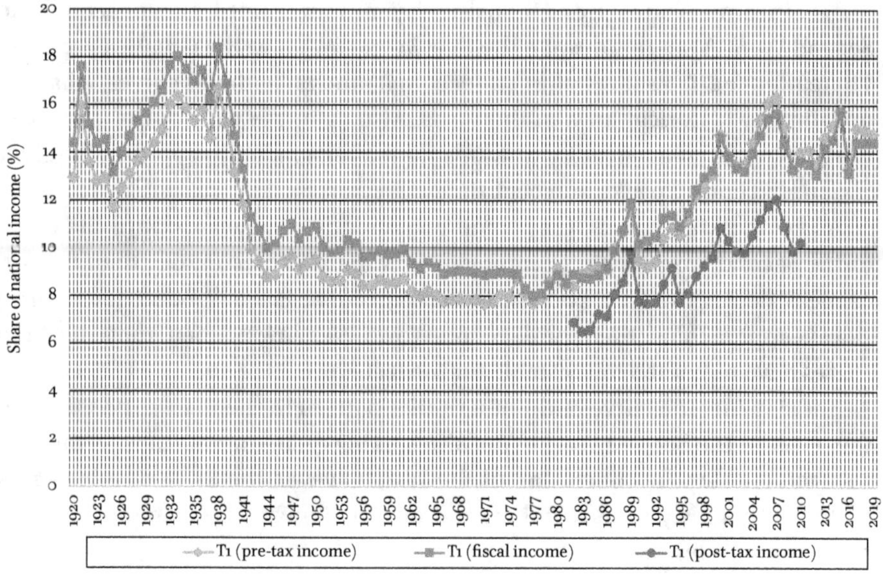

FIGURE 21 T1 income share in Canada, 1920–2019
FIGURE PRODUCED USING DATA FROM *WID.WORLD*

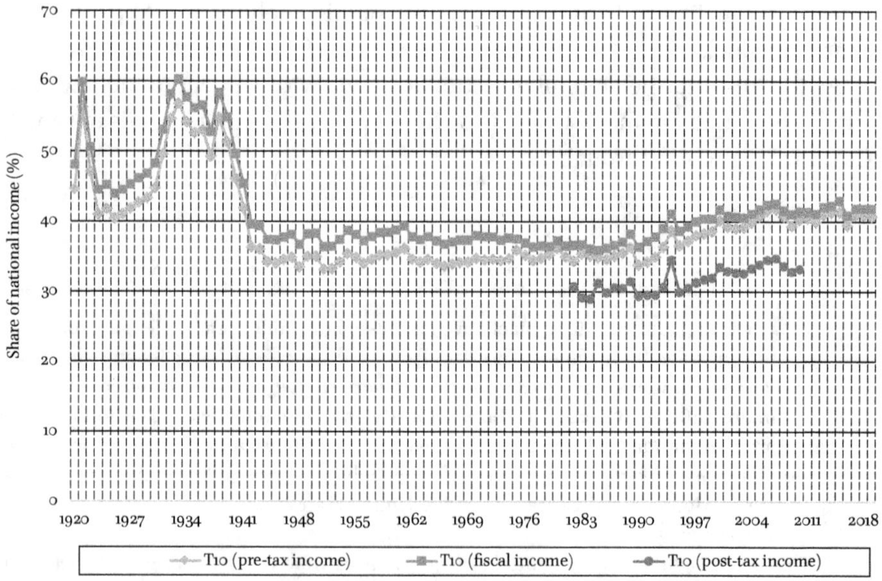

FIGURE 22 T10 income share in Canada, 1920–2019
FIGURE PRODUCED USING DATA FROM *WID.WORLD*

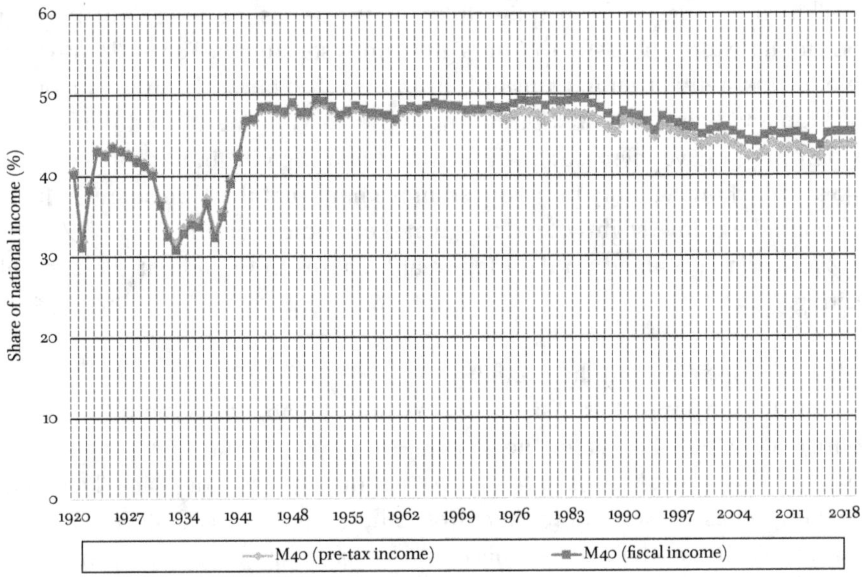

FIGURE 23 M40 income share in Canada, 1920–2019
FIGURE PRODUCED USING DATA FROM *WID.WORLD*

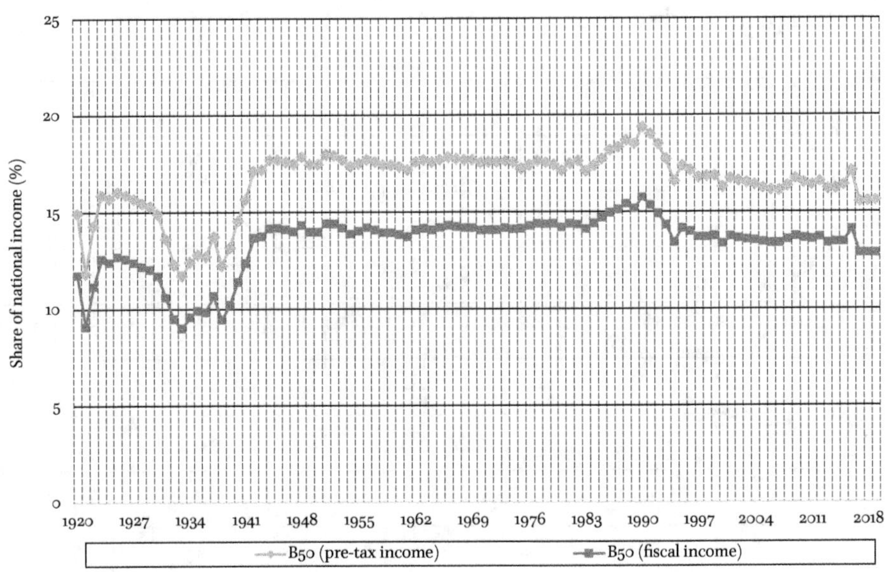

FIGURE 24 B50 income share in Canada, 1920–2019
FIGURE PRODUCED USING DATA FROM *WID.WORLD*

While the actual levels are quite different, the trends are quite similar: the T1 and T10 shares drop persistently (and significantly so) after the Second World War, before consistently trending upwards from the 1980s onwards. Simultaneously, the M40 and B50 shares shoot upwards at the onset of the Second World War, exhibit progressive increases until the 1980s and then begin to drop, with the B50 shares showing more pronounced movement that the M40 shares, which, although they move slightly, tend to stay rather stable over time.

WID.world contained no data for wealth shares in Canada at the time of writing.

2.2.2 East Asia and the Pacific

For current purposes, 'East Asia' refers to China, Japan, Korea (both North and South) and Mongolia. As for the 'Pacific', this region includes Australia, New Zealand, Singapore, Malaysia, Indonesia, Myanmar, Viet Nam, Laos, Thailand, the Philippines, as well as a number of smaller island states. Collectively, 'East Asia and Pacific' as defined here accounts for approximately 30 percent of the global population. As for the distribution of income and wealth within each of these states, *WID.world* contains especially complete data for China, at least from 1978 onwards, which makes up approximately 60 percent of the overall population in the region. Figures 25 through 32 accordingly serve as a good starting point for discussion:

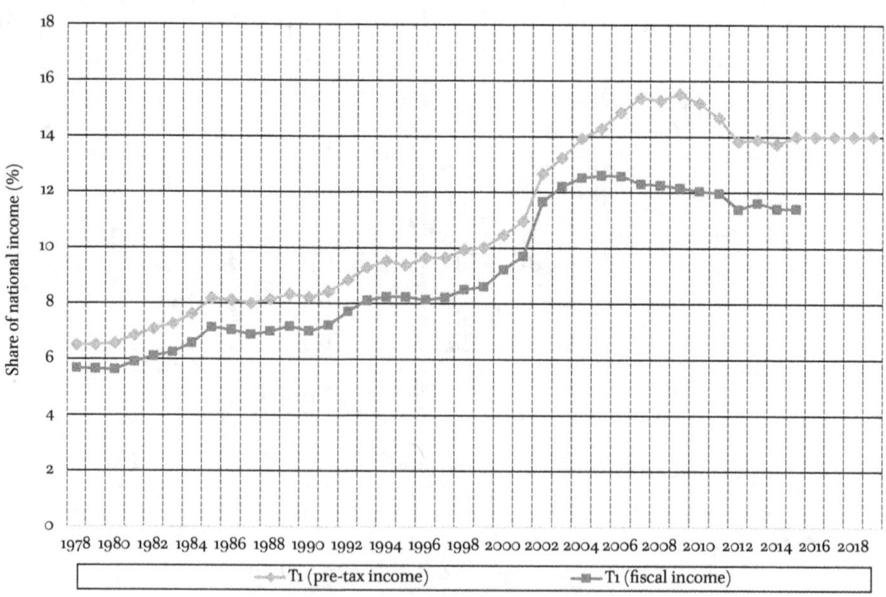

FIGURE 25 T1 income share in China, 1978–2019
FIGURE PRODUCED USING DATA FROM *WID.WORLD*

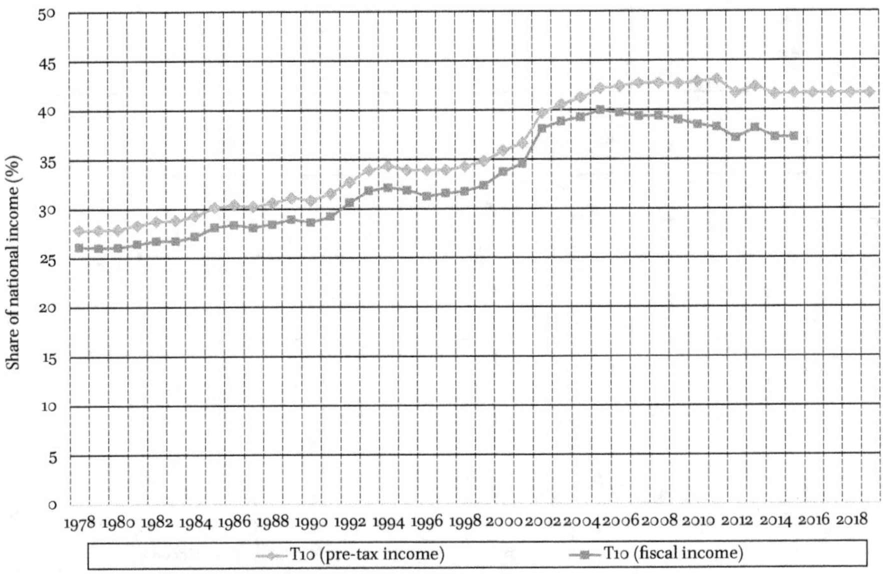

FIGURE 26 T10 income share in China, 1978–2019
FIGURE PRODUCED USING DATA FROM *WID.WORLD*

FIGURE 27 M40 income share in China, 1978–2019
FIGURE PRODUCED USING DATA FROM *WID.WORLD*

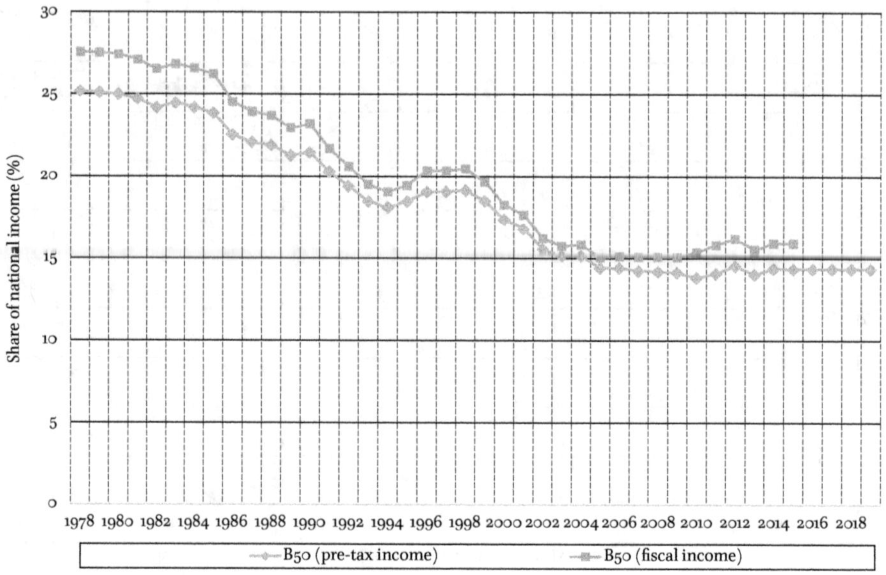

FIGURE 28 B50 income share in China, 1978–2019
FIGURE PRODUCED USING DATA FROM *WID.WORLD*

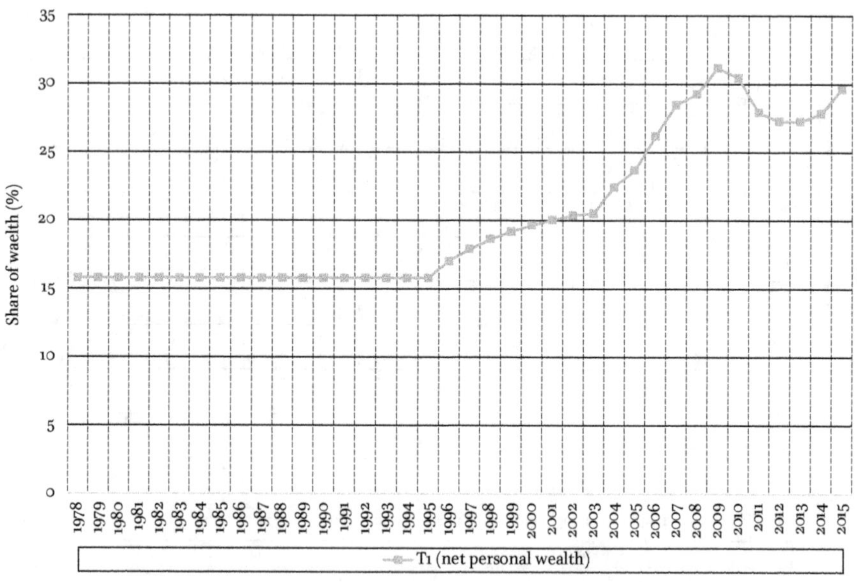

FIGURE 29 T1 wealth share in China, 1978–2015
FIGURE PRODUCED USING DATA FROM *WID.WORLD*

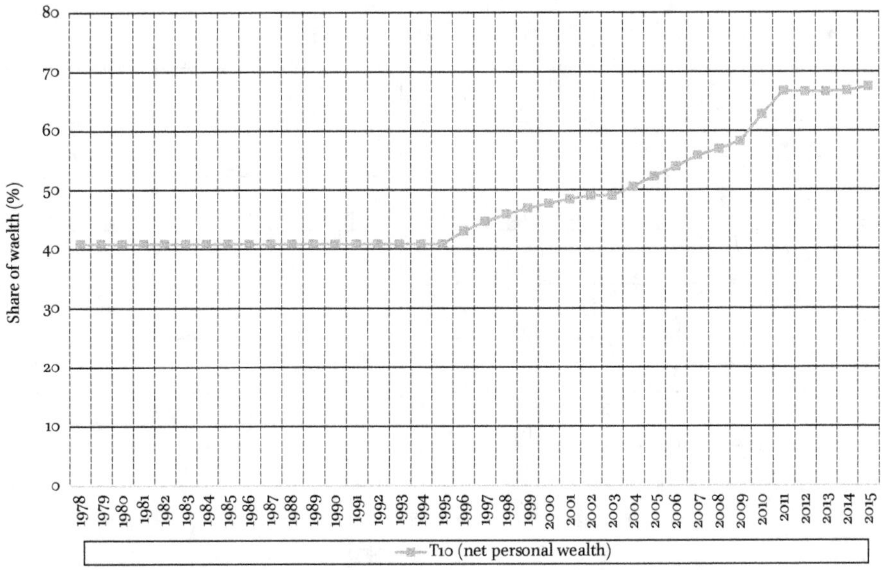

FIGURE 30 T10 wealth share in China, 1978–2015
FIGURE PRODUCED USING DATA FROM *WID.WORLD*

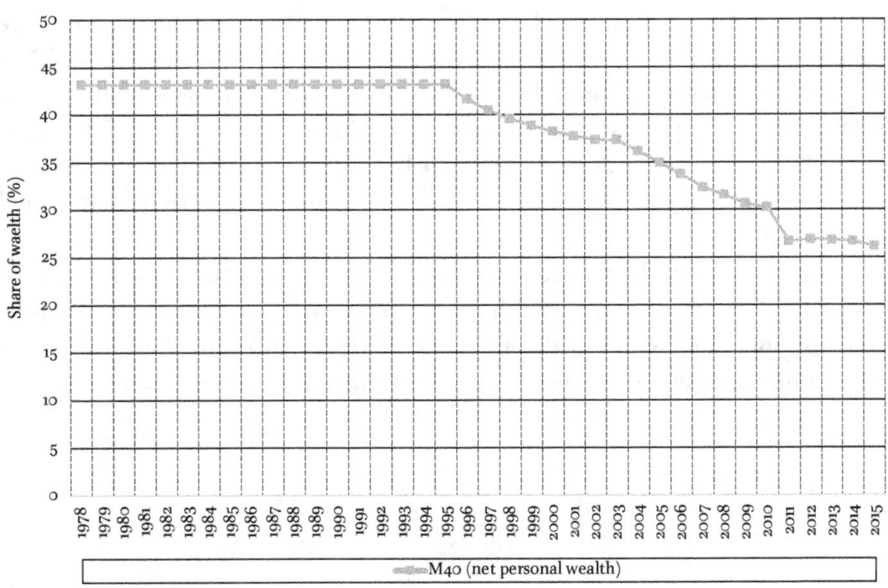

FIGURE 31 M40 wealth share in China, 1978–2015
FIGURE PRODUCED USING DATA FROM *WID.WORLD*

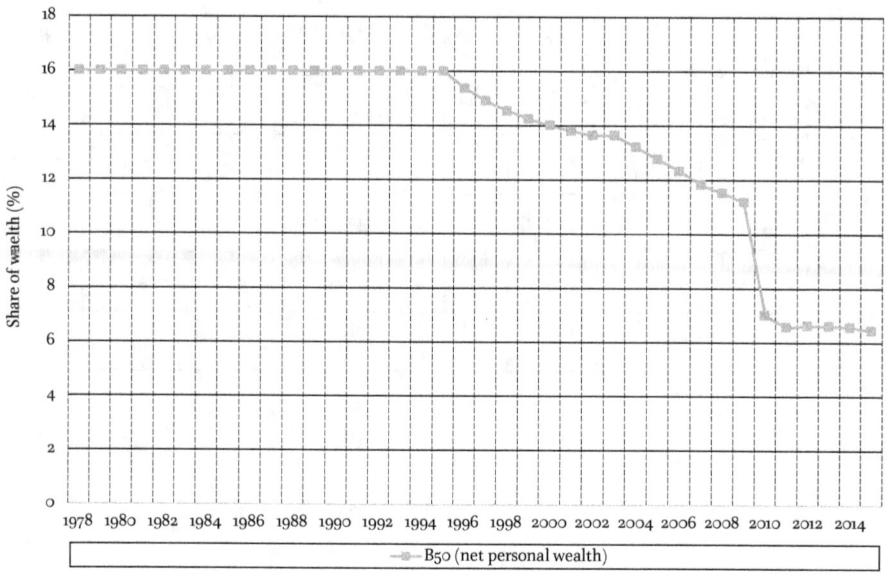

FIGURE 32 B50 wealth share in China, 1978–2015
FIGURE PRODUCED USING DATA FROM *WID.WORLD*

Since 1978, the directional trends in respect of income at the top have been largely similar to those observed in North America; the T1 and T10 shares have risen substantially. As for the M40 and B50 shares, they have also declined appreciably over the course of the last 40 years or so. As for wealth, essentially the same trends have been observed: the T1 and T10 shares have increased significantly, whereas the M40 and B50 shares have declined significantly.

One of the next largest countries in the region is Japan. *WID.world* contains no data on Japanese wealth shares, but it does contain quite complete data on income. Figures 33 through 36 provide us with some insight into the directional changes in respect of income shares in Japan over time:

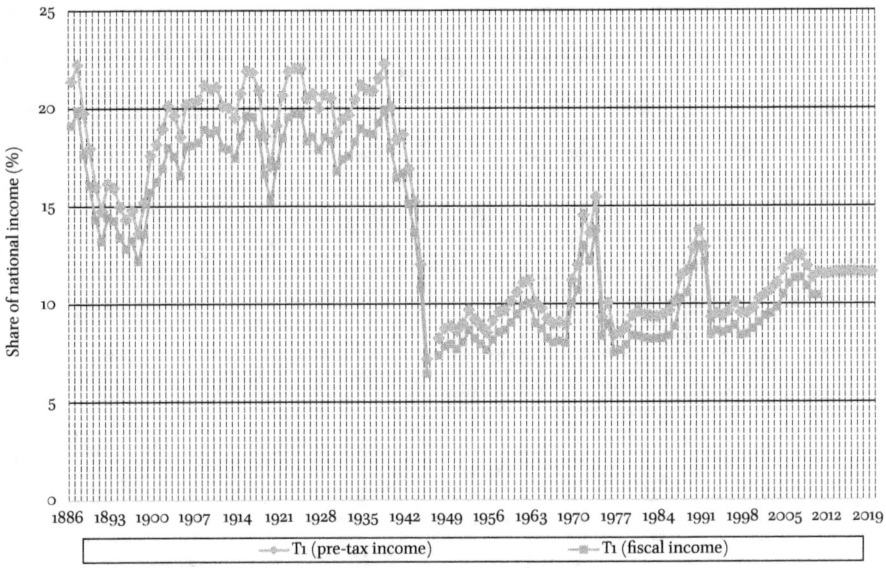

FIGURE 33 T1 income share in Japan, 1886–2019
FIGURE PRODUCED USING DATA FROM *WID.WORLD*

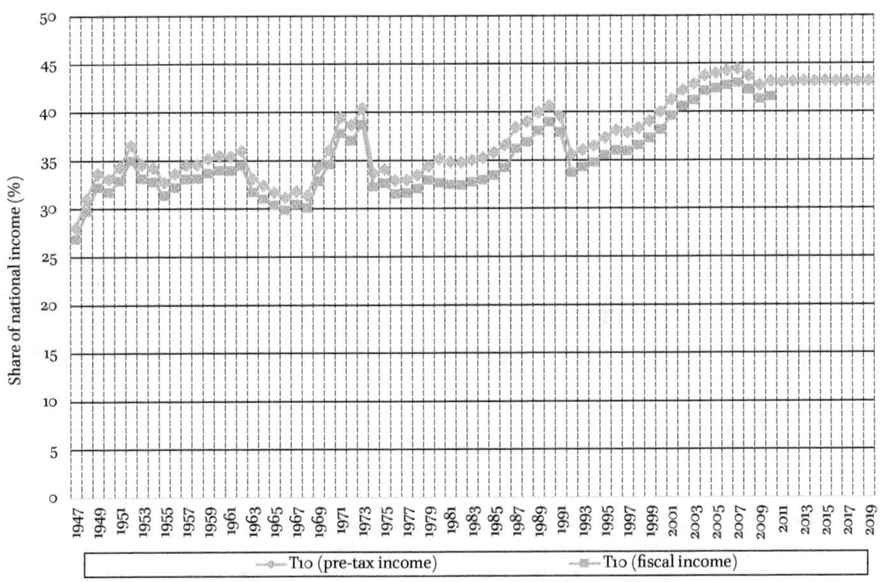

FIGURE 34 T10 income share in Japan, 1947–2019
FIGURE PRODUCED USING DATA FROM *WID.WORLD*

FIGURE 35 M40 income share in Japan, 1980–2019
FIGURE PRODUCED USING DATA FROM *WID.WORLD*

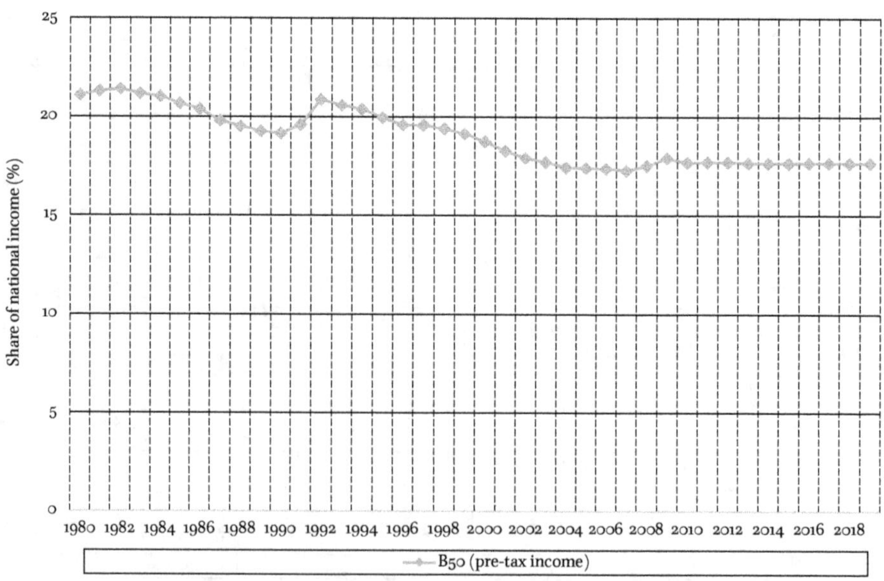

FIGURE 36 B50 income share in Japan, 1980–2019
FIGURE PRODUCED USING DATA FROM *WID.WORLD*

Important for current purposes, the T1 and T10 shares have progressively risen since 1980, whereas the M40 and B50 shares have progressively declined. The T1 and T10 shares in Japan in recent times remain notably below where they once were—but the fact remains that the directional trends since 1980 have been similar vis-à-vis those observed in other parts of the world.

WID.world also contains data for a number of other states in the region. These include Australia, Indonesia, New Zealand, Singapore and South Korea. Again, the Database does not include wealth data for these countries, but Figures 37 through 40 illustrate how income has been distributed among their inhabitants since the end of the Second World War and to the extent that *WID.world* contains the requisite data for each of the countries in question:

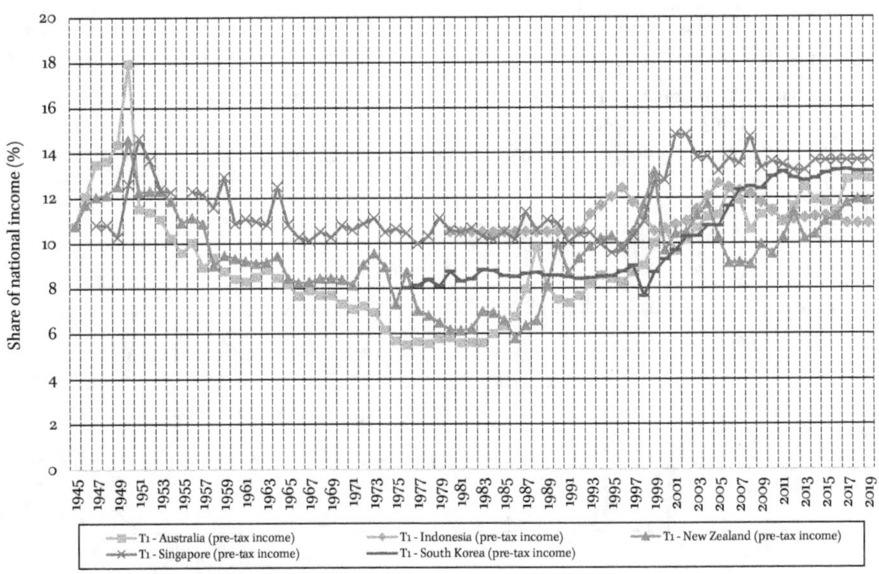

FIGURE 37 T1 income share in Australia, Indonesia, New Zealand, Singapore and South Korea, 1945–2019

FIGURE PRODUCED USING DATA FROM *WID.WORLD*

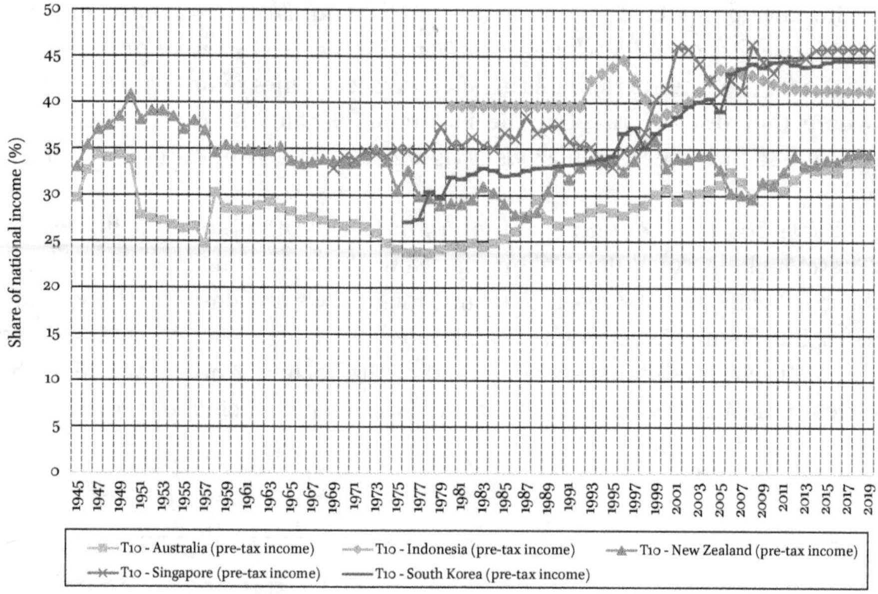

FIGURE 38 T10 income share in Australia, Indonesia, New Zealand, Singapore and South Korea, 1945–2019
FIGURE PRODUCED USING DATA FROM *WID.WORLD*

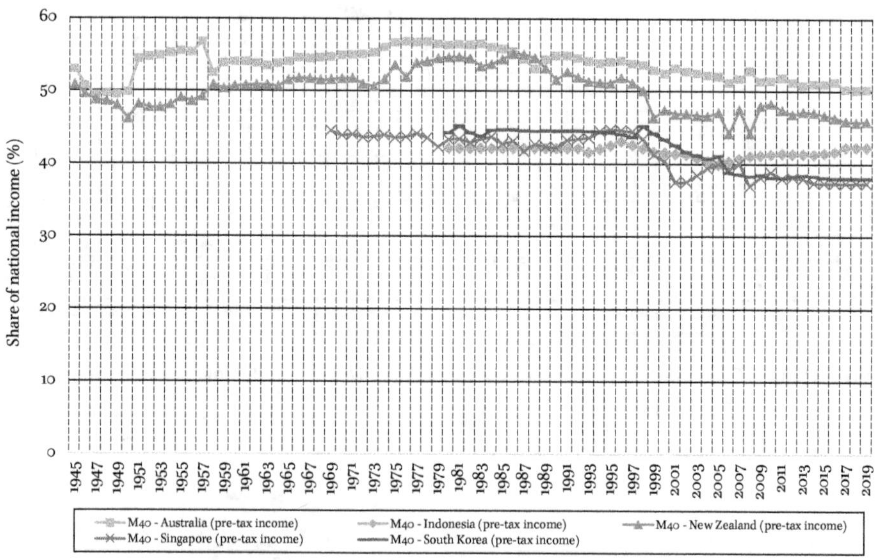

FIGURE 39 M40 income share in Australia, Indonesia, New Zealand, Singapore and South Korea, 1945–2019
FIGURE PRODUCED USING DATA FROM *WID.WORLD*

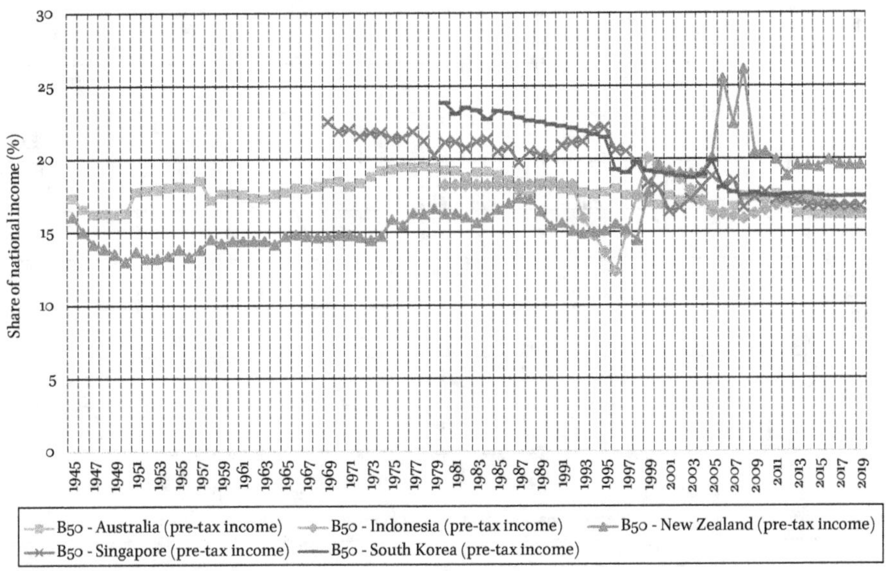

FIGURE 40 B50 income share in Australia, Indonesia, New Zealand, Singapore and South Korea, 1945–2019
FIGURE PRODUCED USING DATA FROM *WID.WORLD*

Again, the same patterns generally emerge. What these figures do show, however, is that the same patterns are not observable in each and every country. In New Zealand, for example, the B50 share rose significantly from 1980 until after the global financial crisis in 2008–2009 (since which it has fallen, but is still higher today than it was in the 1980s), whereas the M40 share has declined significantly. All this has unfolded alongside an increase for both the T1 and T10 shares. Another country in the region which has seemingly gone against the grain is Malaysia. Figures 41 through 44 seem to show that Malaysia has experienced the opposite of what most countries have experienced:

FIGURE 41 T1 income share in Malaysia, 1980–2019
FIGURE PRODUCED USING DATA FROM *WID.WORLD*

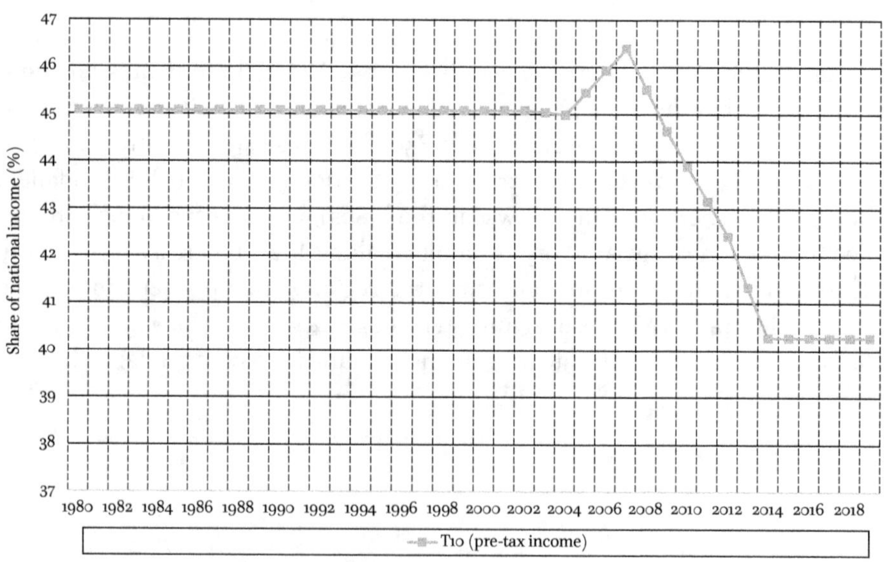

FIGURE 42 T10 income share in Malaysia, 1980–2019
FIGURE PRODUCED USING DATA FROM *WID.WORLD*

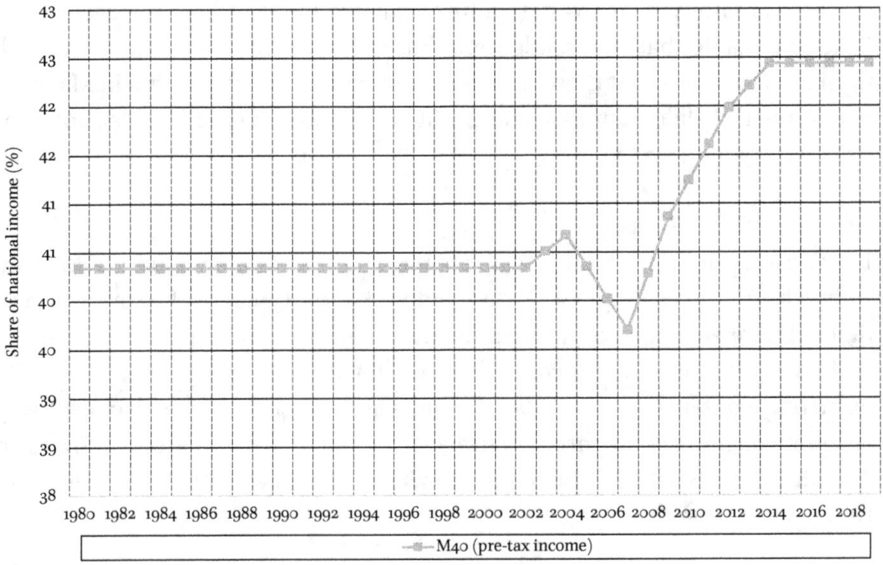

FIGURE 43 M40 income share in Malaysia, 1980–2019
FIGURE PRODUCED USING DATA FROM *WID.WORLD*

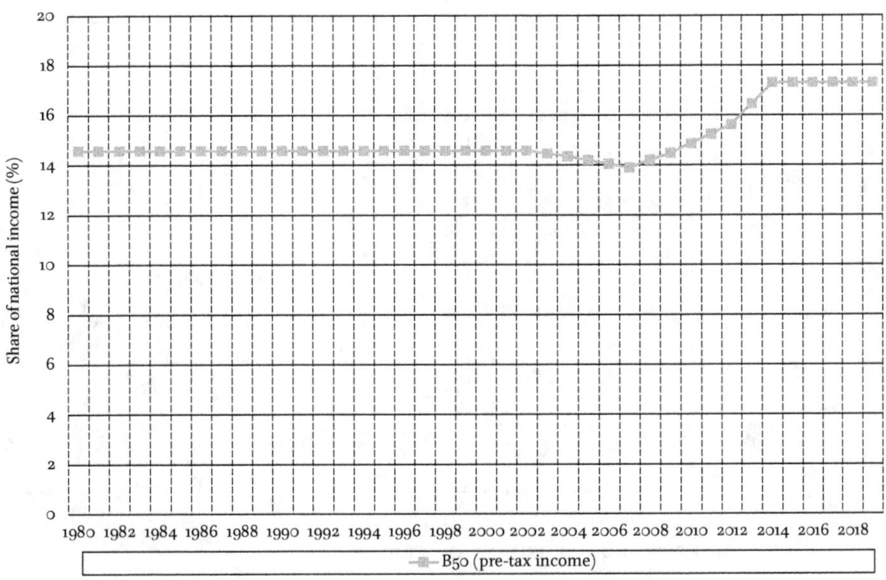

FIGURE 44 B50 income share in Malaysia, 1980–2019
FIGURE PRODUCED USING DATA FROM *WID.WORLD*

There are not very many datapoints available for Malaysia, however, and it is quite possible that the trends were thus quite different in reality. That said, even if one accepts that these figures accurately capture the trends in Malaysia over time, the Malaysian case could still be seen as the type of exception that proves the general rule.

2.2.3 South Asia

For current purposes, 'South Asia' refers to Afghanistan, Bangladesh, Bhutan, India, the Maldives, Nepal, Pakistan and Sri Lanka. Collectively, South Asia as defined here accounts for approximately 25 percent of the global population. As for the distribution of income and wealth within each of these states, *WID.world* only contains pertinent data for India and Bangladesh, which collectively account for more than three quarters of the region's population. *WID.world* contains particularly complete data for India, which allows for the construction of Figures 45 through 52:

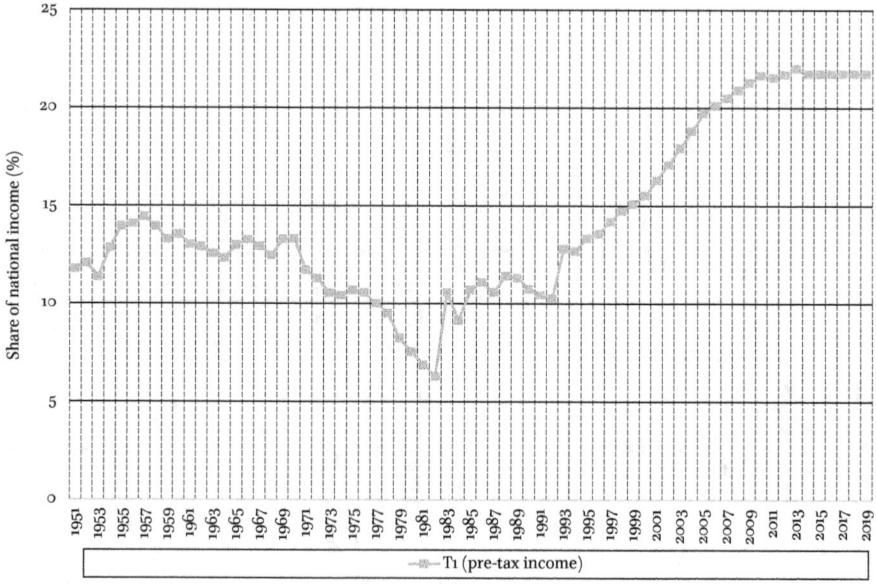

FIGURE 45 T1 income share in India, 1951–2019
FIGURE PRODUCED USING DATA FROM *WID.WORLD*

FIGURE 46 T10 income share in India, 1951–2019
FIGURE PRODUCED USING DATA FROM *WID.WORLD*

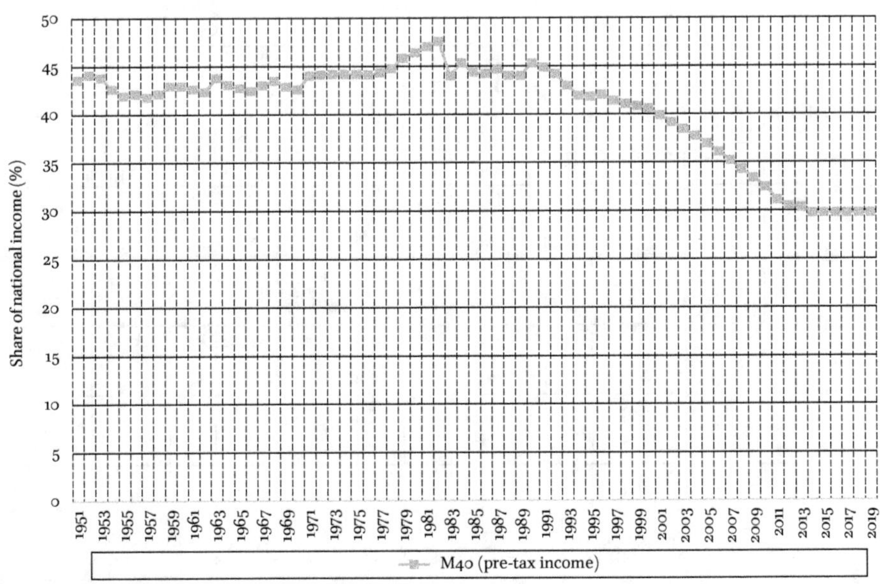

FIGURE 47 M40 income share in India, 1951–2019
FIGURE PRODUCED USING DATA FROM *WID.WORLD*

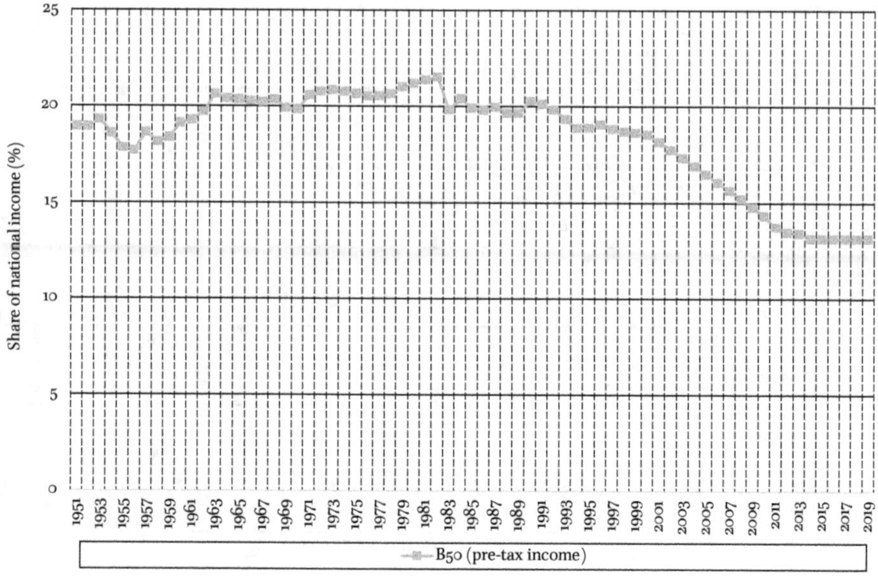

FIGURE 48 B50 income share in India, 1951–2019
FIGURE PRODUCED USING DATA FROM *WID.WORLD*

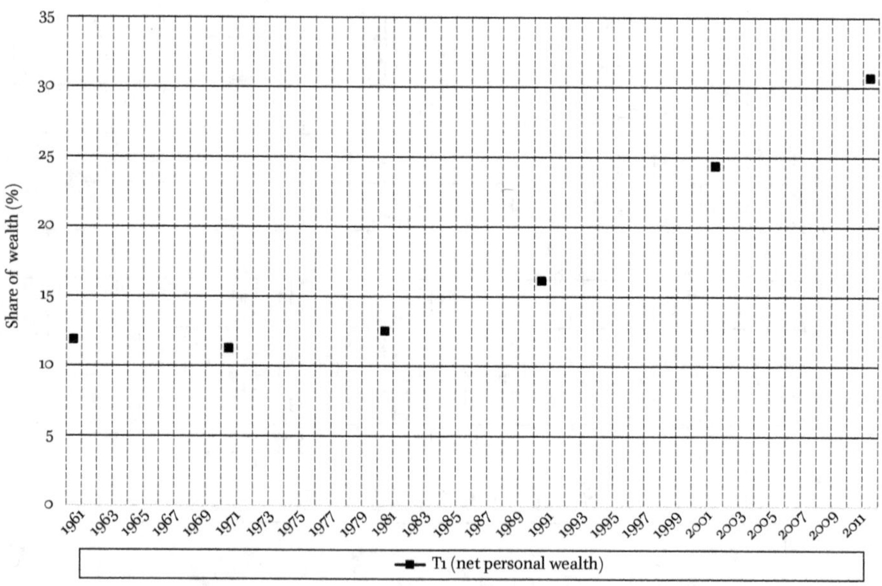

FIGURE 49 T1 wealth share in India, 1961–2012
FIGURE PRODUCED USING DATA FROM *WID.WORLD*

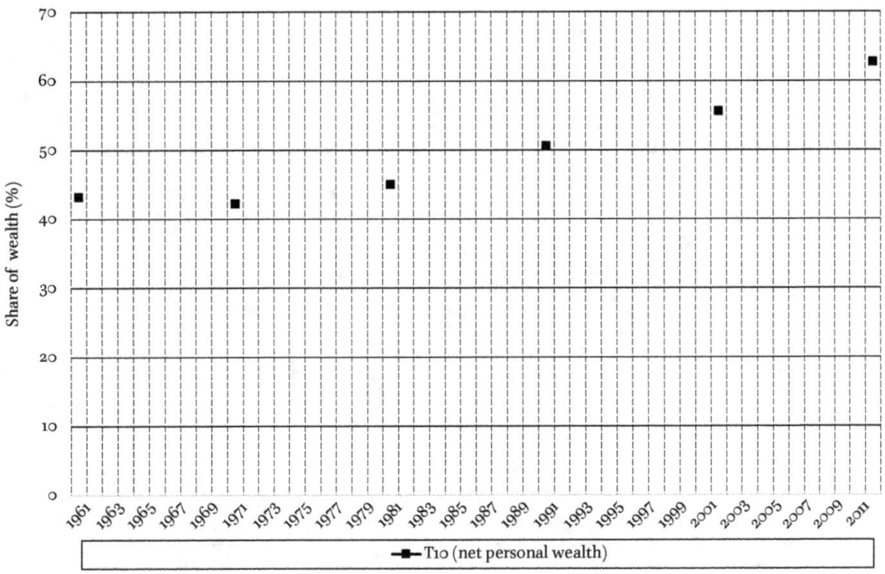

FIGURE 50 T10 wealth share in India, 1961–2012
FIGURE PRODUCED USING DATA FROM *WID.WORLD*

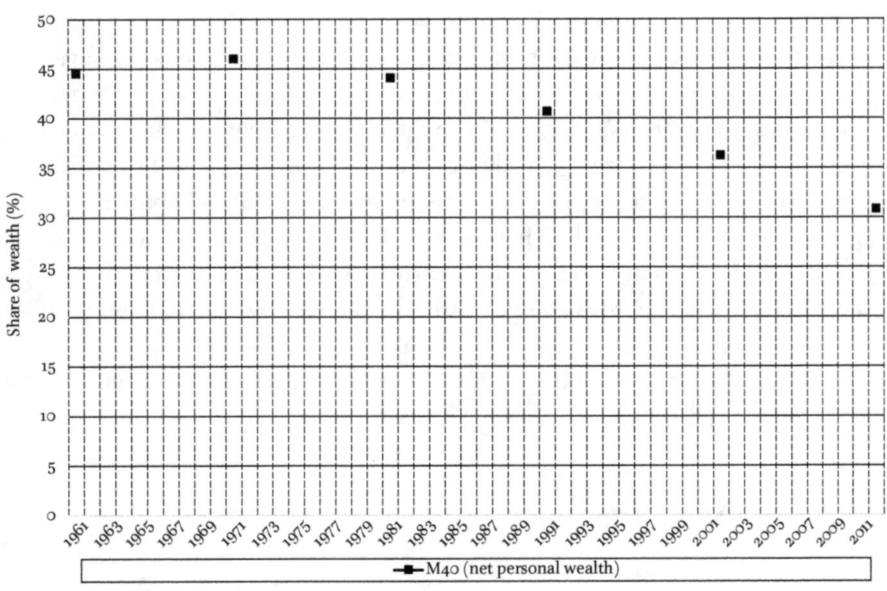

FIGURE 51 M40 wealth share in India, 1961–2012
FIGURE PRODUCED USING DATA FROM *WID.WORLD*

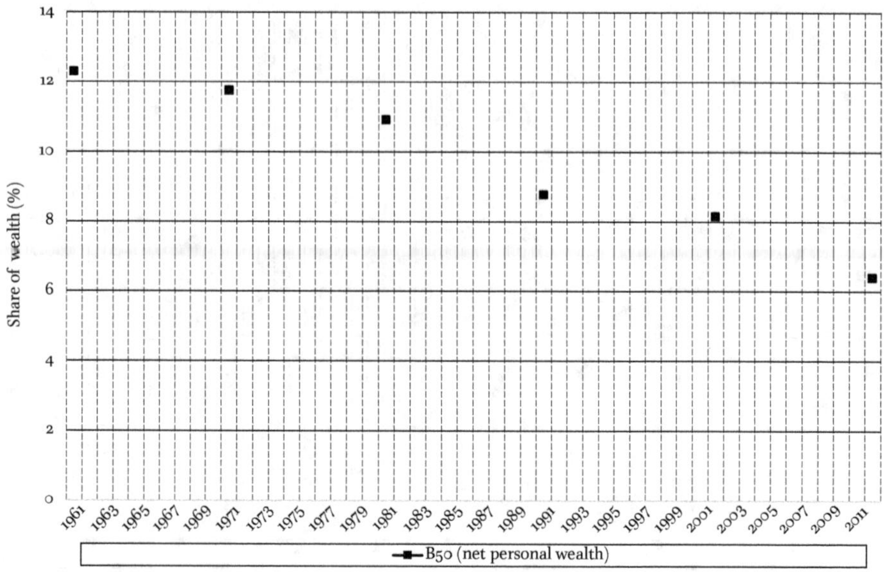

FIGURE 52 B50 wealth share in India, 1961–2012
FIGURE PRODUCED USING DATA FROM *WID.WORLD*

As the graphs illustrate, the evolution of economic distributions in India over time follow similar directional trends to the general trends we have seen thus far. In respect of income, it would seem that in India, too, the T1 and T10 shares started at pre-War highs, after which they fell consistently for around 40 years before rising significantly from around 1980 onwards. Similarly, also, the M40 and B50 shares appear to increase until 1980 and then both show substantial declines in the following three or four decades. As for wealth, the T1 and T10 shares appear to have consistently increased since the 1960s, whereas the M40 and B50 shares have consistently decreased over that same period of time.

Similar, albeit less pronounced, income trends have unfolded in Bangladesh (see Figures 53 through 56):

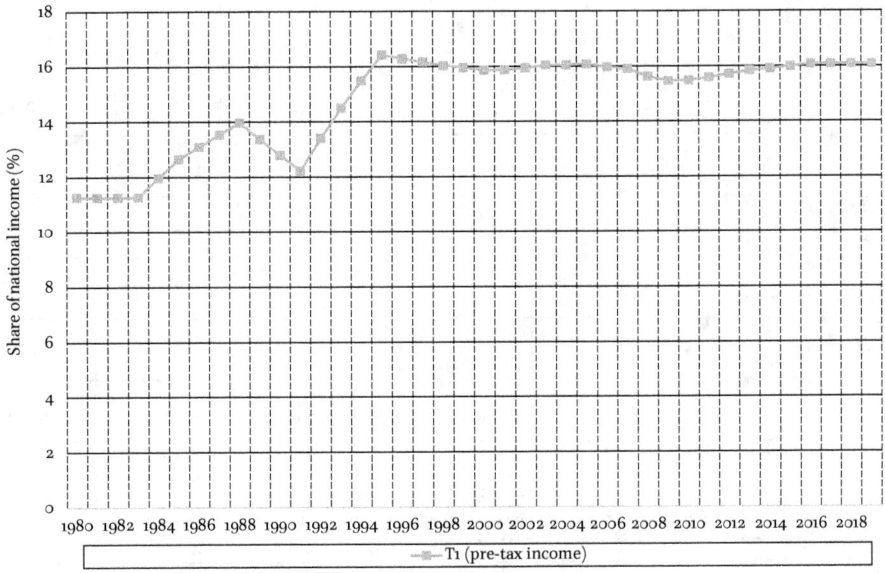

FIGURE 53 T1 income share in Bangladesh, 1980–2019
FIGURE PRODUCED USING DATA FROM *WID.WORLD*

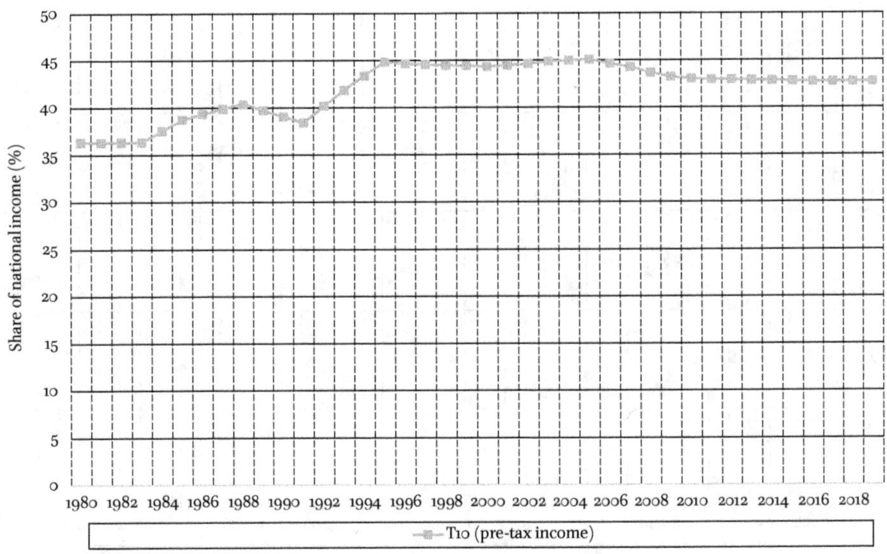

FIGURE 54 T10 income share in Bangladesh, 1980–2019
FIGURE PRODUCED USING DATA FROM *WID.WORLD*

FIGURE 55 M40 income share in Bangladesh, 1980–2019
FIGURE PRODUCED USING DATA FROM *WID.WORLD*

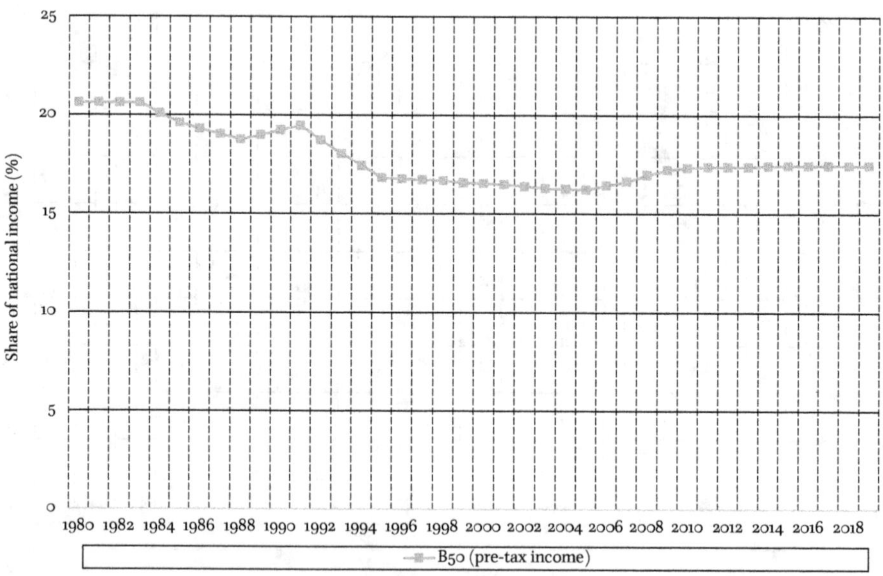

FIGURE 56 B50 income share in Bangladesh, 1980–2019
FIGURE PRODUCED USING DATA FROM *WID.WORLD*

2.2.4 Europe and Central Asia

For current purposes, 'Europe and Central Asia' consists of the 58 countries that are longitudinally situated between Portugal and Russia (both of these countries included). They collectively account for approximately 12 percent of the global population. As for the distribution of income and wealth within these states, *WID.world* contains especially complete data for France and Russia. It also contains income data for a large set of countries in this region, as well as wealth data for the United Kingdom. Figures 57 through 78 accordingly provide a helpful snapshot of economic inequality trends within this region:

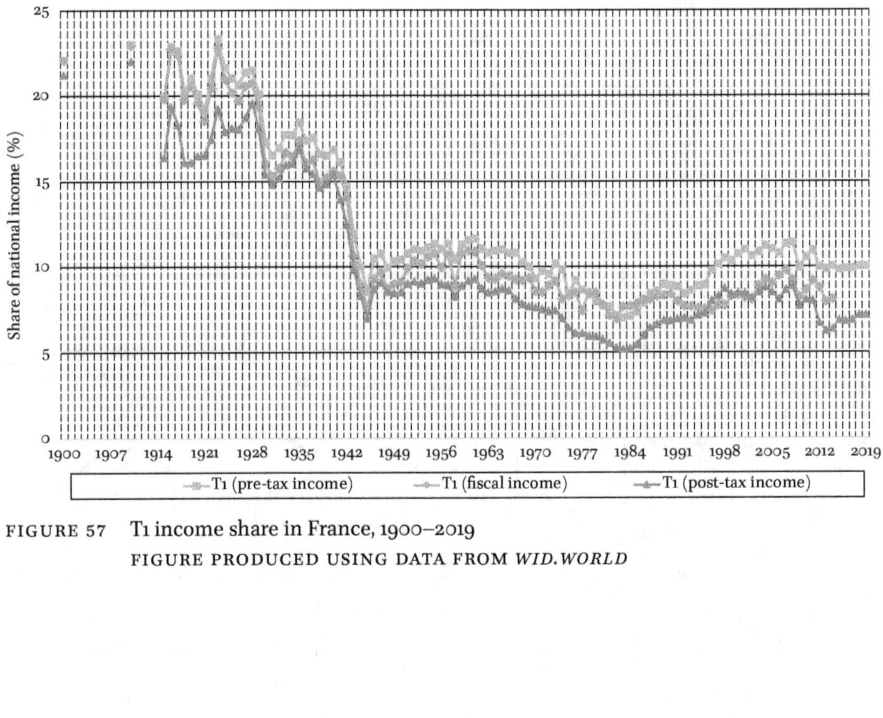

FIGURE 57 T1 income share in France, 1900–2019
FIGURE PRODUCED USING DATA FROM *WID.WORLD*

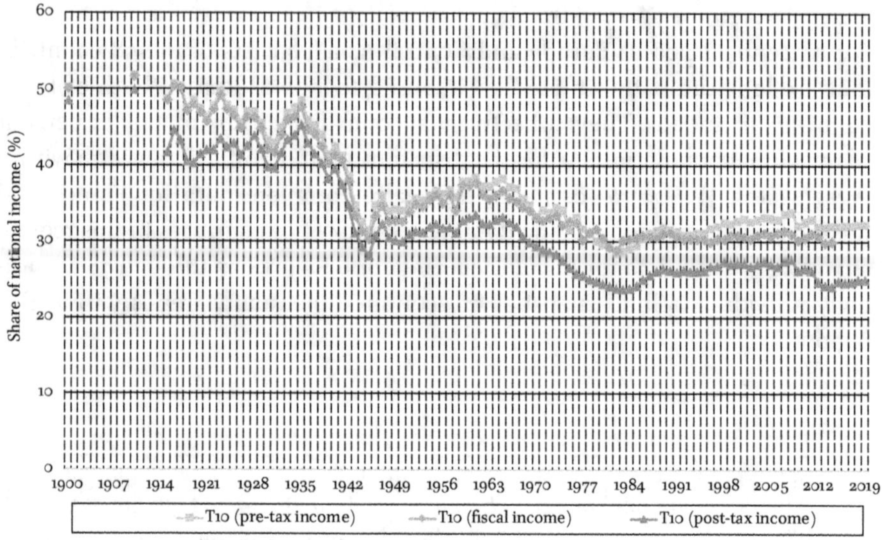

FIGURE 58 T10 income share in France, 1900–2019
FIGURE PRODUCED USING DATA FROM *WID.WORLD*

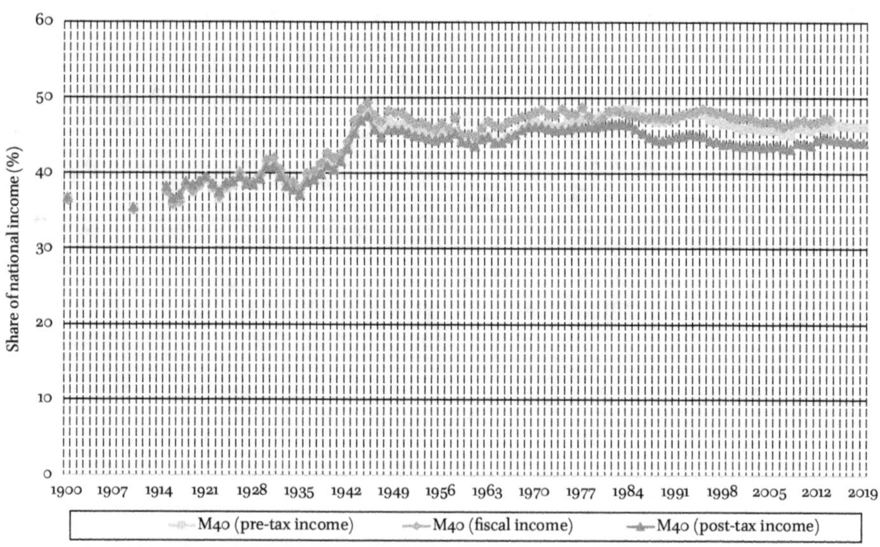

FIGURE 59 M40 income share in France, 1900–2019
FIGURE PRODUCED USING DATA FROM *WID.WORLD*

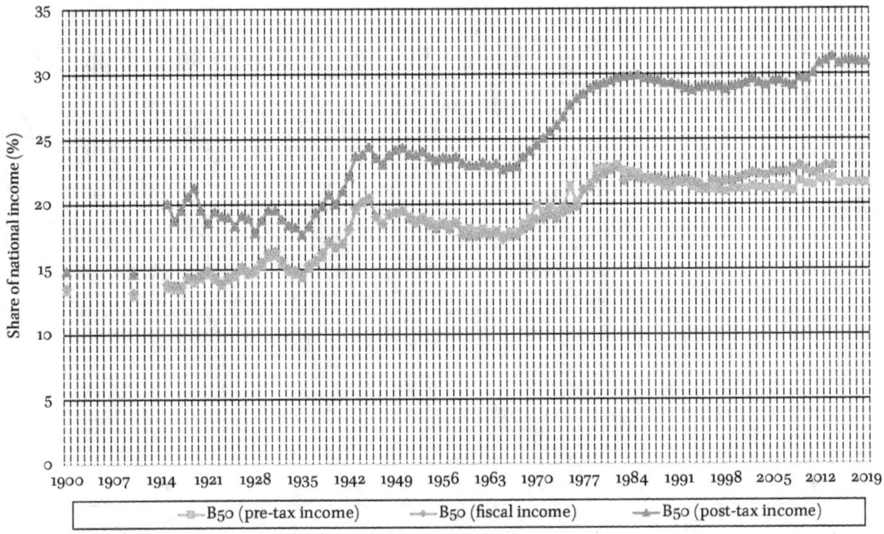

FIGURE 60 B50 income share in France, 1900–2019
FIGURE PRODUCED USING DATA FROM *WID.WORLD*

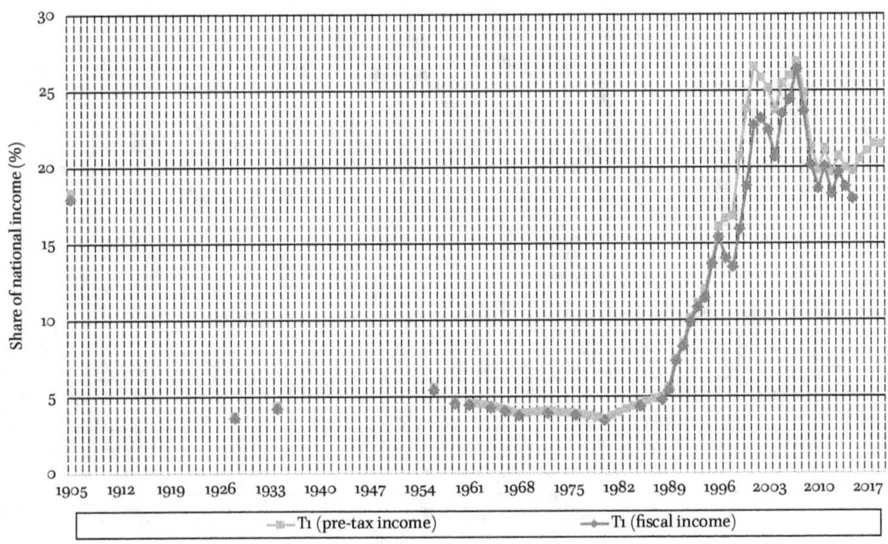

FIGURE 61 T1 income share in Russia, 1905–2019
FIGURE PRODUCED USING DATA FROM *WID.WORLD*

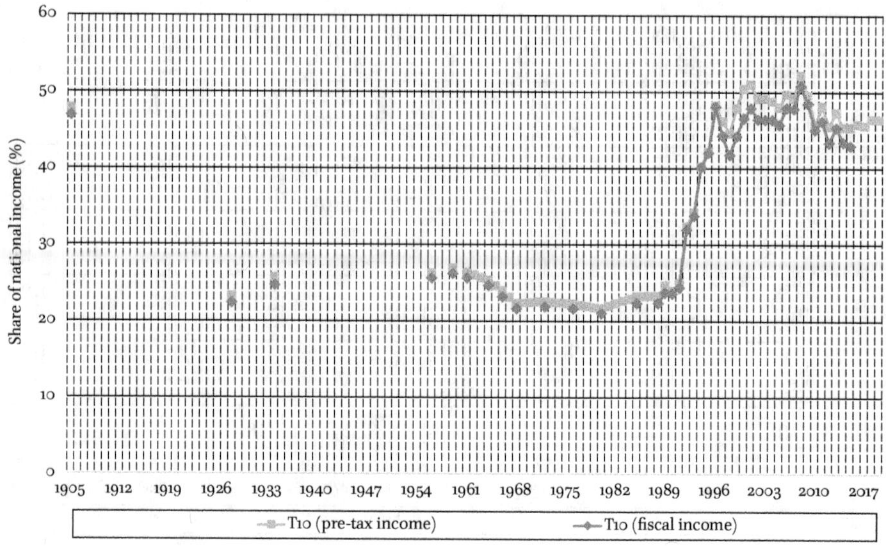

FIGURE 62 T10 income share in Russia, 1905–2019
FIGURE PRODUCED USING DATA FROM *WID.WORLD*

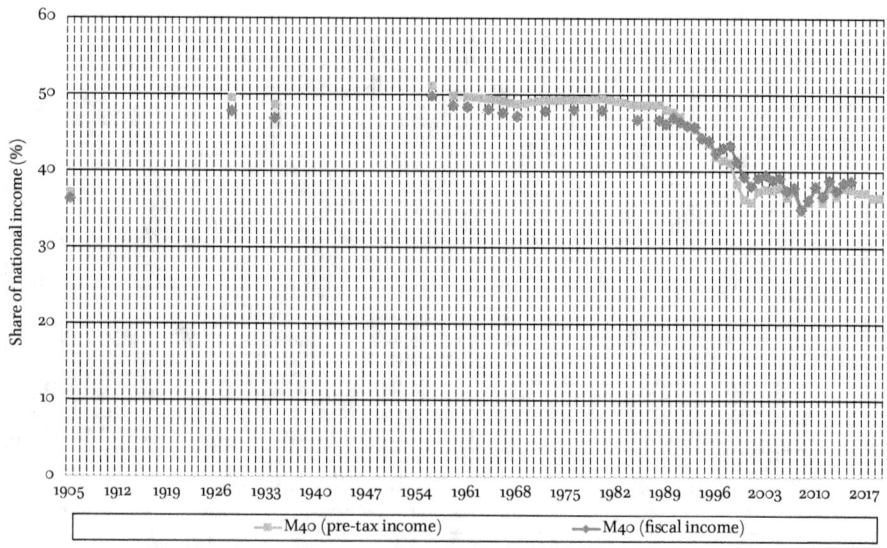

FIGURE 63 M40 income share in Russia, 1905–2019
FIGURE PRODUCED USING DATA FROM *WID.WORLD*

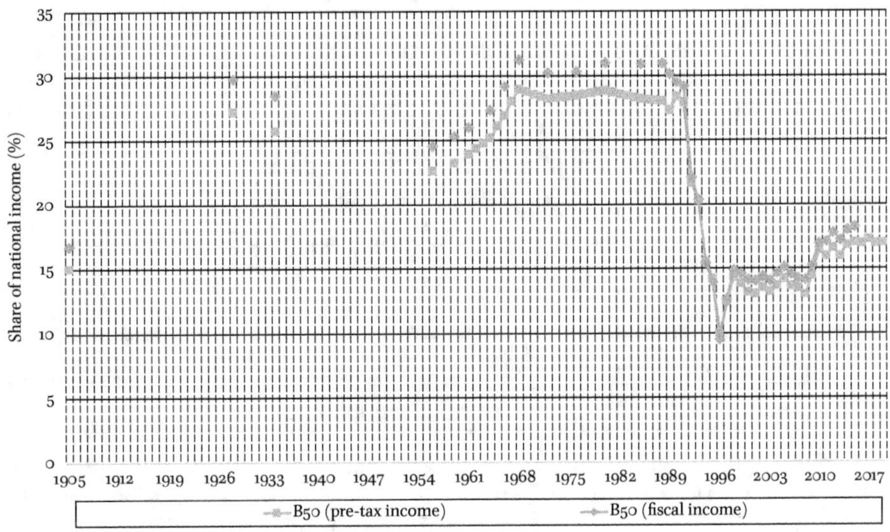

FIGURE 64 B50 income share in Russia, 1905–2019
FIGURE PRODUCED USING DATA FROM *WID.WORLD*

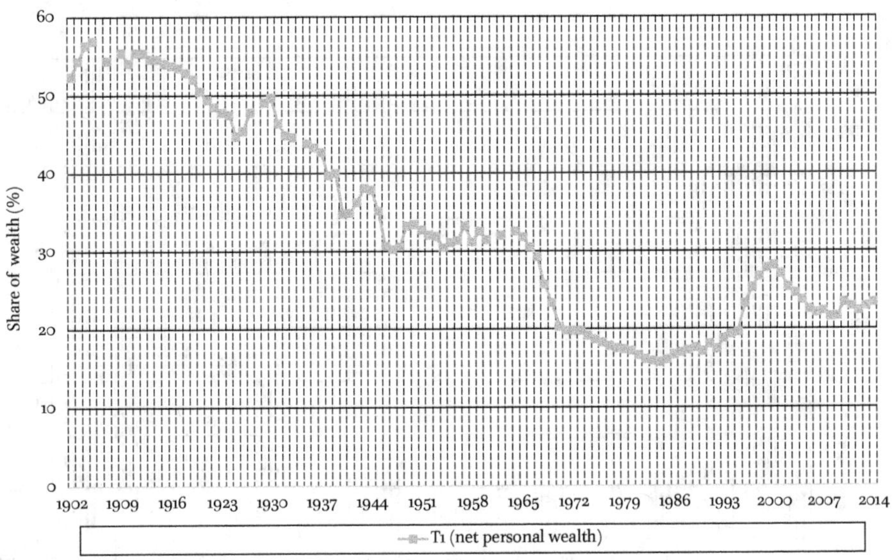

FIGURE 65 T1 wealth share in France, 1902–2014
FIGURE PRODUCED USING DATA FROM *WID.WORLD*

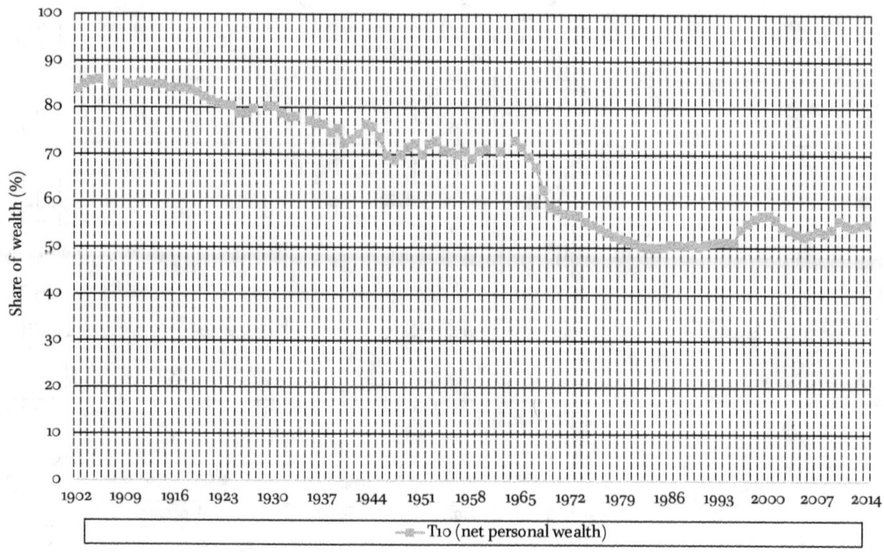

FIGURE 66 T10 wealth share in France, 1902–2014
FIGURE PRODUCED USING DATA FROM *WID.WORLD*

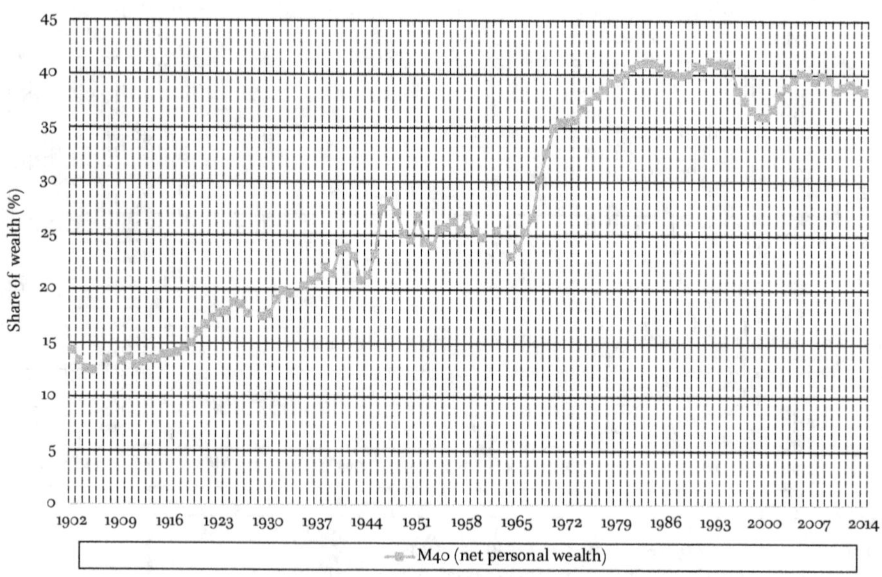

FIGURE 67 M40 wealth share in France, 1902–2014
FIGURE PRODUCED USING DATA FROM *WID.WORLD*

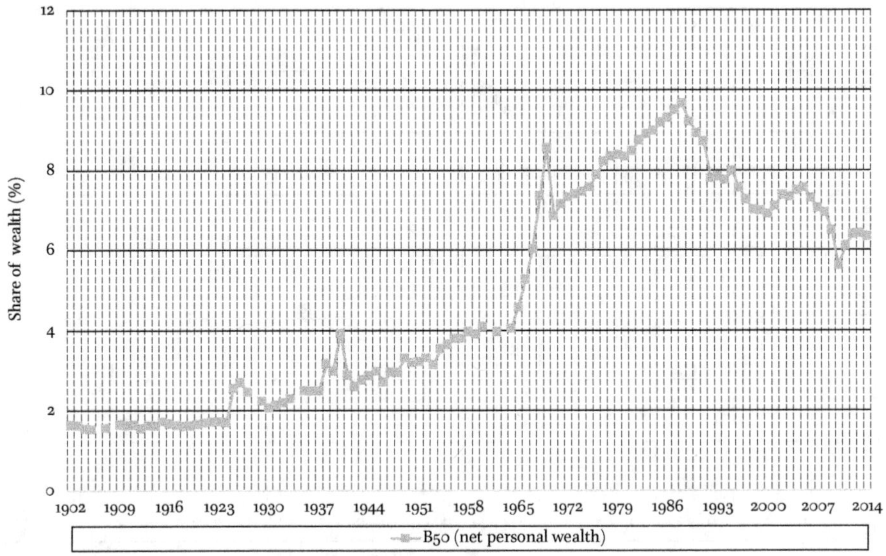

FIGURE 68 B50 wealth share in France, 1902–2014
FIGURE PRODUCED USING DATA FROM *WID.WORLD*

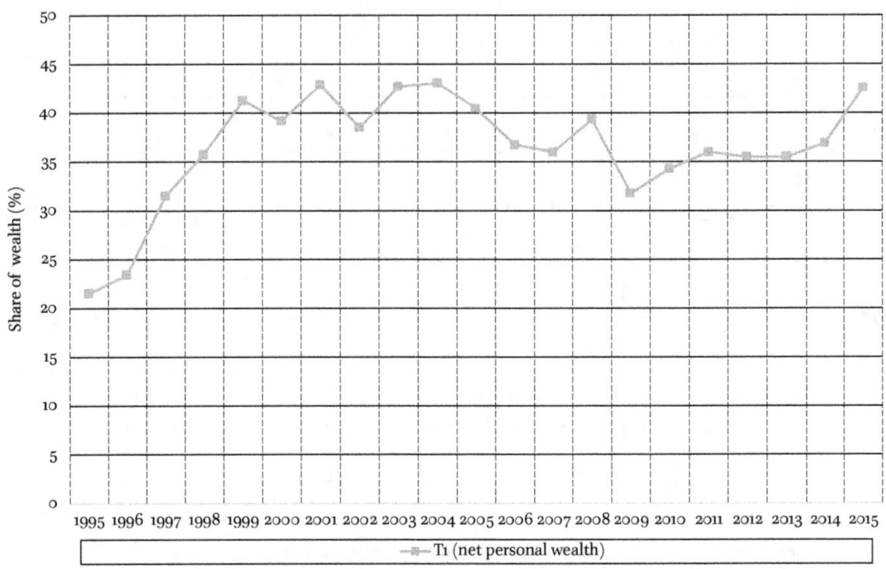

FIGURE 69 T1 wealth share in Russia, 1995–2015
FIGURE PRODUCED USING DATA FROM *WID.WORLD*

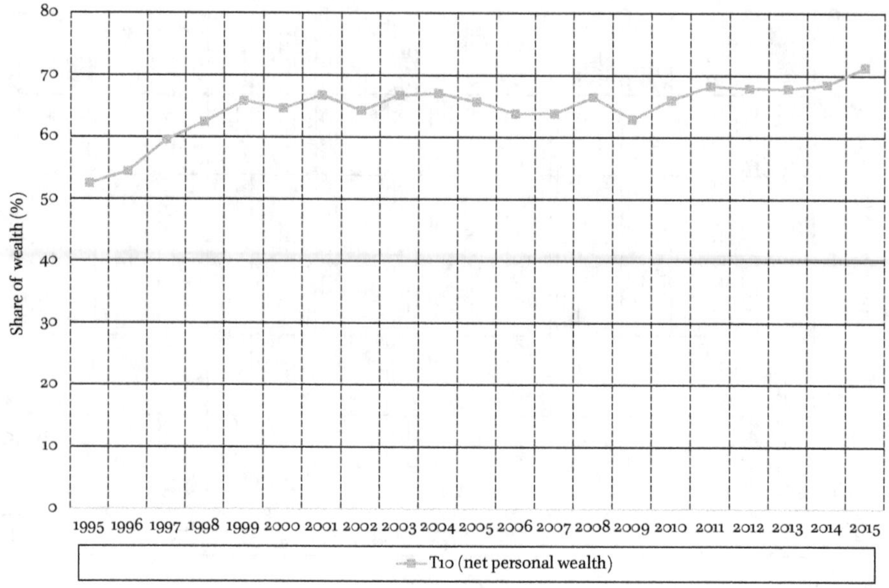

FIGURE 70 T10 wealth share in Russia, 1995–2015
FIGURE PRODUCED USING DATA FROM *WID.WORLD*

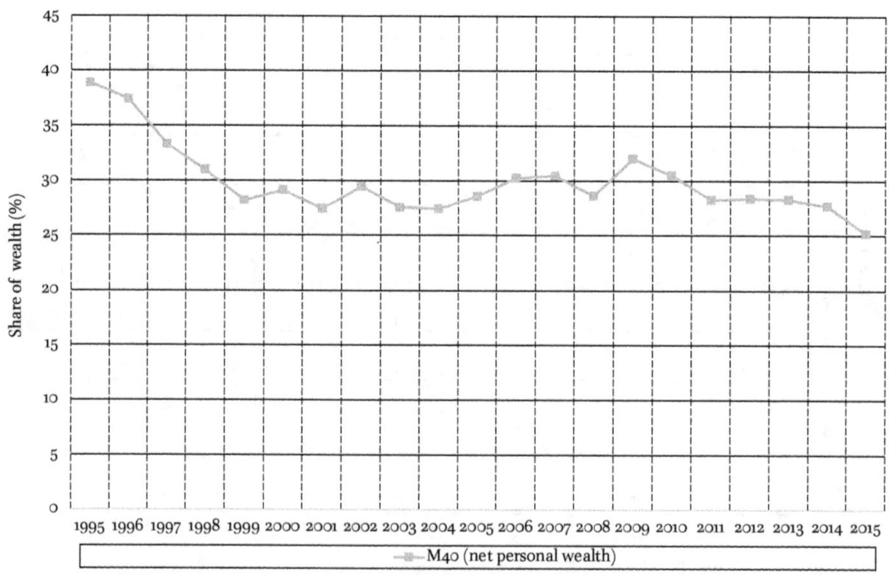

FIGURE 71 M40 wealth share in Russia, 1995–2015
FIGURE PRODUCED USING DATA FROM *WID.WORLD*

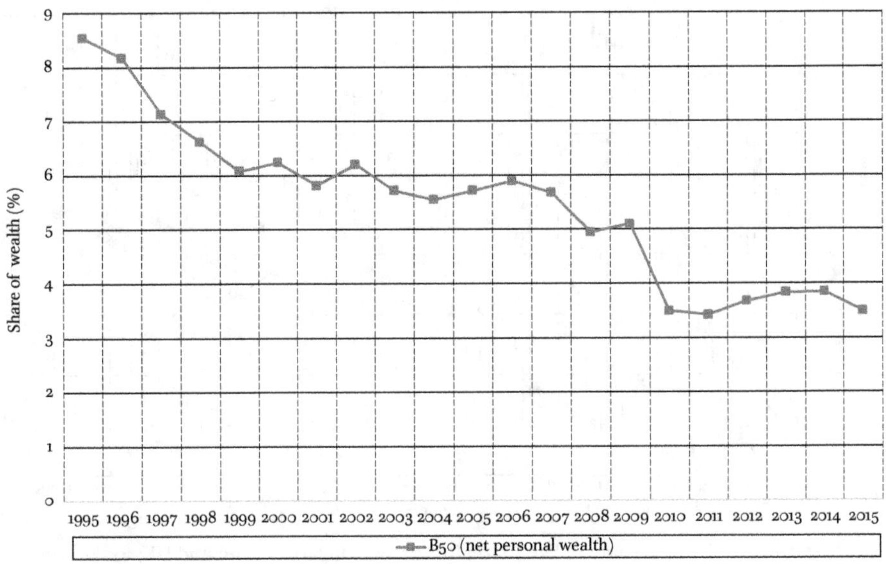

FIGURE 72 B50 wealth share in Russia, 1995–2015
FIGURE PRODUCED USING DATA FROM *WID.WORLD*

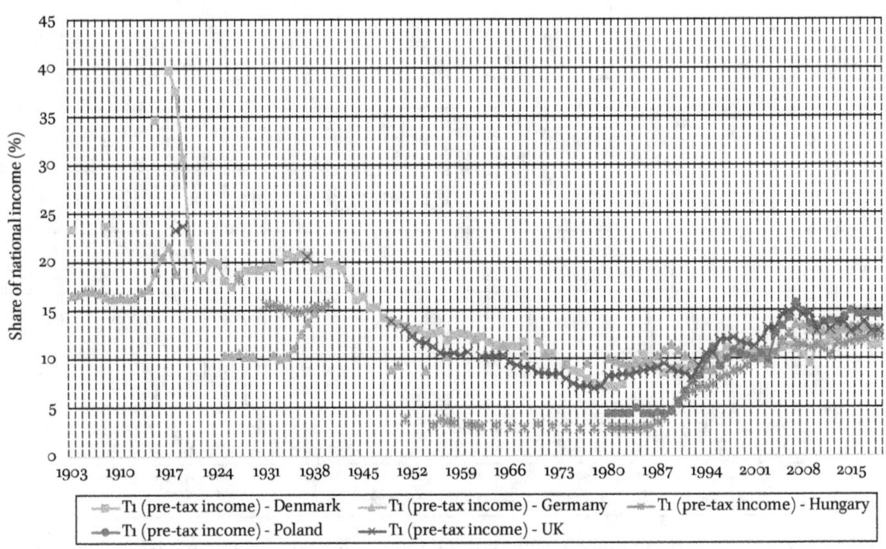

FIGURE 73 T1 income share in Denmark, Germany, Hungary, Poland and UK, 1903–2019
FIGURE PRODUCED USING DATA FROM *WID.WORLD*

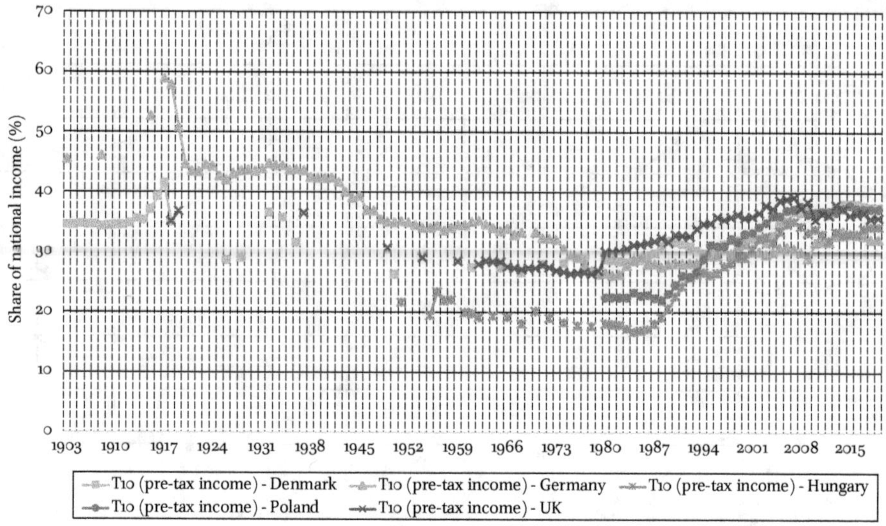

FIGURE 74 T10 income share in Denmark, Germany, Hungary, Poland and UK, 1903–2019
FIGURE PRODUCED USING DATA FROM *WID.WORLD*

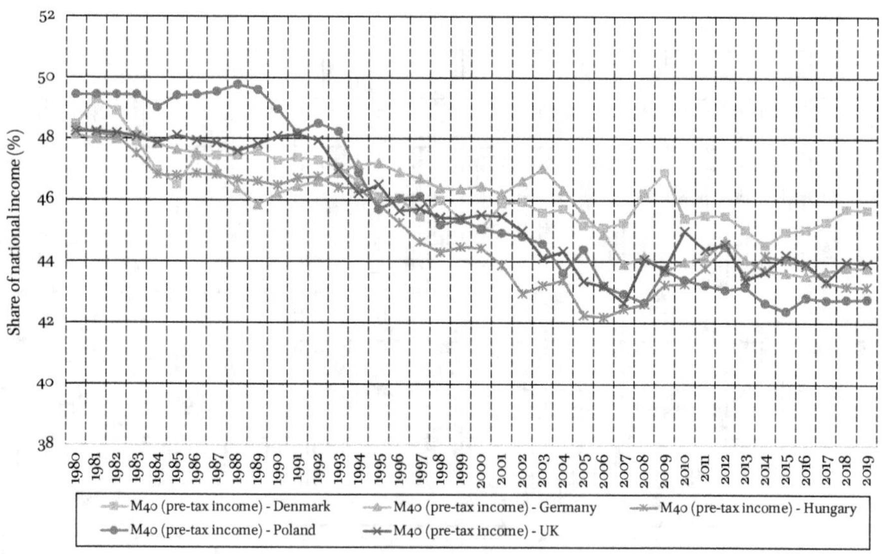

FIGURE 75 M40 income share in Denmark, Germany, Hungary, Poland and UK, 1980–2019
FIGURE PRODUCED USING DATA FROM *WID.WORLD*

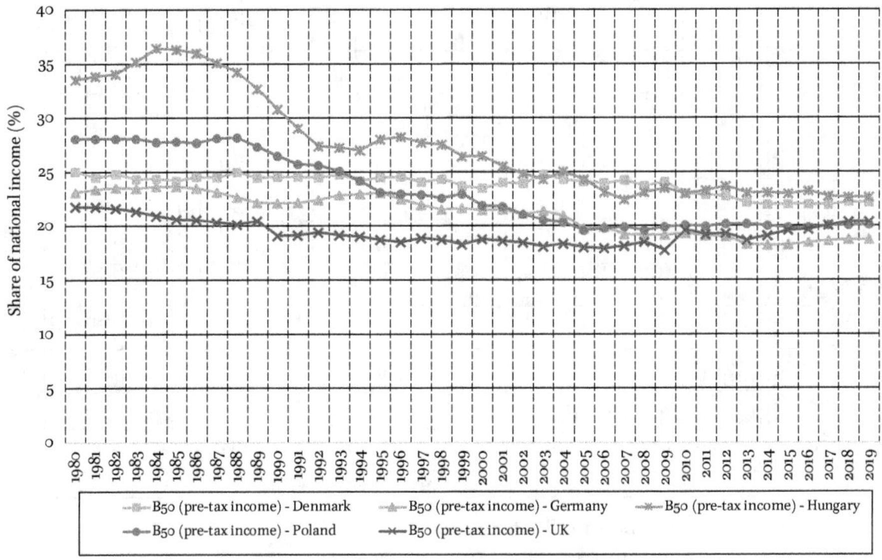

FIGURE 76 B50 income share in Denmark, Germany, Hungary, Poland and UK, 1980–2019
FIGURE PRODUCED USING DATA FROM *WID.WORLD*

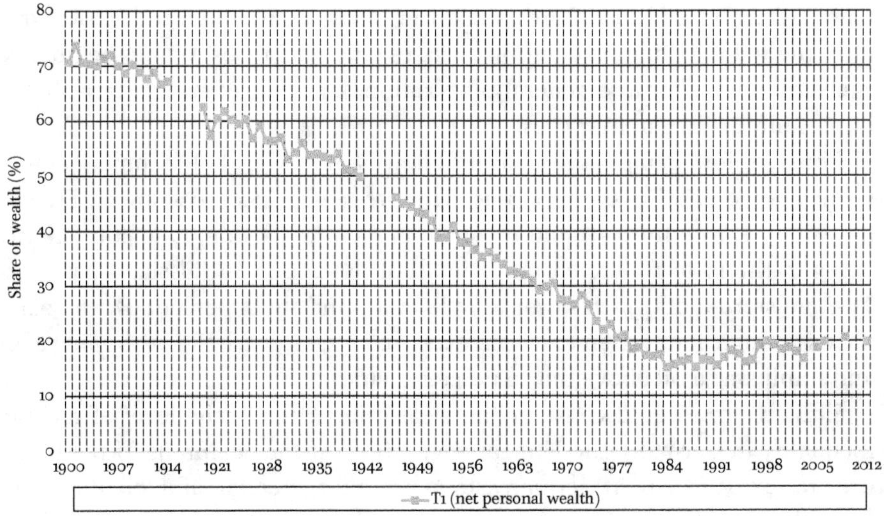

FIGURE 77 T1 wealth share in UK, 1900–2012
FIGURE PRODUCED USING DATA FROM *WID.WORLD*

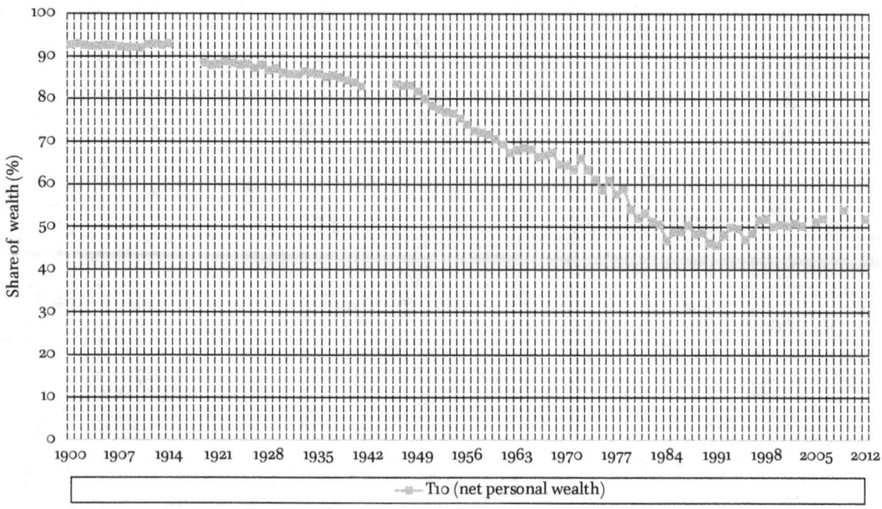

FIGURE 78 T10 wealth share in UK, 1900–2012
FIGURE PRODUCED USING DATA FROM *WID.WORLD*

While there is much nuance to this story, the figures tend to show the same trends that have become all too familiar: falling T1 and T10 shares until the 1980s, rising T1 and T10 shares since the 1980s; rising M40 and B50 shares until the 1980s, falling M40 and B50 shares since the 1980s. While the nuance is clearly important as a general proposition, it is the general pattern that is important for current purposes.

Consider for example the clear differences in the level of income inequality in France and Russia over time. The pre-tax T1 income share in France, for example, rose from around the eight percent mark in 1980 to consistently being in the 10 to 11 percent range in all of the 2000s. In Russia, the pre-tax T1 share started off much lower in 1980 at around three percent. By the early 2000s, though, it has risen to well in excess of 25 percent, before dropping a bit and stabilising a bit above the 20 percent mark.

Similarly, one could consider the clear differences in the level of income inequality in Germany and Hungary over time. At the beginning of the 1980s, the pre-tax B50 share in Germany stood around 23 percent and fell quite consistently over time to around 19 percent by 2019. In Hungary, the B50 share started off much higher in 1980 at around 34 percent and dropped to around 23 percent by 2019.

The levels of inequality and the rate at which these levels have changed over time in different countries are often, though not always, far from the same. The fact remains, however, that the general trends share distinct similarities. The main proposition at the end of the day is simply that economic inequality within countries has risen significantly in most parts of the world, and for most of its people, since the 1980s. This should be viewed against the backdrop of a number of decades of inequality falling nearly everywhere around the world in the decades preceding 1980.

2.2.5 Sub-Saharan Africa

For current purposes, 'Sub-Saharan Africa' consists of 48 countries. They collectively account for approximately 14 percent of the global population. The number of datapoints available on Sub-Saharan African countries are as general proposition lower than those available for countries in the other regions examined thus far. Still, as Figures 79 through 86 show, enough data exist to paint a picture of some of the trends that have unfolded in this region.

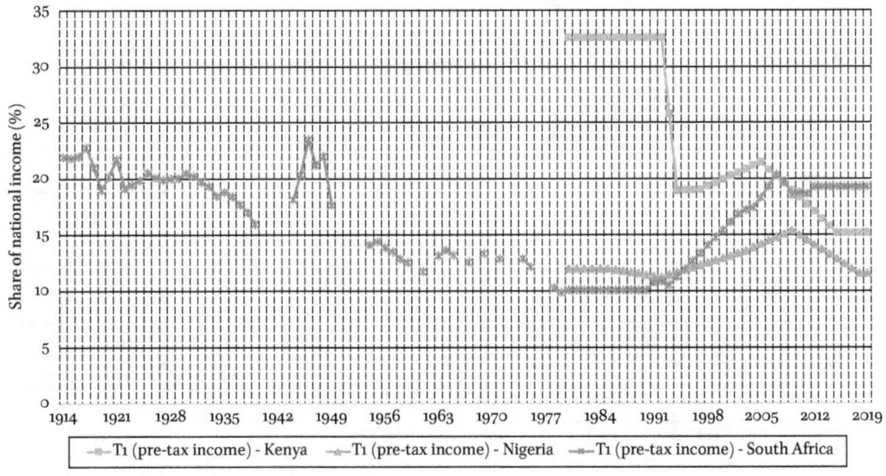

FIGURE 79 T1 income share in Kenya, Nigeria and South Africa, 1914–2019
FIGURE PRODUCED USING DATA FROM *WID.WORLD*

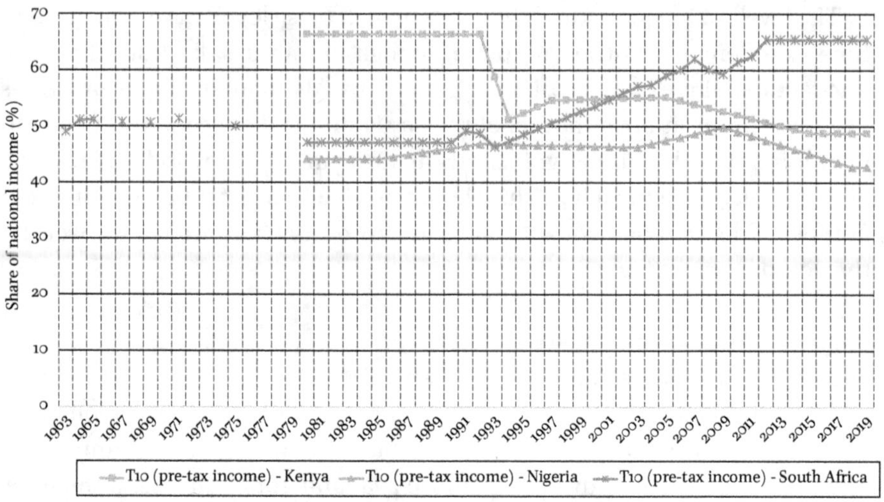

FIGURE 80 T10 income share in Kenya, Nigeria and South Africa, 1963–2019
FIGURE PRODUCED USING DATA FROM *WID.WORLD*

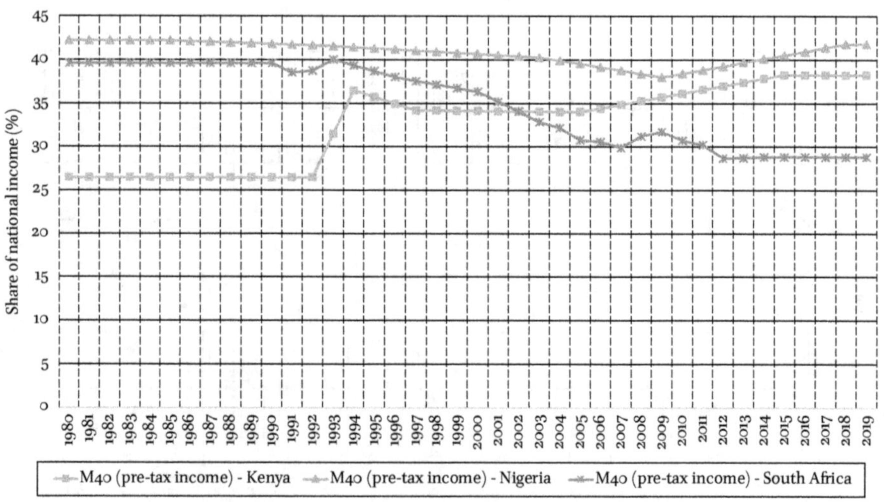

FIGURE 81 M40 income share in Kenya, Nigeria and South Africa, 1980–2019
FIGURE PRODUCED USING DATA FROM *WID.WORLD*

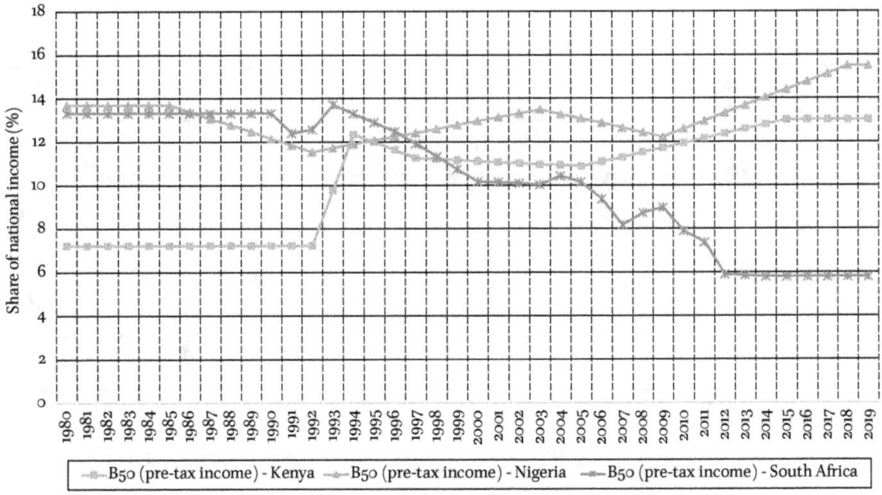

FIGURE 82 B50 income share in Kenya, Nigeria and South Africa, 1980–2019
FIGURE PRODUCED USING DATA FROM *WID.WORLD*

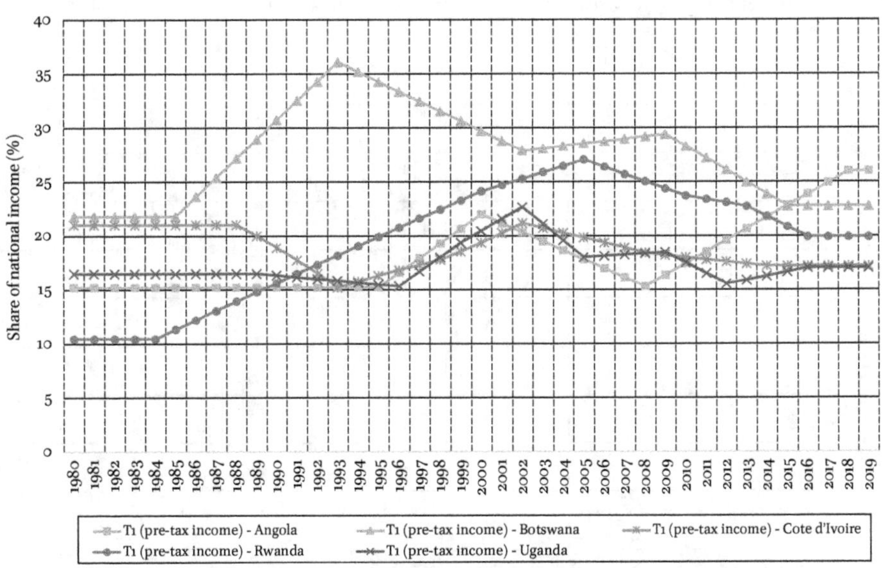

FIGURE 83 T1 income share in Angola, Botswana, Cote d'Ivoire, Rwanda and Uganda, 1980–2019
FIGURE PRODUCED USING DATA FROM *WID.WORLD*

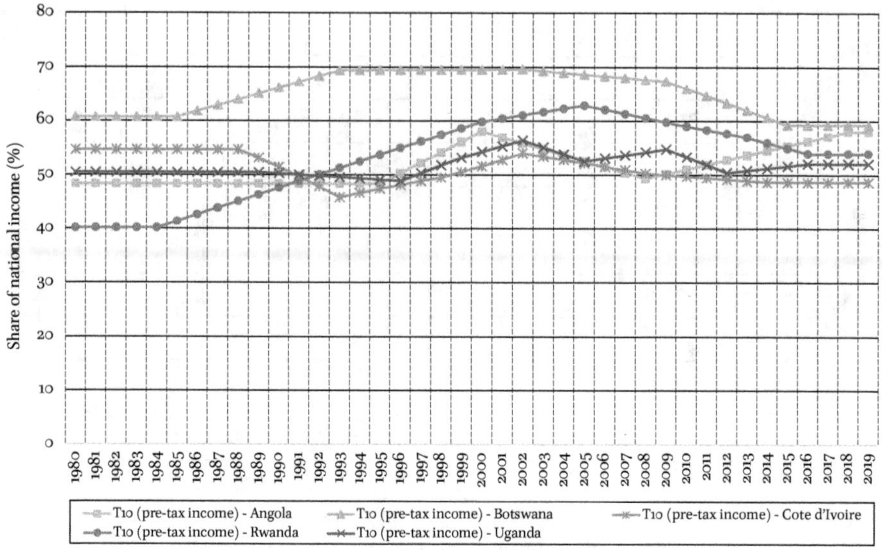

FIGURE 84 T10 income share in Angola, Botswana, Cote d'Ivoire, Rwanda and Uganda, 1980–2019

FIGURE PRODUCED USING DATA FROM *WID.WORLD*

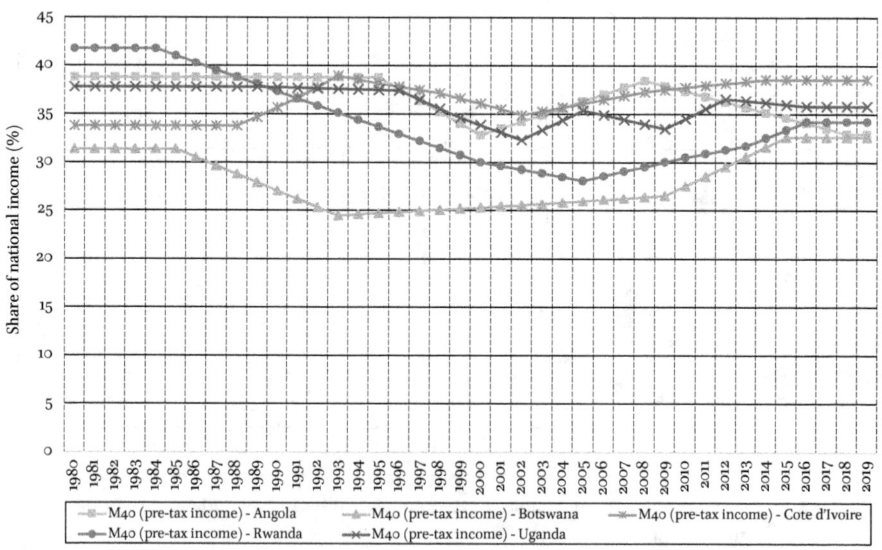

FIGURE 85 M40 income share in Angola, Botswana, Cote d'Ivoire, Rwanda and Uganda, 1980–2019

FIGURE PRODUCED USING DATA FROM *WID.WORLD*

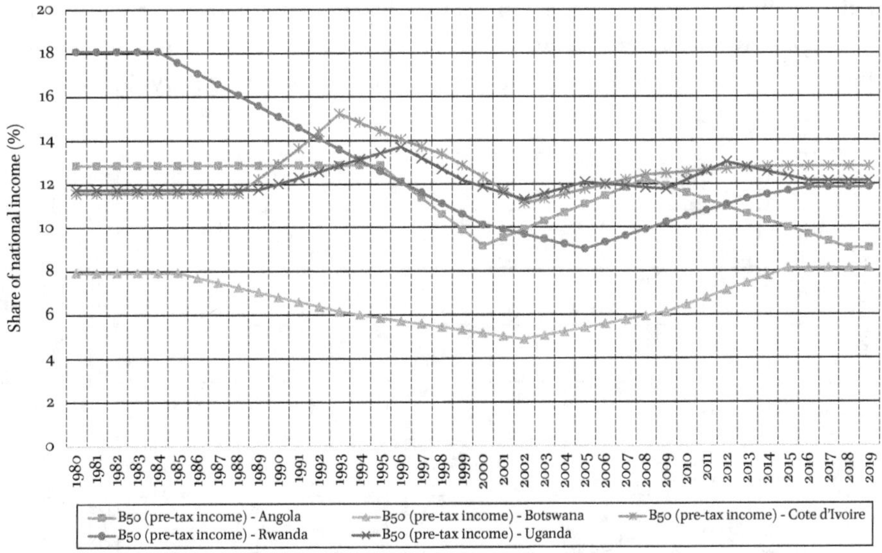

FIGURE 86 B50 income share in Angola, Botswana, Cote d'Ivoire, Rwanda and Uganda, 1980–2019
FIGURE PRODUCED USING DATA FROM *WID.WORLD*

While the same general trends are again visible to a degree, we encounter some notable exceptions in Sub-Saharan Africa. For example, while income inequality in South Africa has clearly risen in significant respects since the 1980s, with the T1 and T10 shares increasing persistently and significantly over time and the M40 and B50 shares concomitantly decreasing (countries like Angola have followed a similar pattern), the exact opposite has been observed in countries like Kenya. Much like Malaysia, however, Kenya seems to be one of the few countries around the world that has seen T1 and T10 income shares decline and M40 and B50 shares rise (albeit that there are not many datapoints available for Kenya). The trends in Sub-Saharan Africa have also been more erratic over time, with a significant number of countries following the same general trend until the 2000s, but then observing the opposite Kenyan- or Malaysian-style trend since then. This is true for countries like Rwanda and Botswana.

2.2.6 Latin America and the Caribbean

For current purposes, 'Latin America and the Caribbean' consists of approximately 32 countries. They collectively account for approximately 9 percent of the global population. As in the case of Sub-Saharan Africa, the number of datapoints available are as general proposition lower than those available for countries in other regions. As Figures 87 through 94 show, insufficient data exist to show clearly how the various trends have unfolded in the region *since even 1980*. All the same, the figures do provide us with a general sense of what income inequality has looked like in the region in contemporary times.

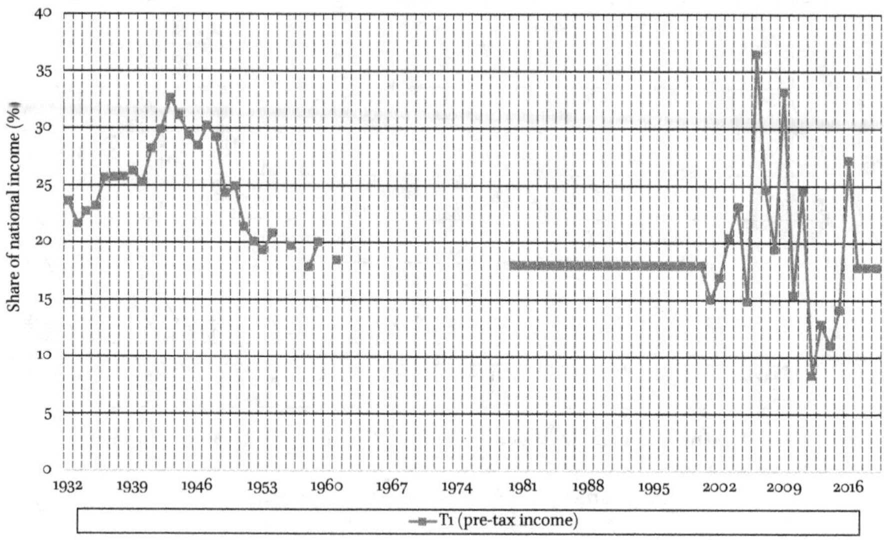

FIGURE 87 T1 income share in Argentina, 1932–2019
FIGURE PRODUCED USING DATA FROM *WID.WORLD*

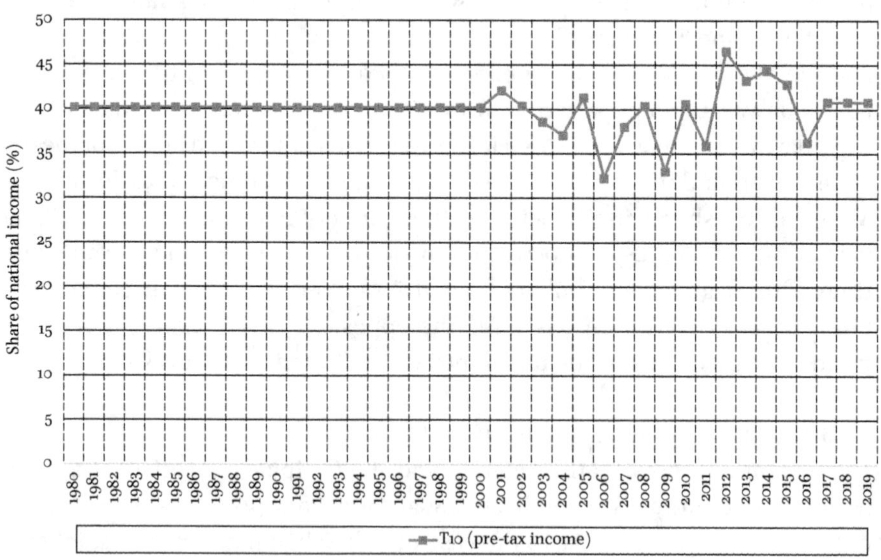

FIGURE 88 T10 income share in Argentina, 1980–2019
FIGURE PRODUCED USING DATA FROM *WID.WORLD*

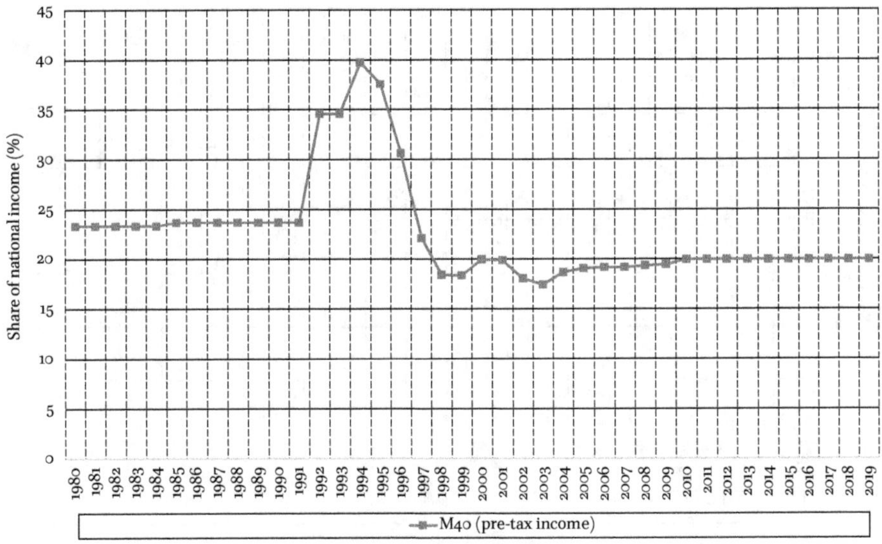

FIGURE 89 M40 income share in Argentina, 1980–2019
FIGURE PRODUCED USING DATA FROM *WID.WORLD*

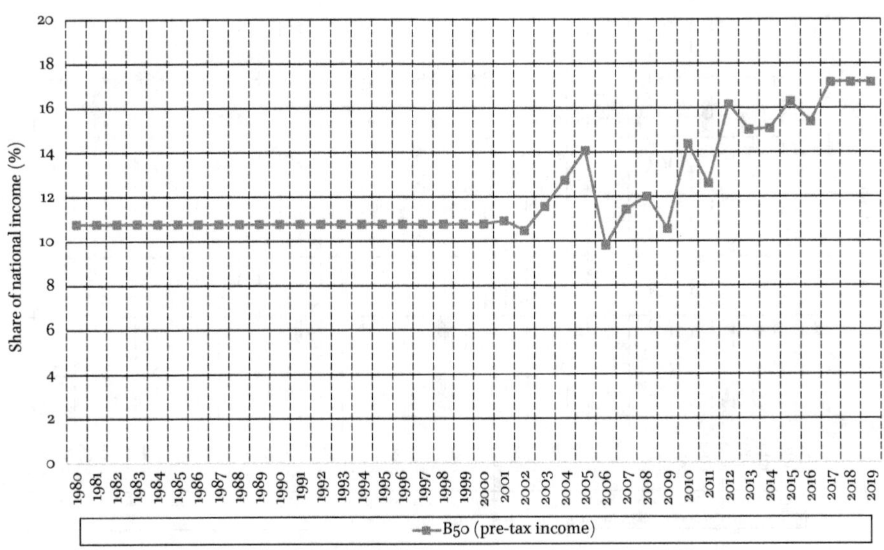

FIGURE 90 B50 income share in Argentina, 1980–2019
FIGURE PRODUCED USING DATA FROM *WID.WORLD*

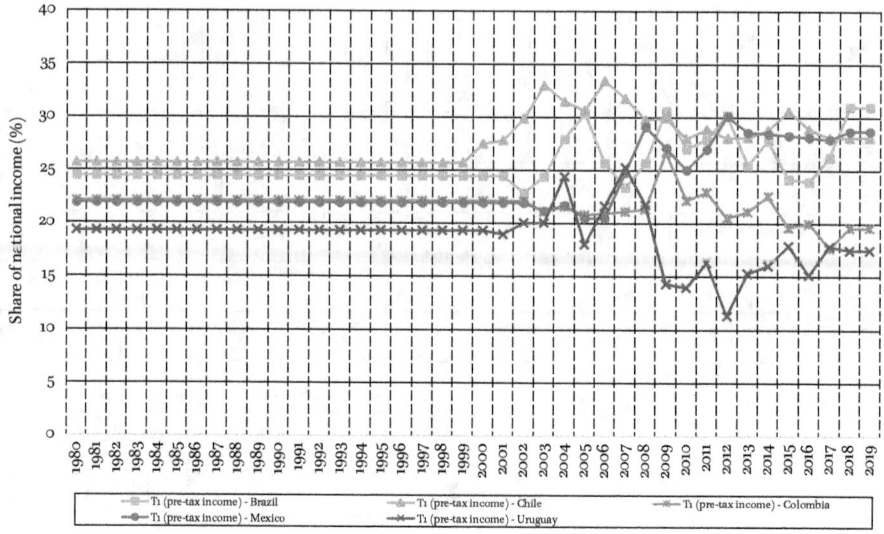

FIGURE 91 T1 income share in Brazil, Chile, Colombia, Mexico and Uruguay, 1980–2019
FIGURE PRODUCED USING DATA FROM *WID.WORLD*

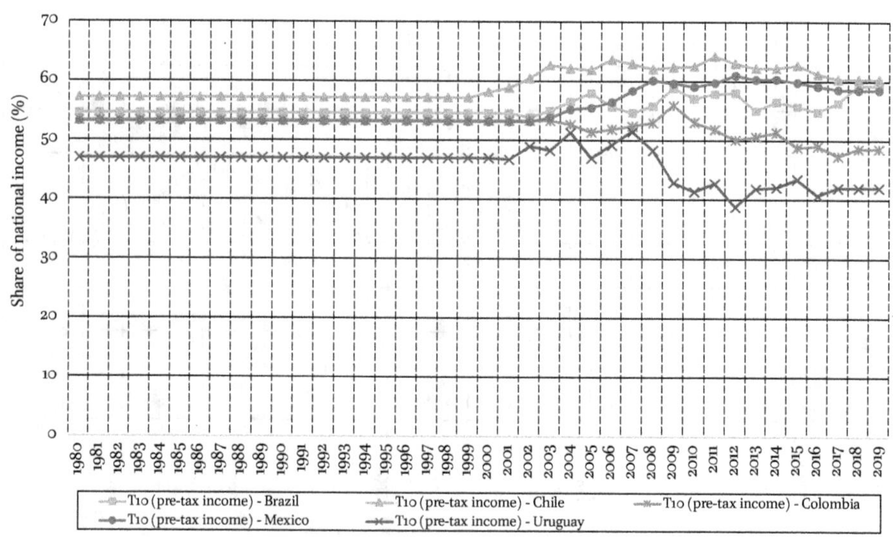

FIGURE 92 T10 income share in Brazil, Chile, Colombia, Mexico and Uruguay, 1980–2019
FIGURE PRODUCED USING DATA FROM *WID.WORLD*

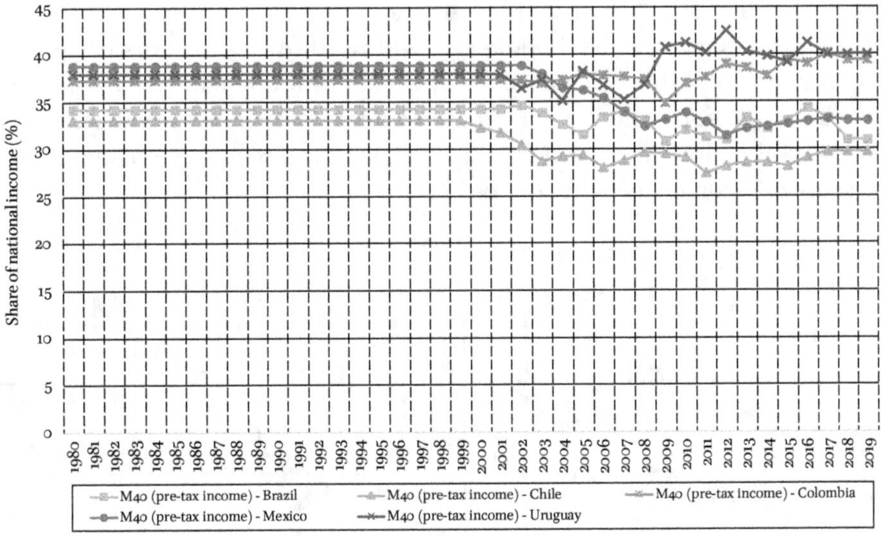

FIGURE 93 M40 income share in Brazil, Chile, Colombia, Mexico and Uruguay, 1980–2019
FIGURE PRODUCED USING DATA FROM *WID.WORLD*

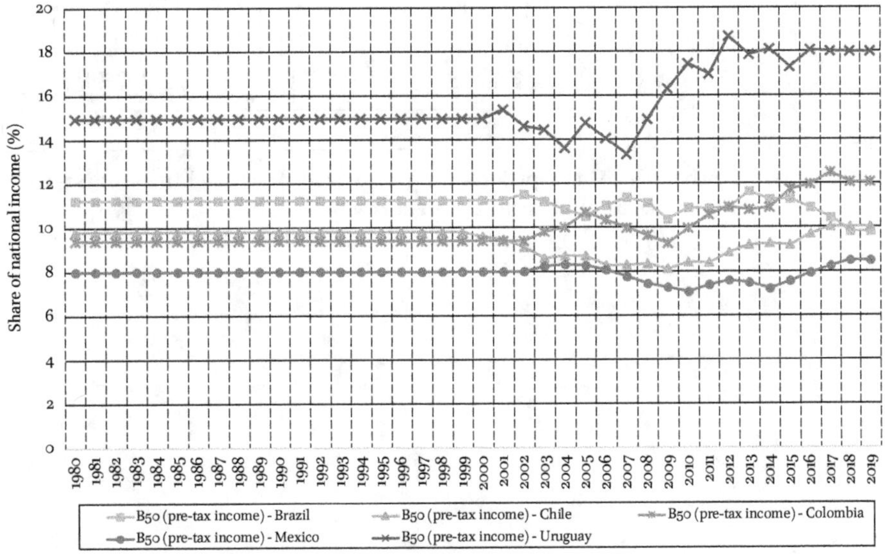

FIGURE 94 B50 income share in Brazil, Chile, Colombia, Mexico and Uruguay, 1980–2019
FIGURE PRODUCED USING DATA FROM *WID.WORLD*

2.2.7 The Middle East and North Africa

For current purposes, the 'Middle East and North Africa' consists of approximately 20 countries. They collectively account for approximately 6 percent of the global population. Again, *WID.world* does not really contain sufficient datapoints to draw firm conclusions, but Figures 95 through 98 provide us with a sense of income inequality trends in the region:

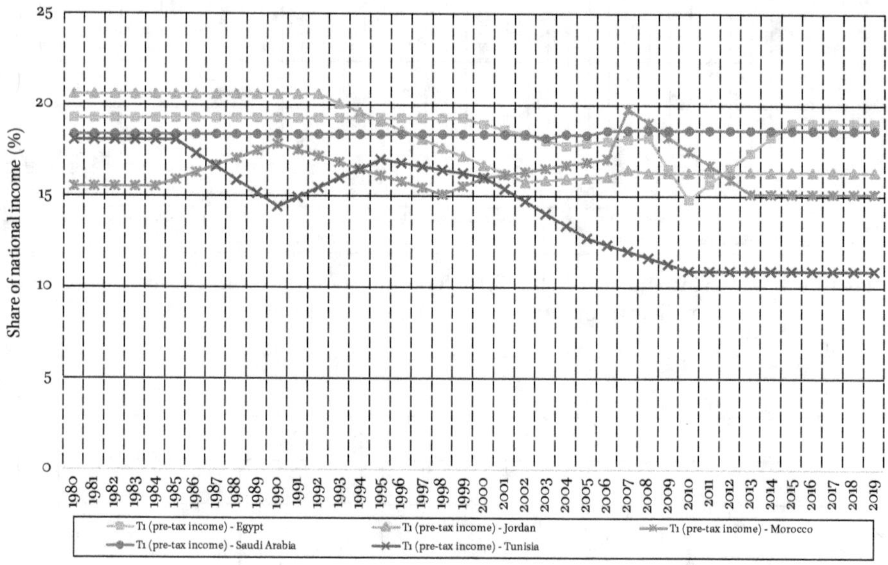

FIGURE 95 T1 income share in Egypt, Jordan, Morocco, Saudi Arabia and Tunisia, 1980–2019
FIGURE PRODUCED USING DATA FROM *WID.WORLD*

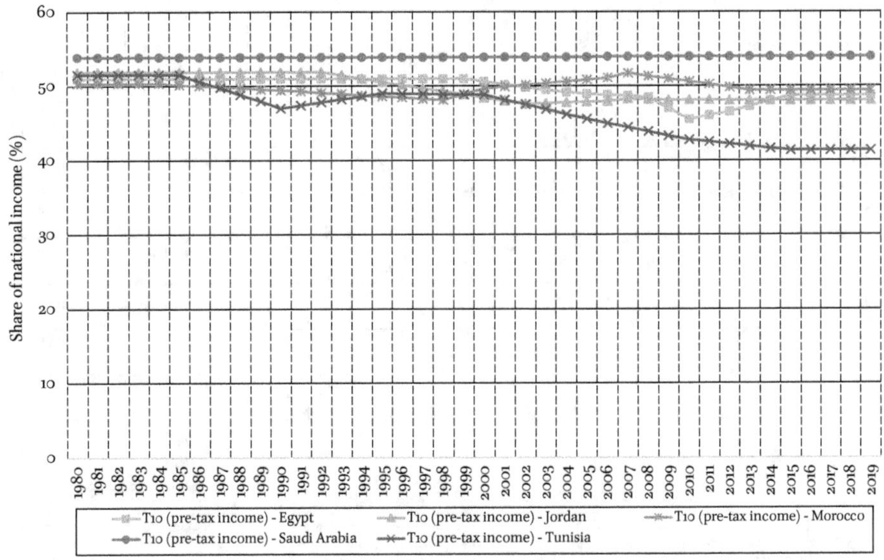

FIGURE 96 T10 income share in Egypt, Jordan, Morocco, Saudi Arabia and Tunisia, 1980–2019
FIGURE PRODUCED USING DATA FROM *WID.WORLD*

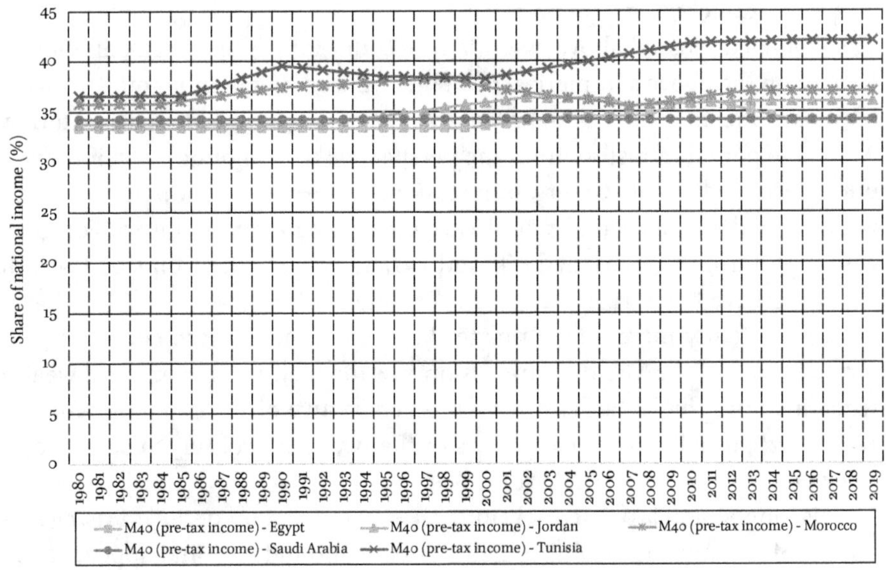

FIGURE 97 M40 income share in Egypt, Jordan, Morocco, Saudi Arabia and Tunisia, 1980–2019
FIGURE PRODUCED USING DATA FROM *WID.WORLD*

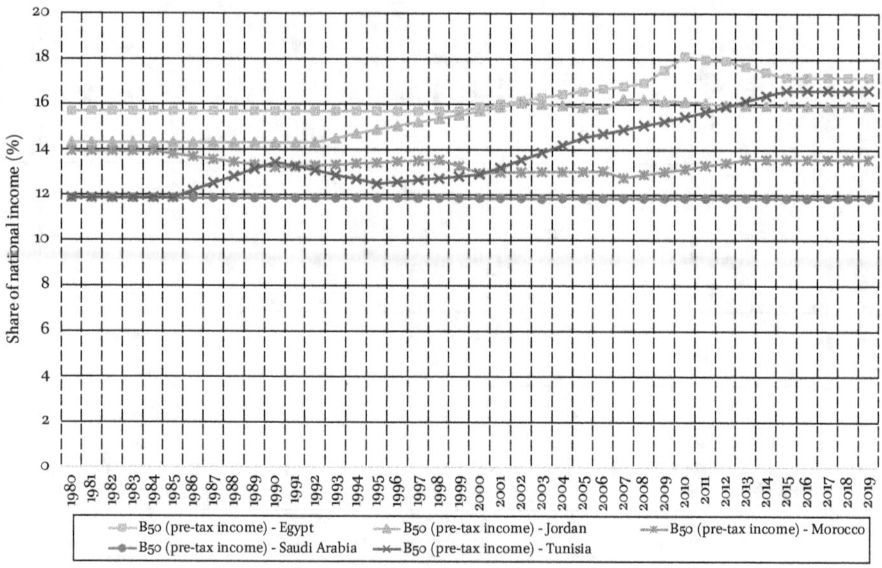

FIGURE 98 B50 income share in Egypt, Jordan, Morocco, Saudi Arabia and Tunisia, 1980–2019
FIGURE PRODUCED USING DATA FROM *WID.WORLD*

2.2.8 Concluding Summary

The regions discussed above essentially account for the entire global population. From the above summaries it can be surmised that within-country distributions of income and wealth have moved fairly similarly in directional terms. A notable period in history from the perspective of economic distributions is often described as the 'Great Compression'.[89] This refers to a period starting with the end of the Second World War and ending in around 1980. For most countries during this period, the T1 and T10 shares for both income and wealth appear to have fallen incrementally over time while the M40 and B50 shares were persistently increasing. Prior to this period, most of the countries that formed a part of the 'Great Compression' saw inequality of income and wealth reach historical highs (at least from the perspective of the data contained in *WID.world*), usually in the early parts of the twentieth century at some point prior to the onset of the First World War.

This monograph is particularly interested in the current period of rising inequality of income and wealth, which started in around 1980 and appears to be ongoing. Based on the discussions above, it can be concluded with reasonable

89 See n 86 above.

certainty that a significant majority of the countries in the world have been experiencing a substantial reversal of the trends witnessed during the Great Compression during this period: the T1 and T10 shares for both income and wealth have, since around 1980, been rising incrementally over time, with the M40 and B50 shares persistently falling. There are some notable exceptions to these trends, which exceptions tend to prove the general rule.

3 The Effects of Changing Distributions of Income and Wealth within States

Having illustrated the distributional trends within states in the previous part (*Part 1*), the discussion turns now to their effects. While there are many effects one might explore, perhaps the most obvious way in which the distribution of income and wealth affects a society in contemporary times is through the distribution of spending or consumption power. It follows that outcomes tied to spending become more unevenly distributed between groups and the persons in those groups over time as economic distributions become more unequal. For example, if health outcomes—such as life expectancy—depend, even if only in part, on how much individuals spend or are capable of spending on their health, then we can expect life expectancy to differ based on where an individual finds herself in the income distribution.

Raj Chetty and his colleagues have quite definitively shown this to be the case in the United States.[90] In their study they divided the population into income quartiles and were able to show that life expectancy is lowest in the lowest quartile, with life expectancy getting progressively higher as one moves up to the next quartiles and with the highest quartile exhibiting the highest life expectancy.[91] This finding also holds for countries other than the United States. For example, a study by Karin Hederos and her colleagues has produced a very similar finding for Sweden, a state where income and wealth are substantially more equally distributed.[92] This sort of finding—whereby outcome

90 Raj Chetty et al, 'The Association between Income and Life Expectancy in the United States, 2001–2014' (2016) 315 *Journal of the American Medical Association* 1750. See also National Academies of Sciences, Engineering, and Medicine, *The Growing Gap in Life Expectancy by Income: Implications for Federal Programs and Policy Responses* (National Academies, Washington, DC 2015).

91 Chetty et al (n 90) 1755–6.

92 Karin Hederos et al, 'Trends in Life Expectancy by Income and the Role of Specific Causes of Death' (2018) 85 *Economica* 606.

heterogeneity for non-economic outcomes within a population increases as economic distributions become more unequal—applies to various other areas as well.

For example, Lucas Chancel and Thomas Piketty have conducted a study examining the distribution of global carbon dioxide emissions amongst the world's population.[93] The results of the study show that within-state carbon dioxide emission distributions are playing an increasingly larger role over time in the overall global distribution.[94] This is because those higher up in the income distributions within states are prone to emit more carbon dioxide than those lower down the distributions, with the increase over time of income inequality within states essentially driving the structural changes they observe in the overall global distribution of carbon dioxide emissions.[95] For current purposes, an upshot of this finding is that as economic distributions within a state become more unequal over time, so too do the distribution of carbon dioxide emissions.[96]

Similar trends are visible with respect to educational outcomes: greater inequality of income and wealth can lead to greater inequality of educational achievement.[97] It is also easy to imagine how these trends affect one another over time. Greater inequality in educational attainment is often cited as a driver of widening gaps in income and wealth over time.[98] This could imply that as

---

93 Lucas Chancel and Thomas Piketty, 'Carbon and Inequality: from Kyoto to Paris, Trends in the Global Inequality of Carbon Emissions (1998–2013) & Prospects for an Equitable Adaptation Fund' (November 2015) <http://piketty.pse.ens.fr/files/ChancelPiketty2015.pdf> accessed 30 September 2021.

94 See generally Chancel and Piketty (n 93).

95 See generally Chancel and Piketty (n 93).

96 See also Zan Yang, Shuping Wu and Hiu Ying Cheung, 'From Income and Housing Wealth Inequalities to Emissions Inequality: Carbon Emissions of Households in China' (2017) 32 *Journal of Housing and the Built Environment* 231.

97 See in this regard, for example, Alex Bell et al, 'Mobility Report Cards: The Role of Colleges in Intergenerational Mobility' (NBER Working Paper 23618, July 2017); Charles T Clotfelter, *Unequal Colleges in the Age of Disparity* (HUP, Cambridge, MA 2017) and Sean F Reardon, 'The Widening Academic Achievement Gap between the Rich and the Poor: New Evidence and Possible Explanations' in Greg J Duncan and Richard J. Murnane (eds), *Whither Opportunity? Rising Inequality, Schools, and Children's Life Chances* (Russell Sage Foundation, New York 2011) 91.

98 See generally, for example, Claudia Goldin and Lawrence F Katz, *The Race between Education and Technology* (HUP, Cambridge, MA 2008). For further examples, see David Coady and Allan Dizioli, 'Income Inequality and Education Revisited: Persistence, Endogeneity, and Heterogeneity' (IMF Working Paper WP/17/26, May 2017) and Steven J Haider and Kathleen McGarry, 'Postsecondary Schooling and Parental Resources: Evidence from the PSID and HRS' (2018) 13 *Education Finance and Policy* 72.

economic inequality rises so does educational inequality, which in turn would lead to greater economic inequality over time, which would lead to greater disparities in life expectancy and in carbon dioxide emissions. These sorts of cross-cutting issues are difficult to disentangle empirically, but the point here is simply to show how as economic distributions become increasingly more unequal over time the population of a state becomes composed of increasingly heterogeneous members: this has clear implications for cooperative propensities,[99] responses to perceived distributive injustices,[100] and ultimately for the type of collective action necessary to solve problems common to the state as a whole.[101]

There is a clear relationship between economic inequality and social cohesion. This much is borne out by the data and appears only logical given that greater economic inequality breeds greater distrust amongst societies and less trust translates into less social cohesion.[102] This also circles back to collective action. As Dan Kahan explains in refuting the logic of Mancur Olson in the latter's famous book *The Logic of Collective Action*:[103]

> Whereas the conventional logic of collective action counsels the creation of appropriate external incentives, the logic of reciprocity suggests the importance of promoting trust. Individuals who have faith in the willingness of others to contribute their fair share will voluntarily respond in kind. And spontaneous cooperation of this sort breeds more of the same, as individuals observe others contributing to public goods and are moved to reciprocate. In this self-sustaining atmosphere of trust, reliance on costly incentive schemes becomes less necessary. By the same token, individuals who lack faith in their peers can be expected to resist

---

99 See, for example, Stephen Mark Rosenbaum et al, 'Income Inequality and Cooperative Propensities in Developing Economies: Summarizing the Preliminary Experimental Evidence' (2016) 43 *International Journal of Social Economics* 1460.

100 See, for example, Jiawen Huang, 'Income Inequality, Distributive Justice Beliefs, and Happiness in China: Evidence from a Nationwide Survey' (2018) 137 *Social Indicators Research* 1 and Germán Reyes and Leonardo Gasparini, 'Perceptions of Distributive Justice in Latin America during a Period of Falling Inequality' (World Bank Policy Research Working Paper 8072, May 2017).

101 See, for example, Lisa R Anderson, Jennifer M Mellor and Jeffrey Milyo, 'Inequality and Public Good Provision: An Experimental Analysis' (2008) 37 *Journal of Socio-Economics* 1010.

102 See Christian Albrekt Larsen, *The Rise and Fall of Social Cohesion: The Construction and De-construction of Social Trust in the US, UK, Sweden and Denmark* (OUP, Oxford 2013) for an excellent description of this relationship.

103 See generally Mancur Olson, *The Logic of Collective Action* (HUP, Cambridge, MA 1965).

> contributing to public goods, thereby inducing still others to withhold their cooperation as a means of retaliating. In this self-sustaining atmosphere of distrust, even strong (and costly) regulatory incentives are likely to be ineffective in promoting desirable [behaviour].[104]

It is also easy to imagine how failure to take collective action on certain issues within a particular state can have an impact beyond its own borders. For example, in the event that a state fails to take collective action in respect of climate change, the impact of that failure will almost certainly be felt elsewhere in the world, if not by the world—humankind—as a whole.[105] Similarly, it is easy to imagine how less trust within a state might make that state less cooperative generally in its relations with the rest of the world. There is a significant body of literature showing that less trust within a society leads to less trust of other societies.[106] This becomes particularly harmful when economic inequality is rising within virtually all states.[107]

Beyond the sorts of effects described above, there are also aggregate-level effects that stem from changing economic distributions. Some of these have been fairly definitively established, such as the relationship between increasing levels of economic concentration and increases in aggregate crime rates.[108]

In other areas, it appears that a relationship may exist, but the exact causal mechanisms remain somewhat murky or heavily disputed. For example, many studies have asserted that increases in income inequality lead to worse levels of aggregate population health measured in terms of life expectancy or child

---

104 Dan M Kahan, 'The Logic of Reciprocity: Trust, Collective Action, and Law' (2003) 102 *Michigan Law Review* 71, 71–2.

105 For example, the failure within the United States to take collective action on climate change has spilled over into the international realm, with likely ramifications for humankind as a whole. This is perhaps best exemplified by its withdrawal from the Paris Agreement on climate change. For an assessment of the impacts of such withdrawal, see Han Chen et al, 'The Global Impacts of US Climate Policy: A Model Simulation Using GCAM-TU and MAGICC' (2018) 18 *Climate Policy* 852.

106 See generally Paul R Brewer, Kimberly Gross and Timothy Vercellotti, 'Trust in International Actors' and Brian Christopher Rathbun, 'Trust in International Relations', both in Eric M Uslaner (ed), *The Oxford Handbook on Social and Political Trust* (Oxford University Press, Oxford 2018).

107 See Part I, Section 3.2 above in this chapter.

108 See, for example, Pablo Fajnzyber, Daniel Lederman and Norman Loayza, 'Inequality and Violent Crime' (2002) 45 *Journal of Law and Economics* 1 and Neil Metz and Mariya Burdina, 'Neighbourhood income inequality and property crime' (2018) 55 *Urban Studies* 130.

mortality rates.[109] Similar relationships have been found to exist with respect to more specific health concerns, such as the aggregate cardio-vascular disease rate within a state,[110] or its mental illness rate.[111] While some authors forcefully assert that causal mechanisms exist in this regard, others are only willing to go as far as recognising some kind of correlation between the two variables.[112] Similar debates exist concerning the relationship between changing economic distributions and other aggregate-level concerns, such as the onset of financial crises,[113] or overall household debt.[114] There are also emerging research agendas, for example concerning the relationship between economic distributions and terrorism.[115]

In this part of the chapter, however, the focus will simply be on some relationships of interest: that between changing economic distributions, economic growth, poverty reduction and mobility (*Section 3.1*), the one between increasing inequality of income and wealth and climate change (*Section 3.2*) and the relationship between changing distributions, conflict, violence and civil war (*Section 3.3*).

3.1 *Economic Growth, Poverty Reduction and Mobility*

During the prominence of Simon Kuznets and his contemporaries in the 1950s, the prevailing argument concerning the distribution of income and economic

109 For an overview of this literature, see Kate E Pickett and Richard G Wilkinson, 'Income Inequality and Health: A Causal Review' (2015) 128 *Social Science & Medicine* 316.

110 See, for example, Daniel Kim et al, 'Is Inequality at the Heart of It? Cross-country Associations of Income Inequality with Cardiovascular Diseases and Risk Factors' (2008) 66 *Social Sciences & Medicine* 1719.

111 See, for example, Vikram Patel et al, 'Income Inequality and Depression: A Systematic Review and Meta-analysis of the Association and a Scoping Review of Mechanisms' (2018) 17 *World Psychiatry* 76 and Wagner Silva Ribeiro et al, 'Income Inequality and Mental Illness-related Morbidity and Resilience: A Systematic Review and Meta-analysis' (2017) 4 *Lancet Psychiatry* 554.

112 For an overview of these arguments, see Owen O'Donnell, Eddy Van Doorslaer and Tom Van Ourti 'Health and Inequality' in Anthony B Atkinson and François Bourguignon (eds), *Handbook of Income Distribution (Volume 2B)* (Elsevier, Amsterdam 2015) 1419, 1499–1512.

113 See, for example, Michael D Bordo and Christopher M Meissner, 'Does Inequality Lead to a Financial Crisis?' (2012) 31 *Journal of International Money and Finance* 2147 and Raghuram Rajan, *Fault Lines* (PUP, Princeton 2010).

114 See, for example, Matteo Iacoviello, 'Household Debt and Income Inequality, 1963–2003' (2008) 40 *Journal of Money, Credit and Banking* 929 and JW Mason, 'Income Distribution, Household Debt, and Aggregate Demand: A Critical Assessment' (Levy Economics Institute Working Paper 901, March 2018).

115 See, for example, Tim Krieger and Daniel Meierrieks, 'Income Inequality, Redistribution and Domestic Terrorism' (2019) 116 *World Development* 125.

growth was that greater income inequality leads to greater aggregate savings as a result those higher up in the income distribution saving proportionately more than those lower down.[116] This, for the purposes of that argument, led to increases in the aggregate rates of investment and growth.[117] As has been alluded to already, although Kuznets had been methodical with respect to data collection, his worked was premised on data which can at best be described as incomplete.[118] Nonetheless, the argument gives the impression—an impression that became and remains deeply rooted in the minds of many—that there is a trade-off between the distribution of income and economic growth; more specifically, it impresses the notion that reducing the inequality of incomes is harmful to economic growth.

Since the early 1990s, the conventional wisdom on the relationship has persistently been challenged at both a theoretical and empirical level.[119] Regarding the latter, Jess Habib wrote in 2003 that '[o]n the empirical side, the evidence on the trade-off between inequality and growth, despite a large number of [then] recent studies, remain[ed] inconclusive'.[120] Since then, and especially after the so-called Great Recession of 2007–8, research into the topic has further intensified; increasingly with the added benefit of improved data. In more recent years, there has been a decided shift in the empirical literature: as a general proposition, the notion that more unequal income distributions are likely harmful to economic growth is gradually coming to be accepted, with a wide range of studies having come to this conclusion.[121]

---

116 See Simon Kuznets, 'Economic Growth and Income Inequality' (1955) 45 *American Economic Review* 1. See also Nicholas Kaldor, 'A Model for Economic Growth' (1957) 67 *Economic Journal* 591.

117 See Kuznets (n 116); Kaldor (n 116).

118 See Chapter 1 of this monograph.

119 See, for example, Daron Acemoğlu and James A Robinson, 'Why Did the West Extend the Franchise? Democracy, Inequality, and Growth in Historical Perspective' (2002) 115 *Quarterly Journal of Economics* 1167; Alberto Alesina and Dani Rodrik, 'Distributive Politics and Economic Growth' (1994) 109 *Quarterly Journal of Economics* 465; Abijhit V Banerjee and Andrew F Newman, 'Occupational Choice and the Process of Development' (1993) 101 *Journal of Political Economy* 274; Oded Galor and Joseph Zeira, 'Income Distribution and Macroeconomics' (1993) 60 *Review of Economic Studies* 35 and Torsten Persson and Guido Tabellini, 'Is Inequality Harmful for Growth?' (1994) 84 *American Economic Review* 600.

120 Jess Benhabib, 'The Tradeoff between Inequality and Growth' (2003) 4 *Annals of Economics and Finance* 329, 330.

121 See, for example, Amparo Castelló-Climent, 'Inequality and Growth in Advanced Economies: an Empirical Investigation' (2010) 8 *Journal of Economic Inequality* 293; Federico Cingano, 'Trends in Income Inequality and its Impact on Economic Growth' (OECD Social, Employment and Migration Working Papers 163, 2014); Era Dabla-Norris et al, 'Causes and Consequences of Income Inequality: A Global Perspective' (IMF Staff Discussion Note SDN/15/13, June 2015); Fernando Delbianco, Carlos Dabús and

In a recent paper that came to a consistent but more nuanced conclusion, Francesco Grigoli and Adrian Robles found strong and robust evidence across a large sample of countries that the relationship between a country's Gini coefficient and its economic growth rate follows an interesting non-linear pattern.[122] In essence, the authors find that there is an 'overhang' value at which point the relationship switches from positive to negative.[123] Simply put, up until a Gini coefficient of a certain level—of approximately 0.27 in respect of incomes after taxes and transfers for the purposes of their study—the observed income distribution or level of inequality is positively associated with economic growth.[124] As the Gini coefficient crosses the threshold of 0.27, however, a higher coefficient begins to be negatively associated with economic growth.[125] Moreover, once the Gini coefficient crosses the threshold its association with economic growth becomes negative at a faster rate as the coefficient grows.[126]

Research has also been conducted into the length or sustainability of economic growth spells. For example, Andrew Berg, Jonathan Ostry and Jermonin Zettelmeyer have found empirical support for the view 'that less equal and cohesive societies experience lower and more volatile growth'.[127] More explicitly for current purposes, this finding translates into the idea that more equal distributions do not only result in greater overall growth over a period of time but also lead to growth being more sustainable over that same period of time.[128] These findings are important for at least two reasons: first, economic growth remains a—if not *the*—stated policy objective of most states around

María Ángeles Caraballo, 'Income Inequality and Economic Growth: New Evidence from Latin America' (2014) 33 *Cuadernos de Economía* 381; Francesco Grigoli, Evelio Paredes and Gabriel Di Bella, 'Inequality and Growth: A Heterogeneous Approach' (IMF Working Paper WP/16/244, December 2016); Daniel Halter, Manuel Oechslin, and Josef Zweimüller, 'Inequality and Growth: the Neglected Time Dimension' (2014) 19 *Journal of Economic Growth* 81; Tom Kennedy et al, 'Does Income Inequality Hinder Economic Growth? New Evidence Using Australian Taxation Statistics' (2017) 65 *Economic Modelling* 119 and Jonathan D Ostry, Andrew Berg and Charalambos G Tsangarides 'Redistribución, Desigualdad y Crecimiento' (2014) 16 *Revista de Economía Institucional* 30.

122 Francesco Grigoli and Adrian Robles, 'Inequality Overhang' (IMF Working Paper WP/17/76, 28 March 2017).

123 Grigoli and Robles (n 122).

124 Grigoli and Robles (n 122).

125 Grigoli and Robles (n 122).

126 Grigoli and Robles (n 122).

127 Andrew Berg, Jonathan D Ostry and Jermonin Zettelmeyer, 'What Makes Growth Sustained?' (2012) 98 *Journal of Development Economics* 149, 163. See also Andrew G Berg and Jonathan D Ostry, 'Inequality and Unsustainable Growth: Two Sides of the Same Coin?' (2017) 65 *IMF Economic Review* 792.

128 See Berg, Ostry and Zettelmeyer (n 127). See also Berg and Ostry (n 127).

the world;[129] and secondly, aggregate economic growth—as a means to certain ends—is often touted for its ability to alleviate poverty.[130]

Insofar as the distribution of wealth is concerned, as a starting point it must be acknowledged that it has been difficult historically to test the relationship between the distribution of wealth and other variables such as poverty reduction or economic growth at least in part because, as Sutirtha Bagchi and Jan Svejnar note, 'nearly all empirical studies use the distribution of income rather than wealth because data on the distribution of wealth do not exist for a sufficient number of countries'.[131] For studies that have been undertaken, this often leads to the use of unreliable proxies.[132] The importance of the question, however, remains: as Martin Ravallion argues, 'wealth inequality is arguably more relevant [as a determinant of growth than income inequality is,] though this has been rarely used due to data limitations'.[133] With continuing improvements in the available data on wealth as described earlier in this chapter, it is be quite probable that something more definitive could be said about wealth in the not-so-distant future. For the purposes of this chapter, however, it should be accepted that what data are currently available have resulted in a literature that is too scant for the purposes of presenting a thoughtful discussion on the relationship between the distribution of wealth and economic growth.[134]

It is further clear that economic distributions—beyond their impact on economic growth—affect poverty alleviation. François Bourguignon, for example, accepts that the distribution of income and how it changes over time has an impact on growth.[135] Growth concomitantly impacts the

---

129 See generally, for example, President of the United States (2017-: Trump), 'Economic Report of the President: Transmitted to the Congress; Together with the Annual Report of the Council of Economic Advisors' (February 2018) <https://www.whitehouse.gov/wp-content/uploads/2018/02/ERP_2018_Final-FINAL.pdf> accessed 30 September 2021; National Planning Commission of South Africa, *National Development Plan: Vision for 2030* (Presidency of South Africa, Pretoria 2011).

130 See, for example, Paul Collier, *The Bottom Billion: Why the Poorest Countries are Failing and What Can be Done About It* (OUP, Oxford 2007) 8–12 and Dani Rodrik, *One Economics, Many Recipes: Globalization, Institutions and Economic Growth* (PUP, Princeton 2007) 1–3.

131 Sutirtha Bagchi and Jan Svejnar 'Does Wealth Inequality Matter for Growth? The Effect of Billionaire Wealth, Income Distribution, and Poverty' (2015) 43 *Journal of Comparative Economics* 505, 505.

132 See Philippe Aghion, Eve Caroli and Cecilia Garcia-Penalosa, 'Inequality and Economic Growth: The Perspective of the New Growth Theories' (1999) 37 *Journal of Economic Literature* 1615, 1617–8.

133 Martin Ravallion, 'Why Don't We See Poverty Convergence?' (2012) 102 *American Economic Review* 504, 506.

134 See, however, Bagchi and Svenjar (n 131).

135 François Bourguignon, 'The Poverty-Growth-Inequality Triangle?' in Research Department, Agence Française de Développement, (ed) *Poverty, Inequality and Growth: Proceedings of the AFD-EUDN Conference*, 2003 (Maggelan & Cie, Paris 2004) 85–98.

distribution over time, and growth and the distribution simultaneously affect poverty and its reduction.[136] The ultimate message here is that the distribution of income—which entails as one a constituent element the distribution of growth over time—and how it changes affect the rate at which poverty is reduced within a state or particular community. In order to illustrate his point, Bourguignon uses Mexican data: he assumes that the Mexican economy will grow at an aggregate rate of three percent and illustrates what distributional changes mean for the rate of poverty reduction.[137] He starts by showing the number of persons living in poverty in Mexico at given point in the early 2000s and then illustrates what the number would look like ten years down the line given that: (a) income remains distributed at a Gini coefficient of 0.55; and (b) income is imagined to be distributed with a Gini coefficient of 0.45.[138] As a third scenario, he shows what percentage of Mexicans would be living in poverty 30 years later in the event that income remains distributed at a Gini coefficient of 0.55.[139] The results he obtains, as illustrated in Figure 99, make his point quite clear:

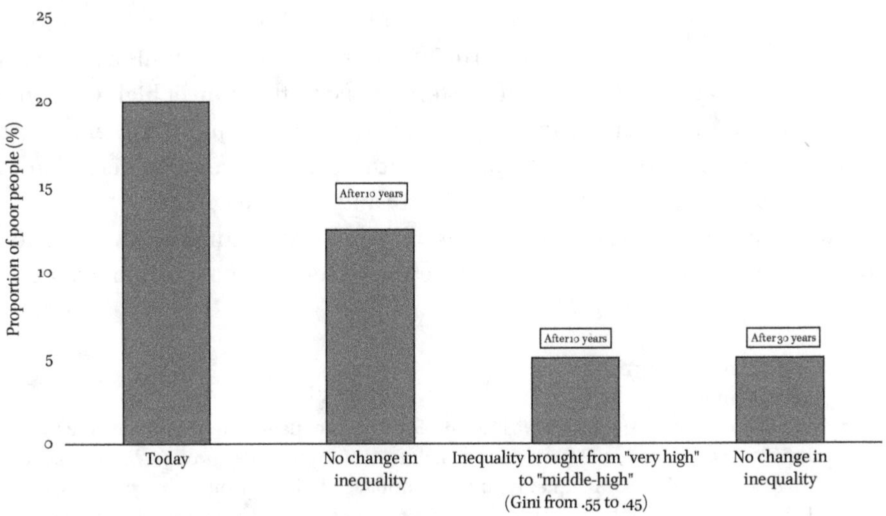

FIGURE 99 Change in poverty in a middle-income country with high inequality: Three percent annual growth in income per capita
REPRODUCED FROM BOURGUIGNON (N 135) 81

136 See Bourguignon (n 135) 76–7.
137 See Bourguignon (n 135) 76–84.
138 See Bourguignon (n 135) 76–84.
139 See Bourguignon (n 135) 76–84.

In order to attain the same level of poverty reduction without the imagined change in the distribution of income would take an additional 20 years to achieve. In light of the discussions above, one might also want to look at the effect that changes in the income distribution would have on the economic growth rate and what any change in growth might mean for poverty reduction in turn. Bourguignon is also careful to suggest that the sort of result depicted above will not necessarily follow in all instances and emphasises the role of the initial income distribution and particular country specifics in the overall process.[140] He also concludes that growth and the distribution of income must be considered simultaneously and that the distribution of income 'matters as much as growth for poverty reduction'.[141] Other empirical studies have since provided support for Bourguignon's contribution.[142]

As for mobility, Katharine Bradbury and Jane Katz surmise that '[m]uch of America's promise is predicated on the existence of economic mobility—the idea that people are not limited or defined by where they start, but can move up the income ladder based on their effort and accomplishments'.[143] The authors continue to question whether 'an individual or family … [can] move out of poverty and rise into the middle class' or whether 'longer-term economic status is limited by where one starts'.[144] In a broad sense, this captures the notion of 'economic mobility'. The literature, of course, entails a broad set of far more specific definitions of the term, making the subject highly complicated to study. As with economic growth and poverty reduction, then, only a sliver of what has become a complex literature will be examined here; that of 'absolute mobility' as defined by Raj Chetty and his colleagues.[145]

At an aggregate level, 'absolute mobility' can be defined as the 'fraction of children earning or consuming more than their parents [within a state or

140 Bourguignon (n 135) 77.

141 Bourguignon (n 135) 82.

142 See, for example, Augustin Kwasi Fuso, 'Growth, Inequality, and Poverty Reduction in Developing Countries: Recent Global Evidence' (2017) 71 *Research in Economics* 306; Augustin Kwasi Fuso 'Inequality and the Impact of Growth on Poverty: Comparative Evidence for Sub-Saharan Africa' (2009) 45 *Journal of Development Studies* 726 and Adriaan Kalwij and Arjan Verschoor, 'Not by Growth Alone: The Role of the Distribution of Income in Regional Diversity in Poverty Reduction' (2007) 51 *European Economic Review* 805.

143 Katherine Bradbury and Jane Katz, 'Trends in U.S. Family Income Mobility, 1967–2004' (Federal Reserve Bank of Boston, working paper 2009) 2 <https://www.bostonfed.org/-/media/Documents/ Workingpapers/PDF/wp0907.pdf> accessed 30 September 2021.

144 Bradbury and Katz (n 143) 2.

145 See Raj Chetty et al, 'The Fading American Dream: Trends in Absolute Income Mobility since 1940' (2017) 356 *Science* 398.

defined geographical area]'.[146] Seen this way, Chetty and his colleagues set out to chart and understand absolute mobility trends in the United States since 1940.[147] What their study ends up showing quite definitively, is that the more unequal the distribution of income becomes over time, the more absolute income mobility is impaired.[148] In other words, the more unequal the distribution of income becomes, the less unlikely it becomes that a child—as a general proposition—will earn greater incomes than his or her parents did.[149]

Chetty and his colleagues show that in order to undo the ongoing trend of decreasing mobility in the United States, for example, fairly modest distributional changes will be far more likely to succeed than increased economic growth, which would have to increase to unrealistic heights in order to begin to reverse the trend (especially given that increasing inequality of incomes appears to have an impact on the rate and sustainability of growth as illustrated above).[150]

3.2 *Climate Change*

Scholars have presented many theories since the 1990s seeking to explain the relationship between income and wealth distributions, on the one hand, and carbon emissions or environmental protection on the other. Many of these theories have centred on the connection of distributions, particularly of wealth, to power and the capacity of the relatively powerful to create environmental 'winners' and 'losers'.[151] One of the more prominent of these theorists is James Boyce, who has depicted social decisions as being 'power weighted'.[152] As Boyce explains:

> [I]nequalities of wealth and power affect valuations of the costs and benefits of environmental degradation via the distribution of purchasing power, the shaping of preferences, and influences on the path of technological change. By each route, greater inequality tends to raise the valuation of benefits reaped by rich and powerful winners, relative to costs imposed on poor and less powerful losers. These valuation effects

---

146 Chetty et al (n 145) 398.
147 Chetty et al (n 145).
148 See Chetty et al (n 145).
149 See Chetty et al (n 145).
150 See Chetty et al (n 145).
151 See, for example, James K Boyce, 'Inequality as a Cause of Environmental Degradation' (1994) 11 *Ecological Economics* 169.
152 See Boyce (n 151) 172–3, 178.

> reinforce the linkage between inequality and environmental degradation under the power-weighted social decision rule.[153]

In the same 1994 paper where Boyce posited this theory, he argued that his hypotheses could be empirically tested.[154] While more than twenty years have since passed, Kyle Knight, Juliet Schor and Andrew Jorgenson bemoan the lack of a subset of these potential empirical studies: those relating to carbon dioxide emissions and climate change.[155] Researchers have, however, progressively begun to examine the relationship between income and wealth distributions and carbon emissions. While this literature is still in its 'nascent' stages (at least insofar as wealth distributions are concerned), it is certainly worth examining some of the results; climate change and its adverse effects have, as noted in the general introduction of this monograph, been recognised as a common concern of humankind and if addressing distributional concerns has a role to play in combatting those effects policy-makers should take them into account.

The literature examining the relationship between the distribution of income and the level of carbon emissions appears to have yielded substantially different results. Studies from the early 2000s tended to show that more unequal distributions were correlated with *less* carbon dioxide emissions per capita.[156] Some researchers thus argued that the likes of Boyce had it the wrong way round: whereas Boyce had suggested that more egalitarian distributions of income would result in less carbon dioxide emissions per capita, the empirical evidence purportedly pointed the other way.[157] This would often lead to the conclusion that there is a possibility of trade-offs existing between attaining a more equal distribution of income and reducing carbon emissions.[158]

Some years later, in the mid-2000s, researchers began to come to the conclusion that the relationship is in fact not significant as they tweaked and

153 Boyce (n 151) 176. Footnote omitted.

154 Boyce (n 151) 178.

155 Kyle W Knight, Juliet B Schor and Andrew K Jorgenson, 'Wealth Inequality and Carbon Emissions in High Income Countries' (2017) 4 *Social Currents* 403, 409.

156 See, for example, Nico Heerink, Abay Malatu and Erwin Bulte 'Income Inequality and the Environment: Aggregation Bias in Environmental Kuznets Curves' (2001) 38 *Ecological Economics* 359 and Martin Ravallion, Mark Heil and Jyotsna Jalan 'Carbon Emissions and Income Inequality' (2000) 52 *Oxford Economics Papers* 651.

157 See, for example, Heerink, Malatu and Bulte (n 156) 75–6.

158 See, for example, Heerink, Malatu and Bulte (n 156) 75–6; Ravallion, Heil and Jalan (n 156) 667.

refined their methodological approaches.[159] In a 2006 study, for example, Simone Borghesi examined the relationship for 97 different countries and concluded that no statistically significant relationship existed between the distribution of income and greater carbon dioxide emissions per capita for the period 1988–1995.[160] More recently, as methods became more sophisticated still, the direction of findings appears to have taken another turn. It is noteworthy that some these studies have relied on income distribution data for a broader range of countries over longer periods of time.[161] As for the carbon emissions, researchers have generally used the same reference point consistently over time: data from the United-States-based Oak Ridge National Laboratory.[162]

A recent, seemingly comprehensive study, undertaken by Nicole Grunewald and her colleagues finds that the relationship between income distribution and carbon dioxide emissions hinges on a particular country's income level.[163] For countries classified by the authors as 'low and middle-income economies', on the one hand, a less equal distribution of income is associated with lower carbon dioxide emissions.[164] On the other hand, in countries deemed 'upper middle-income and high-income economies' a less equal distribution of income is associated with higher carbon dioxide emissions.[165] As the authors note, their findings have implications for the notion that there is a trade-off between distributional changes and the lowering of carbon dioxide emissions: the trade-off referred to above may well exist, but only for countries that have relatively low average incomes.[166]

Recent work by Andrew Jorgenson and his colleagues, based on data spanning a shorter period of time and covering fewer countries, came to essentially

159 See, for example, Simone Borghesi, 'Income Inequality and the Environmental Kuznets Curve' in Marcello Basilli, Maurizio Francini and Alessandro Vercelli (eds), *Environment, Inequality and Collective Action* (Routledge, New York 2006) 32 and Martin Gassebner, Michael J Lamla and Jan-Egbert Sturm, 'Determinants of Pollution: What Do We Really Know?' (2011) 63 *Oxford Economics Papers* 568.

160 See Borghesi (n 159).

161 Compare, for example, Nicole Grunewald et al, 'The Trade-off Between Income Inequality and Carbon Dioxide Emissions' (2017) 142 *Ecological Economics* 249 where the study was undertaken for 138 countries across the period 1960–2008 and Ravallion, Heil and Jalan (n 156) where 42 countries were examined over the period 1975–1992.

162 See, for example, Borghesi (n 159); Grunewald et al (n 161); Ravallion, Heil and Jalan (n 156).

163 Grunewald et al (n 161). The authors looked at the period 1980–2008 for 158 countries.

164 See Grunewald et al (n 161) 254.

165 Grunewald et al (n 161) 254.

166 Grunewald et al (n 161) 254.

the same conclusion as that reached by Grunewald and her colleagues.[167] In two different additional studies, Andrew Jorgenson and his colleagues also examined the relationship at a sub-national level in the United States.[168] In the first of these studies, the authors examined the relationship for (United States) state-level residential carbon emissions; in the second study they performed a similar exercise for all sectors (residential and non-residential) combined. On both occasions the authors came to the conclusion that there was a positive association between less equal income distributions and higher carbon dioxide emissions.[169]

Theoretical hypotheses relating economic distributions to carbon emissions have focused on the distribution of wealth (more or less as a proxy for political power).[170] The empirical studies that have been undertaken thus far, however, have predominantly focused on the distribution of income.[171] As is the case with the literature on distributions, poverty reduction and growth, this may simply be as a result of researchers not having (access to) comprehensive data for a sufficient number of countries to study the relationship in any meaningful way. Fortunately, sufficiently comprehensive data are available for some countries. Given that researchers have slowly begun reaching consensus on the notion that the relationship between the distribution of income and the level of carbon emissions differs among groups of countries when they are sorted in terms of income level, a logical starting point for testing the relationship between wealth distributions and per capita carbon emissions would be for the set of (relatively) rich countries.

---

167 See Andrew K Jorgenson et al, 'Domestic Inequality and Carbon Emissions in Comparative Perspective' (2016) 31 *Sociological Forum* 770. This time, the authors examined the period 1991–2008 for 67 countries.

168 Andrew K Jorgenson et al, 'Income Inequality and Residential Carbon Emissions in the United States: A Preliminary Analysis' (2015) 22 *Human Ecology Review* 93; Andrew K Jorgenson, Juliet B Schor and Xiaorui Huang, 'Income Inequality and Carbon Emissions in the United States: A State-level Analysis, 1997–2012' (2017) 134 *Ecological Economics* 40.

169 Jorgenson et al (n 168); Jorgenson, Schor and Huang (n 168).

170 See, for example, James K Boyce, 'Is Inequality Bad for the Environment?' (2008) 15 *Research in Social Problems and Public Policy* 267; Boyce (n 151).

171 Beyond the studies already referred to above, see also, for example, Jungho Baek and Guankerwon Gweisah, 'Does income inequality harm the environment?: Empirical evidence from the United States' (2013) 62 *Energy Policy* 1434; Jane Golley and Xin Meng, 'Income Inequality and Carbon Dioxide Emissions: The Case of Chinese Urban Households' (2012) 34 *Energy Economics* 1864; Yu Hao, Heyin Chen and Qianxue Zhang, 'Will Income Inequality Affect Environmental Quality? Analysis Based on China's Provincial Panel Data' (2016) 67 *Ecological Indicators* 533 and Hemachandra Padhan et al, 'What Matters for Environmental Quality in the Next-11 Countries: Economic Growth or Income Inequality?' (IZA Institute of Labor Economics Working Paper 11407, March 2018).

This is where Kyle Knight and his colleagues started in another recent study.[172] Examining the period 2000–2010, the authors attempted to discern the relationship between the distribution of wealth—using as proxy the T10 wealth share for 26 high-income countries—and per capita carbon emissions.[173] The authors came to the conclusion that for high-income countries more unequal wealth distributions were associated with higher consumption-based carbon dioxide emissions.[174] These results—having to some extent vindicated Boyce's theory—will likely see responses from scholars elsewhere; clarifying this relationship—that between the distribution of wealth and aggregate carbon emissions—may be of critical importance for climate change mitigation efforts.

3.3 *Conflict, Violence and Civil War*

Walter Scheidel ends his excellent book on the history of economic inequality with the following passage (quoted at the outset of this chapter, but quoted again for ease of reference):

> [M]uch of the world has entered what could become the next long stretch—a return to persistent capital accumulation and income concentration. If history is anything to go by, peaceful policy reform may well prove unequal to the growing challenges ahead. But what of the alternatives? All of us who prize greater economic equality would do well to remember that with the rarest exceptions, it was only ever brought forth in sorrow. Be careful what you wish for.[175]

The 'sorrow' that Walter Scheidel writes of at the end of his book is a reference to what he has termed 'the four horsemen'; that is to say, the four factors that have led to the reduction of inequalities of income and wealth within societies throughout the course of known history: mass mobilization warfare, transformative revolution, state collapse and plague.[176] It is fairly clear that two of them have become almost completely obsolete in contemporary times: ever since the Industrial Revolution, plagues akin to the Black Death experienced in the Middle Ages have not arisen,[177] nor has there, beyond a few examples such as the case of Somalia,[178] been much state collapse to speak of.

172 Knight, Schor and Jorgenson (n 155).
173 See Knight, Schor and Jorgenson (n 155) 407.
174 Knight, Schor and Jorgenson (n 155) 409.
175 Scheidel (n 1) 444.
176 See generally Scheidel (n 175).
177 The recent COVID-19 pandemic, albeit that it has had really severe impacts, does not rise to the level of 'plague' in the sense Scheidel uses the term.
178 See Scheidel (n 175) 8.

Since the start of the twentieth century, the two main sources for reducing the inequality of economic distributions have been mass mobilization warfare and transformative revolution.[179] As Scheidel notes, however, it is not clear—at an empirical level—that distributional changes over time in fact cause large wars or violent revolutions.[180] It accordingly serves us well to traverse briefly some of the literature on the relationship between changing economic distributions within states or societies and with events that may threaten the maintenance of international peace and security.

It is worth recalling that the very first listed purpose of the United Nations, under its Charter, is to 'maintain international peace and security'.[181] Under this mandate, the United Nations has concluded a variety of other agreements. For example, the United Nations Office on Counter-Terrorism notes that '[s]ince 1963 the international community has elaborated 19 international legal instruments to prevent terrorist acts' and that '[t]hose instruments were developed under the auspices of the United Nations and the International Atomic Energy Agency … and are open to participation by all [United Nations] Member States'.[182] It suffices to say that terrorism, loosely defined, is something that is at least notionally dear to the international community; one might accordingly ask whether there is some kind of relationship between distributional changes and changes in the observed level of terrorism.

In a blog post for the *Le Monde* newspaper in 2015, Thomas Piketty made was widely seen as a controversial argument in the following terms:

> Confronted with terrorism, the response must involve security measures. We must hit Daech [ISIS] and arrest those who are members. But we must also consider the political conditions of this violence, the humiliation and the injustices which result in this movement receiving considerable support in the Middle East and today gives rise to murderous vocations in Europe. In the long run, the real issue is the establishment of an equitable model for social development both there and here. … One thing is obvious: terrorism thrives on the inequality in

179 See Scheidel (n 175) 8–9.

180 See Scheidel (n 175) 10.

181 Article 1.1, Charter of the United Nations (UN Charter) (adopted 26 June 1945, entered into force 24 October 1945).

182 See further generally United Nations Office on Counter-Terrorism, 'International Legal Instruments' <http://www.un.org/en/counterterrorism/legal-instruments.shtml> accessed 30 September 2021.

> the Middle-East which is a powder keg we have largely contributed to creating.[183]

In this area, systematic empirical research—of which Piketty is an enthusiastic supporter generally speaking—is sparse. The little available work that exists, however, does tend to suggest—with admittedly little certainty as to how precisely the causal mechanisms operate—that increased levels of income inequality within a state leads to a greater amount of terrorist activities.[184] As one might expect in such a nascent area of research, however, the existing research leaves much to be desired: it does not, as yet, account properly for different definitions of terrorism or for different types of distributions.[185] Given that there is some preliminary evidence for concern, this is an area of research that should be monitored carefully as it develops in precision with time; especially so given that there is a fairly well established theoretical basis for the hypothesised linkages and that interest in data of this sort as well as its collection is continually increasing.[186]

A relationship that has, however, been studied more systematically is that between distributional variables and the onset of conflict, violence and civil war.[187] It suffices to say that any summary of what has become a dense literature over time is likely to over-simplify findings in a field where there is much scope for nuance. For example, much of the literature distinguishes between what are often labelled 'vertical inequalities' (VIs)—that is to say the difference in income or wealth as measured or as estimated between *individuals* within a defined area—and 'horizontal inequalities' (HIs), which refer to differences in income or wealth between *groups*.[188] There are various questions

---

183 See Thomas Piketty, 'Clamping down with law and order will not be enough' (*Le Monde* blog, 24 November 2015) <http://piketty.blog.lemonde.fr/2015/11/24/clamping-down-with-law-and-order-will-not-be-enough/> accessed 30 September 2021.

184 See, for example, Tim Krieger and Daniel Meierrieks, 'Income Inequality, Redistribution and Domestic Terrorism' (2019) 116 *World Development* 125.

185 Some studies are, however, careful to make some distinctions in this regard. See, for example, Roberto Ezcurra and David Palacios, 'Terrorism and Spatial Disparities: Does Interregional Inequality Matter?' (2016) 42 *European Journal of Political Economy* 60, where the authors are careful to limit the scope of their definition of terrorism to one that only includes 'domestic' terrorist acts and examine interregional income inequality.

186 On the theoretical basis, see, for example, the discussions in Krieger and Meierrieks (n 184) 3–7 and Ezcurra and Palacios (n 185) 61–2.

187 See, for example, Frances Stewart (ed), *Horizontal Inequalities and Conflict: Understanding Group Violence in Multiethnic Societies* (Palgrave Macmillan, Basingstoke 2008).

188 See Frances Stewart, 'Horizontal Inequalities and Conflict: An Introduction and Some Hypotheses' in Stewart (ed) (n 187) 3, 12–3.

here to which one could—and should where possible—dedicate much time to unpack. For example, with respect to HIs, how are 'groups' defined?[189] Methodological questions such as this are important—and a great deal has been done to answer them—but much of what follows will be simplified to make the broader point that changing economic distributions within countries have the capacity to contribute—to varying degrees—to events that threaten and/or harm international peace and security.

As a general proposition, VIs have not been found to contribute to the onset of civil conflict or to civil war. To simplify a lengthy discussion, following Ted Robert Gurr's 'relative depravation' theory, which he first appears to have posited in the late 1960s, empirical techniques have been applied over and over again with the aim of proving (or disproving) Gurr's theoretical construct.[190] Different theories have, of course, appeared over time,[191] with empirical studies and various critiques of both theory and measurement following soon after. Even with respects to VIs, the debate continued—and to an extent still does—to flare. An influential study undertaken by Paul Collier and Anke Hoeffler in 2004, using a VI-style measure—that is, the Gini coefficient of either income or land ownership—came to the conclusion, amongst other things, that the change in economic distributions over time do not contribute to the onset of civil war.[192] Some studies have come to similar conclusions.[193] Yet, other studies have come to the conclusion that there VIs do have a contributory impact on the onset of civil war.[194]

More recently, and specifically in light of the work done by Frances Stewart,[195] the focus has shifted away from VIs towards HIs. At their simplest,

189 On this question, see for example the discussion in Stewart (n 188) 7–12.

190 On Gurr's 'relative deprivation' hypothesis, see Ted Robert Gurr, *Why Men Rebel* (PUP, Princeton 1970) 22–56.

191 See, for example, Terry Boswell and William J Dixon, 'Marx's Theory of Rebellion: A Cross-Nation Analysis of Class Exploitation, Economic Development, and Violent Conflict' (1993) 58 *American Sociological Review* 681.

192 See generally Paul Collier and Anke Hoeffler, 'Greed and Grievance in Civil War' (2004) 56 *Oxford Economic Papers* 563.

193 See, for example, Halvard Buhaung and Lars-Erik Cederman, 'Square Pegs in Round Holes: Inequalities, Grievances and Civil War' (2014) 58 *International Studies Quarterly* 418.

194 See, for example, Carles Boix, 'Economic Roots of Civil Wars and Revolutions in the Contemporary World' (2008) 60 *World Politics* 390; Lars-Erik Cederman, Nils B Weidmann and Kristian Skrede Gleditsch, 'Horizontal Inequalities and Ethnonationalist Civil War: A Global Comparison' (2011) 105 *American Political Science Review* 478 and Gudrun Østby, 'Polarization, Horizontal Inequalities and Violent Civil Conflict' (2008) 45 *Journal of Peace Research* 123.

195 See especially Stewart (ed) (n 187). See also Frances Stewart, 'Crisis Prevention: Tackling Horizontal Inequalities' (2000) 23 *Oxford Development Studies* 245.

HIs can be defined as 'inequalities in economic, social or political dimensions or cultural status between culturally defined groups'.[196] While an array of results has come from work on HIs,[197] perhaps the most important of these is that, simplistically put, the probability of conflict, including the onset of civil war, rises when socio-economic—which of course includes an economic distribution component—HIs grow higher over time.[198]

Understanding what causes a complex event such as a civil war naturally remains a difficult task, especially given that the data used in the relevant studies, although they have improved in quantity and quality over time, still remains inadequate at times.[199] The fact remains, however, that there is a growing body of literature that comes to the conclusion that HIs have a strong contributory effect when it comes to the causes of civil war and other similar forms of violence.[200]

4 Conclusions

In concluding this chapter, it should be emphasised that it constitutes a *very* brief description of a subset of issues surrounding economic distributions. This chapter is of necessity a significant truncation. It leaves out many issues that are of general importance when it comes to economic distributions. For instance, this chapter has not discussed much in relation to gender and economic distributions. It has also not dealt comprehensively with race and economic distributions. Further, where it has dealt with a certain issue, it has done so fairly superficially. What, then, has been the point of this chapter? Simply put, it has been as follows: first, it has sought to show that economic distributions have become significantly more unequal in almost all countries around the world since the 1980s; and secondly, it has been to show some of the impacts this has had and will continue to have. With this context sketched, the monograph turns to its main topics of discussion in the next two chapters.

196 Stewart (n 188) 3. For examples of HIs in conflict situations, see Stewart (n 188) 15.

197 See further Frances Stewart, Graham K Brown and Arnim Langer, 'Major Findings and Conclusions on the Relationship Between Horizontal Inequalities and Conflict' in Stewart (ed.) (n 187).

198 Stewart, Brown and Langer (n 197) 287.

199 For an overview of attempts to overcome data-related difficulties, see, for example, Lars-Erik Cederman, Nils B Weidmann and Nils-Christian Bormann 'Triangulating Horizontal Inequality: Toward Improved Conflict Analysis' (2015) 52 *Journal of Peace Research* 806.

200 See, for example, Buhaung and Cederman (n 193); Cederman, Weidmann and Gleditsch (n 194); Cederman, Weidmann and Bormann (n 199); and Østby (n 194).

CHAPTER 3

Recognising the Distribution of Income and Wealth within States as a Common Concern of Humankind

> [A]s for equality, the word must not be taken to mean that the degrees of power and wealth should be exactly the same, but that, as regards personal power, it should not be so great as to make violence possible, and should be exercised only in accordance with social position and the law; and as regards wealth, that no citizen should be rich enough to be able to buy another, and none so poor that he has to sell himself ... Equality, it is said, is a theorists' vision, which cannot exist in practice. But if an abuse is inevitable, does it follow that it should not at least be controlled? It is precisely because the force of things always tends to destroy equality that the force of law should tend always to conserve it.
>
> JEAN-JACQUES ROUSSEAU (1712–1778), *The Social Contract*[1]

1 Introduction

Since the late 1980s the 'common concern of humankind' concept has been contemplated by the international community within the frameworks of various treaty regimes that seek to deal with global problems.[2] In 1992, the United Nations Framework Convention on Climate Change (UNFCCC) was agreed, with the parties acknowledging 'that change in the Earth's climate

1 Jean-Jacques Rousseau, *The Social Contract* (OUP, New York 1994), translated from the original French by Christopher Betts, 87. Footnote omitted.

2 On the history and development of common concern of humankind as a concept in international law, see Laura Sandra Horn, *The Common Concern of Humankind and Legal Protection of the Global Environment* (Unpublished PhD thesis, University of Sydney 2000) 103–93. See also Thomas Cottier, 'The Principle of Common Concern of Humankind' in Thomas Cottier (ed), *The Prospects of Common Concern of Humankind in International Law* (CUP, Cambridge 2021) and Thomas Cottier et al, 'The Principle of Common Concern and Climate Change' (2014) 52 *Archiv des Völkerrechts* 293, 298–303.

 | DOI:10.1163/9789004511750_004

and its adverse effects are a common concern of humankind'.[3] In the same year the Convention on Biological Diversity (CBD) was concluded; signatories on that occasion affirmed that 'the conservation of biodiversity is a common concern of humankind'.[4] Since then, the concept has been used again in the Paris Agreement on Climate Change and its application has been proposed in the International Law Commission's work on the protection of the atmosphere.[5] For many, however, the concept and its implications remain vague.[6] This can—and has in the case of atmospheric protection, for example—lead to its application being rejected in areas where there is potential for recognising novel common concerns of humankind.[7]

It is certainly true that the common concern of humankind concept and its implications are open to a broad range of understandings. Scholars differ, for example, on what the recognition of a common concern of humankind implies for the justification of certain state actions; most authors appear to agree that the recognition of a common concern of humankind constitutes a justification for collective international action, with others suggesting that it also provides a normative justification for action at the national level, and others still proposing that it provides a justification for unilateral action as the term is understood in international law. Academic debate relating to the common concern of humankind concept has also yielded a range of opinions concerning the relationship between the common concern of humankind concept and that of obligations *erga omnes*, the constitutive elements of common concerns of humankinds more generally and on whether the recognition of common concerns of humankind simply amount to justifications for action

3 Preamble, United Nations Framework Convention on Climate Change (UNFCCC) (adopted 9 May 1992, entered into force 21 March 1994) 1771 UNTS 107, 165.

4 Preamble, Convention on Biological Diversity (CBD) (adopted 5 June 1992, entered into force 29 December 1993) 1760 UNTS 79, 143.

5 On the Paris Agreement on Climate Change, see preamble, Paris Agreement (adopted 12 December 2015, entered into force 4 November 2016), I54113 UNTC 1, 89. For a brief overview of the use of the common concern of humankind concept in the work of the International Law Commission (ILC) on the protection of the atmosphere, see Nadia Sánchez Castillo-Winckels, 'Why "Common Concern of Humankind" Should Return to the Work of the International Law Commission on the Atmosphere' (2016) 29 *Georgetown International Environmental Law Review* 131, 132–3.

6 See, for example, in the context of the ILC's work on the protection of the atmosphere, Shinya Murase (Special Rapporteur), *Second Report on the Protection of the Atmosphere*, UN Document A/CN.4/681 (2015) 18; ILC, *Report on the Work of the International Law Commission: Sixty-Seventh Session*, UN Document A/70/10 (2015) 26–7.

7 See Castillo-Winckels (n 5) 132.

or whether they impose duties or responsibilities, including on the scope and precision of such duties and responsibilities.[8]

An under-discussed theme—overlooked perhaps on the basis of apparent scholarly consensus—is that of the relationship between the concept of common concern of humankind and that of state sovereignty. To be sure, the relationship has been discussed.[9] The general consensus amongst scholars appears to be that common concerns of humankind require a 'balancing' of the interests of humankind, or at least those of the international community broadly construed, with the concept of state sovereignty; the implication being that, at least to some degree, the two concepts are at odds with one another.[10]

The approach adopted in this monograph departs from this general consensus: rather than suggest that the common concern of humankind concept is antithetical to sovereignty, it will instead be argued that the recognition of common concerns of humankind is a manner in which states act to *enhance* or *retain* their sovereignty. The recognition of a particular common concern of humankind therefore acts as a definitional instantiation of particular aspects of state sovereignty (or perhaps an attempt at this). Common concerns of humankind are recognised precisely because contemporary understandings of sovereignty at a given point in time are inadequate for addressing specific problems.

The basis for this argument stems from the idea captured by the Latin maxim '*ex post facto ius oritur*'; that is, that law arises out of fact.[11] In the context of climate change, for example, the common concern of humankind concept has been employed, largely, as a response to factual changes, the discovery of which was enabled by progress in the field of climate science, pertaining to the rate at which the climate has been undergoing certain changes and the adverse

---

8 See further below in this chapter for an examination of these debates.

9 See generally, for example, Frank Biermann '"Common Concerns of Humankind" and National Sovereignty' in Diane Hiscox and Johanne Levasseur (eds), *Globalism: People, Profits, and Progress: Proceedings of the 30th Annual Conference of the Canadian Council on International Law* (Kluwer, London 2002). See also Horn (n 2) 135–45; Stephen Stec, 'Humanitarian Limits to Sovereignty: Common Concern and Common Heritage Approaches to Natural Resources and Environment' (2010) 12 *International Community Law Review* 361, 368.

10 See Castillo-Winckels (n 5) 135 and the sources cited there. See also Frank Biermann, '"Common Concern of Humankind": The Emergence of a New Concept of International Environmental Law' (1996) 34 *Archiv des Völkerrechts* 426, 465 and 481; Horn (n 2) 135–45; and Stec (n 9) 368.

11 For a different application of the maxim, see Claus D Zimmermann, *A Contemporary Concept of Monetary Sovereignty* (OUP, Oxford 2013) 9–16.

effects that can be observed as a result of these changes.[12] Upon becoming aware of these factual changes, certain aspects of general state sovereignty—that is, the legal conception of the term—had to be reworked by states; sovereignty had to be asserted in a new way: recognising climate change and its adverse effects as a common concern of humankind, therefore, is in large part simply sovereignty reconstituted; it is representative of an agreement between states to define certain aspects of sovereignty in a particular way so as to enhance the sovereignty of each state that forms part of the agreement.

Seen this way, the need for the legal reconstitution of sovereignty in light of particular factual changes over time can be seen as an important—and often overlooked—constitutive element of common concerns of humankind. The set of changed facts contemplated in this chapter are the shifts in economic globalization that began to be observed in the late 1980s: the world saw major technological advances in information and communications technology (ICT) which are often described as having had—and continuing to have—a 'revolutionary' or 'transformative' impact on the world economy.[13] As illustrated in the previous chapter, most of the states in the world have also seen income and wealth within their respective territories become increasingly unequally distributed.[14] These trends have unfolded simultaneously to the described shifts in economic globalization. This, of course, is not a coincidence.

The overarching aim of this chapter, against the backdrop of contemporary economic globalization, is to contemplate whether the observable near-global changes in the distribution of income and wealth within states and the adverse effects associated therewith could and, if so, should be recognised as a common concern of humankind. In order to accomplish this aim, it is first necessary to describe how economic globalization has changed—factually—since the beginning of the on-going ICT revolution. It is also necessary to distil the

---

12 For a brief overview of the history and development of climate change science, see Spencer Weart, 'The Development of the Concept of Dangerous Anthropogenic Climate Change' in John S Dryzek, Richard B Norgaard and David Schlosberg, *Oxford Handbook of Climate Change and Society* (OUP, New York 2011) 67–81. For a detailed review of the physical science basis of climate change assertions, see generally Thomas F Stocker et al (eds), *Climate Change 2013: The Physical Science Basis, Working Group I Contribution to the Fifth Assessment Report of the Intergovernmental Panel on Climate Change* (CUP, New York 2014). On the impact and effects of climate change over time, see, for example, Christopher B Field et al (eds), *Managing the Risks of Extreme Events and Disasters to Advance Climate Change Adaption: Special Report of the Intergovernmental Panel on Climate Change* (CUP, New York 2012) 109–290.

13 See, for example, Richard Baldwin, *The Great Convergence: Information Technology and the New Globalization* (HUP, Cambridge, MA 2016), 81–2.

14 See Chapter 2 of this monograph.

common concern concept into factors that can be assessed in order to determine what does and what does not constitute a common concern of humankind. Having done these two things, the chapter is then in a position to proceed to contemplate whether changes in the distribution of income and wealth within states and the adverse effects that follow as a consequence thereof are capable of being recognised as a common concern of humankind.

This latter task is the key focus of this chapter. Ultimately, its aim is to illustrate that sovereignty-based objections to the recognition of the adverse effects stemming from the distribution of income and wealth as a common concern of humankind are premised on an understanding of sovereignty that have become outdated given the mentioned changes in economic globalization. The recognition of changes in the distribution of income and wealth and their adverse effects as a common concern of humankind would act to enhance the sovereignty of states in a manner that would allow them to better address issues that are of great importance to humanity as a whole. This argument will be defended throughout this chapter, and indeed the rest of this monograph, with due reference also to the other constitutive elements of common concerns of humankind and to the legal implications that flow from the recognition of common concerns of humankind.

The chapter is structured as follows: having provided a contemporary conceptualization of what will be referred to as 'the distributive aspects of economic sovereignty' in light of the changing nature of economic globalization since the late 1980s (*Part I*), this chapter proceeds to examine the recognition of common concerns of humankind, with a focus on sovereignty as a constitutive element, and what legal implications such recognition entails (*Part II*). In light of the discussions in the first two parts, the final part of this chapter contemplates the recognition of the distribution of income and wealth within states and the adverse effects that flow therefrom as a common concern of humankind (*Part III*).

2 Economic Sovereignty and the Distribution of Income and Wealth Since 'Globalization's Second Unbundling'

This first part of the chapter is part contextual; using Richard Baldwin's framework for explaining economic globalization, it sketches a background against which the distribution of income and wealth can be evaluated in order to determine whether it does, could and/or should be considered a common concern of humankind. It is also part conceptual development. First, Baldwin's framework, with a focus on what he calls 'globalization's second unbundling', is introduced and its impact on the distribution of income and wealth within states is considered (*Section 2.1*). In the second section, the concept of economic sovereignty is discussed and developed conceptually in light of globalization's second unbundling (*Section 2.2*).

2.1 *'Globalization's Second Unbundling' and the Distribution of Income and Wealth within States*

In his book, *The Great Convergence*, Richard Baldwin essentially sketches a history of economic globalization; presenting what he terms a 'three-cascading-constraints' view of the concept.[15] Baldwin distils the history of globalization into three more or less distinct stages: (1) the pre-globalization era; (2) globalization's first 'acceleration' or 'unbundling'; and (3) globalization's second 'acceleration' or 'unbundling'.[16] Others have written similar histories about globalization, but Baldwin's characterisation provides a helpful framework for the purposes of this work; it provides a simple but convincing set of guidelines for understanding the contemporary global economy and how it has come to be.[17]

Baldwin's simplification is essentially that globalization mainly hinges on three factors—or cascading constraints—(1) trade costs (the costs of moving goods); (2) communication costs (the costs of moving ideas); and (3) face-to-face costs (the costs of moving people).[18] In the pre-globalized world, which only stopped existing in around 1820, production and consumption generally occurred in the same geographical area.[19] This came as a result of all three factors being costly—trade costs were high, communication costs were high and face-to-face costs were high; trade was mostly limited to trade within particular communities that were geographically close to one another and the same could be said of communication and the movement of people, both of which activities predominantly occurred between people in close proximity.[20]

Globalization's first unbundling came in three phases. The first of these started in around 1820 with the 'steam revolution' and ended with the First World War; the second phase was the interwar period, with the third phase

15 See Baldwin (n 13) 113–41.
16 See Baldwin (n 13) 4–6.
17 See also, however, Part I of John H Dunning and Sarianna M Lundan, *Multinational Enterprises and the Global Economy* (2ed Edward Elgar, Cheltenham 2008) 3–200; Ronald Findlay and Kevin H O'Rourke, *Power and Plenty: Trade, War, and the World Economy in the Second Millennium* (PUP, Princeton 2008).
18 See Baldwin (n 13) 8–10.
19 On the pre-globalized era, see Chapter 1 of Baldwin (n 13) 21–46.
20 Baldwin (n 13) 114–20.

lasting from the end of the Second World War until the late 1980's.[21] In short, the consequences of this unbundling as a whole were a substantial reduction in trade costs and an ever-widening income gap between developed and developing countries.[22] Importantly, only the nature of one of the three cascading constraints changed significantly: trade costs dropped, but communication costs and face-to-face costs remained high.[23] It was with this reality in mind that the base for the current international economic law regime was designed and implemented: the post-war economic order—which started being formed in the 1940s and continues to underpin contemporary economic globalization—was accordingly built to deal with the circumstances associated with globalization's first unbundling.

Globalization's second unbundling started occurring in the late 1980s with the start of the 'ICT revolution'.[24] What made this globalization's 'second unbundling' was the fact that the nature of the second cascading constraint began to change—communication costs fell and it progressively, and very rapidly, became virtually costless to move ideas around the globe.[25] Baldwin calls this state of affairs—where trade and communication costs are low, but the costs associated with moving people remain high—the 'New Globalization'. We remain is this era today and central questions for the purposes of this chapter relate to how the New Globalization is different from what preceded it and what this means for economic sovereignty and the distribution of income and wealth within states.

Most important for current purposes is Baldwin's chapter titled 'What's Really New?'[26] In this chapter, Baldwin illustrates how globalization has changed since the second unbundling began in the late 1980's; at the beginning of the chapter he writes that '[t]he newness of the New Globalization' can be found in two integral parts of the second unbundling: (1) fragmentation and offshoring in manufacturing and service sectors; and (2) the technology flows that 'follow the jobs sent offshore'.[27] Importantly, the New Globalization was mostly made possible by rapid technological change in ICT; but this had a clear knock-on effect on trade—the costs associated with which continued

21 Baldwin (n 13) 47–9.

22 See Baldwin (n 13) 57–62. See also Chapter 3 of Branko Milanovic *Global Inequality: A New Approach for the Age of Globalization* (HUP, Cambridge, MA 2016) 118–155.

23 See Baldwin (n 13) 75–6.

24 Baldwin (n 13) 81–5.

25 See Baldwin (n 13) 130–2.

26 See Baldwin (n 13) 142–76.

27 Baldwin (n 13) 142.

to fall—predominantly due to the new configurations it made available for the organization of production.[28]

A lot of attention has been paid to the topic of how the organization of production has changed.[29] Gerald F Davis, for example, in his aptly titled book *The Vanishing American Corporation*, writes of the 'Nikefication' of American industry.[30] Davis describes the process as follows:

> The new model for the corporation was to be like Nike. Nike designs and markets sneakers from its headquarters in Oregon, but hires contractors in East Asia to produce them. Its "core" involves developing intellectual property, not manufacturing physical goods, and it has become one of the most valuable brands in history. Pressed by investors and enabled by the growth of generic suppliers, firms in industry after industry followed a path of Nikefication. Businesses like Sara Lee and Apple jettisoned production to focus on design and brand management. Computers, pet food, pharmaceuticals, shoes, and even government services are increasingly produced by contractors, not the company whose name is on the label.[31]

In essence, as Baldwin points out, whereas the frontline of competition used to be national borders they are today better thought of as 'cross-national production networks'; more often referred to as 'global value chains' (GVCs).[32] The implications of GVC proliferation have been far reaching. Comparative advantage—in the David Ricardo sense—essentially underpinned globalization for the entirety of its 'first unbundling'.[33] This traditional conception of comparative advantage is based on the idea that goods are made in one state, relying on inputs that are from that same state.[34] Where the GVC-era is different, is in how it has led to a situation where goods are no longer made in one state; trade in part and components—in intermediate goods—have risen extensively since Globalization's second unbundling started.[35]

28 See Baldwin (n 13) 149–54.

29 See, for example, Gerald F Davis, *The Vanishing American Corporation: Navigating the Hazards of a New Economy* (Berrett-Kohler Publishers, Oakland 2016).

30 See Chapter 6 of Davis (n 29) 69–80.

31 Davis (n 29) 69.

32 Baldwin (n 13) 145.

33 See Chapter VII in David Ricardo, *On the Principles of Political Economy and Taxation* (John Murray, London 1817).

34 See Baldwin (n 13) 145–53.

35 Baldwin (n 13) 150.

Additionally, capital has become more mobile over time and there has been a drastic proliferation in the amount of foreign direct investment (FDI) between countries. This is indicative of production facilities, personnel and know-how moving across borders.[36] As production continued to become more dispersed, related services also gained in relative importance as there was suddenly a need for a greater focus on the coordination of networks spanning far larger geographical areas than before.[37] The upshot of all these changes is that comparative advantage became progressively 'de-nationalized'.[38] What this means, in essence, is that the traditional comparative advantage—whereby production all occurs within one state—no longer holds in the same way it did before.[39] Commercial competition is no longer between national corporations; multinational GVCs compete with other multinational GVCs instead, with each GVC comprising workers and firms from a multitude of different states.[40]

As Baldwin puts it, 'international commerce became more *multifaceted*—involving flows of goods, services, intellectual property, capital and people—and ... those flows became more *entangled* in the sense that they are generated by the same cause (production unbundling)'.[41] This makes the tasks of all actors involved in the economy more complicated because national progress is not prioritised by all actors in a world of de-nationalized comparative advantage.[42] Labour unions, for example, have a more difficult time organising because in the event that—as is the case in a large number of countries—unions are organised by sector, it could be that union members have conflicting interests vis-à-vis other members of their own union.[43] It also means that the interests of states and firms are increasingly less aligned with one another.[44] Often, firm and national interests even directly conflict with one another.[45]

Related to the organisation of production are multiple other changes that have surfaced since globalization's second unbundling. Most of these stem from the ICT revolution in the sense that new technology ushered in an era of greater capital mobility. For example, the ICT revolution and other factors

36 Baldwin (n 13) 150.
37 Baldwin (n 13) 150.
38 Baldwin (n 13) 145.
39 Baldwin (n 13) 145.
40 Baldwin (n 13) 145.
41 Baldwin (n 13) 150. Emphasis original.
42 Baldwin (n 13) 145.
43 Baldwin (n 13) 169.
44 Baldwin (n 13) 170.
45 Baldwin (n 13) 170.

further enabled financial services to be provided more efficiently across borders at a greater scale. One result of this has been a proliferation of tax havens. Up until the 1980s, the lone offshore financial centre appears to have been Switzerland.[46] Since then, a majority of capital flows offshore have been to new centres, predominantly located in Europe, Asia and the Caribbean.[47] This raises an array of additional tax complications that cannot easily be resolved within a particular state's borders. As with the organization of production, this often brings the interests of firms (and, in this case, of wealthy individual's as well) into stark contrast with those of its (or their) 'home' state.

While there are a number of other changes perhaps worth discussing—and some of these are discussed further below—the point is ultimately that the development of ICT has resulted in an economic system that is far more global in reach than the system that preceded it and that the nature of the relationship between states and firms has changed accordingly. The manner in which goods and increasingly services are produced combined with the various other corollaries of the uptake of ICT has left the world with a unique set of governance challenges. One such challenge is the manner in which income and wealth are distributed within states in a world where firms and capital are increasingly de-coupled from states.

The post-Second-World-War economic system was fashioned during the latter stages of globalization's first unbundling. It was premised on the traditional conception of comparative advantage, the understanding being that economic interdependence would promote mutual prosperity—and thereby peace—with international trade playing a central role. In essence, at the international level the goal was to make the global economic pie as large as possible whilst trying to provide a level playing field for states and *their* firms. The distribution of income and wealth between states was accordingly increasingly subjected to international legal rules, first through the GATT and later through the WTO and its various covered agreements.

Distributive matters within states, however, were left entirely to the states themselves to deal with as a domestic issue.[48] This meant the development

46 For a succinct overview of the history of offshore finance, see Chapter 1 in Gabriel Zucman, *The Hidden Wealth of Nations: The Scourge of Tax Havens* (University of Chicago Press, Chicago 2015), translated from the original French by Teresa Lavender Fagan.

47 Zucman (n 46) 24.

48 See generally Ethan B Kapstein, 'Distributive Justice as an International Public Good' in Inge Kaul, Isabelle Grunberg and Marc A Stern (eds), *Global Public Goods: International Cooperation in the 21st Century* (OUP, New York 1999) 88–115.

of various forms of welfare states.[49] Governments around the world also took on more and more distributive functions, especially after human rights gained traction as a concept after the War. Healthcare became something governments were involved in;[50] as did housing,[51] and the provision of trade adjustment assistance amongst various other functions with distributive impacts.[52] Moreover, until the 1980s the post-War globe was characterised by steady or declining levels of inequality of income and wealth within states, at least in developed democracies, but also in countries such as India, China and Russia, amongst others.[53]

Since globalization's second unbundling, however, and as illustrated in Chapter 2, the distribution of income and wealth has changed dramatically within states, with a large majority of the world's citizens now living in countries where distributions have become more unequal since the 1980s.[54] In the ICT world of de-nationalized comparative advantage and increasing capital mobility, the post-Second-World-War economic framework is unable to deliver what it was intended to deliver. This is predominantly because it was not designed with globalization's second unbundling in mind.

Moreover, as Baldwin notes, globalization also became 'wilder' during its second unbundling: the shocks associated with globalization grew substantially in size and they happened a lot faster than ever before.[55] This meant that—and still means that—the distributive and redistributive issues that

---

49 See Kapstein (n 48) 94–7. See also generally Asa Briggs, 'The Welfare State in Historical Perspective' (1961) 2 *European Journal of Sociology* 221; Frank Nullmeier and Franz-Xaver Kaufmann, 'Post-War Welfare State Development' in Francis G Castles et al (eds), *The Oxford Handbook of the Welfare State* (OUP, Oxford 2012) 81–104; Chapter 4 in Christopher Pierson, *Beyond the Welfare State? The New Political Economy of Welfare* (Penn State University Press, University Park, PA 1991) 99–166.

50 See, for example, Peter Greengross, Ken Grant and Elizabeth Collini, *Helpdesk Report: The History and Development of the UK National Health Service 1948–1999* (DFID Health Systems Resource Centre, London 1999) for a history of the development of the National Health Service in the United Kingdom.

51 For an overview of public housing provisioning covering a large number of states in historical and contemporary perspective, see Jie Chen, Mark Stephens and Yanyun Man (eds), *The Future of Public Housing: Ongoing Trends in the East and the West* (Springer, Heidelberg 2013).

52 On trade adjustment assistance, see for example JF Hornbeck, *Trade Adjustment Assistance (TAA) and Its Role in U.S. Trade Policy* (Congressional Research Service, Washington, DC 2013) for an overview of the historical development of trade adjustment assistance in the United States.

53 See Chapter 2 above in this monograph.

54 See Chapter 2 above in this monograph.

55 See Baldwin (n 13) 165–75.

states were required to deal with increased in importance, became more demanding and also became more complicated to resolve. At the same time, functions that were previously carried out by states could now only be carried out by states in cooperation with other states. The idea that distributive issues within states can be competently handled—as a matter of *fact*—as a purely national concern is quickly losing traction.

2.2 *Conceptualising the Distributive Aspects of Contemporary Economic Sovereignty*

The term 'sovereignty' has a certain notoriety to it; often invoked as between nations but rarely with a common understanding as to the meaning of the word or its implications, 'sovereignty' has been a contested concept for most of its existence. For current purposes, it would be of little worth to engage in the larger sovereignty debate. Rather, it suffices to say that the view taken here is that state sovereignty is an 'essentially contestable concept' as this term was understood by Walter Bryce Gallie.[56] That is to say that sovereignty as a concept is normative in nature, intrinsically complex and a-criterial.[57] Amongst other things, this implies—as Samantha Besson has put it—that 'sovereignty is as once a state of affairs, a question pertaining to the nature and justification of that state of affairs and a justification of it'.[58] With this in mind, the aim here is to attempt to conceptualize a subsidiary notion; what will be referred to here as the 'distributive aspects of economic sovereignty'.

2.2.1 An Outline of 'Economic Sovereignty' and Its Relation to the Provision of Public Goods

Economic Sovereignty. There have been earlier attempts—both in name and in kind—at describing the state of affairs which the term 'economic sovereignty' entails, questioning its nature and justification and offering justifications for its use. In a 1985 article, for example, Vaughan Lowe presented an outline of what he then considered could be some of the methods which might be adopted in

56 See generally WB Gallie 'Essentially Contested Concepts' (1956) 56 *Proceedings of the Aristotelian Society* 167.

57 See Samantha Besson, 'Sovereignty in Conflict' (2004) 8 *European Integration online Papers (EIoP)* 1, 7. See also Dan Sarooshi, 'The Essentially Contested Nature of the Concept of Sovereignty: Implications for the Exercise by International Organizations of Delegated Powers of Government' (2004) 25 *Michigan Journal of International Law* 1107, 1108–1109; Dan Sarooshi, *International Organizations and Their Exercise of Sovereign Powers* (OUP, New York 2005) 3–5; and Zimmermann (n 11) 19–20.

58 Besson (n 57) 22. See also Zimmermann (n 11) 19–24 for a detailed analysis of contemporary monetary sovereignty as an 'essentially contested concept'.

order to define the concept in greater detail.[59] For each of these methods Lowe asserted that 'the essential argument is that, if it can be shown that there are certain rights or powers which are considered to be essential components of a State's sovereignty, then other States ought not to exercise their own powers so as to undermine those rights or powers'.[60] Lowe was quick to add the following:

> It must be admitted at once that in the case of most, if not all, of the components of economic sovereignty this requirement of restraint imposed on third States is not the direct and logically necessary consequence of the very existence of the first State's economic rights. Rather, it will be necessary to base the duty of restraint on the more general principles of self-determination and of non-intervention in the domestic affairs of another State—themselves corollaries of the sovereign equality and independence of States which is a fundamental datum of contemporary international law.[61]

The first method Lowe refers to in order to give some content to the term economic sovereignty is the 'recognition approach'.[62] This approach is based on the presumption that 'certain economic powers' are considered to be 'conditions upon which the recognition of States or governments can depend'; Lowe consequently asserts that 'it would be reasonable to regard these powers as components of a State's economic sovereignty'.[63] The second method is the 'responsibility approach'.[64] Under this approach, it is assumed that states —

> have the right, free from the deliberate interference of third States, to control persons and companies within their territory in relation to matters which they are generally regarded as being entitled to bind themselves by treaty to regulate in a certain way and in respect of which they may therefore become internationally responsible.[65]

Having set out both theories and provided examples as evidence of the exercise of economic sovereignty, Lowe reaches the following conclusion:

---

59 See A Vaughan Lowe, 'The Problems of Extraterritorial Jurisdiction: Economic Sovereignty and the Search for a Solution' (1985) 34 *International and Comparative Law Quarterly* 724, 740–6.

60 Lowe (n 59) 740.

61 Lowe (n 59) 740.

62 See Lowe (n 59) 741.

63 Lowe (n 59) 741.

64 See Lowe (n 59) 742.

65 Lowe (n 59) 742.

> [A]t the heart of the concept of economic sovereignty is the right of a State to regulate the structure of its own economy. There may be ancillary rights, such as the right to regulate the activities of all businesses within its territory and the terms of trade within its territory: inevitably, its precise scope will be a matter for debate.[66]

As part of the right to regulate the structure of its own economy, one of the ancillary rights a state has is surely that of the provision of public goods.[67] This holds in terms of Lowe's recognition approach in the sense that the capacity and actual provision of public goods is a *raison d'être* of states, which exist precisely because public goods are undersupplied or not supplied at all in the absence of states. The right to supply public goods also holds under Lowe's responsibility approach because states are entitled to bind themselves by treaty as part of public goods provision, for example by agreeing to cooperate with other states, including in the provision of funding for example, such that public goods may be produced in each of the states that are party to the agreement.

Max Huber's oft-cited statement from his award in the *Island of Palmas* case perhaps makes this point more lucidly. He wrote that '[s]overeignty in the relations between States signifies independence. Independence in regard to a portion of the globe is the right to exercise therein, to the exclusion of any other State, the functions of a State'.[68] With respect to public goods, the assertion here is that their supply is a, if not *the*, quintessential function of a state. This implies that economic sovereignty has long included the right of a state to regulate its own economy in order to influence how income and wealth are distributed within its borders. Lester Thurow has, after all, argued persuasively that the distribution of income within a society—a state for current purposes—is a pure public good.[69] A brief rehearsal of his argument is warranted here. Thurow introduces his article with the following:

> Although the social welfare function—in other words, some value judgment—must ultimately be invoked to determine society's optimum distribution of income, there is a subsidiary problem. Is every initial

66 Lowe (n 59) 744. Emphasis added.

67 The concept 'public goods' is used here as it was used by Paul Samuelson. See Paul A Samuelson, 'A Pure Theory of Public Expenditure' (1954) 36 *Review of Economics and Statistics* 387.

68 *Island of Palmas Case (Netherland v USA)* (1928), 2 UNRIAA 829.

69 Lester C Thurow, 'The Income Distribution as a Pure Public Good' (1971) 85 *Quarterly Journal of Economics* 327.

> distribution of income a Pareto optimum, or is some redistribution necessary to achieve a Pareto optimum?[70]

He subsequently suggests that there are a variety of reasons to come to the conclusion that arbitrary initial distributions are not Pareto optimal and proceeds to an explanation. Amongst other reasons, Thurow posits that '[t]he distribution of income itself may be an argument in an individual's utility function [and that t]his may come about because there are externalities associated with the distribution of income'.[71] On the assumption that both parts of this statement are true, Thurow categorises the distribution of income as a pure public good.[72] This is because everyone in a given society faces the same aggregate income distribution—exclusion is impossible—consumption is non-rivalrous in that no person can be excluded of any benefits that result from a particular income distribution and each person must consume the same quantity.[73] In light of the conclusion of his argument, Thurow in part concludes as follows:

> To the extent that individuals are interested in the income distribution because of externalities rather than simple tastes for equality or inequality, the public good approach focuses attention on the need for research in an area that is between economics and sociology. What are the empirical effects of the income distribution on crime, social stability, political stability, or any other characteristic of society? Perhaps the impact is significant; perhaps it is insignificant. We just do not know.[74]

With four and a half decades having since passed, we now have a better sense of the empirical effects Thurow referred to; an array of these have already been outlined in Chapter 2.[75] That Chapter also outlined a range of empirical effects that flow from the distribution of wealth as well as some findings relating to public perception of the distribution of income and wealth.[76] To be sure, there is much left to learn about the consequences of income and wealth distributions. It is also fairly clear, however, that there is sufficient evidence for us to conclude that the distribution of income and the distribution of wealth both

70 Thurow (n 69) 327.
71 Thurow (n 69) 327.
72 Thurow (n 69) 328.
73 Thurow (n 69) 328–9.
74 Thurow (n 69) 335–6.
75 See Chapter 2 above in this monograph.
76 See Chapter 2 above in this monograph.

constitute pure public goods.[77] It also follows, therefore, that, as a function of having economic sovereignty, states have the right to provide public goods, including by exercising ancillary rights in order to influence the distribution of income and wealth within its territory.

2.2.2 Towards a Contemporary Concept of the Distributive Aspects of Economic Sovereignty

In referring to the conceptualisation of economic sovereignty here as 'contemporary', the aim is to suggest that the concept needs to be updated in light of globalization's second unbundling as described above. The central issue to this discussion is the capacity of states—as a matter of fact—to address problems that stem from the distribution of income and wealth by directly pursuing alterations of the distributions themselves as economic sovereigns. This entails addressing some of the positive aspects of economic sovereignty; those that relate to the competences that states exercise and how effectively they are able to do so. The view of sovereignty adopted here, however, is that the concept also has a normative component that warrants some discussion: that of distributive justice.

It also serves the discussion well to distinguish at this point between internal and external economic sovereignty. While there is clearly no bright line distinguishing one from the other, the former refers to sovereignty over the internal affairs of a state, while the latter refers to sovereignty as it operates vis-à-vis other sovereigns.[78] These notions align well conceptually with Lowe's

---

77 The distribution of income and wealth has also been shown to affect the provision of other public goods. See, for example, J Mohan Rao, 'Equity in a Global Public Goods Framework' in Inge Kaul, Isabelle Grunberg and Marc A Stern (eds), *Global Public Goods: International Cooperation in the 21st Century* (OUP, New York 1999) 68, 79–85. For experimental evidence in this regard, see, for example, Lisa R Anderson, Jennifer M Mellor and Jeffrey Milyo, 'Inequality and Public Good Provision: An Experimental Analysis' (2008) 37 *The Journal of Socio-Economics* 1010; Annarita Colasante and Alberto Russo, 'Voting for the Distribution Rule in a Public Good Game with Heterogeneous Endowments' (2017) 12 *Journal of Economic Interaction and Coordination* 443; and Stephen Mark Rosenbaum et al, 'Income Inequality and Cooperative Propensities in Developing Economies: Summarizing the Preliminary Experimental Evidence' (2016) 43 *International Journal of Social Economics* 1460. It accordingly follows that states have the right to act in order to ensure the alteration of the distribution of income and wealth within their own territory not only because certain distributions constitute public goods as such, but also because it may be necessary to do so to ensure better provision of other public goods.

78 See Besson (n 57) 9. See also Vaughan Lowe, 'Sovereignty and International Economic Law' in Wenhua Shan, Penelope Simons, and Dalvinder Singh (eds), *Redefining Sovereignty in International Economic Law* (Hart Publishing, Portland OR 2008) 79–80.

'recognition' and 'responsibility' approaches as described earlier; the 'recognition' approach essentially seeks to define what is essentially the internal economic sovereignty of a state, whereas the 'responsibility' approach more or less captures the essence of external economic sovereignty. It is, of course, fairly clear to most scholars that the two concepts cannot be kept distinct from one another in practice: internal and external sovereignty are basically different sides of the same coin.[79]

The competences entailed by economic sovereignty that have distributive implications. At present there is no agreed upon set of competences entailed by the concept of economic sovereignty, even less so with respect to the distributive aspects. Some competences—capacities or powers—are beyond contestation: it can hardly be doubted, for example, that as part of its general economic sovereignty a state has the right to make and enforce rules relating to taxation within its own territory; the very existence of a state clearly depends on its ability to raise taxes.[80] To return to Huber's construction of sovereignty, taxation is clearly a function of a state which it must be allowed to pursue independently, not only as an end in of itself but also such that it can fulfil its other sovereign functions independently.

The sovereign right of taxation clearly entails distributive aspects: deciding who should be taxed, what should be taxed and deciding how the revenues derived through taxation should be spent carry clear implications for the distribution of income and wealth within a state. First, it impacts the actual distribution of income and wealth, whether this is simply as a function of revenue collection or through the manner in which the revenue collected is spent. The taxation decisions of a state also have consequences for how the distribution of income and wealth are perceived by citizens and accordingly for the legitimacy of that state. This is predominantly a matter of fairness and justice, something that is taken up further below.

Beyond taxation, there are other economic functions of a state that have distributive effects. The manner in which a state exercises its monetary sovereignty, for example, affects the supply of money in an economy and, ultimately,

79 See, for example, Besson (n 57) 9–10. See also Zimmermann (n 11) 25 for a brief illustration of the manner in which internal and external sovereignty overlap and come into conflict in the context of the monetary stability competence encompassed by a state's monetary sovereignty.

80 See, for example, Allison Christians, 'Sovereignty, Taxation and Social Contract' (2009) 18 *Minnesota Journal of International Law* 99, 104–114.

inflation.[81] Inflation has historically had substantial impacts on the distribution of aggregate income and wealth.[82] Similarly, labour market regulation also has distributional impacts, most directly on the distribution of income. An obvious example, perhaps, is when a state makes a law imposing a minimum wage.[83] The implementation of competition or antitrust laws may also have distributive effects; these laws are after all, at least in part, concerned with avoiding abuses of market power and the existence of—and increase in—market power has been shown to have significant distributive effects in respect of both income and wealth.[84] Various other activities—state functions—that may properly be linked with economic sovereignty have been shown to have distributive impacts. Examples include allowing foreign direct

---

81 On monetary sovereignty as a concept, see Zimmermann (n 11) 7–36.

82 See, for example, Thomas Piketty, *Capital in the Twenty-First Century* (HUP, Cambridge, MA 2014), translated by Arthur Goldhammer, 133–4. See also Andres Erosa and Gustavo Ventura, 'On Inflation as a Regressive Consumption Tax' (2002) 49 *Journal of Monetary Economics* 761 wherein the authors posit that inflation is effectively a regressive consumption tax and that the distributional consequences of inflation should accordingly be taken into account in setting monetary policy. A wide range of additional channels have also been identified whereby monetary policy—that is the exercise of monetary sovereignty—has distributive effects. See, for example, Adrien Auclert, *Monetary Policy and the Redistribution Channel* (NBER, Cambridge, MA 2017).

83 While it seems fairly obvious that the imposition of a minimum wage law will have distributional consequences, the precise effects, however, remain less clear. For two examples of attempts at clarifying these effects, see Arindrajit Dube, 'Minimum Wages and the Distribution of Family Incomes' (IZA Institute of Labor Economics Discussion Paper 10572, February 2017) <http://ftp.iza.org/dp10572.pdf> accessed 30 September 2021; Kevin Rinz and John Voorheis, 'The Distributional Effects of Minimum Wages: Evidence from Linked Survey and Administrative Data' (Center for Administrative Records Research and Applications (CARRA) Working Paper 2018-02, March 2018) <https://www.census.gov/content/dam/Census/library/working-papers/2018/adrm/carra-wp-2018-02.pdf> accessed 30 September 2021.

84 See Anthony B Atkinson, *Inequality: What Can Be Done?* (HUP, London 2015) 123–7; Sean Ennis, Pedro Gonzaga and Chris Pike, 'Inequality: A Hidden Cost of Market Power' (OECD Discussion Paper 2017) <https://www.oecd.org/daf/competition/Inequality-hidden-cost-market-power-2017.pdf> accessed 30 September 2021; Jason Furman and Peter Orszag, 'A Firm-Level Perspective on the Role of Rents in the Rise in Inequality' (Presentation at 'A Just Society' Centennial Event in Honor of Joseph Stiglitz, 2016) <https://obamawhitehouse.archives.gov/sites/default/files/page/files/20151016_firm_level_perspective_on_role_of_rents_in_inequality.pdf> accessed 30 September 2021; and Joseph Stiglitz, *The Price of Inequality: How Today's Divided Society Endangers Our Future* (WW Norton, New York 2012) 28–51.

investment to flow in or out of a state,[85] and formulating corporate laws in a particular way.[86]

Distributive justice as a normative component of economic sovereignty. Ultimately there are many possible normative components of economic sovereignty. Traditionally, most states have sought to prioritise economic growth—that is to say aggregate economic growth without due consideration for distributions—as a predominant normative goal in their exercise of economic sovereignty.[87] Growth, in turn, hinges on the manner in which states exercise the various competences their respective economic sovereignty is comprised of; the rate of growth also has an impact—it feeds back in a way—on how state's exercise their economic sovereignty. Growth acts as 'regulatory guideline' and 'legitimacy benchmark' for most, if not all, states;[88] but it is not the only normative component of economic sovereignty.

Since the start of the ICT revolution, calls for distributive justice around the globe have intensified.[89] To be sure, 'distributive justice' here is intended to be a normative term, but its contents are intended to be variable.[90] At the same time, even if the content of different conceptions of distributive justice are more or less the same, proposed approaches for its attainment yield as much disagreement as its contents do; it may even be the case that the approach

85 See, for example, Changkyu Choi, 'Does Foreign Direct Investment Affect Domestic Income Inequality?' (2006) 13 *Applied Economics Letters*, 811; Teresia Kaulihowa and Charles Adjasi, 'FDI and Income Inequality in Africa' (2017) *Oxford Development Studies* (*online*) <10.1080/13600818.2017.1381233> accessed 30 September 2021; Jai S Mah, 'Foreign Direct Investment, Labour Unionization and Income Inequality of Korea (2012) 19 *Applied Economics Letters* 1521 and Xiaodong Wu, 'Foreign Direct Investment and Income Inequality' in Hung-Gay Fung, Pei Changhong and Kevin H Zhang, *China and the Challenge of Economic Globalization: The Impact of WTO Membership* (Routledge, New York 2006) 61, 61–82.

86 See, for example, Matthew T Bodie, 'Income Inequality and Corporate Structure' (2015) 45 *Stetson Law Review* 69; J Adam Cobb and Flannery G Stevens, 'These Unequal States: Corporate Organization and Income Inequality in the United States' (2017) 62 *Administrative Science Quarterly* 304; and Gerald F Davis and J Adam Cobb, 'Corporations and Economic Inequality around the World: The Paradox of Hierarchy' (2010) 30 *Research in Organizational Behaviour* 35.

87 On the normative underpinnings of economic growth, see Lisa Herzog, 'The Normative Stakes of Economic Growth; Or, Why Adam Smith Does Not Rely on "Trickle Down"' (2015) 78 *Journal of Politics* 50.

88 These phrases are used as they are by Zimmermann. See Zimmermann (n 11) 24–7.

89 See Chapter 2 above in this monograph.

90 As an illustration of the variability of distributive justice as a normative concept, see generally Fred Feldman, *Distributive Justice: Getting What We Deserve from Our Country* (OUP, Oxford 2016); John E Roemer, *Theories of Distributive Justice* (HUP, Cambridge, MA 1996).

forms a part of the content itself.[91] To further complicate matters, distributive justice and economic growth may have perceived conflicting prescriptions for how economic sovereignty should be exercised.

The idea of conflicting prescriptions is fairly well—if vaguely—captured by the concept of 'sustainable development' and the Sustainable Development Goals (SDGs) set by the international community.[92] Amongst other things, for example, SDG 10 indicates that the international community seeks to 'progressively achieve and sustain income growth of the bottom 40 percent of the population at a rate higher than the national average' by 2030.[93] What this indicates is that distributive aims have not supplanted growth as a normative goal but should be considered as developing the notion of growth in a different direction. In any event, there is an increasing body of literature that suggests that broadly there exists no trade-off between economic growth and more equal distributions of income and wealth.[94]

The need for a cooperative conception of economic sovereignty. 'Cooperative sovereignty' for the purposes of this work follows the conception adopted by Samantha Besson, amongst others.[95] As Besson puts it:

> [G]radually the exercize of sovereignty has turned from an individual exercize into a cooperative enterprise. This corresponds to the more general development of multilevel governance in a post-national

91 See further below in this chapter.

92 UN General Assembly, 'Transforming our World: the 2030 Agenda for Sustainable Development', UNGA Resolution A/RES/70/1 (21 October 2015) <http://www.refworld.org/docid/57b6e3e44.html> accessed 30 September 2021. As mentioned above, it is worth noting that there exists a lengthy tradition of nations seeking to reduce inequality of incomes and wealth *between* states and that the goals associated with such movements have sometimes been read as implying that there should be less economic inequality within states. It is similarly the case that there have in the past been pushes to reorient our understanding of growth, particularly insofar as it applies between states. On the issue of equity in international law, see generally Thomas Cottier, *Equitable Principles of Maritime Boundary Delimitation* (CUP, Cambridge 2015). On the issues discussed here, see specifically 21–8. See also Thomas Cottier, 'Equity in International Law' in Thomas Cottier, Shaheeza Lalani and Clarence Siziba, *Intergenerational Equity: Environmental and Cultural Concerns* (Brill | Nijhoff, Leiden 2019).

93 UN General Assembly (n 92) 21.

94 See, for example, Andrew G Berg and Jonathan D Ostry, 'Inequality and Unsustainable Growth: Two Sides of the Same Coin?' (2017) 65 *IMF Economic Review* 792; Francesco Grigoli and Adrian Robles, 'Inequality Overhang', IMF Working Paper (28 March 2017).

95 See Besson (n 57) 13; Franz Xaver Perrez, *Cooperative Sovereignty: From Independence to Interdependence in the Structure of International Environmental Law* (Kluwer, The Hague 2000); Zimmermann (n 11) 31–5.

> constellation; sovereign political entities can no longer exercize their traditional competences and functions alone, especially, but not only, when these overlap within the same territory and apply to the same legal political community. … In these conditions, sovereign authorities need to collaborate with other sovereign political and legal entities when applying the same rules and principles in this pluralist constitutional order and this gives rise to a … cooperative form of sovereignty. This form of sovereignty triggers duties of cooperation on the part of entities which cannot ensure the protection of all the values they should protect, as much as on the part of the entities which can help the former protect those values they share. … Only when understood in this cooperative way, can sovereignty be the reflexive and dynamic concept it is, stimulating constant challenging of the allocation of power, thus putting into question others' sovereignty as well as one's own. This common exercize of political sovereignty is then reflected in the structure of the relationship between the different legal orders at stake; none of them is ultimately and entirely submitted to another. This kind of legal cooperation reveals the possibility of a non-hierarchically organized plurality of legal orders, which may individually remain hierarchical in their internal structure or in their relationship to international law, but which relate to one another in a heterarchical way.[96]

Economic sovereignty as conceptualised here accepts the premise that sovereignty is divisible; it should accordingly be seen as comprising various different parts of general state sovereignty, including fiscal sovereignty, monetary sovereignty and the other parts of general state sovereignty relevant to the distribution of income and wealth, particularly—but not limited to—those relating to the regulation of a 'national' economy. Seen this way, economic sovereignty is only effective as a concept in the event that there operates alongside it a functioning principle of subsidiarity; that is to say a principle of power allocation. In this regard, Besson writes that 'the principle of subsidiarity implies a *test of efficiency* in power allocation. In each case, the sovereign authority will be that authority which can realize the objective in the most efficient way'.[97]

The view taken here is that the competence of states to affect changes to the distribution of income and wealth within their own territories is tied to

96 Besson (n 57) 13. Emphasis original, original footnotes omitted.

97 Besson (n 57) 12. Emphasis original.

their exercising their economic sovereignty in accordance with the normative idea of distributive justice. It is this tie that leads to a call for understanding economic sovereignty as a cooperative enterprise: to the extent that cooperation is necessary to affect the actual distribution of income and wealth in order to attain distributive justice within a state, economic sovereignty can only be made meaningful through cooperation. Moreover, ensuring a certain distribution of income or wealth can, as described above, be viewed as a public good. It does not necessarily follow, however, that in doing so a state also ensures the attainment of distributive justice. The distributive justice and public goods components should accordingly be thought of as existing alongside one another, with each aspect requiring different albeit it overlapping types of cooperation.

3 The Recognition of Common Concerns of Humankind as Sovereignty Redefined

This second part traces the development of common concern of humankind as a concept in both the theory and practice of international law. This exercise is undertaken in two parts. First, the development of common concern of humankind as a concept in international law is briefly discussed in order to provide the relevant background context in which the remainder of the discussions in this chapter are grounded (*Section 3.1*). Subsequently the discussion turns to a key issue for the purposes of this chapter and indeed this work as a whole: that of the recognition of common concerns of humankind and the legal implications of such recognition (*Section 3.2*). Finally—and in the light of several theoretical lacunae identified in Section 3.2—a general theory for the recognition of common concerns of humankind in international law is proposed (*Section 3.3*).

3.1 *The Development of the Common Concern of Humankind Concept in International Law*

On 6 December 1988, the UN General Assembly resolved, in a document titled 'Protection of global climate for present and future generations of mankind', welcomed 'with appreciation the initiative taken by the Government of Malta in proposing for consideration by the Assembly the item entitled "Conservation of climate as part of the common heritage of mankind" ', and '[c]onvinced that climate change affects humanity as a whole and should be confronted within a global framework so as to take into account the vital interests of all mankind', recognised 'that climate change is a common concern of mankind, since climate is an essential condition which sustains life on earth'.[98] This was the first of several intermediate—but concrete—steps towards the recognition of the common concern of humankind concept in international law.

Subsequently, the term 'common concern of mankind' having been used in multiple UN documents in 1989 and 1990,[99] during the course of a United Nations Environmental Programme (UNEP) meeting of legal experts held in Malta in 1990, the origin, contents, rationale and implications of the concept were debated by attendees as part of a precursory exercise, the purpose of which was to establish a normative basis for the upcoming United Nations Conference on Environment and Development (UNCED) to be held in 1992.[100] By the time of the group's next meeting in 1991, a 'growing interest of States' in the concept was identifiable, particularly 'within the context of negotiations on legal instruments on climate change and conservation and sustainable use of biological diversity'.[101] At the third and final meeting of the group before the occasion of the UNCED in 1992, the group lent its support to the idea that the common concern of humankind concept was 'sufficiently flexible to warrant its general acceptance as providing a broad basis for the consideration of global environmental issues'.[102]

At the UNCED in 1992, the concept found support and was included in the preambles to both the UN Framework Convention on Climate Change (UNFCCC) and the Convention on Biological Diversity (CBD).[103] The text of the UNFCCC '[acknowledges] that change in the Earth's climate and its adverse effects are a common concern of humankind' and notes the parties' '[concern] that human activities have been substantially increasing the atmospheric concentrations of greenhouse gases, that these increases enhance the natural greenhouse effect, and that this will result on average in an additional warming

98 UN General Assembly, *Protection of Global Climate for Present and Future Generations* (UNGA Resolution 43/53, 27 January 1989) 28 ILM 1326, 1326–7.

99 See Mostafa K Tolba, 'The Implications of the "Common Concern of Mankind Concept" on Global Environmental Issues' (1991) 13 *Revista IIDH* 237.

100 Antônio Augusto Cançado Trindade, *International Law for Humankind: Towards a New* Jus Gentium (Martinus Nijhoff Publishers, Leiden 2010) 344–5.

101 Cançado Trindade (n 100) 345.

102 Cançado Trindade (n 100) 346. Flexibility had at that time become necessary as most states had voiced concern with Malta's invocation of the common heritage concept in its original proposal to the General Assembly in 1988, with states noting their view that the common heritage concept was inappropriate in the context of climate change. See Daniel Bodansky, 'The United Nations Framework Convention on Climate Change: A Commentary' (1993) 18 *Yale Journal of International Law* 451, 465.

103 See Cançado Trindade (n 100) 346.

of the Earth's surface and atmosphere and may adversely affect natural ecosystems and humankind', whereas the CBD '[affirms] that the conservation of biological diversity is a common concern of humankind' and notes the parties' '[concern] that biological diversity is being significantly reduced by certain human activities'.[104]

The common concern of humankind concept has also subsequently been discussed in the context of the International Law Commission's Draft Guidelines on the Protection of the Atmosphere. Until it was removed by the Commission in 2015, Draft Guideline 3 affirmed that '[t]he atmosphere is a natural resource essential for sustaining life on Earth, human health and welfare, and aquatic and terrestrial ecosystems, and hence the degradation of the atmosphere is a common concern of humankind'.[105] In the literature on common concern of humankind, explorations of possible additional common concerns of humankind can also be found; authors having examined an array of issues for potential common concern of humankind status, including land degradation,[106] the sustainable management of soils,[107] the availability and use of fresh water,[108] the conservation of plant biodiversity,[109] technology transfer in pursuit of climate change mitigation,[110] the protection of human rights,[111] maritime resource allocation and the protection of the oceans,[112] monetary

---

104 See UNFCCC, preamble; CBD, preamble.

105 See Shinya Murase (Special Rapporteur), *Second Report on the Protection of the Atmosphere*, UN Document A/CN.4/681 (2015) 18; ILC, *Report on the Work of the International Law Commission: Sixty-Seventh Session*, UN Document A/70/10 (2015) 26–7. For a criticism of the removal of Draft Guideline 3, see Castillo-Winckels (n 5).

106 See Ben Boer, 'Land Degradation as a Common Concern of Humankind' in Federico Lenzerini and Ana Filipa Vrdoljak (eds), *International Law for Common Goods: Normative Perspectives on Human Rights, Culture and Nature* (Hart Publishing, Oxford 2014) 289.

107 See Harald Ginzky, 'The Sustainable Management of Soils as a Common Concern of Humankind: How to Implement It?' in Harald Ginzky et al (eds), *International Yearbook of Soil Law and Policy 2017* (Springer, Cham 2017).

108 Edith Brown Weiss, 'The Coming Water Crisis: A Common Concern of Mankind' 1 (2012) *Transnational Environmental Law* 153.

109 See Aline Jaeckel, 'Intellectual Property Rights and the Conservation of Plant Biodiversity as a Common Concern of Humankind' (2013) 2 *Transnational Environmental Law* 167.

110 See Zaker Ahmad, 'Trade-Related Measures to Spread Low Carbon Technologies: A Common Concern Based Approach' in Thomas Cottier (ed), *The Prospects of Common Concern of Humankind in International Law* (CUP, Cambridge 2021).

111 See Iryna Bogdanova, 'Reshaping the Law of Economic Sanctions for Human Rights Violations: The Potential of Common Concern of Humankind' in Thomas Cottier (ed), *The Prospects of Common Concern of Humankind in International Law* (CUP, Cambridge 2021).

112 See Judith Schäli, 'Marine Plastic Pollution as a Common Concern of Humankind' in Thomas Cottier (ed), *The Prospects of Common Concern of Humankind in International*

stability,[113] financial stability,[114] migration,[115] and global forest protection,[116] amongst others.

3.2 *The (Non-)recognition of a Common Concern of Humankind and Its Legal Implications*

As discussed above, only two common concerns of humankind have thus far been explicitly recognised in treaty law; one is the field of climate change and one in the field of biodiversity. It thus becomes a worthwhile exercise looking as precisely as possible at their subject matter. In the area of climate change, it is the 'change in the Earth's climate and its adverse effects' that are recognised as a common concern of humankind by the UNFCCC.[117] As for in the realm of biodiversity, it is the 'conservation of biological diversity' that has been affirmed as a common concern of humankind in the text of the CBD.[118] Understanding fully what is being protected in these conventions is clearly helpful for understanding what can in fact be recognised as a common concern of humankind, how that might happen and what implications, if any, such recognition will have.

Change in the Earth's climate and its adverse effects. As Jutta Brunnée points out with respect to the UNFCCC, it is not the Earth's climate that is afforded common concern of humankind status, but rather the *change* in the Earth's climate and its *adverse effects*.[119] The second paragraph of the preamble to the UNFCCC also goes on to state that the parties to the Convention are—or

---

Law (CUP, Cambridge 2021) and Judith Schäli, 'Intergenerational Justice and the Concept of Common Concern in Marine Resource Allocation and Ocean Governance' in Thomas Cottier, Shaheeza Lalani and Clarence Siziba (eds), *Intergenerational Equity: Environmental and Cultural Concerns* (Brill | Nijhoff, Leiden 2019).

113 See Lucia Satragno, 'International Monetary Stability as a Common Concern of Humankind' in Thomas Cottier (ed), *The Prospects of Common Concern of Humankind in International Law* (CUP, Cambridge 2021).

114 See Federico Lupo-Pasini, 'Financial Stability as a Common Concern of Humankind' in Thomas Cottier (ed), *The Prospects of Common Concern of Humankind in International Law* (CUP, Cambridge 2021).

115 See Thomas Cottier and Rosa Maria Losada, 'Migration as a Common Concern of Humankind' in Thomas Cottier (ed), *The Prospects of Common Concern of Humankind in International Law* (CUP, Cambridge 2021).

116 See Jutta Brunnée and André Nollkaemper, 'Between the Forests and the Trees—An Emerging International Forest Law' (1996) 23 *Environmental Conservation* 307.

117 UNFCCC, preamble.

118 CBD, preamble.

119 Jutta Brunnée, 'Common Areas, Common Heritage, and Common Concern' in Daniel Bodansky, Jutta Brunnée and Ellen Hey (eds), *The Oxford Handbook of International Environmental Law* (OUP, New York 2007) 565.

at the very least were at the time of the UNFCCC's enactment—'[c]oncerned that human activities have been substantially increasing the atmospheric concentrations of greenhouse gases, that these increases enhance the natural greenhouse effect, and that this will result on average in an additional warming of the Earth's surface and atmosphere and may adversely affect natural ecosystems and humankind'. This pronouncement gives additional meaning to the terms 'change' and 'adverse effects' contained in the first paragraph of the preamble. It is human activity that has been increasing the atmospheric concentrations of greenhouse gases and driving the *change* in the Earth's climate. The *additional* warming of the Earth's surface and atmosphere that will result from this *change* may result in *adverse effects* to natural ecosystems and to humankind.

Conservation of biological diversity. As Brunnée has observed with respect to this common concern of humankind too, it is the *conservation* of biological diversity that is afforded common concern status in the third paragraph of the preamble to the CBD and not biological diversity itself.[120] This distinction is clear from context given that the first paragraph of the preamble indicates that the parties to the Convention are—or at least were—'[c]onscious of the intrinsic value of biological diversity and of the ecological, genetic, social, economic, scientific, educational, cultural, recreational and aesthetic values of biological diversity and its components'. The second paragraph reinforces the distinction, illustrating that the parties were '[c]onscious also of the importance of biological diversity for evolution and for maintaining life sustaining systems of the biosphere'. Finally, the sixth paragraph spells out that the parties were '[c]oncerned that biological diversity is being significantly reduced by certain human activities'.

As with climate change, then, it appears clear that common concern of humankind status is afforded in respect of a particular *change* and the *adverse effects* flowing from it. In the biodiversity context, it is significant reduction in biological diversity caused by certain human activities that amounts to a change; the adverse effects of this change are the losses of the intrinsic value of biological diversity as described in the first two paragraphs to the preamble of the CBD. Together, the change and the adverse effects make up the common concern of humankind; the 'conservation of biological diversity'.

Constitutive elements of common concerns of humankind. In order to guide and structure this next part of the discussion, the following conceptual characterisation of Antônio Augusto Cançado Trindade, now a Judge of the International

120 Brunnée (n 119) 565.

Court of Justice, is a helpful starting point. In his tome *International Law for Humankind: Towards a New* Jus Gentium, Cançado Trindade writes as follows:

> Six constitutive elements of the concept of common concern of mankind have been identified, namely: first, the concentration of the concept—devoid of proprietary connotations—in truly fundamental questions for all humankind, pursuant to the notion of commonness; second, the necessary engagement, in the treatment of such questions of common interest, of all countries, all societies and all the social segments within the countries and the societies; third,—as already pointed out ... —the long-term temporal dimension (underlying the term humanity), to encompass both the present and the future generations; fourth, the emphasis on the element of protection, on the basis of considerations of humanity and of ordre public, transcending reciprocity; fifth, the attention primarily to the causes of the problems (both for their prevention and for the responses to be given); and sixth, the equitable sharing of responsibilities as an instrumental principle in the application of the concept of common concern of mankind.[121]

Writing in the *Oxford Handbook of International Climate Change Law*, Friedrich Soltau distils common concerns into the following 'fundamental characteristics':

> (a) the interests concerned extend beyond those of individual states and touch on values or ethics of global significance;
> (b) threats to the interests concerned are marked by their gravity and potential irreversibility of impacts; and
> (c) safeguarding the interests involved requires collective action and entails collective responsibility.[122]

Moreover, in note to the Group of Legal Experts that met prior to the 1992 conclusion of the UNFCCC and the CBD, the UNEP Secretariat provided the following information:

> 'Common concern' concept has at least two important facets: spatial and temporal. Spatial aspect means the common concern implies

121 Cançado Trindade (n 100) 351.

122 Friedrich Soltau, 'Common Concern of Humankind' in Cinnamon P Carlane, Kevin R Gray and Richard G Tarasofsky (eds), *The Oxford Handbook of International Climate Change Law* (OUP, New York 2016) 207–8.

> co-operation of all states on matters being similarly important to all nations, to the whole international community. Temporal aspect arises from long term implications of major environmental challenges which affect the rights and obligations not only of present but also future generations. ... One more aspect of the 'common concern' is a social dimension. Common concern presumes involvement of all structures and sectors of the society into the process of combatting global environmental threats. i.e. legislative, judicial and governmental bodies together with private business, non-governmental organizations, citizen groups.[123]

While there is much to quibble about when it comes to the constitutive or definitional elements—the common concern of humankind concept is after all still subject to much debate and no definitive understanding of the terms has yet to be settled on, whether in treaty practice, treaty application or by scholars of the concept—these passages can be distilled into four headings by which we might structure a discussion on what constitutes a common concern of humankind and what the implications of recognising something as such may entail: (1); the substance of, and space covered by, the concept of common concern of humankind; (2) the temporal element of common concerns of humankind; (3) the recognition and mode of recognition of a common concern of humankind; and (4) the legal implications of recognising a common concern of humankind. Through examining a combination of legal and scholarly sources below, the aim is to provide a plausible understanding of what might allow for the recognition of a common concern of humankind and what legal implications, if any, may flow therefrom.

3.2.1 The Substance of, Space Covered by, and Location of Common Concerns of Humankind

Human-driven change and its adverse effects. As already touched on above, the common concerns of humankind explicitly identified thus far in treaty law relate to an identifiable *change* in the nature of an object and the *adverse effects* that stem from that change over time. Seen this way, it is clear that the climate is not a common concern of humankind; nor is biodiversity per se.[124] It is also clear that the change must cause adverse effects in order for a

123 Tolba (n 99) 239.

124 The protection of a natural resource per se is better captured by the concept of 'common heritage of humankind'. On the common heritage of humankind, see generally Kemal Baslar, *The Concept of the Common Heritage of Mankind in International Law* (Kluwer Law International, The Hague 1998); Cançado Trindade (n 100) 327–44.

common concern of humankind to arise. As Dale Jamieson has put it, '[e]ven if we accept that climate change is occurring, as we should, we do not yet have a problem', continuing that '[d]ramatic changes occur all the time that we do not consider to be problems (e.g. summer changes to autumn, black holes devour stars)' and that '[w]hat is minimally required for a *change* to be a problem [or a concern] is that it *adversely affects* what we care about'.[125]

The word 'adverse' (of fortune, events, etc.), originally, meant 'contrary, opposing, harmful, hostile *to* a person or thing'; today, 'adverse' (of conditions, circumstances, etc.) means 'unfavourable; preventing success, development, or well-being'.[126] It accordingly follows that what constitutes a common concern of humankind, entails, at least in part, a normative decision as to whether the identifiable effects of the change in the nature of the object in question can be termed 'adverse'. Climate change is a common concern of humankind because the change over time in the nature of the Earth's climate has certain effects *and* those effects have been deemed *adverse* by the international community.

This brings the manner in which a common concern of humankind is framed acutely into focus. As Jamieson continues:

> Some people would say that if the climate change that is now under way were due to purely natural (i.e. non-anthropogenic) factors, then it would not be a problem. There are two distinct grounds one might have for this view. Some people may think that it is necessary for a change to be a problem that it is caused by human agency. On this view, natural occurrences that affect us adversely are unfortunate, but they are not problems. A second, more plausible ground is that if we cannot in some way remedy a change that adversely affects us, then the change is not a problem. On this view, problems imply solutions. For example, dying prematurely of a curable disease is a problem; being mortal is not. There are people who think that nothing can be done about climate change. If they also have the view that problems require solutions, then they do not think that climate change is a problem, however regrettable they may think it is that it is occurring. Of course they are wrong in thinking that

125 Dale Jamieson, 'The Nature of the Problem' in John S Dryzek, Richard B Norgaard and David Schlosberg, *Oxford Handbook of Climate Change and Society* (OUP, New York 2011) 38–54. Emphasis added.

126 See 'adverse, adj. and n'. in Oxford English Dictionary Online (OUP, online March 2018) <http://0-www.oed.com.innopac.wits.ac.za/view/Entry/2960?rskey=CWwsNB&result=1&isAdvanced=false> accessed 30 September 2021.

> we cannot respond to climate change in ways that make a difference. But what counts as making a difference depends enormously on what exactly we think the problem is.[127]

The second paragraph of the preamble to the UNFCCC is consistent with these arguments in that it clarifies that the international community is '[c]oncerned'; not purely because the climate is changing and that there are adverse effects as a result, but rather because 'human activities have been substantially increasing the atmospheric concentrations of greenhouse gases, that these increase enhance the natural greenhouse effect, and that this will result on average in an additional warming of the Earth's surface and atmosphere and may adversely affect natural ecosystems and humankind'. In other words, the concern is with human activities that are within our control; the focus of a common concern of humankind is human-driven changes that have adverse effects. Indeed, the UNFCCC defines 'climate change' only as changes to the climate which can be 'attributed directly or indirectly to human activity'.[128]

The above analysis with respect to the UNFCCC applies with equal force to the CBD, which asserts that the international community is '[c]oncerned that biological diversity is being significantly reduced by certain *human* activities'.[129] The conservation of biological diversity is a common concern of humankind in a similar way to climate change in that it is being reduced by human activity; this again amounts to a change, i.e. a change in the extent to which biodiversity is being diminished. The adverse effects of this change are also captured in the preamble to the CBD: the loss of biodiversity and its components equates to a loss of the various values listed in its first paragraph as well as to a loss of something which is important 'for evolution and for maintaining life sustaining systems of the biosphere'.[130]

The scope of the adverse effects. The next logical question, perhaps, goes to the scope of the adverse effects. Must each and every person that comprises humanity, for example, feel or be affected directly the adverse effects of the loss of biodiversity? Or must the adverse effects of climate change simply affect a large portion or majority of human beings? Treaty law is not explicit when it comes to answering questions pertaining to the scope of common concerns of humankind; nor have they all been thoroughly addressed in the literature. The

127 Jamieson (n 125) 39.
128 UNFCCC, Article 1.2.
129 CBD, preamble. Emphasis added.
130 CBD, preamble.

manner in which Duncan French has dealt with the scope of adverse effects is a helpful starting point.[131]

French starts by asserting that 'matters are of common concern not simply because they impact upon the environment per se, but because the scale and extent of the impact potentially affects all of humanity, both present and future generations'.[132] He then points to the 1994 Desertification Convention, mindful of the fact that it was concluded shortly after the CBD and the UNFCCC, and contrasts the concepts employed in that convention with that of common concern of humankind, questioning as he does so how the two regimes differ.[133] The preamble to the Desertification Convention provides, in relevant part, as follows:

> The Parties to this Convention,
> Affirming that human beings in affected or threatened areas are at the centre of concerns to combat desertification and mitigate the effects of drought,
> Reflecting the urgent concern of the international community, including States and international organizations, about the adverse impacts of desertification and drought,
> Aware that arid, semi-arid and dry sub-humid areas together account for a significant proportion of the Earth's land area and are the habitat and source of livelihood for a large segment of its population,
> Acknowledging that desertification and drought are problems of global dimension in that they affect all regions of the world and that joint action of the international community is needed to combat desertification and/or mitigate the effects of drought,
> Noting the high concentration of developing countries, notably the least developed countries, among those experiencing serious drought and/or desertification, and the particularly tragic consequences of these phenomena in Africa,
> …
> Expressing concern over the impact of desertification and drought on affected countries in Central Asia and the Transcaucasus,

131 See Duncan French, 'Common Concern, Common Heritage and Other Global(-ising) Concepts: Rhetorical Devices, Legal Principles or a Fundamental Challenge' in Michael Bowman, Peter Davies and Edward Goodwin (eds), *Research Handbook on Biodiversity and Law* (Edward Elgar Publishing, 2016 Cheltenham) 342–9.

132 French (n 131) 345.

133 French (n 131) 346.

> …
>
> Have agreed as follows … [134]

Moreover, the full title of the Convention also contains a helpful indicator in that it includes the phrase 'to Combat Desertification *in Those Countries* Experiencing Drought and or Desertification'.[135] This leads French to the following remarks:

> True, there are such phrases as "human beings … are at the centre of concerns", "urgent concern" and "problems of global dimension … affect[ing] all regions of the world", which in layman's terms may come close to saying the same thing—but, importantly, nowhere is combating desertification itself said to be of common concern. And if one looks more closely at these preambular paragraphs, one can see the global nature of the problem is tempered with a decidedly regional perspective. Only those human beings in "affected or threatened areas" are of concern; the "urgent concern" is intergovernmental—of States and international organisations—not of humankind; and the areas under threat affect a "large segment", but not the whole, of the world's population.[136]

To the extent that the 'adverse impacts of desertification and drought' can be seen as falling short of a common concern of humankind based purely on the subject and geographical scope of these adverse impacts, certain inferences can be drawn concerning the subject and geographical scope of common concern of humankind. For example, through contrasting 'humankind' with 'human beings in affected or threatened areas', it might then be surmised that the scope of common concerns of humankind are not geographically limited; that common concerns of humankind are not limited to 'human beings in affected or threatened areas'. Similarly, one might contrast the Desertification Convention's 'a large segment of … [the Earth's] population' with 'humankind' and come to the conclusion—even though the phrase 'large segment' is ambiguous—that the adverse effects that form a part of a common concern of humankind, or the potential for there to be such adverse effects, must affect at least 'a large segment' of all the human beings on Earth.

---

134 United Nations Convention to Combat Desertification in those Countries Experiencing Serious Drought and/or Desertification, Particularly in Africa (adopted 14 October 1994, entered into force 26 December 1996) 1954 UNTS 3, 108–11. Emphasis added.

135 French (n 131) 346. Emphasis original.

136 French (n 131) 346.

Beyond the subject and geographical scope, there appears to be consensus among scholars that the location of common concerns of humankind, including their adverse effects, may be within the territorial jurisdiction of recognised nation states as well as beyond these jurisdictions. In other words, the adverse effects that result from a particular change are of equal concern for the purposes of common concern of humankind regardless of whether they arise within or beyond the territorial jurisdiction of states.[137] This has brought to the fore the apparent clash between the common concern of humankind concept and the concept of territorial sovereignty as alluded to above.

The nature of the adverse effects. 'Common concern of humankind' can be read as something that is of concern to all or parts of humankind; but this does not imply that each and every member of humankind need necessarily be affected in the same manner in order for something to constitute a common concern of humankind.[138] A range of additional questions arise which go to the nature of the adverse effects that are guarded against by the application of the common concern of humankind concept. One such question is whether common concern of humankind lends itself to events linked to specific subject-matters or whether common concerns of humankind can be recognised regardless of subject-matter provided that certain prerequisites have been met. Once this issue has been resolved, additional questions remain about the nature of the adverse effects. These stem predominantly from the wide range of possible events which may be considered 'adverse' and the remaining ambiguity as to who it is that must be the subject of the adverse effects.

Environmental lawyers have often hinted that common concerns of humankind pertain to environmental concerns to the exclusion of concerns from other fields. Jutta Brunnée, for example, has argued that 'the concept is targeted more narrowly at specific *environmental* processes or protective actions' and that 'whether the *environmental* concern relates to the global commons or to resources within the territories of individual states, it is the fact that all states derive common benefits from protective action that elevates it to a matter of common concern'.[139] Nadia Sánchez Castillo-Winckels has argued elsewhere that one of two common features of common concerns is 'the interest to protect humanity and the *global environment* from harm'.[140] She further argues that treaty practice shows that 'what the international community is trying

137 See, for example, Brunnée (n 119) 564–7.

138 See UNFCCC, preamble where a subset of humanity are considered to be 'particularly vulnerable to the adverse effects of climate change'.

139 Brunnée (n 119) 564–7. Emphasis added.

140 Castillo-Winckels (n 5) 147. Emphasis added.

to avoid by recognizing certain issues as common concerns of humankind is harm to humanity (human health and well-being, food security, cultural heritage) and to the *global environment* (changes in weather patterns due to global warming, and the loss of genetic, species and ecosystem diversity)'.[141]

In the context of the relationship between common concern of humankind and obligations *erga omnes*, Duncan French has argued that 'there is no doubt that obligations *erga omnes* (*partes*), in particular, and common concern have real potential to be mutually reinforcing concepts, the former providing a general framework for the *environmental-specificity* of the latter'.[142] As the above-cited authors—and the common concern literature more generally—make fairly clear, it is taken somewhat for granted that common concern of humankind is a concept that covers predominantly environmental matters and that in recognising future common concern of humankind a link to the 'environment' or the 'global environment' should be present.[143] There is nothing inherent to common concern of humankind as a concept, however, which provides a proper justification for restricting their recognition by subject-matter.

As for the nature of the adverse effects, and if we proceed on the assumption that the source of the adverse effects is unconstrained by subject-matter restrictions, it is fairly clear that the common concern of humankind concept is aimed at protecting against consequences of a particular gravitas. This said, serious conceptual issues remain concerning the highly abstract, highly contestable notion of 'adverse effects'. Are effects 'adverse' if, and only if, they threaten, whether directly or indirectly, the very existence of humanity or a large part thereof? Or could effects also be considered 'adverse' if they merely threaten something held dear by most of humankind? There are, as yet, no clear answers to these questions; but the UNFCCC and the CBD provide some helpful guidance.

For example, in Article 1.1 of the UNFCCC 'adverse effects of climate change' is a term defined as 'changes in the physical environment or biota resulting from climate change which have significant deleterious effects on the composition, resilience or productivity of natural and managed ecosystems or on the operation of socio-economic systems or on human health and welfare'. Equally broad, perhaps, are the adverse effects that the CBD aims to protect against. In the preamble, the CBD makes clear that the adverse effects that stem from

141 Castillo-Winckels (n 5) 147. Emphasis added.

142 French (n 131) 354. Emphasis added.

143 See also Cançado Trindade (n 100) 344 where it is asserted that 'The emphasis of this latter [i.e. common concern of humankind] falls upon concerted actions in equitable sharing of burdens (in *environmental* protection)'. Emphasis added.

a loss of biodiversity include biodiversity's importance 'for evolution and for maintaining life sustaining systems of the biosphere', but also its 'intrinsic value' *and* 'the ecological, genetic, social, economic, educational, cultural, recreational and aesthetic values of biological diversity and its components'.

While this still leaves much scope for debate on what exact types of effects are sufficiently 'adverse' in order for them to form part of a common concern of humankind, it does allow for the conclusion to be drawn that there need be no tangible physical harm or threat of harm to humanity or a part thereof in order for certain events to be considered 'adverse' and therefore as part of a common concern of humankind. This conclusion can be reached for a number of reasons, including because the CBD protects against the loss of certain values, such as the aesthetic value of biodiversity for example, which do not involve physical harm of any kind. Similarly, the UNFCCC—while also protecting against physical harms such as degradations to human health—protects against potential harm that might be done to the 'operation of socio-economic systems'.[144]

A final issue to be dealt with under the heading of the nature of the adverse effects is actuality and risk. The recognised common concerns of humankind in the UNFCCC and the CBD appear to suggest that it is the *actual* adverse effects that stem from the given change that is considered to be a part of a common concern of humankind. As a forward-looking concept, however, it would be logical to assume that common concern of humankind also anticipates *future* adverse effects and attempts to protect human beings from them materialising in the first place. To do otherwise would to a large degree be to deprive common concern of humankind of its potential efficacy because actors responding to the common concern of humankind would be perpetually looking to protect humanity from harm that has already taken place. This brings into sharper focus the notion of risk of *future* adverse effects and the role of uncertainty. It also brings into focus the changing nature of the notion of 'adverse effects' and the capacity of treaty law to effectively deal with this. As these issues are essentially temporal, they are dealt with under the next subsection.

3.2.2 The Temporal Elements of Common Concerns of Humankind

Present and future generations. As Cançado Trindade has put it, common concerns of humankind 'transcend the level of strictly inter-State relations, focusing on the needs and aspirations of humankind as a whole, encompassing present and future generations'.[145] There appears to be consensus among scholars

144 See UNFCCC, preamble.

145 Cançado Trindade (n 100) 344.

on this point; it stems from the idea that 'humankind' refers to humanity as a whole over time and thereby incorporates 'humankind' as it is now but also 'humankind' as it will be for the duration of the existence of a particular common concern of humankind.[146] There is little room for objection here, save to emphasise that it is not necessarily *all* future generations that are encompassed; a necessary implication—hopefully—of trying to solve a problem is that it may in fact be solved and, in the common concern of humankind context, the adverse effects of concern may cease to exist. It is therefore safe to conclude that common concerns of humankind encompass present and an *indeterminate number of* future generations.

The changing nature of adverse effects over time. As noted earlier in this chapter, the recognised common concerns of humankind in the UNFCCC and the CBD appear to suggest that it is the *actual* adverse effects that stem from the given change that is considered to be a part of a common concern of humankind. Even the actual adverse effects of climate change and the loss of biodiversity, however, are dependent on a large number of factors and have presumably changed considerably over time, even in the relatively short period since the enactment of the UNFCCC and the CBD. How the adverse effects develop over time, of course, depends on the observed rate of change of the climate or of the loss of biodiversity. It is for these reasons that common concern of humankind entails the dynamic notion of *rate*; rate implying that it is the actual adverse effects *as the change in rate occurs* that are of common concern.

In the context of climate change, for example, it would be fairly senseless to attempt to respond to the adverse effects that result from climate change based on the rate at which the climate was changing in the 1980s, a time since when the number of annual climate-related natural disasters have more than doubled.[147] Similarly, it would make little sense to ignore the impact of technological change on climate change mitigation efforts over time. common concern of humankind is inherently a dynamic concept and, as a result, factual information and judgments made in response to factual changes must necessarily be re-evaluated as time passes in order for the common concern of humankind concept to have any sense of credibility or for it to be effective in solving problems.

---

146 See, for example, Cançado Trindade (n 100) 344; Brown Weiss (n 108) 164–5; Castillo-Winckels (n 5) 146; French (n 131) 345.

147 See John Hay and Nobuo Mimura 'The Changing Nature of Extreme Weather and Climate Events: Risks to Sustainable Development' (2010) 1 *Geomatics, Natural Hazards and Risk* 3, 3.

This implies a clear preference on the part of the international community for the development of effective monitoring and evaluation mechanisms in relation to particular common concerns of humankind.[148] The text of the preamble to the UNFCCC, for example, notes that the parties are conscious of 'the valuable analytical work being conducted by many States on climate change and of the important contributions of the World Meteorological Organization, the United Nations Environment Programme and other organs, organizations and bodies of the United Nations system, as well as other international and intergovernmental bodies, to the exchange of results of scientific research and the coordination of research' and accordingly recognises 'that steps required to understand and address climate change will be environmentally, socially and economically most effective if they are based on relevant scientific, technical and economic considerations and continually re-evaluated in the light of new findings in these areas'. Similarly, in the preamble to the CBD indicates that the parties are aware of 'the urgent need to develop scientific, technical and institutional capacities to provide the basic understanding upon which to plan and implement appropriate measures'.

Both the UNFCCC and CBD accordingly set up regimes for the evaluation and consistent re-evaluation over time of the problems they seek to solve. The CBD, through its Article 7, makes the identification and monitoring of certain issues mandatory for the parties to the Convention. Moreover, Article 12 makes mandatory certain research and training activities. Likewise, the UNFCCC, through its Article 5, makes certain actions related to 'research and observation' mandatory. These obligations are further supported by the important underlying principle of cooperation between contracting parties in order to ensure the effective evaluation and systematic re-evaluation of the rates of change encompassed by the specific common concerns of humankind and the adverse effects stemming from such rates of change.

Additionally, as noted above, an evaluation of what constitutes the actual and future adverse effects necessarily entails elements of uncertainty and the management of risks. In the preamble to the UNFCCC, for example, it is noted 'that there are many uncertainties in predictions of climate change, particularly with regard to the timing, magnitude and regional patterns thereof'. The CBD notes that the parties, in a comparable fashion to the UNFCCC, are aware of 'the general lack of information and knowledge regarding biological diversity'. This makes clear that in order for a common concern of humankind to be recognised in treaty law, it is not necessary for there to be certainty as to

148 Soltau makes the same argument in respect of obligations *erga omnes*. See Soltau (n 122) 207.

the exact adverse effects that may stem from a particular rate change and how these (potential) effects may develop over time; a certain level of risk combined with some form of actual effects appears to be sufficient.

3.2.3 The (non-)Recognition and Mode of Recognition of Common Concerns of Humankind

At the end of the previous subsection, and throughout this chapter more generally, reference has been made to the 'recognition' of common concerns of humankind. The notion of recognition, or perhaps 'identification', itself raises certain interesting questions. For example, as Jutta Brunnée has put it:

> One may ask whether common concerns must be identified by treaty to engender particular legal consequences. Indeed, must they be specifically identified at all? Or is it enough that an issue is of concern to all or a large number of states, and that its resolution requires global cooperation? Clearly these latter features place an issue within the range of potential common concerns.[149]

Brunnée also points out, as various others have, that common concerns of humankind have thus far been identified primarily through treaty law.[150] She also continues to note, however, two particular difficulties with the status quo:

> The first relates to the need for sufficient international consensus on whether a given issue, say global forest protection, is indeed of common concern. There is no reason why such consensus could not find expression in customary international law. Yet treaty negotiations may be more conducive to forging the consensus ... When widely ratified, a treaty may also forestall further debates about this threshold issue. The second difficulty arises from the need to clarify the precise legal ramifications of common concerns. For example, even if it were agreed that global forest protection is of common concern, absent a treaty, the legal implications would be subject to debate. Of course, over time, a growing number of treaties can also help crystallize the legal consequences that generally attach to common concerns and, thereby contribute to the development of a customary framework.[151]

149 Brunnée (n 119) 564–7.
150 See Brunnée (n 119) 564–7; French (n 131) 354–6.
151 Brunnée (n 119) 564–7.

This brings into focus more closely the actions required for something to be recognised as a common concern of humankind which has legal implications. While it certainly is preferable for common concerns of humankind to be explicitly identified or recognised as having legal implications through the adoption of treaties, it is also obvious that the adverse effects that ensue from certain events will have to—and will in fact—be addressed in some form or another, whether there is an existing treaty regime in place or not. Tracing the exact contours of the different arguments in this regard is beyond the scope of this work. In short, the view taken here is that common concern of humankind recognition should occur through treaty law for a number of reasons.

Chief amongst these reasons are the benefits and/or drawbacks of the (lack of) legal certainty, especially as the recognition of common concerns of humankind touches on difficult normative issues that pertain to humanity at large.[152] Alongside these certainty gains there are also legitimacy gains that can only be derived through treaty recognition.[153] The difficulty of reaching consensus on global issues may lead to a desire to circumvent treaty-making in the face of problems that need urgent solving; doing so, however, is likely to lead to more harm than good. In any event, as will be argued further below, the recognition of a common concern of humankind is only a starting point for solving global problems. Without connecting the recognition of a common concern of humankind to concrete legal rules, the efficacy of the concept is seriously constrained.[154]

3.2.4 The (Potential) Legal Implications of Common Concerns of Humankind: An Overview

The legal implications of recognising a common concern of humankind remain, at best, unclear. In the literature on common concern of humankind there is a fair deal of agreement on certain legal implications, while a substantial divergence in understanding remains on others. In the world of contemporary treaty-making, too, there remains a fair deal of scepticism about the common concern of humankind concept, ostensibly because of a lack of clarity as to its precise legal implications. For example, in 2015 the ILC dropped its reference to common concern of humankind from its current work on its Draft Guidelines on the Protection of the Atmosphere on the basis that the legal

152 See Brunnée (n 119) 564–7; French (n 131) 354–6.

153 See generally, in this regard, John O McGinnis and Illya Somin, 'Should International Law be Part of Our Law?' (2007) 59 *Stanford Law Review* 1175.

154 This does not, however, render the exercise of recognising a common concern of humankind without specifying concrete legal rules meaningless. See French (n 131) 354–6.

consequences of the concept were insufficiently clear at that point in time.[155] A more precise understanding of what legal implications flow from common concerns of humankind accordingly appears to be a necessity in order for a broader application of the concept to come to fruition.

This logic is fairly peculiar given the substance of common concerns of humankind; assuming, as it does, that recognition must necessarily happen contemporaneously with the coming into effect of precise legal obligations or responsibilities. While it may for various reasons be desirable for precise legal obligations to flow at the moment of recognition, it is worth pondering an alternative in the form of 'mere' recognition. If there is evidence to the effect that a particular rate problem—such as climate change—is causing certain adverse effects—such as an increase in the amount of natural disasters—then some form of recognition should follow based squarely on the problem *itself* regardless of what the legal consequences of recognition are. Should the recognition of a common concern of humankind not stem from concern with the adverse effects rather than from concern about what precise legal consequences should flow once something has been deemed a concern?

Dinah Shelton has argued that 'common concern, *l'interot general*, is a general concept which does not connote specific rules and obligations, but establishes the general basis for the concerned community to act'.[156] This should not be taken to mean that common concerns of humankind do not imply any duties or obligations whatsoever, but merely that common concerns of humankind at best imply general duties, the precise nature of which should be established by the international community by way of agreement. This perhaps makes matters of common concern of humankind difficult to enforce, but the concept's strength thus far can be found not in its enforcement capacity but rather it its capacity to facilitate new forms of institutional cooperation. It is in this light that the legal implications of the recognition of common concerns of humankind should be viewed.

Duties to cooperate. It is fairly uncontroversial by now that the recognition of a common concern of humankind implies duties of cooperation. In fact, one might go as far as to say that the necessity of cooperation to solve the problem at issue forms a part of the *raison d'être* of the concept of common concern of humankind. It is in part because common concerns of humankind cannot be handled in isolation that they are recognized as common concerns of humankind in the first place. The parties to the UNFCCC have acknowledged 'that the global nature of climate change calls for the *widest possible cooperation* by all

155 See Castillo-Winckels (n 5) 132.
156 Dina Shelton, 'Common Concern of Humanity' (2009) 5 Iustum Aequum Salutare 33, 38.

countries and their participation in an effective and appropriate international response'.[157] As for the parties to the CBD, they have stressed 'the importance of, and the need to promote, international, regional and global cooperation among States and intergovernmental organizations and the non-governmental sector for the conservation of biological diversity and the sustainable use of its components'.[158] While the precise form that cooperation should take still remains somewhat unclear, the duty to cooperate forms a central part of the common concern of humankind concept and clearly flows as a legal consequence from the recognition of a common concern of humankind.[159] Unless concrete rules are enacted, however, the duty remains a general one.

'Responsibilities at home'.[160] It has additionally been argued that the invocation of 'humankind' implies certain duties or obligations at a national level.[161] Edith Brown Weiss has quite persuasively argued that common concerns of humankind are aimed at *aggregate* protection at a global level; ergo, international cooperation at a global scale is insufficient to adequately address the problem that a particular common concern of humankind seeks to solve.[162] It therefore follows logically that in order for common concern of humankind not to be deprived of its potential efficacy it must necessarily imply a duty to take certain actions at the national level. This notion is clearly reflected in both the UNFCCC and the CBD: the former, particularly in Article 4, provides for national commitments in respect of climate change mitigation; the latter, in Articles 8 through 10, provides for certain national-level obligations connected to the conservation of biodiversity. As with the duty to cooperate, it is fairly difficult to decipher the precise boundaries of the duty to act at the national level: this does not detract from the existence of a general duty to act 'at home', with some specificity being added by particular treaty rules.[163]

'Responsibilities abroad'.[164] As with obligations *erga omnes*, the issue of enforcing common concerns of humankind remains an important one insofar as the efficacy of the concept hinges on particular actions being taken. This brings more sharply into focus the notion of unilateral action taken in pursuit of ensuring compliance with the legal obligations that stem from common concerns of humankind. This is by far the most controversial issue

157 UNFCCC, preamble. Emphasis added.
158 UNFCCC, preamble.
159 See Cottier et al (n 2); Brunnee (n 119); Shelton (n 156).
160 This phrase is used here in the same general sense as in Cottier et al (n 2).
161 See Brown Weiss (n 108) 164.
162 Brown Weiss (n 108) 164.
163 See Cottier et al (n 2).
164 This phrase is used here in the same general sense as in Cottier et al (n 2).

discussed under the legal implications of the recognition of common concerns of humankind and is framed either in terms of the discretion to act, in terms of responsibilities to act or obligations *erga omnes*. As Thomas Cottier et al argue, '[common concern of humankind as a principle] also authorises the taking of action in relation to facts relating to the Common Concern produced outside the proper jurisdiction of a State. At the same time, the principle is suitable for limiting the scope of extraterritorial action taken in regard to climate change mitigation'.[165] The authors continue to point out that while the recognition of a common concern of humankind 'provides the foundations of authorisation to act, the most difficult question relates to the problem of to what extent the principle [of common concern of humankind] also entails obligations to act'.[166]

Common but differentiated responsibilities. As Judge Cançado Trindade has pointed out, '[i]t should not pass unnoticed,—and it should perhaps be stressed,—that, in this conceptual construction [of common concern], what was kept in mind was not the sharing of resources or benefits, but rather of *responsibilities*'.[167] In essence, various authors are agreed; common concerns of humankind are foremost about common or shared problems and the allocation of responsibility for solving such problems.[168] While it still makes sense to recognise common concerns of humankind where they arise without any reference to *how* responsibility should be shared—as opposed to simply acknowledging that they should be shared in some manner or form—it becomes difficult to operationalize common concerns of humankind in a meaningful way without agreeing to a mechanism dealing with how responsibility should be shared.

One such mechanism often discussed in relation to common concerns of humankind is the concept of 'common but differentiated responsibilities (CBDR)'. Jutta Brunnée argues that this concept 'may fairly be described as the flipside of the concept of common concern'.[169] In sum, the concept is premised on the idea that different actors contribute in different ways to the problem itself and that different actors have differing capacities—based on their respective levels of social and economic development—to contribute to solving the shared problem.[170] CBDR accordingly stands for the proposition that all

165 Cottier et al (n 2) 318.
166 Cottier et al (n 2) 319.
167 Cançado Trindade (n 100) 351. Emphasis original.
168 See Cançado Trindade (n 100) 344.
169 Brunnée (n 119) 564–7.
170 See, for example, Cottier et al (n 2) 303.

actors should take responsibility for the same problem, with the aggregation of all actors taking on different levels of responsibility vis-à-vis one another in accordance with their respective levels of causation and their respective capacities to contribute to solving the shared problem at issue.[171] What the CBDR discussion here serves to clarify is that the obligations and responsibilities implied by the recognition of a common concern of humankind are in part defined with reference to concepts that are external—but related—to that of common concern of humankind itself.

3.3 *Towards a General Theory for the Recognition of Common Concerns of Humankind in International Law*

The rationale that underlies the need for a general theory for the recognition of common concerns of humankind has been well captured by Duncan French within the CBD context:

> [W]hat we are looking for here is whether one can identify reasons that support its [that is, biodiversity's] inclusion in the panoply of issues that justify the nomenclature of common concern. If one cannot do this, and it is therefore not possible to provide normative coherence as to why certain issues are of common concern and others are not, there is a real risk that the discussion descends into little more than retrospective realpolitik.[172]

As argued above, the most obvious commonality between common concerns of humankind, both existing and potential, is the implications that their recognition entail for state sovereignty. The position taken here is accordingly that a central element—or perhaps even *the* central element—for the recognition of common concerns of humankind is the need for a reconceptualization of state sovereignty; identifying areas where current conceptions of sovereignty have become dated or where a new definition of the term is required in order to enhance sovereignty such that global problems of particular significance can be solved is therefore a good starting point for identifying potential common concerns of humankind. This is the core focus of this section and for Part III below.

To understand the recognition of common concerns of humankind in this way is a way in which to give the concept a normative coherence that it would

171 See, for example, Cottier et al (n 2) 303.

172 French (n 131) 344.

otherwise lack. As discussed above, however, the need for redefining sovereignty is not the only potential constitutive element related to common concern of humankind recognition. The need for redefinition must also stem from a problem that affects, or has the capacity to affect, all—or at least a very large part—of humankind; the relevant problem should generally concern a rate, a change in which results in effects that are deemed 'adverse' by the entire international community. All the caveats and consequences described above relating to common concern of humankind recognition would apply as well. With this context sketched, the aim here is to posit a general theory of the process for the recognition of common concerns of humankind in international law.

There is currently no general process by which common concerns of humankind are recognised. The process described here is a proposal, the purpose of which is to provide a pathway for the common concern of humankind concept to find wider application in international law. It is by no means meant to stand in opposition to existing lists of constitutive elements of common concerns of humankind, but rather to complement and refine existing accounts in as simple a manner possible. As a general proposition, then, common concern of humankind recognition should entail three steps: (1) an identification process that will be referred to here as 'framing'; (2) once 'framed', the potential common concern of humankind should be tested against the threshold question of whether current constructions of state sovereignty in the area(s) related to the potential common concern of humankind need to be redefined in order for the 'framed' common concern of humankind to be successfully managed; and (3) if the threshold question is answered in the affirmative, the common concern of humankind must be recognised through a process of law. Each of these three steps will be examined in greater detail in turn.

3.3.1 Framing a Common Concern of Humankind

'Framing' as used in this context denotes the following two-step process: (1) identifying a rate 'problem' that affects humankind, or a large part thereof; and (2) identifying the effects and potential effects that stem from the identified rate problem. 'Framing' in this sense should—as far as possible—be a purely factual exercise undertaken without any sort of normative judgment. For the purposes of this inquiry, a 'rate' is simply '[a]n amount, quantity, or value, considered relative to another; the relationship between two values'.[173] In essence, a 'rate' refers to a *change* in the nature of a particular object,

173 See 'rate, *n.1*' in Oxford English Dictionary Online (OUP, online March 2018) <http://0-www.oed.com.innopac.wits.ac.za/view/Entry/158412?rskey=Ul7VvI&result=2&isAdvanced=false#eid> accessed 30 September 2021.

whether tangible or intangible, over the course of time. A simple example is 'climate change', which is seen—in ordinary terms—as 'an *alteration* in the regional or global climate; [especially] ... the *change* in global climate patterns increasingly apparent *from the mid to late 20th* [*century*] ... *onwards* and attributed largely to the increased levels of atmospheric carbon dioxide produced by the use of fossil fuels'.[174]

The latter part of the above definition of 'climate change'—relating to what climate change can be attributed to—is unimportant for identifying it as a rate problem. In other words, while the cause of climate change is important in deciding whether it constitutes a common concern of humankind—and is an issue that is addressed at a later stage of the recognition analysis—it does not matter for this stage what causes climate change. It simply matters that it is an identifiable rate with particular consequences that can be objectively established as fact as a change in the identified rate occurs. Put differently, certain effects can be determined as a matter of fact. Naturally, perhaps, there will be a temptation even at this stage to begin to classify the rate change and its effects in normative terms. Such efforts should be kept for the normative stage of the identification process; that is, it should be saved for the recognition phase.

In the context of climate change, for example, 'framing' would entail (1) identifying that the climate has the capacity to change in nature, does in fact change in nature over time and that these changes have certain effects on humankind or a large part of humankind; and (2) identifying as precisely as possible what the effects of a changing climate are. Similarly, in the context of biodiversity, 'framing' would involve (1) identifying that the level of biodiversity in the world has the capacity to change over time, does in fact change over time and that changes in the level of biodiversity has certain effects; and (2) identifying as precisely as possible what the effects of a changing level of biodiversity are. In both of the above-described cases, potential common concerns of humankind have now been framed and we can proceed to ask the threshold question: does state sovereignty in these areas need to be redefined in order to manage the rate changes and effects identified?

3.3.2 The Threshold Question: Does State Sovereignty Need Redefinition?

'Cooperative sovereignty' and the related concept of subsidiarity have already been discussed above. This second stage of the recognition of common

174 See 'climate, *n.1*' in Oxford English Dictionary Online (OUP, online March 2018) <http://0-www.oed.com.innopac.wits.ac.za/view/Entry/34319?redirectedFrom=climate+change#eid119694526> accessed 30 September 2021.

concerns of humankind entails asking whether a cooperative conception of state sovereignty is necessary in order to effectively manage the framed potential common concern of humankind. Put differently, the question is simply whether the current construction of state sovereignty in a particular field allows states to affect—at a factual level—the rate change identified and accordingly the effects (including those with normative implications) that flow from the change in that rate. Turning again to the climate change context, the question becomes whether a more traditional form of sovereignty—one that does not entail cooperation as part of sovereignty itself—allows for states to alter the rate at which the climate is changing and thereby alter the effects that stem from the rate at which the climate is changing.

In the event that cooperative sovereignty is unnecessary, there is no need for the recognition of a common concern of humankind because states will already have the necessary competences to address the rate change and its effects. For example, states are competent on current constructions of sovereignty to adequately fund a wide range of public goods. States can, for example, affect the rate at which crimes are committed; they can alter the rate at which their respective populations are educated to a certain level; they can build roads, railways and airports; they can establish and run a military; they can provide systems for the adequate settlement of a broad array of disputes—all of this, and much more, can be achieved without redefining sovereignty as a cooperative enterprise.

3.3.3 Recognition of the Common Concern of Humankind through a Process of Law

For this part of the inquiry, it is necessary, finally, to make certain normative judgments. The normative work of the common concern of humankind concept is done—almost entirely—by the word 'adverse'. The last real hurdle—and certainly the most difficult to overcome—is reaching agreement amongst actors in the international law arena that the effects identified at the framing stage are of sufficient concern to a large part of humanity in order for them to be deemed 'adverse'. Once there is agreement on this point, common concern of humankind designation should necessarily follow unless states are unconcerned with addressing a particular set of adverse effects. It is also at this stage that the underlying causes of the rate change and its effects enters the fray; the causes and the ability of the international community to address them do, after all, affect perceptions as to what effects are and are not 'adverse' in nature.

Returning to climate change once again, it is clear from the UNFCCC, as discussed above, that the effects of climate change are deemed 'adverse', at least in part, because they are caused by reversible human activity. This does not mean that the effects themselves are reversible; in the common concern of humankind context it is potentially irreversible effects that more likely to be deemed 'adverse'.[175] For example, in the biodiversity context, permanent losses of biological diversity—which is itself considered to be intrinsically valuable—are more likely to be considered 'adverse'. Similarly, in the climate change context, damage done to natural ecosystems may be irreversible inasmuch as once particular ecosystems have been destroyed they cannot be reproduce subsequently.

This does not mean, however, that the effects need necessarily be irreversible in order to be considered 'adverse'. Equally adverse in the climate change context, perhaps, is the threat that changes in the climate pose for natural water sources, food security and human security, amongst others. Ultimately, the process of recognising that certain effects are 'adverse' leaves the international community with wide discretion to recognise common concerns of humankind. While one might propose a set of factors to guide contemplation in this regard—such as the irreversibility and scale of the effects—what is and is not deemed 'adverse' is up to the collective will of the international community.

4 Changes in the Distribution of Income and Wealth within States: To Recognise as Common, as Concern or as Common Concern?

The third and final part of this chapter brings together the two parts that precede it. This exercise is structured into three sections. First, building on the general process for the recognition of common concerns of humankind elucidated in Part II above, the increasingly unequal distribution of income and wealth within states is framed as a potential common concern of humankind with due reference to the adverse effects of this phenomenon—a rate problem—over time and across space (*Section 4.1*). In the second section, the threshold issue—as identified in Part II above—of the need for 'cooperative sovereignty' is applied to the potential common concern of humankind framed in Section A (*Section 4.2*). Finally, having come to the conclusion that the threshold requirement is currently being met, or may alternatively be met in the near future, the potential modes of recognising changes in the distribution of income and wealth within states as a common concern of humankind are explored (*Section 4.3*).

175 See Soltau (n 122) 208.

4.1 *Framing Changes in the Distribution of Income and Wealth within States as a Common Concern of Humankind*

For the UNFCCC parties, 'change in the Earth's climate and its adverse effects are a common concern of humankind'.[176] For the parties to the CBD, 'the conservation of biological diversity is a common concern of humankind'.[177] For the purposes of this section, it will be argued, along similar lines, that 'the change, over time, in the distribution of income and wealth within states and the adverse effects stemming therefrom is a common concern of humankind'. In an analogous way to the concern is expressed through the CBD 'that biological diversity is being significantly reduced by certain human activities' and that concern is voiced 'that human activities have been substantially increasing the atmospheric concentrations of greenhouse gases, that these increases enhance the natural greenhouse effect, and that this will result on average in an additional warming of the Earth's surface and atmosphere and may adversely affect natural ecosystems and humankind' in the UNFCCC, the concern here expressed be that 'income and wealth within states are being increasingly unequally distributed'.

The distribution of income and wealth are both rates that constantly change over time. One could represent these distributions in many ways that illustrate how these rates change over time: one could, for example, use a composite measure such as the Gini coefficient or the Palma Ratio; alternatively—and this is the method preferred here—one could look at the share of the bottom 50 percent of income or wealth recipients in conjunction with the share of the next 40 percent and the top 10 percent and how these shares change over time.[178] Moreover, as was also illustrated in Chapter 2—as a factual matter—a large majority of humankind are citizens of states currently experiencing a rise in concentration of income and wealth.

As for the effects of these rate changes, they too have been documented in Chapter 2. Again, it should be stressed here that these assertions are intended to be purely factual, much in the same way that the climate change and its effects can be expressed in an objective factual manner without making any normative judgments; or in the same way as the change in the level of overall biological diversity on Earth and the effects of such change over time can objectively be expressed as factual information to the extent that contemporary research methods permit. At this point of the inquiry, the question of whether the effects stemming from the changes in the distribution of income

176 UNFCCC, preamble.

177 CBD, preamble.

178 See Chapter 2 above in this monograph for a lengthier discussion.

and wealth are deleterious or adverse is irrelevant: the point at this stage is simply to ascertain the facts of the matter.

4.2 *Illustrating That the Distribution of Income and Wealth Requires a Cooperative Conception of Sovereignty*

Plato had already taken what is a highly pointed stance on economic distributions by today's standards in his *Laws*.[179] Writing in the fourth century BC, Plato poignantly demonstrated the unparalleled power of law as a discipline to alter the distribution of income and wealth in a society in a deliberate and systematic fashion. His *Laws* is made up of 12 different books and consists of a dialogue between three fictional characters: one dubbed the 'Athenian Stranger', an ordinary Spartan citizen named Megillos and a lawmaker from Crete called Clinias.[180] Through the Athenian Stranger, Plato initiates the dialogue by questioning the other men whether a god or a man should be credited as the author of their laws.[181] What follows during the rest of the dialogue is essentially an attempt at answering this question, but the dialogue additionally allows the Athenian Stranger to contemplate the design of his ideal political order in practical terms. In Book V, the dialogue turns to contemplate an array of issues, including how many people an ideal society should be made up of and who should own how much property and wealth.[182] The answers are incredibly concrete.

Taking from Book V only that which is necessary to make this point, the following (admittedly simplified ideas) can be gleaned about Plato's notion of an ideal society: (1) out of what appears to essentially amount to mathematical convenience, it would be made up of no more than 5040 citizens;[183] (2) equality of material possessions (wealth) is desirable in theory, but considered impossible as a practical matter;[184] (3) acquisition of wealth is constructed so as to be based on merit, at least to the extent possible;[185] (4) honours and offices are determined in proportion to a man's wealth;[186] (5) there will be four classes based on wealth alone;[187] (6) there will be level of wealth that each

---

179 Plato, *Laws, Volume I: Books 1–6* (William Heinemann Ltd., London 1926), translated from the original Greek by R.G. Bury.
180 See Plato (n 179) vii-xvii.
181 See Plato (n 179) vii-xvii..
182 See Plato (n 179) 323–92.
183 Plato (n 179) 356–9.
184 Plato (n 179) 360–5, 378–9.
185 Plato (n 179) 378–9.
186 Plato (n 179) 378–9.
187 Plato (n 179) 378–9.

person should be allotted at a minimum, based on the limit of poverty;[188] and (7) no person will be allowed to acquire more than four times the minimum allotment in wealth.[189] Most importantly of all, all of these characteristics are to be backed by the coercive power of law: any wealth acquired in excess of the limit, for example, would in one way or another be handed over to the state and 'the gods who keep [it]'.[190]

As illustrated earlier in this chapter, applying this sort of legislative scheme—whether its attainment is in fact desirable is of little moment—is not realistically possible. Exercising sovereignty in order to ensure particular distributions of income and wealth within a state can only be done in cooperation with other states: sovereignty needs to be updated; it should be seen as a cooperative enterprise whereby distributive competences can only be exercised—and achieving distributive justice can only be attained—within states through international cooperation given the contemporary state of economic globalization. Again, as with the framing stage described above, this is a factual inquiry that can be made without taking a particular normative stance about the desirability of states being able to enhance their internal economic sovereignty.

This remains the case regardless of one's conception of distributive justice. Whether one takes a similar approach to the one of Plato as described above, whether one prefers a more Rawlsian understanding of distributive justice,[191] or whether one takes the view that an economic system can be considered as providing for distributive justice only when government interference with the free market is at a minimum,[192] the fact remains that in contemporary times distributive justice can only realistically be achieved through cooperation between sovereign entities. This notion is interrogated in greater detail with respect to discrete aspects of distributive justice in Chapter 4.

5 Conclusions

The distribution of income and wealth within a state, as has been illustrated throughout this monograph, depends on a very large number of factors,

188 Plato (n 179) 378–381.

189 Plato (n 179) 380–1.

190 Plato (n 179) 380–1. Plato also spoke to additional rules relating, for example, to the coining of money, foreign aid and immigration. See generally Plato (n 179) 323–93.

191 See generally John Rawls, *A Theory of Justice* (*Revised Edition*) (HUP, Cambridge, MA 1999); more specifically, see 228–335.

192 For the defence of such a view, see generally, for example, Milton Friedman, *Capitalism and Freedom* (University of Chicago Press, Chicago 1962); more specifically, see 161–176.

ranging from technology, to labour regulation to taxation, amongst many other factors. Making one single normative claim about the distribution of income and wealth within a state is accordingly a highly complex task; to do so for all nations, far more so still. Consider for a moment the international rules relating to the protection of foreign investment. Even within this one field of international law, it is a complex exercise to cover all the potential normative aspects relating to the distributive aspects of foreign investments. The normative claims relating to taxation are, of course, a different set of claims entirely. What these differing sets of normative claims have in common, however, is that they are all related—albeit it to differing degrees—to the distribution of income and wealth within states.

In light of the above, it may be necessary to recognise a distributional common concern in respect of a number of areas of international law, each with its own modalities and particularities. Consideration of each possibility in this regard is well beyond the scope of this monograph. This monograph is restricted to contemplating the potential of recognising a distributional common concern in the area of international corporate taxation. Before turning to this topic, however, a detour is necessary in order for us to consider the most important contemporary actor insofar as the distribution of income and wealth—and all other common concerns of humankind—is concerned: the *multinational enterprise*.

Acknowledgements

A condensed version of this chapter has been published as a book chapter: see Alexander Beyleveld, 'Exploring the Recognition of New Common Concerns of Humankind: The Example of the Distribution of Income and Wealth within States' in Thomas Cottier (ed) *The Prospects of Common Concern of Humankind in International Law* (CUP, Cambridge 2021).

CHAPTER 4

Recognising a Distributional Common Concern in the Area of Corporate Taxation

> It is commonly believed that the corporation is a creature of the state and that the state grants not only corporate life and personality but also powers and privileges to the corporation and that without the power granted by the state, the corporation would be helpless. ... The corporation ... [however] drafts its own constitution and, in effect, creates itself, without any meaningful participation by the state. The corporation did not seize this broad power from the state by force; nor can we conclude that the exercise of broad powers by the corporation necessarily dilutes the sovereignty of the state. However, it should be noted that this lofty status of the corporation is one which most states can never hope to attain. The corporation often has far more power to govern its own affairs without accountability to outside influences and without domination by external sources than does the state.
>
> The closing decades of the nineteenth century provided considerable evidence that the large corporation could not be controlled effectively by the state of its incorporation nor by the states where it carried on its activities. The federal government has, with greater or lesser success, tried to exercise control over some aspects of corporate life. Even where successful, these attempts only emphasize the breadth of the departure of the myth from the true account; though a creature of one state, the only substantial attempts at control of the corporation have come from another. ... What machinery does a state have for exercising control over large, intricately organized corporations with subsidiaries of many origins and nationalities? Even a national government finds itself somewhat short of operative instrumentalities in this connection.
>
> But the myths persist that the corporation is a creature of the state, that the state grants powers and privileges to the corporation, and that the corporation is subject to the control of the state. ... What is important is that legislators, corporate officers, incorporators and

 | DOI:10.1163/9789004511750_005

the public think about and deal with corporate issues in terms of what is rather than in terms of what is not.

DOW VOTAW (1920–2004), 'The Mythology of Corporations'[1]

•••

[L]and is a subject which cannot be removed; whereas stock easily may. The proprietor of land is necessarily a citizen of the particular country in which his estate lies. The proprietor of stock is properly a citizen of the world, and is not necessarily attached to any particular country. He would be apt to abandon the country in which he was exposed to a vexatious inquisition, in order to be assessed to a burdensome tax, and would remove his stock to some other country where he could either carry on his business, or enjoy his fortune more at his ease.

ADAM SMITH (1723–1790), *The Wealth of Nations*[2]

1 Introduction

The words of Dow Votaw cited above have aged well. Votaw's 'The Mythology of Corporations' was published in 1962, well before 'globalization's second unbundling'. The technological advances we have seen since that unbundling started in the 1980s, however, have considerably increased the importance of the phenomena Votaw described. This is because firms have become significantly more global as a result of technological change. Their reach has extended further outwards from their 'home' states. The desire to regulate the multinational firm has increased, but the ability of states to do so autonomously has declined significantly.

Corporations, especially 'multinational corporations' as certain firms are often labelled, have long attracted a large amount of heavy criticism. Some have, for example, depicted them as representing 'new' colonisers. They are sometimes fingered as greedy profit mongers who break all the rules for the

1 Dow Votaw, 'The Mythology of Corporations' (1962) 4 *California Management Review* 58, 61–3. Footnotes omitted; emphasis original.

2 Adam Smith, *The Wealth of Nations: Books IV-V* (Penguin Books, London 1999) 442.

sake of material gains and exploit their workers and customers alike. They are occasionally seen as undercutting smaller firms to the extent that those firms cannot compete and go out of business. They are accused, at times, of 'sending' jobs offshore and unfairly engaging in regulatory arbitrage. They are said to be and do all these things and much more to the detriment of the many and the enrichment of the few. They have also been vigorously defended against these varied charges. On balance, advocates argue, they move us forward; they bring development and progress, making the world a better place for most that live in it.

Corporations and multinational firms also simply *are*: at a given moment we can, with some difficulty, describe their various attributes and actions. Whether our description is accurate or not, there is no need to take a position on whether corporations or multinational firms are good or bad or something in between. This is not what this chapter is about. Instead, this chapter is concerned with understanding what corporations *are* and highlighting that this definitional issue in and of itself raises many tricky questions for global governance generally, including for proponents of the Doctrine of Common Concern of Humankind. The first preoccupation of this chapter, in Part I, is thus to describe what corporations *are* and to illustrate what they *are not* by distinguish them from other concepts, such as the multinational *enterprise*. This discussion sets the scene for this chapter's first point: namely that it is the multinational enterprise—which should be viewed as an *institution*—that merely uses various constructed *corporate forms*—corporations, companies or similar types of fictions—to structure its business and other operations. As an institution, the 'multinational'—a word used here as shorthand for the term 'multinational *enterprise*'—wields a unique form of power, power which it often asserts authoritatively and autonomously from the human beings that have an interest in it.

With this point made, the chapter moves on, in Part II, to its second major exploration: that is, to the extent to which multinational *enterprises*, which in their current form cannot exist without the *corporate form*, as global institution, enable and contribute to the occurrence of certain global phenomena, particularly the distribution of income and wealth within the different states of the world. What this discussion should reveal is this chapter's second point: that is that multinational enterprises are the *institutional* actors that contribute *most directly* to common concerns of humankind and particularly to the distributional common concern argued for in this monograph.

This second point leads tidily into the chapter's third area of contemplation, which is the problematic issue of *responsibility* for solving the problems that sit as the heart of the various common concerns of humankind. This discussion, captured in Part III, starts from the premise that it is states—and not multinational enterprises or other institutions—that are ultimately responsible, at least *most directly*, for taking steps to address common concerns of humankind. Given that multinational enterprises are the institutional actors that *contribute most directly* to the problems animating common concerns it is implicit that an *effective* Doctrine of Common Concern of Humankind must necessarily entail an understanding of how state responsibility is parsed into helpful actions—whether proactive or reactive—on the part of multinationals. The third aim of this chapter, therefore, is to devise a 'responsibility-action' framework for thinking about this process.

Coming up with a responsibility-action framework entails answering a number of questions, the most pertinent of which—and therefore the ones addressed in this chapter—are as follows: (1) what is the main purpose of the multinational enterprise and the corporate form it so heavily relies on for its continued existence? (2) In light of their main purpose, to what extent should states attempt to regulate multinational enterprises in executing the responsibilities states take on in relation to common concerns of humankind? Or, put slightly differently, to what extent can states be satisfied that common concern problems will be solved given current levels of regulation (or lack thereof) imposed on multinationals? (3) Are states capable of imposing the necessary levels of regulation unilaterally or is cooperation with other states necessary? This chapter answers these questions by thinking about how the responsibility-action framework might be applied in the context of a distributional common concern of humankind.

The chapter then proceeds to consider corporate taxation as it pertains to multinationals. As has already been illustrated, the income and wealth shares of individuals at the top of these distributions have increased substantially since the 1980s in countries around the world. As an increasing amount of evidence suggests, these individuals have also been able to effectively—sometimes perfectly legally—use low-tax jurisdictions in order to pay significantly lower taxes. The upshot of this is that the true extent of the inequality of income and wealth is to a significant extent concealed. As alluded to earlier, if offshore wealth is not accounted for in measuring the wealth share of the top 0.01 percent of persons within a given state, their true share may be dramatically underestimated, sometimes by more than 100 percent.[3] It also means that states collect much less revenue than they intend to and are to an extent

3 See Annette Alstadsæter, Niels Johannesen and Gabriel Zucman, 'Tax Evasion and Inequality' (2019) 109 *American Economic Review* 2073.

constrained in any tax actions they take to affect the distribution of income and wealth.

Of greater importance for this chapter, however, is that corporate profits have risen handsomely since the start of globalization's second unbundling, reaching historical highs in recent years in both absolute and relative terms. Simultaneously, the average statutory corporate income tax rate—viewed from a global perspective—has at least halved: while in 1985 it was at 49 percent, in 2018 it sits at a mere 24 percent.[4] This latter number still masks a fair deal of variance in rates between the countries of the world. For example, as at 2018, Brazil's statutory corporate tax rate stood at 34 percent; India's stood at 35 percent. Other countries' rates were closer to the average: China's, for example, stood at 25 percent; as did Austria's. In countries such as Bermuda or the Cayman Islands, the rate stood at zero. Multinational firms, especially the larger ones, have become particular effective at shifting their profits to low-tax jurisdictions—mostly legally—thereby greatly reducing their overall global tax burden.

In such a world, the tax sovereignty of individual states has become increasingly less meaningful from both positive and normative standpoints. From a positive standpoint, there are essentially two arguments why corporate tax rates have been falling so drastically. The more common argument is that states have been '[competing] harder for productive capital, [thereby] … pushing corporate tax rates down'.[5] A less common argument is that multinational firms 'artificially' shift their profits to low-tax jurisdictions to minimize their tax liability.[6] The stance taken here is that these arguments are not necessarily mutually exclusive, with both arguments possibly providing a partial explanation for overall general trends. Even in the event that these arguments were mutually exclusive, however, the outcome would still be the factual erosion of the functional elements of tax sovereignty as it is clear that states cannot effectively set their own corporate tax rates without considering the behaviour of other states.[7]

The factual reality has, in turn, led to a status quo wherein the inability of states to counter the practises of multinational firms is increasingly vulnerable to critique from an array of normative standpoints. From the perspective of

4 Thomas Tørsløv, Ludvig Wier and Gabriel Zucman, 'The Missing Profits of Nations' (NBER Working Paper 24701, 5 June 2018) <http://gabriel-zucman.eu/files/TWZ2018.pdf> accessed 30 September 2021, 1.

5 Tørsløv, Wier and Zucman (n 4) 1.

6 See Tørsløv, Wier and Zucman (n 4).

7 See further below in this chapter where this is discussed in greater detail.

an 'equal sacrifice' theory of taxation, the erosion of the functional taxation capacity of states also results, by necessary implication, in the erosion of the ability of states to exercise its powers of taxation in a manner which is normatively sound. This is exemplified by the fact that in a large number of countries multinational firms face a lesser tax burden than domestic firms. It also means that states are in a way forced to shift the burden of taxation to other parts of the tax base, which, in turn, results in the violation of the equal sacrifice principle or alternatively in increased borrowing, with the latter having an implication for distributive justice between different generations.

From a Rawlsian perspective, moreover, it could be asserted that the factual erosion of tax sovereignty affects the background institutions necessary for justice.[8] More specifically, for John Rawls, amongst these institutions is a 'distribution arm' which has two functions: first, 'gradually and continually to correct the distribution of wealth and to prevent concentrations of power detrimental to the fair value of political liberty and fair equality of opportunity';[9] and second, it is there to 'raise the revenues that justice requires'.[10] The factual erosion of tax sovereignty as thought of here—as a function of the activities of multinational firms—makes it more difficult for a state to achieve either of these purposes, thereby depriving that state of the institutions necessary for it to ensure distributive justice.[11]

The above examples are illustrations of the broader idea that tax sovereignty is better viewed from a cooperative viewpoint. Starting from this premise, the aim of the remaining parts of the chapter become to show how the recognition of a distributional common concern of humankind could act as part of the foundation for the enactment of a global treaty regime to address various problems arising in connection to taxation, especially insofar as it pertains to multinational firms. In other words, the final task of the chapter is to imagine a process of law—including the normative arguments that would underpin such a process—whereby a distributional common concern of humankind might be recognised over time in the area of multinational corporate taxation.

In light of the above, the remainder of the chapter proceeds to consider three further issues. First, some of the more important reasons behind falling corporate tax rates are set out, with a particular emphasis on what this means for revenue collection and, more importantly, the distribution of income and wealth within states (*Part IV*). Next it is illustrated that—at least insofar as

8 See John Rawls, *A Theory of Justice (Revised Edition)* (HUP, Cambridge, MA 1999) 242–51.
9 Rawls (n 8) 245.
10 See Rawls (n 8) 246.
11 This claim is examined more carefully below.

it pertains to multinational firms—tax sovereignty is best conceived of as cooperative sovereignty, both from positive and normative perspectives (*Part* v). Finally, the chapter contemplates the potential implications and utility of recognising a distributional common concern of humankind in the area of multinational corporate taxation (*Part* vi).

2 The Multinational as Global Institution and Use of the Corporate Form

This part presents the definitional claims that are necessary to properly frame the substantive discussions that follow in the subsequent parts of this chapter. These questions, although they have complex answers, are fairly simple. The first of these concerns what *corporations* are. The second question pertains to what *multinational enterprises* are. The answers to these respective questions provide the necessary context for Part ii of this chapter which follows.

The meaning of the term 'corporation' being a contestable one, it is helpful to clarify at the outset how it is used in this chapter and the chapters that follow it. For current purposes, a 'corporation' is a legal construction. Upon 'incorporation', a corporation becomes a legal object that exists, in our collective imagination at least, separately from the human beings that caused it to come into existence and for the furtherance of whose aims it was created.[12] It—the legally constructed device—is bestowed with the capacity for rights and obligations and the ability to exercise and perform them to the extent that they have been acquired.[13] Even though the corporation, which does not have a physical existence, operates through the actions of physical proxies, the pertinent law allows for the pretence that it—and not *someone* else—'does' things. It, for example, often enters into contracts. It also usually owns assets.[14] But it remains a fiction: it exists as an idea and only to the extent that a particular law or set of laws dictates.

This understanding, while perhaps reflective of legal jargon, is largely consistent with dictionary entries that might properly be used as comparators. For example, the *Oxford English Dictionary* contains a legal definition amongst other definitions under the entry for 'corporation'. A 'corporation' in this sense is '[a] body corporate legally authorized to act as a single individual'—where

12 See Peter T Muchlinski, 'Corporations in International Law' in *Max Planck Encyclopaedia of International Law* (OUP online, June 2014) 2.

13 See Muchlinski (n 12) 2.

14 See Muchlinski (n 12) 2.

a 'body corporate' is in turn, in rather circular fashion, defined as '[a]n entity legally authorized to act as a single individual and having legal rights and duties; a corporation'—or it is 'an artificial person created by royal charter, prescription, or act of the legislature, and having authority to preserve certain rights in perpetual succession'.[15] What most definitions of the term omit, including the one offered above, is information about the *reach* of any particular authorisation or incorporation: they do not speak to *how far* the fiction is authorised to exist.

In order to unpack this point properly, it is useful to understand an 'enterprise' as something conceptually distinct from a 'corporation'. The former refers to '[a] commercial or industrial undertaking; a firm, a company, [or] a business'.[16] An 'enterprise' is a physically-existing commercial operation which may or may not establish one or many corporations—which only exist notionally or in the world of legal abstractions—in furtherance of its objectives. Unlike in the case of a corporation, then, it is easy, for example, to identify what makes an enterprise 'multinational' or 'national' or 'regional'. The reach of an enterprise is an empirically determinable fact: the commercial operation reaches as far as its actual tangible and intangible activities. As for the reach of a corporation, this can only ever be a question of law because it only exists as far as it is permitted to exist by the laws responsible for its construction.

An upshot of the above logic is that 'multinational enterprises' clearly exist but that the extent to which corporations can be described as 'multinational' is a question without an obvious answer. It is true that '[b]usiness corporations have a fundamentally similar set of legal characteristics—and face a fundamentally similar set of legal problems—in all jurisdictions'.[17] It is also clear that they share a 'common structure' in many different states.[18] A fairly standard description is that corporations consist of 'five core structural characteristics', namely: '(1) legal personality, (2) limited liability, (3) transferable shares, (4) centralized management under a board structure, and (5) shared ownership by contributors of equity capital'.[19] What is unclear, however,

---

15 See 'corporation, *n*'. in Oxford English Dictionary Online (OUP, online) <http://0-www.oed.com.innopac.wits.ac.za/view/Entry/158412?rskey=Ul7VvI&result=2&isAdvanced=false#eid> accessed 30 September 2021.

16 See 'enterprise, *n*'. in Oxford English Dictionary Online (OUP, online) <http://0-www.oed.com.innopac.wits.ac.za/view/Entry/158412?rskey=Ul7VvI&result=2&isAdvanced=false#eid> accessed 30 September 2021.

17 John Armour et al, 'What is Corporate Law?' in Reinier Kraakman et al, *The Anatomy of Corporate Law: A Comparative and Functional Approach* (3ed OUP, Oxford 2017) 1.

18 See Armour et al (n 17) 1–28.

19 Armour et al (n 17) 5.

is where precisely these features begin and end. Consider, for example, The Boeing Company, which is a business primarily engaged in making airplanes. On its website, Boeing emphasizes the extent to which it sees itself being tied to the United States; its supposed 'home' state:

> The Boeing Company—the world's largest aerospace company and America's largest exporter—assembles commercial airplanes and [defence] ... products and also builds aerospace components in the United States. Among Boeing's 137,000 employees in all 50 states (as of January 2017) are more than 50,000 factory employees and more than 45,000 engineers. Boeing's market success plays a key role in supporting high-value aerospace jobs across its supply chain and across the United States. In 2016 alone, Boeing paid nearly $45 billion to more than 13,600 businesses, supporting an additional 1.3 million supplier-related jobs in the United States. These businesses include suppliers for our commercial and [defence] ... production, non-production vendors and subsidiaries of companies to which Boeing made other payments.[20]

It is fairly clear from this passage that Boeing means to present itself as a predominantly American enterprise. It largely *is* an American enterprise—loosely speaking. If one were to ask what Boeing's nationality was, the answer would perhaps justifiably be 'American'. From a corporations perspective, however, it is difficult—and perhaps harmful—to characterize Boeing this way. This is because the corporation registered as 'The Boeing Company' in Delaware has notified the United States Securities and Exchange Commission that it has 282 subsidiaries scattered throughout the globe.[21] Some of its subsidiaries are in other parts of the United States, such as New York and California. There are, however, further Boeing subsidiaries in Canada, Ireland, Brazil, China, the United Kingdom, Spain, Japan, Germany, Norway, the Virgin Islands, India, South Korea, Saudi Arabia and Bermuda, amongst various other locations.[22]

Virtually all other well-known large enterprises have similar stories. Boeing's largest competitor is Airbus, which similarly sees itself as an enterprise that is predominantly rooted in one place—the European Union—but

---

20 The Boeing Company, 'Boeing's U.S. Footprint' <https://www.boeing.com/company/general-info/#/global> accessed 30 September 2021.

21 SEC, 'EXHIBIT (21)—List of Company Subsidiaries The Boeing Company and Subsidiaries'<https://www.sec.gov/Archives/edgar/data/12927/000119312505038602/dex21.htm> accessed 30 September 2021.

22 See SEC (n 21).

has operations and dealings scattered throughout the world.[23] Electronics businesses such Apple and Samsung have similarly intricate globally scattered supply chains. As do virtually all of the major automobile manufacturers. The same holds true for contemporary internet service providers, such as Microsoft and Google. Less well-known businesses have similar supply chains and are accordingly similarly scattered across the globe. What all these enterprises have in common is that they are all, by virtue of the geography of their respective operations, regulated—because they predominantly operate through the corporate form—by a range of national corporate and other laws even though they each operate, at least for the most part, *as a single business enterprise*.

John Ruggie has written a helpful article on multinationals where he characterises them as 'global institution'.[24] Ruggie's account is split up into essentially four parts and does an excellent job of taking the above discussion further. The first part entails describing what a multinational enterprise *is*. The next topic Ruggie addresses is the notion of the power of multinationals. The third topic he deals with is the idea of the authority of multinationals. Finally, and of great importance for current purposes, Ruggie looks into the concept of the 'relative autonomy' of multinationals. Ruggie's ideas set out in his article provide us with language which is helpful in describing the features of multinationals.

Ruggie starts off by noting that, '[s]urprisingly, there is no legally precise and universally accepted definition of the multinational enterprise'.[25] While Ruggie is correct that there is no such definition, it is rather odd that he finds this to be surprising given what he subsequently describes. His starting point is a definition currently deployed by the OECD within a specific instrumental context. That definition, which Ruggie describes as 'minimalist', reads as follows:

> [Multinationals] usually comprise companies or other entities established in more than one country and so linked that they may coordinate their operations in various ways. While one or more of these entities may be able to exercise a significant influence over the activities of others, their degree of autonomy within the enterprise may vary widely from one multinational enterprise to another.[26]

---

23 See Airbus SAS, 'Worldwide presence: At home around the world' <https://www.airbus.com/company/worldwide-presence.html> accessed 30 September 2021.

24 John Gerard Ruggie, 'Multinationals as Global Institution: Power, Authority and Relative Autonomy' (2018) 12 *Regulation & Governance* 317.

25 Ruggie (n 24) 318.

26 See Ruggie (n 24) 318.

Next, Ruggie delves into one of the many distinctions that make the idea of a multinational enterprise such a complicated one: that between the multinational enterprise the *legal entity* and the multinational enterprise the *economic entity*. Ruggie's choice to use the word 'entity' is an interesting one, for an 'entity', in one sense, is a '[b]eing, ... [or an] existence, as opposed to non-existence'; that is 'the existence, as distinguished from the qualities or relations, of anything'.[27] An 'entity' is '[t]hat which constitutes the being of a thing'; it is an 'essence, ... [or an] essential nature'.[28] In this sense an entity is '*concrete*'.[29] An entity has 'a *real* existence' in this sense.[30] When an entity is not concrete, it may be purely 'rational'—it may exist only as an 'object of reason'.[31] A philosophical definition of the word 'ens'—from the Latin term '*ens*', from which the English word 'entity' originates—is perhaps more specific: an 'ens' is '[a]n entity regarded apart from any predicate but that of mere existence' but it is also 'the *predicable* "ens" regarded as an abstract notion'.[32] As this discussion evolves, it should thus be noted that a multinational enterprise can never be a mere entity—it will always constitute an array of *entities and non-entities—each of which can be conceived of from multiple disciplinary perspectives—and how they relate to one another*. It is precisely this conceptual complexity that makes it perfectly understandable that we remain far away from universal agreement on the meaning of the term 'multinational enterprise'.

Ruggie's distinction between legal and economic understandings of multinational enterprises, however, remain pertinent, and his framework for understanding multinational enterprises, mostly apt. Ruggie notes that, broadly

27 See 'entity, *n*'. in Oxford English Dictionary Online (OUP, online) <http://o-www.oed.com.innopac.wits.ac.za/view/Entry/158412?rskey=Ul7VvI&result=2&isAdvanced=false#eid> accessed 30 September 2021.

28 See 'entity, *n*'. in Oxford English Dictionary Online (OUP, online) <http://o-www.oed.com.innopac.wits.ac.za/view/Entry/158412?rskey=Ul7VvI&result=2&isAdvanced=false#eid> accessed 30 September 2021.

29 See 'entity, *n*'. in Oxford English Dictionary Online (OUP, online) <http://o-www.oed.com.innopac.wits.ac.za/view/Entry/158412?rskey=Ul7VvI&result=2&isAdvanced=false#eid> accessed 30 September 2021.

30 See 'entity, *n*'. in Oxford English Dictionary Online (OUP, online) <http://o-www.oed.com.innopac.wits.ac.za/view/Entry/158412?rskey=Ul7VvI&result=2&isAdvanced=false#eid> accessed 30 September 2021. Emphasis added.

31 See 'entity, *n*'. in Oxford English Dictionary Online (OUP, online) <http://o-www.oed.com.innopac.wits.ac.za/view/Entry/158412?rskey=Ul7VvI&result=2&isAdvanced=false#eid> accessed 30 September 2021.

32 See 'ens, *n*'. in Oxford English Dictionary Online (OUP, online) <http://o-www.oed.com.innopac.wits.ac.za/view/Entry/158412?rskey=Ul7VvI&result=2&isAdvanced=false#eid> accessed 30 September 2021. Emphasis again is my own.

speaking, from an economic viewpoint, multinational enterprises can be viewed from two vantage points: the actor-based view and network-based view of multinationals.[33] To illustrate the former, Ruggie considers the *French* 'supermajor' oil and gas firm Total.[34] He describes it as follows:

> [Total is] the French oil and gas company whose global headquarters is just a short taxi ride from the OECD in Paris, and whose organization illustrates the conventional integrated multinational. By market capitalization, Total ranks as the fourth largest publicly traded integrated oil and gas company in the world .... It operates in 130 countries and has 100,000 direct employees. Its business segments cover every aspect of the oil and gas industry, from exploration, development, production, refining, and petrochemicals to marketing, trading, and shipping. It is also active in specialty chemicals and aims to become a global leader in new energies.
>
> The Total "group" comprises nearly 900 subsidiaries and equity affiliates. But the reach of the enterprise doesn't stop there. As part of its marketing business, Total's service station network includes more than 16,000 outlets in 110 countries, all carrying the Total brand. Reflecting local circumstances and sometimes requirements, they fall into three categories: owned and operated by an in-country subsidiary, owned by a subsidiary but operated by independent dealers, and dealer owned and operated. Beyond that set of relationships are countless suppliers of products and services, as well as distributors other than service stations that are contractually connected to individual corporate entities within the Total group.[35]

Towards the end of this description, Ruggie already begins, knowingly or not, to describe the network view, that is, as Ruggie puts it, viewing the multinational as economic concept 'through the lens of the contractual ecosystems they continue to generate'.[36] As Ruggie continues, '[t]hese are variously called transnational production networks, supply chains, or global value chains'.[37]

---

33 Ruggie (n 24) 318. The manner in which Ruggie explains this is somewhat confusing. At first, he seems to suggest that there are two 'forms' of multinationals. It becomes clear, however, that what he means is that there are two ways of *viewing* or *looking at* multinationals as economic concept. See Ruggie (n 24) 318–9.

34 Ruggie (n 24) 318.

35 Ruggie (n 24) 318. Ruggie's references omitted.

36 Ruggie (n 24) 319.

37 Ruggie (n 24) 319.

From his subsequent exposition of his understanding of these terms, it becomes clear that Ruggie's view of the economic multinational definitional comports with how the concept has been conceived of in Chapter 3 of this monograph. It is from this viewpoint that this monograph adopts a contextual understanding upon which it builds its arguments pertaining to the economic sovereignty of states and their distributive autonomy.[38] To illustrate his understanding of the network view of the multinational, Ruggie starts by looking at *American* coffee shop giant Starbucks, which he asserts 'lies at the simple end of that spectrum'.[39] In order to illustrate, Ruggie quotes a United Nations Conference on Trade and Development Report, which in turn describes Starbucks as follows:

> [Starbucks] directly employs 150,000 people; sources coffee from thousands of traders, agents and contract farmers across the developing world; manufactures coffee in over 30 countries, mostly in alliance with partner firms, usually close to final market; distributes coffee to retail outlets through over 50 major central and regional warehouses and distribution centres; and operates some 17,000 retail stores in over 50 countries across the globe.[40]

Next, Ruggie discusses Apple, the *American* technology behemoth. More specifically, he discusses the iPhone 6—as opposed to the economic activity of Apple more generally—in the following terms:

> The Apple iPhone 6 illustrates a producer-led production network. As of 2014, its components were produced by 785 suppliers in 31 countries (comparecamp.com 2014). The product is designed in the United States (US) and assembled in China, which also had the largest number of suppliers in 2014 at 349, nearly half the total. Some 60 suppliers were US-based, several themselves multinationals, some headquartered in other countries. Many US suppliers also outsourced fabrication of components to companies in Japan, South Korea, and Taiwan, which in turn are sourced from yet other (and lower cost) locations in South East Asia.[41]

---

38 See Chapter 3 of this monograph on economic sovereignty and distributive autonomy.

39 Ruggie (n 24) 319.

40 See Ruggie (n 24) 319. This description of Starbucks is from 2013 and is thus somewhat dated. The point the description was used to make, however, remains the same.

41 Ruggie (n 24) 319.

It is important that Ruggie singled out the iPhone 6, because other parts of Apple's business are not producer-led. Apple's online stores, such as its App Store and its iTunes Store, for example, predominantly relies on others—musicians, filmmakers, app developers and various other content and platform producers—to produce the main product. In that scenario, Apple provides a platform that fits together with the main product which it produces—the iPhone. Looking at Apple as a whole, then, from a network or GVC perspective, results in Apple being significantly larger. It also results in it being a multinational significantly more complex in nature.[42] As Ruggie further explains:

> [Production networks] illustrate a fundamental transformation that has taken place in the production process of many if not most sectors. Multinational enterprises "are increasingly able to fine-slice activities and operations in their value chains and place them in the most cost-effective location, domestically and globally" ... . The electronics and automobile industries led the way, largely because components can be broken down into so many discrete parts and are easy to transport. But garments and footwear were also early movers, and the list today includes food and beverages, chemicals, mining, furniture, and a host of others. In view of the complexity of managing these transactions, the role of services looms large (logistics, telecommunications, legal services, data processing, accounting, and human resources management, among others). Although a single product emerges at the end, production networks are inherently multi-sectoral, drawing upon inputs from several sectors simultaneously. In a word, these are mini—and in many cases not-so-mini—trans-national economic systems. Product and process standards are set by the lead firm and then cascade across its network and down the supply chains.[43]

This largely comports the view of economic globalization proffered by Richard Baldwin and adopted in Chapter 3. Where Ruggie goes further is in his acknowledgement that '[t]he links among the various parties can take a variety of legal forms: they can be among subsidiaries or affiliates of the same corporate group, joint ventures, different types of non-equity relationships (contract manufacturing, licensing, franchising), and arms-length purchases—or any combination thereof'.[44] Having acknowledged some of the major economic

42 Ruggie does acknowledge that other forms of multinationals exist. See Ruggie (n 24) 319.

43 Ruggie (n 24) 319.

44 Ruggie (n 24) 319.

consequences of the multinational,[45] Ruggie begins to explain why the distinction between the economic and legal concepts is such an important one. In his words:

> These, then, are two snapshots of the 21st century multinational seen in terms of the organization of their transnational economic activity. But importantly, this is not how the law conceives of them—far from it. When we think of a multinational we think of the likes of Exxon, GE, Unilever, Sinopec, Google, Coca-Cola, Toyota, Novartis, and so on down the list of well-known names as one company, with unity of command, operating under a single global vision and strategy, optimizing worldwide operations for efficiencies, market share, and profits. We are not wrong to think this. Those organizations do exist in the everyday world of economic activity. But they don't exist as entities in the law.[46]

Ruggie explains simply why this is important:

> Where no equity nexus exists, as in the Starbucks and iPhone examples, relations between producers/buyers and their suppliers are governed by the private law of contracts. In the case of an integrated firm like Total, each of its 900 subsidiaries and affiliates is a separate legal entity, subject to the laws of the particular jurisdiction in which it is incorporated. Through equity relations they are ultimately linked to a "corporate parent," which is itself a separate legal entity. Hence, Robé … insists that the first step in fully understanding the multinational in relation to governance issues is to grasp this fundamental disjuncture between economic reality and legal form. The multinational as economic organization orchestrates and controls the entirety of its global operations. The group of firms or enterprises that make up the multinational as an economic organization is structured using the corporate form; but legally the group itself is not a corporation. Why is this distinction so crucial? Because national law for the most part governs the separate legal entities, not the single economic enterprise.
>
> The "parent company" enjoys limited liability even if it wholly owns all of its subsidiaries. This means that the corporate parent is generally not liable for risks incurred by a subsidiary, or monetary damages imposed on

45 See further, Ruggie (n 24) 319.

46 Ruggie (n 24) 319–20.

> a subsidiary, beyond the extent of its investment in it. Moreover, a subsidiary or affiliate may have subsidiaries and affiliates of its own, based on the same principle of limited liability. Some subsidiaries may be listed on stock exchanges in their own right, with the corporate parent remaining the majority or controlling shareholder. In all such cases, the parent company is not liable for harm caused by subsidiaries, other than in exceptional situations such as demonstrable negligence, fraud, or other illicit conduct that the corporate parent directed or of which it had knowledge and did nothing to stop. That would provide grounds for what is known as "piercing the corporate veil." But it remains the exception domestically and even more so across national borders. As one widely quoted criticism—and witticism—has it: "Piercing seems to happen freakishly. Like lightning it is rare, severe, and unprincipled".
>
> The main body of national law governing corporations is domestic corporate law and securities regulation, plus whatever civil and criminal provisions in other areas of substantive law and regulations may be applicable to corporations. But domestic law is only able to reach beyond its national borders in limited circumstances ... . However this plays out, as a general rule, unilateral extraterritorial jurisdiction is typically also contested and resented by the other states into whose jurisdiction it reaches.[47]

This leads Ruggie to conclude this section of his analysis with the following two paragraphs:

> Finally, the multinational enterprise barely exists under international law; indeed, some scholars have gone so far as to describe it as "invisible".... For its part, international human rights and humanitarian law generally applies to states, and the latter has been expanded to include natural persons accused of war crimes and certain crimes against humanity .... International human rights law may "contemplate" multinational corporations ... and in some instances even "specify" appropriate conduct, as ILO labor conventions, for example, clearly do. But it imposes the correlative duties on states, not on companies directly. States then have to ratify the relevant instrument, enact it within their individual jurisdictions, and enforce it as a matter of domestic law. States face considerable collective action problems, however, being economic actors themselves,

47 Ruggie (n 24) 320.

whether in promoting or attracting foreign investment, which goes a long way toward explaining the relative weakness of public international law in this domain.

Thus, Larry Catá Backer concludes, in a masterful understatement: "from a public law perspective, the framework for the regulation of multinational enterprises can be viewed most charitably as in flux" … . The fact that public law (national and international) does not generally encompass the economic unity of the multinational firm is the single most important contextual factor shaping its power, authority, and relative autonomy. Twenty-first century corporate globalization is built on foundational principles of corporate law that date back to the 19th century when they were intended to facilitate capital formation among natural persons: attributing legal personhood to corporations, investors' limited liability, and permitting one corporation to own another while still construing them to be separate legal entities.[48]

2.1 *Multinationals and Power*

Insofar as power is concerned, Ruggie understands the concept as did Dahl—'[i]n political science', writes Ruggies, 'power is not treated as a "thing:" it is inherently relational, typically defined as the ability of A to get B to do something that B otherwise would not do'.[49] With this definition in mind, Ruggie draws on a typology devised by Doris Fuchs in order to illustrate the extent of the political power wielded by multinationals.[50] In terms of Fuchs' typology, there is 'instrumental power', 'structural power' and 'discursive power'.[51] A brief discussion on each of these is warranted.

2.1.1 Instrumental Power

Essentially, according to Ruggie, 'instrumental power involves the employment of specific resources to achieve one's aims'.[52] He cites as examples 'political campaign contributions; the asymmetry in knowledge and privileged access to decision-making that business may have, particularly where standards are set by private bodies or "clubs" of state representatives …; and lobbying'.[53] As

48 Ruggie (n 24) 320–1.

49 Ruggie (n 24) 321 relying on Robert Dahl, 'The Concept of Power' (1956) 2 *Behavioral Science* 201.

50 Ruggie (n 24) 321.

51 Ruggie (n 24) 321 relying on Doris Fuchs, *Business Power in Global Governance* (Lynn Rienner, Boulder, CO 2007).

52 Ruggie (n 24) 321.

53 Ruggie (n 24) 321. Reference omitted.

'its evolution closely tracks corporate globalization itself', Ruggie in his article focuses on lobbying.[54] Specifically, Ruggie makes three important points about lobbying: '[t]he first two may be peculiarly prevalent in the US, but they may also involve foreign corporations listed in the US as well as having other international spillover effects'.[55] The third, however, 'is a direct result of corporate globalization everywhere'.[56]

The first point Ruggie makes about corporate lobbying goes to the 'sheer magnitude' of the act, both directly and indirectly.[57] Briefly put, corporate lobbying is ubiquitous and the size of spending on it is gigantic in both absolute terms as well as in relation to spending on other types of lobbying.[58]

Ruggie's second point is that significant asymmetries exist in respect of 'whose views get heard in the policy process, and who wins in court when regulators are challenged'.[59] In short, 'economic elites and organized groups representing business interests have substantial independent impacts on U.S. government policy' whereas the median voter has 'only a miniscule, near-zero, statistically non-significant impact upon public policy'.[60] The same is largely true in Europe.[61]

Ruggie also sees litigation as essentially having become 'an extension of lobbying' and points out that law firms are 'of course … involved in both'. As Ruggie explains, multinationals and other large business interests are capable of following a particular path: the interest can '[l]ose in Congress when legislation is written, then pressure the agency drafting the regulations, and finally, sue the regulator for issuing regulations that are depicted as being too "intrusive," too "costly," or violate some constitutional right that the same Supreme Court has attributed to corporations as legal persons', with this process also being capable of having 'significant international consequences'.[62]

Ruggie's third and final point about the instrumental power of multinationals is perhaps the most important for current purposes: '[t]he most direct change in corporate lobbying that globalization has brought about', he writes, 'is, of course, to expand its locus to the international level'.[63] He subsequently

54 Ruggie (n 24) 321.
55 Ruggie (n 24) 321.
56 Ruggie (n 24) 321.
57 Ruggie (n 24) 321–2.
58 See further Ruggie (n 24) 321–2.
59 Ruggie (n 24) 322.
60 Ruggie (n 24) 322.
61 Ruggie (n 24) 322.
62 Ruggie (n 24) 322.
63 Ruggie (n 24) 322.

describes a number of examples of international institutions, such as the European Union, the World Trade Organization and the World Health Organization, that have become embroiled in what have become focused international lobbying efforts on the part of multinationals, often through enlisting the services of other multinationals—usually consultancies—to do the actual lobbying.[64]

2.1.2 Structural Power

'In general terms', Ruggie continues, 'structural power refers to the ability of "business" or a specific business entity to affect outcomes in its [favour] without having to exercise instrumental power to achieve it'.[65] For Ruggie, '[m]ultinationals enjoy a number of intrinsic sources of structural power'.[66] Above all, Ruggie points out, 'states are territorially fixed entities competing for investments while multinationals typically have locational options, in some measure even in the extractive sectors'.[67] Additionally, 'the juridification of private international commercial relations has expanded immensely through the so-called new lex mercatoria or merchant law, which has the effect of "delocalizing" not only commercial transactions but also related [law-making] and enforceable dispute settlement.[68]

Ruggie's non-exhaustive list of examples of multinationals' structural power includes 'the right of foreign investors to sue governments under binding international arbitration, included in BITs and investment chapters of free trade agreements' and consequent 'regulatory chill impact';[69] 'transfer pricing through related-party trade';[70] 'the existence of tax havens';[71] and, finally, 'how little is known about trade flows at the firm level, and what impact this may have on official trade policy'.[72]

2.1.3 Discursive Power

Discursive power 'refers to the ability by business and business associations to frame and define public interest issues in their [favour]—that is, to shape ideas that then come to be taken for granted as the way things should be done,

64 See further Ruggie (n 24) 322.
65 Ruggie (n 24) 323 and the sources cited there.
66 Ruggie (n 24) 323.
67 Ruggie (n 24) 323.
68 Ruggie (n 24) 323. References omitted.
69 See further Ruggie (n 24) 323–4 and the sources cited there.
70 See further Ruggie (n 24) 324 and the sources cited there.
71 See further Ruggie (n 24) 324 and the sources cited there.
72 See Ruggie (n 24) 324–5 and the sources cited there.

even for non-business entities like governments'.[73] In other words, '[d]iscursive power is the ability to influence outcomes through promoting ideas, setting social norms and expectations, and even shaping identities'.[74] Moreover, '[i]ts exercise involves persuasion and emulation, not coercion'.[75] Examples of multinationals exercising their discursive power range from the conducting of focus groups and sponsoring TV advertisements, to the promotion of concepts, such as 'free markets' and 'limited government'.[76]

2.2 *Multinationals and Authority*

Ruggie concludes his discussion on corporate power by stating that 'the institution of the multinational has considerable transnational instrumental, structural, and discursive power' and acknowledges that 'the three are dynamically related'.[77] As Ruggie further points out, '[c]ontrary to early theorizations of these developments, however, this does not necessarily come at the expense of the territorial state as a political institution …; the two are too closely interwoven to support that argument'.[78] Therefore Ruggie turns to concept of authority because '[e]xamining multinationals' source and exercise of authority sheds further light on this relationship'.[79]

Ruggies starts off this conversation with the following passage:

> The boundary between power and authority is blurry. The key difference between them lies in the voluntary suspension of individual judgment based on a widely accepted and institutionalized belief that the authoritative entity is entitled or has the right to prescribe. Weber's (1978) classic categorization of the sources of authority differentiated between charismatic, traditional, and legal sources. He had the long-term evolution of domestic western society in mind. Leaving charisma aside, it seems clear that multinational enterprises today draw upon and embody a combination of traditional and legal authority. The "traditional" sources of multinationals' authority are the principles of private property rights and freedom of contract sacrosanct and codified in the liberal societies in which they first emerged as constitutional prerogatives of autonomous

---

73 Ruggie (n 24) 321.
74 Ruggie (n 24) 325.
75 Ruggie (n 24) 325.
76 See Ruggie (n 24) 325 and the sources cited there.
77 Ruggie (n 24) 326.
78 Ruggie (n 24) 326.
79 Ruggie (n 24) 326.

> natural persons. Today they form the foundational authoritative basis for the agglomeration of worldwide multinational enterprises … . Crucially, even states that lack political liberal institutions domestically, such as China, adhere to this transnational authority structure so as to be in a position to participate in and benefit from the global economic system. Core elements of this traditional source of authority are enshrined in, elaborated by, and enforced through public and private law, including obligations under the WTO and international investment agreements.[80]

He immediately adds some provisos, however:

> 'Let me not be misunderstood. The host state is the public authority in any particular country. It has the right to determine certain parameters of the operations of a multinational's local subsidiaries, affiliates, and contractual parties. Compliance with applicable laws is a formal requirement, although it is not always rigorously enforced or elements may be waived altogether, as in export processing zones. The state can require the multinational to take on local joint venture partners. It can require permits the company needs in order to operate. It negotiates the taxes and royalties the company must pay. It can refuse access to particular sites. Competition authorities can regulate mergers and acquisitions. A number of states have gone so far as to demand that multinationals share encryption keys of their communication systems with local authorities, or use Internet servers located in the host country.[81]

As Ruggie subsequently explains, however, 'this isn't the whole story of the relationship between the public authority of the state and the private authority of the multinational'.[82] He makes his point using the example of Disney:

> To take a specific example, Disney had to share the keys to the Magic Kingdom to seal its deal with the Chinese government for the new $5.5 billion Shanghai Disney Resort. According to a New York Times report …, Disney had to dial back on several demands, including a TV channel it was eager to have for cross-branding purposes, and it had to give the government a majority stake in the resort, as well as a minority share

80 Ruggie (n 24) 326–7.

81 Ruggie (n 24) 327.

82 Ruggie (n 24) 327.

> in the Disney management company that runs the property. Disney's CEO Robert A. Iger notably describes the arrangement as "authentically Disney and distinctly Chinese." For good measure, when Disney's blockbuster musical "The Lion King" opened at the resort, it included a new character, the Monkey King. This is a figure of Chinese legend recently popularized in a Hong Kong fantasy film, but based on a classic 16th century novel by Wu Cheng'en entitled Journey to the West. The Chinese government, in turn, committed to providing Disney special protection from intellectual property piracy, which remains common in China.
>
> These examples illustrate the obvious point that states possess authority in their dealings with multinationals. Specific outcomes will vary depending on the balance of interests and power; not every country is China, and not every company Disney. But they also illustrate a fundamental institutional fact: a dynamic interplay between two different centers of power, each with its own basis of authority. One is transnational and rests on private property rights, and the other is territorial and rests on sovereignty. The power of each in some measure is constrained by the authority of the other. Neither supplants the other. They coexist: "authentically Disney and distinctly Chinese."[83]

This accurately captures how multinational authority works in certain instances and highlights the point that states are not powerless in a world of powerful multinationals. Importantly, however, it also makes very clear that in order for to states to successfully pursue their interests vis-à-vis multinationals requires states to have the requisite authority to offset that of multinationals. It is also worth appreciating that this is just one of many parts of the equation: that the *reach* of states is limited by respect for the principle of sovereign equality should also be borne in mind; as should it that multinationals tend to wield a more cohesive type of authority than states and, as discussed in the next section, that they possess relative autonomy, whereas as states do not.

Ruggie describes these ideas well:

> Multinationals have authority over themselves. This is not as trite as it may sound when we consider the number of multinationals in the world today; the number of countries in which many operate; the range of activities they encompass; the already vast and still expanding private

83 Ruggie (n 24) 327.

transnational legal order they have generated; and their capacity to affect workplace conditions, the welfare of communities, and even national economic prospects around the world. The difference between the multinational as a single economic organization and the group of separate entities recognized under the law is critical to understanding the scope of multinationals' authority over "themselves."

The economic organization, acting through one legal "self" (often called the corporate "parent"), has the authority to create and structure the other legal "selves" (which of course are integral parts of the single economic organization) in such a way as to optimize the entire group's interests throughout its transnational sphere of operation, as well as to limit its liabilities. The economic organization sets the strategic objectives for the entire enterprise. It decides where and how to allocate its assets, which is based not only on such factors as market size, labor costs, or promising natural resource deposits, but also on selecting or constructing favorable regulatory environments through the global market for legal norms. For some purposes, this now includes the possibility of combining the most favorable regulations of different countries within ... a single contract. ... The economic organization sets terms of employment. It sets product and performance standards. It institutes codes of conduct. In doing so, multinationals have authority that states lack. For example, through their codes of conduct they can require suppliers in host states to adhere to social and environmental standards that, if imposed by the country importing those products, the host state could challenge as a non-tariff barrier under the WTO. The ability of multinationals to enforce such "internal" decisions across countries is the envy of states and intergovernmental organizations.

The authority of multinationals is not limited to their subsidiaries and affiliates. It also extends to contractors, franchisees, and other types of non-equity counterparties. In some industries, such as consumer electronics, toys, and ready-made garments, suppliers (and their subcontractors) may serve multiple multinationals simultaneously, and thus are subject to multiple and sometimes conflicting corporate authorities. Thus, workers in the same factory can be subject to different labor standards, for example, while each may differ from poorly enforced local labor laws, if they exist at all. ...

The vast web of non-equity relationships in global production networks are structured through the private law of contracts and are subject to private international commercial arbitration. Through its International Court of Arbitration, the Paris-based International Chamber of Commerce hosts the world's leading facility. This has transformed business lawyers and arbitration centers into institutionalized global "governors."

In sum, saying that multinationals have authority over themselves is actually saying a lot. Their authority is clearest and most direct when it is administered internally within the corporate group. From there it radiates outward across networks and down supply chains via the private law of contracts. The ultimate boundaries of multinationals' authority, therefore, are difficult to discern, not unlike the gradual frontier zones in early modern Europe before clear national boundaries were fixed. ...[84]

2.3 *The 'Relative Autonomy' of Multinationals*

A final and crucial point Ruggie draws our attention to is at whose behest multinationals exercise their authority.[85] 'Common sense suggests that it must be their owners', writes Ruggie, continuing to note that some multinationals are family owned or privately held, with a number of them also being state owned.[86] But the bulk of multinationals entail some form of public traded companies about whom it has often been said—and this is a view frequently expressed by corporate lawyers—that they are owned by their *shareholders*.[87] But as Ruggie most eloquently notes, 'there are two problems with this premise in today's world':[88]

> First, many investors move into and out of individual stocks of large corporations several times a day or hold them very short periods of time—sometimes mere seconds—using a variety of trading algorithms and automated means to make a quick return. Hedge funds are the single largest trader in US equity markets. ... Five of the world's most heavily traded equity securities are exchange-traded funds. ... These and other such investors are not "owners" in any traditional sense of the term; they have no per se interest in the corporations whose shares they are trading. They are speculators and arbitrageurs, daytraders, flashtraders, or indexers who buy the whole market or some slice of it without "valuing" the price of any one stock as a normal owner would want to do.
>
> The second problem runs deeper. Legal scholars in particular have long struggled with the question of share-holder ownership of the public

84 Ruggie (n 24) 327–8. References omitted.
85 Ruggie (n 24) 328.
86 Ruggie (n 24) 328.
87 Ruggie (n 24) 328.
88 Ruggie (n 24) 328.

corporation and what exactly it means. … From a very different analytical point of view, economics Nobel laureate Eugene Farma stated long ago: "ownership of capital should not be confused with ownership of the firm". … However, Friedman's … property conception of the firm, coupled with principal—agent theory, … and the shareholder primacy norm … dominated theory, and to some extent, US practice, for the past generation. It now seems to be on the wane. … Robé, for one, rejects the idea that anyone owns the large public corporation: After the process of incorporation, shareholders have no right of access to the assets of the corporation; they do not enter into any contract in its name. No liability can arise for them from the corporate activity. They do not run the corporation and do not own it."

And unless a shareholder has a controlling interest, shareholders' rights are limited: "a right to dividends; and the right to participate in shareholder assemblies and vote on rare decisions … But owning shares does not give title to the corporation or to a portion of the corporation". … Even the right to dividends, should the enterprise generate a profit, is subject to the discretion of directors, acting in the corporation's interest. All of this is true of national firms, not only multinationals. The difference, of course, is that multinationals exercise the power and authority they have transnationally, in a global system that lacks a central regulator, and in some cases across more than 200 national jurisdictions.

Clearly, directors and management of a publicly traded firm need to keep investors sufficiently happy to avoid having them sell off their shares, causing a drop in the company's market value (and in executive compensation). The owners of shares thereby constitute a market force that constrains directors' and management decisions. Moreover, holders of large blocks of shares, such as institutional investors, can exercise influence through board elections and more informal means. But neither of these situations makes them owners of the firm.

Thus, there appear to be two possible answers to the question of who owns publicly traded firms: they own themselves, or no one does—and in effect they amount to the same thing. There appears to be only one answer to the question on whose behalf multinationals exercise their authority: their own. In sum, the institution of the multinational has come to constitute not only a significant center of global power but with the exception of state-owned enterprises, also a relatively autonomous transnational authority structure.[89]

---

89 Ruggie (n 24) 328–9. References omitted.

This part has relied heavily on John Ruggie's work and on his words. It has done so because I do not have better words to describe the multinational than does John Ruggie and those authors—particularly Jean-Philippe Robé—that he relies on. Save for critiquing some of Ruggie's phrasing and adding references to other sources that provide greater detail on certain points, I cannot really take the debate on what the multinational *is* much further. The predominant point of this part, however, has been to lay the groundwork for the next part, where, using Ruggie's words for describing the multinational, I hope to illustrate a point that is, perhaps for good reason, not often enough made well: that is, that the multinational as institutional actor in a world as economically globalized as our contemporary world is *the* influential actor among many actors when it comes to the manner in which income and wealth are distributed around the world.

3 The Multinational as the Most Direct Institutional Actor: The Example of Changing Distributions of Income and Wealth within States

Pinning down *the* exact cause of economic inequality is a bit of a silly exercise. Economic distributions are affected by such a large array of factors that one should be somewhat sceptical of statements such as 'technology is *the* reason for rising economic inequality' or 'economic globalization is *the* cause of increased levels of income inequality'. The truth of the matter is that the distribution of income and wealth is far more complex than most of us like to think. Actual distributions of income and wealth are affected by a very wide range of factors and it is worth acknowledging that much at the outset of this discussion.

What also cannot be denied, however, is that, as far as *actors* on the global stage go, multinationals are *the* key actor when looking at how income and wealth is distributed both within and among nations. The typical reasons given for increasing economic inequality tend to be related to technological progress,[90]

90 See, for example, Andrew McAfee and Erik Brynjolfsson, *The Second Machine Age: Work, Progress, and Prosperity in a Time of Brilliant Technologies* (WW Norton, New York 2016). See also Anton Korinek and Joseph E Stiglitz, 'Artificial Intelligence and Its Implications for Income Distribution and Unemployment' (NBER Working Paper 24174, December 2017) <https://www.nber.org/papers/w24174> accessed 30 September 2021.

globalization,[91] unionization,[92] minimum wages and other employment practices,[93] taxation of various kinds,[94] and corporate concentration.[95] Multinationals are single-handedly the most important and most direct actor in each and every one of these fields.

There are essentially two sets of actions that explain how this works: actions taken by multinationals that have an effect within firms and actions taken by multinationals that have an effect among firms. In other words, either an action affects the manner in which income is distributed *among* firms in a 'national' economy or it affects how income is distributed *within* firms in that economy. As a result, this part of the chapter explores a number of factors that contribute to changing economic distributions in three parts. First, it examines how multinationals contribute to within-firm inequality (*Section 3.1*). It then turns to the issue of between-firm inequality and the various ways in which multinationals contribute to its exacerbation (*Section 3.2*). Finally, it briefly illustrates how the within- and between-firm components interact with one another (*Section 3.3*).

3.1 *Multinationals and within-firm Economic Inequality*

Explaining the first way in which a particular firm alters the distribution of economic inequality within that firm is simple: it has employees (loosely speaking) and it pays those employees. For example, if ABC Limited has ten employees,

---

91 See Martin Ravallion, 'Inequality and Globalization: A Review Essay' (2018) 56 *Journal of Economic Literature* 620 for a review of some of the arguments made in this regard.

92 See, for example, Economic Policy Institute, 'Union Decline and Rising Inequality in Two Charts' (Working Economics Blog) <https://www.epi.org/blog/union-decline-rising-inequality-charts/> accessed 30 September 2021.

93 See, for example, Oren M Levin-Waldman and Paul Lerman, 'Is the Minimum Wage an Effective Response to Income Inequality?' (2017) 60 *Challenge* 574.

94 See, for example, Thomas Tørsløv, Ludvig Wier and Gabriel Zucman, 'The Missing Profits of Nations' (NBER Working Paper 24701, 5 June 2018) <http://gabriel-zucman.eu/files/TWZ2018.pdf> accessed 30 September 2021.

95 See Anthony B Atkinson, *Inequality: What Can Be Done?* (HUP, London 2015) 123–7; Sean Ennis, Pedro Gonzaga and Chris Pike, 'Inequality: A Hidden Cost of Market Power' (OECD Discussion Paper 2017) <https://www.oecd.org/daf/competition/Inequality-hidden-cost-market-power-2017.pdf > accessed 30 September 2021; Jason Furman and Peter Orszag, 'A Firm-Level Perspective on the Role of Rents in the Rise in Inequality' (Presentation at 'A Just Society' Centennial Event in Honor of Joseph Stiglitz, 2016) <https://obamawhitehouse.archives.gov/sites/default/files/page/files/20151016_firm_level_perspective_on_role_of_rents_in_inequality.pdf> accessed 30 September 2021; and Joseph Stiglitz, *The Price of Inequality: How Today's Divided Society Endangers Our Future* (WW Norton, New York 2012) 28–51.

the amount it pays its highest earner as a percentage of all salaries will be equivalent to the T10 among its employees. So if ABC Limited spends a total of 1000 widgets paying its ten employees in a given year and pays one person 600 of those widgets, that person will constitute the T10 of earning among the employees in question. The T10 figure will be 60 percent because that one person, X, earns 60 percent of the salary bill. The B90 will thus be 40 percent. If in the next year ABC Limited spends 1500 widgets paying the salary bill for the same ten workers and pays X 750 widgets, now the T10 will be 50 percent because X is now earning 50 percent of the total salary bill. The B90 accordingly rises to 50 percent.

Within-firm distributions are also affected by how the firm apportions its profits and losses between employees (again, in a loose sense) and shareholders. We now have two variables in our ABC Limited model. One can imagine a scenario where ABC makes 2000 widgets in profit in a given year. It might have a policy that says 'pay all widgets made in profit above 1000 to shareholders'. Of the 2000, then, it would pay 1000 to its shareholders. If there are two equal shareholders, each would receive 500. If we assume that X, the CEO, also gets 500, then out of 12 people, 3 of them collectively receive 1500—75 percent—meaning that the remaining 9 employees are left with 500 or 25 percent. In other words, the T25 (top three out of 12 people) is 75 percent for that year and the B75 (the bottom nine of 12 people) is 25 percent.

This scenario also illustrates in a simple way how the within-firm distribution could be tied to performance. If ABC made 1000 widgets the following year, for example, because it performed badly in that year, then the shareholders would receive nothing in that year. This would see both shareholders fall to the bottom of the pile. It would also see X—let us assume she still makes the same salary—take home 50 percent of the total income—up from 25 percent in the previous year. It would also push the next two highest earning employees into the T25.

We should also not forget that the performance may directly affect wealth as well—through the increase or decrease of the price of ABC's shares. Room should also be left in this model for taxation and redistribution. If 25 percent of ABC's profits had to be paid to a revenue authority, then in the year that it made 2000 widgets in profits, 500 would go to that revenue authority. It could hypothetically redistribute the entire 500 to the B75—the nine lowest earning employees. This would decrease the shareholders' cut to 250 each, but leave X's cut unchanged at 500. The T25 would accordingly drop to 50 percent from 75 percent and the B75 would rise from 25 percent to 50 percent.

This simple model also allows one to think about how firms might respond to external circumstances. For example, would ABC change its distribution rule if X—due to taxation, or a minimum wage rule, or higher salaries for other employees negotiated through their union—makes less than a certain amount? Or would it perhaps change the distribution rule if the shareholders make less than a certain amount? The academic studies that have been undertaken on these types of issues tend to be rather complicated and often—perhaps understandably—get lost in econometric detail. It is always helpful to come back to a simple model in order to understand what *actually happens within individual firms*. The same applies to between-firm inequality.

This is important to remember when contemplating how the *multinational* fits into the picture, which has yet to be explained. First, multinationals are themselves firms and make the kinds of decisions describe in our simple model above. Multinationals tend to be large firms and account for a significant portion of global employment. They also account for a substantial majority of international trade and make up a large portion of the world's stock-markets. As a result, multinationals, through payments to their employees and shareholders, and through increases and decreases to their stock price, have a very significant impact on the distribution of income and wealth overall.

Multinationals, however, are also a global institution as Ruggie has shown us. This means that multinationals, as opposed to purely domestic firms, also have the power, the authority and the relative autonomy necessary to impact the rules that apply to them and other firms in the 'domestic' economy. They do this through lobbying. They do this through litigation. They do this through leveraging their relative autonomy. This is not to disparage the behaviour of multinationals; it is simply to suggest that they—as most rational actors probably would—tend to use their power in such a way as to further their own interests.

3.2 *Multinationals and between-firm Economic Inequality*

Multinationals also increase economic inequality between firms. The foremost way in which they do this is through leveraging their status as multinationals. Perhaps it is better to explain it as multinationals leveraging the fact that they are *not domestic firms*: multinationals can by definition achieve certain things that domestic firms cannot achieve simply because they are multinationals. This for example means that multinationals are able to pay less tax than their domestic competitors purely because they are multinationals. Multinationals also have access to multiple labour markets, putting them at a distinct competitive advantage vis-à-vis domestic firms. Amongst other things, they are also able to avoid a significant number of domestic regulations, they are more able to develop economies of scale, they have access to a greater number of customers, they are the recipients of a greater number of investment incentives, they are more capable of expanding the size of their operations (often in anti-competitive ways), they have more sway over regulators and policy-makers, and, because they tend to be larger than domestic firms, they are better positioned to afford the services of proficient lawyers and consultants and the advice that they provide as to the most profitable manner in which to structure their businesses.

All the above is important because the level of competition between multinationals and domestic firms has trended consistently downward over time. This accounts for a significant portion of increases in economic inequality because it means that between-firm inequality increases which, in turn, means that two people that have the same job title—one in a domestic firm and one in a multinational—get paid increasingly unequally over time. In essence, ABC Limited has a domestic competitor called XYZ (Pty) Limited. In year one, ABC pays its accounting officer 200 widgets; XYZ pays its accounting officer 100 widgets. In year two, ABC pays its accounting officer 220 widgets; XYZ pays its accounting officer 105 widgets. By year ten, if we apply the same wage increase every year, ABC pay its accounting officer 472 widgets and XYZ pays its accounting officer 155 widgets. In other words, in year one the ABC accounting officer was paid twice the XYZ accounting officer but by year ten the ABC accounting officer gets paid three times as much as his counterpart that does more or less the same job but at a larger scale.

Alternatively, the call centre operator at ABC gets paid 30 widgets per year and the call centre operator at XYZ gets paid 30 widgets per year. ABC subsequently outsources its call centre function to a low-wage jurisdiction and pays its new call centre operator 5 widgets. It also dismisses its original call centre operator and the difference of 25 widgets either goes to shareholders or to expanding operations or to increasing the accounting officer's pay. XYZ keeps paying its call centre operator 30 widgets per year for the next ten years in order to try and keep competing with ABC. ABC's former call centre operator is unemployed and subsequently gets a different job that pays less than 30 widgets per year.

Multinationals also compete with *other multinationals*. They compete for top managerial 'talent' and skilled employees and they compete to see who can achieve a lower wage bill. This means that those employees at the upper end of multinational distributions do a lot better and those at the lower end tend—due to technology, outsourcing and monopsonistic employment practices—to do worse over time. What multinationals do also spills over to what domestic firms do because domestic firms usually compete with multinationals. This means that the only way domestic firms can offset the inequality exacerbating effect of multinationals in this regard is by *both* competing with multinationals—a difficult task—*and* by reducing inequality within their own ranks. For obvious reasons this tends not to occur. It is also not normatively desirable, particularly given than the inequality between domestic firms and multinationals has been and is likely to continue increasing and because multinationals tend to exhibit greater within-firm inequality than domestic firms do.[96]

3.3 *The Inseparability of within-firm Inequality and between-firm Inequality*

What is often missed in analyses on this topic is the idea that it is difficult to fully separate out within-firm and between-firm inequality when it comes to multinationals. This is because the two phenomena interact to the point where are basically inseparable. For example, when it comes to high and disproportionately increasing executive pay it cannot really be said that this is a within-firm *phenomenon*. While it is true that the inequality increasing event—paying a CEO of a multinational significantly more than the average employee of that multinational and increasing the gap between the CEO and the average employee significantly over time—occurs *within* multinationals, it is also clear that it is increasing *between-firm* inequality that enables multinationals to pay their executives so much more. Similarly, multinationals are able to increase within-firm inequality as much as they do *because* they pay less taxes vis-à-vis the domestic firms they compete with. Increasing within-firm inequality by outsourcing or automating jobs also has the effect of increasing between-firm inequality. It thus does not serve this conversation well to think of the economic inequality-increasing effects of multinationals as separate categories—it all comes down to the manner in which multinationals operate and, as we will see in the next part of this chapter, the manner in which they are regulated. With this clarification having been made, one can more helpfully traverse the specifics of some of the main causes of multinational-led increases in economic inequality within states.

3.3.1 Technological-enabled Economic Globalization

As discussed in Chapter 3, the economic globalization that has been experienced in recent times is perhaps best described by Richard Baldwin as globalization's 'second unbundling'. In essence, this refers to the unbundling of production and the consequent rise of the GVC—that is, the rise of the

96 See Holger M Mueller, Paige P Ouimet and Elena Simintzi, 'Wage Inequality and Firm Growth' (2017) 107 *American Economic Review* 379.

multinational. As Baldwin points out, globalization's second unbundling was *enabled by* technology. Technological change is thus not entirely separable from the globalization it spawned. In a sense globalization is simply shorthand for *the kind of technological advances* that are often blamed for rising economic inequality. But it is also more than that: it includes the legal frameworks that allowed for deeper integration of markets.

Seen this way, economic globalization is both driven and enacted by the multinational. States also have a say in economic globalization through the laws that they enact within their own borders and among one another, but in contemporary times those laws tend to be *reactive*. The large web of 'private' contracts that underpin the multinational, as described by Ruggie, however, is constructed *proactively*. Multinationals are accordingly both the chief architects and primary implementers of economic globalization.

It can be rather frustrating to read that 'globalization is the cause of increasing inequality': globalization is a phenomenon, not an actor and its most significant actor is unquestionably the multinational. Thus when the evidence suggests, as it does, that 'economic globalization' has been a significant driver of increasing economic inequality within states, we should understand this to mean that *the behaviour of multinationals* (and, to a significantly lesser extent, the behaviour of states) has been a significant driver of increasing economic inequality.[97]

3.3.2 Technological Change *Per Se*

There is also a different kind of technological change that is not directly related to economic globalization. In essence, this kind of technological change is best described as an attempt to automate activities hitherto performed by humans. While automation today operates in a world that is significantly globalized, and can often be fuelled by globalization, economic globalization is conceptually distinct from automation. All the same, the main wielder of these types of technology is unquestionably the multinational. Multinationals invest gigantic amounts in research and development; they also channel state spending on research and development. More importantly, however, they are at the forefront of implementing new technologies. Even in instances where technology is not developed by a multinational that technology—if useful in one way or another—inevitably ends up being owned by a multinational and deployed by it.

97 This is not to suggest that multinational *deliberately seek* to increase economic inequality. More economic inequality within states, however, follows as a natural consequence of how multinationals have behaved.

This sort of technological change has also been shown to increase economic inequality within states and is slated to further exacerbate it in years to come.[98] As with globalization, 'technological change' is not self-perpetuating—there are actors that see to it that technological change occurs and there are actors that use technological advances, usually to their own advantage, in ways that increase economic inequality. The primary actor in this regard, again, is the multinational. An obvious example is Uber Technologies, an 'American' ride-hailing multinational. While it is undoubtedly true that the technology underlying Uber's products is ultimately what enabled the disruption of the ride-hailing sector, it was the *multinational* that decided to implement the technology in such a way that exacerbates inequality. It was the *multinational*, for example, that decided to treat its drivers as independent contractors. It was the *multinational* that opposed the unionization of its drivers. It is the *multinational* that is attempting to develop the autonomous vehicles that will eventually replace its drivers entirely.

3.3.3 Market Power: Product Market Concentration, Corporate Consolidation, Monopolies and Monopsonies

Zia Qureshi summarises the 'product market concentration, corporate consolidation, monopolies and monopsonies' case for increase economic inequality well:

> Increased concentration of market power shifted income away from labor. Dominant firms not only acquired more monopoly power in product markets to increase markups and extract higher rents, but they also acquired more monopsony power to dictate wages in the labor market. As the labor income share was squeezed, the share of "pure profits" or rents—profits in excess of competitive market conditions—soared. It is estimated that such profits in the U.S. rose from three percent of national income in 1985 to 17 percent in 2015.
>
> Higher rents and rise in financial wealth increased income inequality as the beneficiaries of these gains belonged disproportionately to upper income groups. These developments reinforced the distributional effects of technological change and globalization favoring capital and higher level skills.[99]

98 See, for example, Korinek and Stiglitz (n 90).

99 See Zia Qureshi, 'Today's Economic Puzzles: A Tale of Weakening Competition' (Brookings Institute, April 2018) <https://www.brookings.edu/blog/up-front/2018/04/05/todays-economic-puzzles-a-tale-of-weakening-competition/> relying on Gauti B Eggertsson, Jacob A Robbins and Ella Getz Wold, 'Kaldor and Piketty's Facts: The Rise of Monopoly

The main culprit in this story, unsurprisingly, is the multinational.[100] Product market concentration is seen as having increased significantly in a majority of markets around the world. This is sometimes looked at in terms of the largest three or four firms. For example, in a 2016 *The Economist* article, the magazine team pointed out that:

> [D]ata make it possible to distinguish between sectors of the economy that are fragmented, concentrated or oligopolistic, and to look at how revenues have fared in each case. Revenues in fragmented industries—those in which the biggest four firms together control less than a third of the market—dropped from 72% of the total in 1997 to 58% in 2012. Concentrated industries, in which the top four firms control between a third and two-thirds of the market, have seen their share of revenues rise from 24% to 33%. And just under a tenth of the activity takes place in industries in which the top four firms control two-thirds or more of sales. This oligopolistic corner of the economy includes niche concerns—dog food, batteries and coffins—but also telecoms, pharmacies and credit cards.[101]

The concentrated and oligopolistic sectors in particular are dominated by large multinationals. It should also be clear by now that they dominate in significant part *because* they are multinationals. In 1985, *cross-border* mergers and acquisitions (M&A) accounted for approximately 10 percent of total M&A spend globally.[102] Over the last decade or so, that number has been between 30 percent and 50 percent.[103] Not only has foreign direct investment (FDI) increased significantly since the start of globalization's second unbundling,

---

Power in the United States' (NBER Working Paper, No 24287, February 2018) <https://www.nber.org/papers/w24287.pdf> accessed 30 September 2021 and Mordecai Kurz, 'On the Formation of Capital and Wealth: IT, Monopoly Power and Rising Inequality' (25 June 2017) <https://papers.ssrn.com/sol3/papers.cfm?abstract_id=3014361> accessed 30 September 2021.

100 It is of course true that states *could* have done more to prevent some of these trends, but the failure of state intervention does not change the fact that it was multinationals that made the decisions that would lead to these trends and implemented them.

101 *The Economist*, 'Business in America: Too Much of a Good Thing' (26 March 2016) <https://www.economist.com/briefing/2016/03/26/too-much-of-a-good-thing> accessed 30 September 2021.

102 Milan Babic, Jan Fichtner and Eelke M Heemskerk, 'States versus Corporations: Rethinking the Power of Business in International Politics' (2017) 52 *International Spectator* 20, 25.

103 Babic, Fichtner and Heemskerk (n 102) 25.

an increasing share of the FDI goes toward cross-border consolidation. This is indicative of markets becoming more globalized over time and, as already pointed out above, multinationals are right at the centre of this process. The ever-increasing list of studies that illustrate the impact of market power on the distribution of income and wealth should therefore all be read with the idea of the multinational as central actor in mind.

3.3.4 Executive Compensation

Putting aside the normative questions, it should be remain clear that the multinational is responsible for the explosion in executive compensation that has been observed since the 1980s. In 1978, the CEO-to-worker compensation ratio for the largest 350 firms in the United States was approximately 30.[104] Since 2000, the same ratio has consistently been in excess of 200 and has been as high as 343.5.[105] Moreover, they are also responsible for the even greater explosion of salaries at the very top of the income scale in particular. In the later 1970s and during the 1980s, CEOs of the top 350 American firms made lots of money in relative terms. In fact, the average salary was between two and three times as high as that of *other* T0.1 salary recipients.[106] Since the early 1990s, however, this has increased to between four and *eight* times as high as that of other T0.1 salary recipients.[107]

This is not where things stop either. Multinationals also use their discursive power to set the tone for the rest of our economies. As Dean Baker, Josh Bivens and Jessica Schieder explain:

> The high pay of CEOs in corporate America also affects pay structures elsewhere in the economy. It is common for top executives at universities, foundations, and private charities to receive pay in the range of $1 million a year, and in some cases two or three times this amount. ... The rationale is that a person running a corporation the size of Harvard University or the American Red Cross could easily be making $10 or $15 million a year if they opted for a managerial job in the corporate sector. With the pay

104 Dean Baker, Josh Bivens and Jessica Schieder, 'Reining in CEO Compensation and Curbing the Rise of Inequality' (Economic Policy Institute Report, Washington DC, 4 June 2019) <https://www.epi.org/files/pdf/168855.pdf> accessed 30 September 2021.

105 Baker, Bivens and Schieder (n 104) 5.

106 Baker, Bivens and Schieder (n 104) 5.

107 Baker, Bivens and Schieder (n 104) 6.

> of corporate CEOs as a reference point, working for $1 million a year can even seem like a sacrifice.
>
> As in the corporate sector, the high pay for a CEO at a nonprofit also affects the pay of other top officers. If a university president is getting over $1 million a year, then the provost and deans of major schools might be earning somewhere close to $1 million each. The high pay for those at the top comes to some extent at the expense of pay for those at the middle and bottom of the wage ladder.
>
> High pay in the corporate sector also affects pay in government. While wages at the top of the government pay ladder are usually held down by statute, people are often hired on contracts by which their effective pay may be many times higher than the pay of top government employees.
>
> In addition, the much higher pay available in the corporate sector is a huge factor in the problem of "revolving door" officials, who spend a few years in a regulatory position and then go to work for the industry they were regulating; this pattern can lead to conflicts of interest—resulting in degradation of regulatory enforcement and increased potential for corruption—as regulators may be (consciously or unconsciously) courting future employers even as they are regulating them. This route is much more attractive to government workers in a context in which private-sector employment can pay millions of dollars a year while public-sector pay tops off at around $200,000. The story would be quite different if high-level public officials could only expect to earn twice or perhaps three times their pay in the corporate sector, as opposed to 10 times or more.[108]

None of this would occur in the absence of multinationals operating the way they have been doing and continue to do. This is a conclusion that can be reached without reference to preferences over how much executives and CEOs *should* be paid and how much these amounts should grow with time vis-à-vis other occupations.

3.3.5 Taxes

Finally, and most importantly for the purposes of this monograph, multinationals avoid paying taxes. This much is beyond doubt. This issue is addressed in detail below in this chapter.

---

108 Baker, Bivens and Schieder (n 104) 6–7. Footnote omitted.

4 Parsing State Responsibility in Respect of a Distributional Common Concern into Multinational Action

This part of the chapter begins with a broad question: that is, given that states remain the primary actors and take on the bulk of the responsibilities under international law, both in general and in respect of recognised common concerns of humankind, how are such responsibilities translated into actions on the part of multinationals in a world where multinationals are the ones carrying out more than a majority of the tasks that contribute to the problem in respect of which the states took on the responsibilities? This part subsequently deals with the more specific question of how it could be that state commitments to recognising a distributional common concern of humankind could be parsed into helpful behaviour on the part of multinationals in solving the problems at the core of the concern. There are essentially two routes states can take in parsing responsibility in this regard, each of which is discussed in this part: they could act in such a way that alters the multinational and the corporate form itself (*Section 4.1*) or they could accept that multinationals are what they are and attempt to regulate them using areas of law other than corporate law (*Section 4.2*).

4.1 *To Change or Not to Change the Multinational and Corporations? Framing the Purpose of Corporate Law and Corporations*

Armour and his colleagues begin a discussion on this topic as follows:

> What is the goal of corporate law, as distinct from its immediate functions of defining a form of enterprise and containing the conflicts among the participants in this enterprise? As a normative matter, the overall objective of corporate law—as of any branch of law—is presumably to serve the interests of society as a whole. More particularly, the appropriate goal of corporate law is to advance the aggregate welfare of all who are affected by a firm's activities, including the firm's shareholders, employees, suppliers, and customers, as well as third parties such as local communities and beneficiaries of the natural environment. This is what economists would characterize as the pursuit of overall social welfare. ... We speak here of maximizing the "aggregate welfare" of society more as a loose metaphor than a precise yardstick. There is no coherent way to put a number on society's aggregate welfare, much less to maximize that number—and particularly so when many benefits are in appreciable part nonpecuniary. What we are suggesting here might be put more

> precisely in the language of welfare economics as pursuing Kaldor-Hicks efficiency within acceptable patterns of distribution.[109]

The authors thereafter proceed to point out, however, that '[a]t least in theory, … the pursuit of overall social welfare may be compatible with different *immediate goals* for corporate law'.[110] What this statement reflects is the conceptual distinction between the goal(s) of corporate law and the manner in which that goal is pursued. The overall goal and the immediate goals are therefore different but strongly interrelated concepts. The distinction is important in this context because the overall goals and the immediate goals of corporate law must necessarily be the prerogative of a given sovereign. Through the laws of a state, the corporate form is made available in order to promote and fulfil the immediate goals of corporate law such that overall goals can in turn be fulfilled.

Using Armour and his colleagues' understanding, the overall aim of corporate law would be seen as advancing aggregate societal welfare. This would presumably mean that corporate law should aim to assist a society in getting closer to Kaldor-Hicks efficiency within 'acceptable patterns of distribution'.[111] In order for the immediate goals of corporate law to be set, then, one would assume that Kaldor-Hicks efficiency would first have to be defined; as would the 'acceptable patterns of distribution'. Thereafter, the immediate goals of corporate law could be determined.

Armour and his colleagues acknowledge that the immediate goal of corporate law—that is, the best way in which to pursue the overall goal of corporate law—can be thought of in a number of ways. For example, the immediate goal of corporate law may simply be to reduce the costs of contracting among the corporation's contractual constituencies.[112] It may be even more narrowly defined as the idea that 'the corporation serves the best interests of its shareholders or, more specifically, to maximize financial returns to shareholders or, more specifically still, to maximize the current market price of corporate shares'.[113]

Regardless of the view one takes on the overall and immediate goals of corporate law, it should be clear that the concept of 'corporate responsibility' cannot properly be given meaning without appropriate reference being made to

109 Armour et al (n 17) 22–3.

110 Armour et al (n 17) 23. Emphasis added.

111 It is fairly clear that Armour and his colleagues are not of the view that the aim of corporate law is to *achieve* Kaldor-Hicks efficiency on its own. See Armour et al (n 17) 23–4.

112 Armour et al (n 17) 23.

113 Armour et al (n 17) 23.

both these types of goals. The phrase 'corporate responsibility' often appears to be conflated with the more frequently used 'corporate social responsibility'. One might look to online search forms for proof of this proposition. Searching for the phrase 'corporate responsibility', or even the more specific ' "corporate responsibility" ', tends to yield results that pertain to items associated—usually very specifically—with what has come to be known, in a very broad or general sense, as 'corporate social responsibility'. One of the aims of this part of the chapter is to suggest that it is necessary to have a more descriptive as opposed to normative discussion about corporate responsibility. After all, as Dow Votaw pointed out as long ago as 1973:

> One … social issue bears the label "corporate social responsibility" or just "social responsibility." The term is a brilliant one; it means something, but not always the same thing, to everybody. To some it conveys the idea of legal responsibility or ability; to others, it means socially responsible [behaviour] in an ethical sense; to still others, the meaning transmitted is that of 'responsible for', in a causal mode; many simply equate it with a charitable contribution; some take it to mean socially conscious; many of those who embrace it most fervently see it as a mere synonym for 'legitimacy', in the context of 'belonging' or being proper or valid; a few see it as a sort of fiduciary duty imposing higher standards of [behaviour] on businessmen than on citizens at large. Even the antonyms, socially 'irresponsible' and 'non-responsible', are subject to multiple interpretations.
>
> Whatever the interpretation, and this brief list by no means exhausts the possibilities, the term has received much attention during the last few years. Corporation presidents and chairmen of the board rarely make public statements without giving it prominence. The editors of Fortune and other business periodicals devote whole issues to it. Politicians are enchanted by its broad appeal. Every oil spill and smog alert brings it to the front page of the daily newspaper. It has become the title of college courses and purports to be a proper subject for scholarly research. Pages written about social responsibility would fill a small library. With few exceptions, however, these pages contain little that might truly be described as analysis of this now ubiquitous social phenomenon or of its implications. Peter Drucker wrote recently in this connection: "The time for sensations and manifestos is about over; now we need rigorous analysis, united effort, and very hard work."[114]

---

114 Dow Votaw, 'Genius Becomes Rare: A Comment on the Doctrine of Social Responsibility Pt. 1' (1972) 15 *California Management Review* 25, 25.

Some of this work has been done over the subsequent decades, but the truth of the matter is that the phrase 'corporate social responsibility' still suffers from the exact same defect. While it has grown significantly as a field and has definitely had an impact on how corporations and multinationals are governed, corporate social responsibility remains a very blunt and ineffective instrument insofar as achieving deliberate goals are concerned. The view taken here, therefore, is that in respect of parsing state into multinational action generally, and specifically in respect of common concerns of humankind, corporate social responsibility is an inappropriate frame. At best, corporate social responsibility as presently conceived of by most means that it only successfully achieves goals that are inherently or have become compatible with the autonomously set goals of multinationals.

In light of this view, this chapter refers simply to 'corporate responsibility', that is as something distinct from 'corporate social responsibility' as presently conceived of by scholars and practitioners. 'Corporate responsibility' refers to the responsibility *imposed* on corporations, either through *corporate law proper* or through other laws that aim to *regulate* the behaviour of corporations. Either way, corporate responsibility is *imposed*. For example, Armour and his colleagues claim as follows:

> It is sometimes said that the goals of core corporate law should be even narrower. In particular, it is sometimes said that the appropriate role of corporate law is simply to assure that the corporation serves the best interests of its shareholders or, more specifically, to maximize financial returns to shareholders or, more specifically still, to maximize the current market price of corporate shares. Such claims can be viewed in two ways.
>
> First, these claims can be taken at face value, in which case they neither describe corporate law as we observe it nor offer a normatively appealing aspiration for that body of law. There would be little to recommend a body of law that, for example, permits corporate shareholders to enrich themselves through transactions that make creditors or employees worse off by \$2 for every \$1 that the shareholders gain.
>
> Second, such claims can be understood as saying, more modestly, that focusing principally on the maximization of shareholder returns is, in general, the best means by which corporate law can serve the broader goal of advancing overall social welfare. In general, creditors, workers, and customers will consent to deal with a corporation only if they expect themselves to be better off as a result. Consequently, the corporation—and, in particular, its shareholders, as the firm's residual claimants and risk-bearers—have a direct pecuniary interest in making sure that

> corporate transactions are beneficial, not just to the shareholders, but to all parties who deal with the firm. We believe that this second view is—and surely ought to be—the appropriate interpretation of statements by legal scholars and economists asserting that shareholder value is the proper object of corporate law.[115]

If we accept this to be true, corporate responsibility as conceived of in this monograph would be limited to increasing shareholder value. This would still leave much room for debate about what precisely corporations would be responsible for because different shareholders value different things. More importantly, whether the enforcement of corporate responsibility amounted to something good would depend largely on whom the shareholders of corporations would be and what constitutes 'value' for those shareholders. In essence, therefore, in the context of economic distributions, corporate responsibility would be defined by the creation of value for shareholders. Since the 1980s the wealth T10 in economies such as the United States, which as shown in Chapter 2 overlaps significantly with the income T10, have consistently owned in excess of 80 percent of total stock market wealth.[116] Corporate responsibility constituted this way, even if enforced, would thus be unable to meaningfully contribute to the reduction of economic inequality unless the T10 class acted incredibly altruistically and against their own economic interests.

The alternative from a corporate law perspective would be to impose a different kind of corporate responsibility by making one simple but incredibly significant change to corporate law: changing how it conceives of the corporate form. There would be obvious difficulties with taking such an approach. First, in order for any changes of this sort to be effective, there would have to be significant coordination among states. Multinationals would not only be able to resist any coordination efforts, they would also autonomously be able to reconstitute themselves in order to avoid the application of such changes. The view taken here is that it is currently improbable that states will significantly change their corporate laws. Coordination among states of this sort would be even less likely. For present purposes, then, it will be assumed that the corporate form will for the foreseeable future remain more or less unchanged. It is in any event preferable to impose corporate responsibility through regulation external to corporate law.

---

115 Armour et al (n 17) 23.

116 See generally Edward N Wolff, 'Household Wealth Trends in The United States, 1962 to 2016: Has Middle Class Wealth Recovered?' (NBER Working Paper, No 24085, November 2017) <https://www.nber.org/papers/w24085> accessed 30 September 2021.

4.2 *Taming the Multinational through Imposing Corporate Responsibility through Cooperative Regulation*

Ultimately, the view taken here is that common concerns of humankind, including the distributional common concern argued for in this monograph, requires that states impose corporate responsibility such that multinationals adjust their behaviour so that the problems at the core of the various common concerns may be solved. This requires states to cooperate and to coordinate far more effectively than they currently do in respect of an array of different areas of regulation. There are a number of regulatory channels beyond corporate law where states could cooperate in order to reduce economic inequality within their own borders.

States could do this through better coordination of their competition laws, for example, including on issues such as cross-border M&A. States could also cooperate more effectively on international investment incentives, amongst a number of other things. In this monograph, however, the focus will be on coordination and cooperation in respect of taxation. The reasons behind this choice are simple: first, as will be shown further below, there is clearly *some* appetite on the part of a significant number of states around the world for moving forward on international tax coordination and cooperation; secondly—and more importantly—taxation has been the single most effective way of reducing economic inequality historically;[117] and finally, because international law for the time being essentially remains the law as between nations; that is, the law as between *states*. If states are incapable of effectively taxing—whether they are heading in this direction is something taken up later in this chapter—they can no longer properly be considered states. Without states, there can be no international law, which would leave us with the need for an entirely different project altogether.

5 Taxation of Multinational Firms and the Distribution of Income and Wealth within States

As noted in the introduction to this chapter, the global average statutory corporate tax rate has fallen from 49 percent in 1985 to 24 percent in 2018.[118]

117 See generally Thomas Piketty, *Capital in the Twenty-First Century* (HUP, London 2014), translated by Arthur Goldhammer. See also Walter Scheidel, *The Great Leveler: Violence and the History of Inequality from the Stone Age to the Twenty-First Century* (PUP, Princeton 2017).

118 Tørsløv, Wier and Zucman (n 4) 1.

Most arguments attempting to explain this trend pertain to the various iterations of 'tax competition'. Tax competition is by definition a non-cooperative enterprise. Loosely defined, tax competition is 'non-cooperative tax setting by independent governments competing for a mobile tax base'.[119] The cause for governments engaging in such practices is much-debated in the economics literature, both theoretically and empirically. This literature entails a great deal of nuance, an understanding of which is helpful but engagement with which is beyond the scope of this monograph.[120] In any event, as eluded to in the introduction above, it is unnecessary to resolve this debate to make the point that some form of cooperation or coordination among states may be desirable.

It is helpful, however, to distinguish between at least two different strands of argument: (1) the 'productive capital' thesis; and (2) the more recently developed 'profit shifting' thesis. It should be reiterated that these arguments need not necessarily exclude the validity of the other as a general proposition. That said, in the case of certain countries it appears fairly clear that corporate tax rates are set low deliberately so as to attract shifted profits.[121] While the focus here is the latter of the two arguments, a brief rehearsal of the first argument provides helpful context.

The 'productive capital' thesis is basically the proposition that corporate tax rates are on the decline because 'globalization makes countries compete harder for productive capital, pushing corporate tax rates down'.[122] Through corporate tax cuts in combination with more efficient provision of public services and infrastructure, so the argument goes, states may attract more productive capital, which in turn raises the productivity of workers and with it their wages.[123] Corporate taxes have accordingly become lower as a result of increased economic globalization because it has made capital more sensitive to differences in tax rates, which in turn has led to the onset of more intense competition between states for scare productive capital.[124]

119 Gaëtan Nicodème, 'Corporate Tax Competition and Coordination in the European Union: What Do We Know? Where Do We Stand?' (European Economy, European Commission Directorate-General for Economic and Financial Affairs, Economic Papers No 250, June 2006) <https://ec.europa.eu/economy_finance/publications/pages/publication718_en.pdf> accessed 30 September 2021, 12.

120 See, however, Michael Keen and Kai Konrad, 'The Theory of International Tax Competition and Coordination' in Alan J Auerbach et al (eds), *Handbook of Public Economics* (Vol 5, Elsevier, Amsterdam 2013) for a thorough overview of many of these arguments.

121 See generally Tørsløv, Wier and Zucman (n 4) and Thomas Rixen, 'Tax Competition and Inequality: The Case for Global Tax Governance' (2011) 17 *Global Governance* 447.

122 Tørsløv, Wier and Zucman (n 4) 1.

123 Tørsløv, Wier and Zucman (n 4) 1.

124 Tørsløv, Wier and Zucman (n 4) 1.

The 'profit shifting' thesis illustrates that the 'productive capital' thesis is at best a partial explanation for why states lower their corporate tax rates. The former line of argument stems from the recent empirical observations of Thomas Tørsløv, Ludvig Wier and Gabriel Zucman.[125] The authors observe that nearly 40 percent of 'multinational profits' were 'artificially' shifted to 'tax havens' in 2015.[126] Through a systematic review of corporate tax data, they come to the conclusion that it is the tax avoidance of multinationals through profit shifting—as opposed to states competing for productive capital due to increased globalization—that has and continues to drive corporate tax rates down around the world.[127] Importantly for the purposes of this discussion, the authors make the point that '[t]he redistributive consequences of this process [that is, lower corporate tax rates that result from profit shifting] are major, and different from than in the textbook model of tax competition. Instead of increasing capital stocks in low-tax countries, boosting wages along the way, profit shifting merely reduces the taxes paid by multinationals, which mostly benefits their shareholders, who tend to be wealthy'.[128]

It is worth emphasising a few points that arise through comparing the 'productive capital' and 'profit shifting' theses. First, it should be noted that underling the 'productive capital' argument is the idea that there may be a good economic rationale for retaining the status quo as it pertains to tax competition between states: the 'winning' states—those that end up attracting the capital in question—potentially see jobs created in their territory, or they realise productivity and wage growth. This potentially compensates for the

125 See Tørsløv, Wier and Zucman (n 4).

126 See Tørsløv, Wier and Zucman (n 4) 1. The authors define 'multinational profits' as 'profits made by multinational companies outside of the country where their parent is located' (see Tørsløv, Wier and Zucman (n 4) 3). The 'artificial' shifting of profits refers to the shifting of accounting profits (Tørsløv, Wier and Zucman (n 4) 1). 'Tax havens' are certain low-tax countries or territories identified by the authors (see Tørsløv, Wier and Zucman (n 4) Table 2).

127 Tørsløv, Wier and Zucman (n 4). See also Ludvig Wier and Hayley Reynolds, 'Big and "Unprofitable": How 10% of Multinational Firms Do 98% of the Profit Shifting' (WIDER Working Paper 2018/111) <https://sa-tied.wider.unu.edu/sites/default/files/pdf/WP-24-Decmber-2018-Wier-Reynolds.pdf> accessed 30 September 2021.

128 Tørsløv, Wier and Zucman (n 4) 1. As an example of this, the authors point to Google Alphabet and the fact that it made $19.2 billion in revenue in Bermuda. The firm hardly employs any workers in Bermuda, nor does it own tangible assets of any kind in Bermuda. The corporate tax rate in Bermuda is zero. The authors point out that '[c]ontrary to the central postulate of the tax competition model, Bermuda does not have much to gain from attracting paper profits that don't improve wages for the population and that it taxes at 0%' (see Tørsløv, Wier and Zucman (n 4) 1–2).

lower tax rate by increasing the size of the pot of taxable income and wealth. The appeal of this explanation, of course, is further supported by the idea of efficient allocation: simply put, because states compete more intensely with one another, productive capital is more efficiently allocated, which is better for everyone. The validity of this argument can, of course, be debated, but, ultimately, the point is that the acceptance of the 'productive capital' thesis as the *only* explanation for declining tax rates does not necessarily incentivise states to engage in corrective action.

As for the 'profit shifting' thesis, there may be an economic rationale in favour of retaining the status quo position, but there is no overall unifying idea like efficiency undergirding it. Moreover, states are essentially incentivised to lower their corporate tax rates purely to increase revenue collection and, additionally, in so doing, those states that do substantially lower their rates—and see substantial revenue increases as a result of base expansion—do so at the expense of the tax revenues of other states that do not lower their rates. As a result, states that have higher rates—'non-haven' countries—lose as much as 29 percent of their corporate tax revenue while states that have lower rates—'tax havens'—increase their collected revenue by up to 100 percent.[129]

The second point worth emphasising is that much of the focus of the tax competition literature is primarily on the loss and/or gain of revenue, as opposed to on the distribution of income and wealth.[130] Revenue is certainly an important issue, including for the distribution of income and wealth. That said, corporate tax revenue observed as fraction of national income over time—as it often is in the tax competition literature—is more helpful from a distributional perspective if we know, for example, what fraction of national income is going to corporate profits over time, what the implications of tax competition are for capital's share of national income over time or what the competition implications of tax competition are for firms of different sizes over time. It should not be neglected that the observation that resulted in most of the tax competition literature coming about was about the decline of corporate tax rates. In other words, while it is important to examine where revenue is being lost based on current rates, it is of at least equal importance to examine whether rates can be prevented from declining further or be raised in response to distributional concerns.

---

129 See Tørsløv, Wier and Zucman (n 4) generally and especially Table 2.

130 Although Tørsløv, Wier and Zucman make it clear that they are aware that there are likely to be substantial distributional consequences in the event that their theory is correct (see Tørsløv, Wier and Zucman (n 4) 1, 5).

Thomas Rixen has convincingly explained the distributional effects of international tax competition.[131] He starts with a premise that accords with the view of Tørsløv, Wier and Zucman discussed above: 'tax competition is a reality: there is limited competition for FDI and fierce competition for mobile paper profits'. However, Rixen continues, '[a]s long as tax revenue remains more or less stable, one may think that there is no reason to do anything about tax competition'.[132] He quickly interjects subsequently that 'this reasoning neglects a crucial externality that countries impose on one another, namely, domestic and international inequality'.[133]

From the viewpoint of economic distributions within states, Rixen points out that the mechanism states engage to respond to tax competition is often a version of the so-called tax cut-cum-base broadening policy.[134] This is an attempt, essentially, 'to both defend against and compensate for the outflow of paper profits'.[135] The lowering of statutory tax rates and concurrent broadening of the tax base means that states avoid the revenue losses that would ensue if the rate was changed but the size of the base remained the same.[136] The upshot of this sort of policy, however, is that it alters the distribution of the tax burden among different types of taxpayers within a particular state.[137] The burden shifts from highly profitable multinationals to smaller domestic firms, from mobile to immobile economic factors (that is, from mobile capital to immobile capital and labour) and increasingly to consumers through consumption taxes.[138]

Moreover, as Rixen points out, the progressiveness of personal income taxes may also be undermined as a result of competitive downward pressure on corporate taxes.[139] Without the corporate tax rate acting as a 'backstop' for personal income tax, and if the statutory corporate rate is lower than the personal rate, individuals are incentivised to incorporate their income so as to benefit from a corporate veil.[140] In order to prevent this from happening, the relevant authorities reduce the top personal income rate, thereby rendering the personal tax system less progressive.[141] For all these reasons, tax competition and

131 Rixen (n 121) 449–54.
132 Rixen (n 121) 451.
133 Rixen (n 121) 451.
134 Rixen (n 121) 451.
135 Rixen (n 121) 451. Footnote omitted.
136 Rixen (n 121) 451.
137 Rixen (n 121) 451.
138 Rixen (n 121) 451–2.
139 Rixen (n 121) 452.
140 Rixen (n 121) 452.
141 Rixen (n 121) 452.

profit shifting result in higher levels of income and wealth inequality within states. The appropriate context for discussion having been sketched above, the chapter now turns to the topic of tax sovereignty.

6 Tax Sovereignty as Cooperative Sovereignty

As economic integration increases globally and economic activity is increasingly structured across borders and jurisdictions, various states may lay claim to jurisdiction to tax the same income or wealth. This is not a new concern. Existing bilateral double taxation treaties (DTTs) are based on model agreements developed under the auspices of the League of Nations between 1927 and 1946, the predecessor of the United Nations.[142] Today, much like with bilateral investment treaties (BITs), the existing network of DTTs spans more than 2500 agreements in total.[143] As Reuven Avi-Yonah points out, DTTs 'are remarkably similar in the topics covered (even the order of articles are always the same) and in their language', with '[a]bout 75% of the actual words of any given DTT [being] ... identical with the words of any other DTT'.[144] Elsewhere Avi-Yonah goes as far as to argue that, due to the similarities of DTTs and state practice in certain areas, certain rules contained in DTTs have become customary international law.[145]

What this does is to give the appearance that there is already a fair deal of cooperation among countries with respect to tax matters. While this may be true insofar as it concerns certain rules and processes, it is also clear that there are many areas where there is incomplete, little or no cooperation. For example, while most states—through the use of DTTs—cooperate with one another to allow for income earned in source country X to be taxed in residence country Y,[146] the existence of a DTT between two countries does not signify that they have a shared conception of how other issues, such as transfer pricing for example, should be dealt with. Nor do states necessarily cooperate

---

142 See Reuven S Avi-Yonah, 'Double Tax Treaties: An Introduction' in Karl P Sauvant and Lisa E Sachs (eds), *The Effects of Treaties on Foreign Direct Investment: Bilateral Investment Treaties, Double Taxation Treaties, and Investment Flows* (OUP, Oxford 2009) 99.

143 See Avi-Yonah (n 142) 99.

144 See Avi-Yonah (n 142) 99.

145 See generally Reuven S Avi-Yonah, 'International Tax as International Law' (2004) 57 *Tax Law Review* 483. See also Reuven S Avi-Yonah, 'The Deemed Dividend Problem' (2004) 4 *Taxation of Global Transactions* 33, 35.

146 Avi-Yonah suggests that this is in fact the animating purpose of DTTs. See Avi-Yonah (n 142) 99–100.

with one another fully in respect of other matters, such as on issues of transparency or the exchange of information.

With this backdrop sketched, the aim of this second part of this chapter is to illustrate that the thesis set out in Chapter 3 with respect to cooperative sovereignty could and should be extended to the realm of corporate taxation.[147] In essence, the argument is that a new understanding of tax sovereignty is necessary in order for states to be able to carry out their taxation function, both at a positive or functional level as well as at a normative level. States can only truly be sovereign in respect of matters of taxation if they cooperate with other sovereigns. Without cooperation, all states have less individual sovereignty over taxation within their respective jurisdictions, not more. This argument is presented in two parts, with the positive elements of the argument addressed first (*Section 6.1*) and the normative elements addressed thereafter (*Section 6.2*).

6.1 *The Positive Elements of Tax Sovereignty*

To recall, as Max Huber put it his award in the *Island of Palmas* case, '[s]overeignty in the relations between States signifies independence. Independence in regard to a portion of the globe is the right to exercise therein, to the exclusion of any other State, the functions of a State'.[148] Taxation being one function of a state, the phrase 'positive elements of tax sovereignty' is intended to refer to the capacity of states to effectively set particular tax rules for its portion of the globe independently without interference from other states and to enforce those rules. As a result of changing factual circumstances—particularly those associated with 'globalization's second unbundling'—states can only remain sovereign over their tax affairs in a functional sense through cooperation with other states. Rixen sums this up tidily, arguing that 'if governments want to retain *de facto sovereignty* (attain their substantive policy goals of efficiency and equity), they will have to share some their *de jure sovereignty* (the legal right to design their own tax systems) with other governments in order to regulate tax competition'.[149] A few examples make this point quite plain.

---

147 On the cooperative sovereignty thesis, see Chapter 3 above in this monograph.

148 *Island of Palmas Case* (*Netherland v USA*) (1928), 2 UNRIAA 829.

149 Rixen (n 121) 448. See also Thomas Rixen, 'Institutional Reform of Global Tax Governance: A Proposal' in Peter Dietsch and Thomas Rixen (eds), *Global Tax Governance: What is Wrong with it and How to Fix It* (ECPR Press, Colchester 2016); Peter Dietsch, *Catching Capital: The Ethics of Tax Competition* (OUP, Oxford 2015); Peter Dietsch, 'Rethinking Sovereignty in International Fiscal Policy' (2011) 37 *Review of International Studies* 2107; Peter Dietsch, 'Whose Tax Base? The Ethics of Global Tax Governance' in Peter Dietsch and Thomas Rixen (eds), *Global Tax Governance: What is Wrong with it and How to Fix It* (ECPR Press, Colchester 2016); Peter Dietsch and Thomas Rixen, 'Redistribution, Globalisation and

Setting corporate tax rates. As the above discussion on tax competition evinces, the setting of corporate tax rates with the aim of collecting a certain amount of revenue has become an increasingly difficult to achieve with any semblance of independence. The corporate tax rate in tax havens like Ireland or Luxembourg interferes with the revenue raising capacity of other non-haven states such as Germany or Colombia.[150] Notionally, states obviously still retain the ability to set tax rates at a percentage of their choosing. In reality, however, due to tax competition, they no longer have the capacity to effectively collect the revenue a particular rate was intended to raise when all states concurrently pursue their own goals with respect to revenue. In other words, while some states may 'win' in terms of revenue—that is, while some states may effectively attain their revenue goals—they necessarily do so at the expense of the sovereignty of other states in most instances.[151]

The same logic applies to setting tax rates with particular distributive goals in mind. For example, if corporate profits dramatically increase as a fraction of national income, as they have in many countries around the world since the onset of the ICT Revolution, and a state wishes to shift the tax burden accordingly—away from workers who are now necessarily receiving a smaller fraction of national income for example—it can no longer realistically do so effectively *and* independently. Consider the United States for example. Since the mid-1980s corporate profits *after* taxation as a share of gross national product (GDP) has risen from approximately 3.5–4 percent of GDP to around 9–11 percent of GDP in recent years.[152] The share of corporate tax revenue as a percentage of GDP, however, has remained consistently between 2.5 and 3.5 percent during the same timeframe and under the same statutory corporate tax rate.[153] Given what is now known about tax competition, it appears arguably clear that it could not have acted on its own to change this.[154]

Multi-Level Governance' (2014) 1 *Moral Philosophy and Politics* 61 and Peter Dietsch and Thomas Rixen, 'Tax Competition and Global Background Justice' (2014) 22 *Journal of Political Philosophy* 150.

150 See Tørsløv, Wier and Zucman (n 4) Table 2.

151 Rixen puts it differently: '[T]ax havens … profit from tax competition. While there is little real economic activity taking place in these countries, their economies prosper because they operate as tax shelters, commercializing their tax sovereignty' (see Rixen (n 121) 453).

152 United States Bureau of Economic Analysis, 'Corporate Profits after Tax (without IVA and CCAdj) [CP]' (Figure created by Federal Reserve Bank of St Louis) <https://fred.stlouisfed.org/series/CP, July 18, 2018> accessed 30 September 2021.

153 See Tørsløv, Wier and Zucman (n 4) Figure 10.

154 This is not to suggest that the United States made any attempt to do this. Moreover, the point being made is not that the United States was unable to make any difference to the situation whatsoever. Rather, the point is that the extent to which it could unilaterally

Transparency and information. Whether international rules on taxation are substantively coordinated in a desirable manner or not, transparency and information remain critical for the enforcement of existing rules.[155] For example, if a particular state taxes by virtue of residence it can only effectively enforce its own tax rules in the event that it knows how much taxable income or wealth is received and/or held by its residents during the relevant period in question. If a particular resident holds some of her wealth abroad, and it is accepted that she is required to pay a particular amount of tax on that wealth, taxes can only be levied on the wealth in question to the extent that the taxing state is aware of the wealth in question and has sufficient information about that wealth in order to determine that resident's tax liability.

Transparency and information are also necessary for substantive rule-making. In deciding how to tax their own citizens and enterprises, states need to be able to identify their tax base is and they need to have pertinent information about the nature of the income and wealth received or owned by the constituent parts of that base. The simple example of raising revenue makes this clear. Either a state can determine in advance that it would like to raise a certain amount of revenue by a given date—in which case it should ideally be well informed about its tax base in order to determine how much to tax who—or perhaps one could argue that states can only really determine what amount of revenue is realistically capable of being raised in the event that it has full or sufficient information at its disposal.

Moreover, from an economic distributions perspective, the impact of the tax practices of multinationals (as well as individuals) on income or wealth inequality can only be determined—or at least accurately determined—with proper data.[156] While fairly accurate estimates can be attained using existing data in conjunction with methods to fill the necessary gaps—and this should certainly be done in the absence of perfect information—the more accurate an empirical picture can be established of the relationship, the easier it is to formulate policies to address any issues that arise and the more effectively rules and procedures can be devised to execute those policies.

---

make a difference in this regard was likely substantially limited by the actions of other states.

155 On this point, see further Carlo Garbarino and Sebastiano Garufi, 'Transparency and Exchange of Information in International Taxation' in Andrea Bianchi and Anne Peters (eds), *Transparency in International Law* (CUP, Cambridge 2013) 172, 172–8.

156 This point is made by Gabriel Zucman in a different form at the outset of his book. See Gabriel Zucman, *The Hidden Wealth of Nations: The Scourge of Tax Havens* (University of Chicago Press, Chicago 2015) 2–4, translated from the original French by Teresa Lavender Fagan.

Transfer pricing manipulation (TPM). The term 'transfer pricing', loosely speaking, refers to 'the pricing of cross-border intrafirm transactions between related parties'.[157] As for TPM, Eden puts it simply:

> **Transfer price manipulation**—as distinct from transfer pricing—is the over- or under-invoicing of related party transactions in order to avoid government regulations (e.g. under-invoicing to avoid paying ad valorem tariffs) or to exploit cross-border differences in these rates (for example, shifting deductible expenses to the high tax location and revenues to the low tax location in order to reduce overall corporate tax payments). It is not transfer pricing that is the problem; it is the potential for transfer price manipulation that governments fear and want to prevent through regulation. However, what one party sees as legitimate forms of price setting may be seen by the other as evasive and illegitimate manipulation.[158]

While there are multiple reasons why multinationals engage in TPM,[159] for the purposes of this chapter the focus is on TPM as a tool used by multinationals to reduce their overall tax burden. An example provided by Dunning and Lundan makes it fairly clear how multinationals could go about doing this:

> Suppose, for example, that an affiliate of [a multinational] located in Country A earns $10 million of taxable income on which it has to pay a 50% tax; another affiliate in Country B earns $10 million of taxable income, on which it has to pay a 20% tax. Suppose, too, that the affiliate in Country A imports goods from an affiliate in Country B worth $25 million at arm's-length prices and exports goods to Country B worth $20 million at arm's-length prices. Then, its total tax bill is $7 million ($5 million paid in Country A and $2 million in Country B) and its net profit is $13 million.
>
> Clearly, in this situation, given a free choice, the [multinational] would prefer to declare all its profits in Country B and pay $3 million less tax. One way of achieving this (if known about and permitted by the authorities of Country A) is for the affiliate in Country A to sell goods or services to the affiliate in Country B at a lower than arm's-length price and

157 Lorraine Eden, 'Taxes, Transfer Pricing, and the Multinational Enterprise' in Alan M Rugman and Thomas L Brewer (eds), *The Oxford Handbook of International Business* (OUP, Oxford 2001) 591, 591.

158 Eden (n 157) 592–3. Emphasis original.

159 See John H Dunning and Sarianna M Lundan, *Multinational Enterprises and the Global Economy* (2 ed Edward Elgar, Cheltenham 2008) 622–3.

buy goods and services from that affiliate at a higher than arm's-length price.[160]

As one might imagine, the rules related to transfer pricing are often complex and are likely to result in conflicts about which rules should prevail because, as with any cross-border transaction, there are at least two countries involved, with each country often having different interests and with transfer pricing methodologies accordingly being applied in the different countries.[161] Dunning and Lundan sum up the complexity, noting that while research often focuses on the deleterious welfare consequences for host states, home states have equally compelling reasons to be concerned as well.[162] The authors continue to explain that '[w]hile a loss of value added of one country will usually result in an equivalent gain of value added to another country, it is quite possible that TPM may result in a loss of value added in one country and a redistribution of value added in another, which is unacceptable to both'.[163] The authors also add that, '[o]n the other hand, where administered prices by [multinationals] replace non-competitive arm's-length prices, or where they are used to combat government policies which are market distorting, they may increase, rather than reduce, economic welfare'.[164]

Hybrid mismatch arrangements (*HMAs*). As the Organisation for Economic Co-operation and Development (OECD) notes, '[t]hese are arrangements exploiting differences in the tax treatment of instruments, entities or transfers between two or more countries'.[165] The OECD continues to note that HMAs 'often lead to "double non-taxation" that may not be intended by either country, or may alternatively lead to a tax deferral which if maintained over several years is economically similar to double non-taxation'.[166] This may, in turn, lead to significant reductions in the overall tax burden of taxpayers that utilise HMAs.[167] Anecdotally, the OECD points to various examples from different

160 Dunning and Lundan (n 159) 621. Reference and footnote omitted.

161 Eden (n 157) 592.

162 Dunning and Lundan (n 159) 620.

163 Dunning and Lundan (n 159) 620–1.

164 Dunning and Lundan (n 159) 621. Reference omitted.

165 OECD, 'Hybrid Mismatch Arrangements: Tax Policy and Compliance Issues' (Report published under the auspices of the Secretary-General of the OECD, March 2012) 1 <http://www.oecd.org/ctp/aggressive/HYBRIDS_ENG_Final_October2012.pdf> accessed 30 September 2021.

166 OECD (n 165) 1.

167 OECD (n 165) 1.

countries where HMAs were reportedly used to reduce taxes in transactions worth several billions of dollars.[168]

At a very basic level, HMAs generally rely on one or several of the following elements: 'hybrid entities', whereby entities 'are treated as transparent for tax purposes in one country and as non-transparent in another country';[169] dual residence entities;[170] 'hybrid instruments', whereby instruments are usually treated as a debt in one country but as an equity in another;[171] and 'hybrid transfers', whereby most frequently a particular transaction involving an asset is considered a transfer of ownership in one country, but as a collateralised loan in another.[172] In making use of these concepts, HMAs result in situations, for example, whereby one deduction may be claimed twice in two different countries for income tax purposes despite the fact that both deductions arose from the same contractual obligation.[173] Similarly, HMAs often result in situation whereby a deduction is created in one country, but is not included as part of taxable income in the other country.[174] HMAs are also used to generate tax credits in foreign countries where they would otherwise not be available.[175]

Without cooperation between states concerning transparency and information exchange, TPM and HMAs individual state become less effective at fulfilling their taxation function. In other words, if sovereignty is not understood as a cooperative enterprise, tax sovereignty no longer signifies complete independence to *effectively* levy taxes free from external interference. Recalling Besson's description of sovereignty as 'at once a state of affairs, a question pertaining to the nature and justification of that state of affairs and a justification of it',[176] it is clear that tax sovereignty not being viewed as cooperative sovereignty deeply weakens the justification for the current state of affairs. Alternatively, it can be stated positively: tax sovereignty as cooperative sovereignty is more justifiable as an argument for what sovereignty is if the purpose of tax sovereignty is, as asserted here, to retain the maximum amount of independence for each state, simultaneously, to be able to set its own tax rules and enforce them.

---

168 OECD (n 165) 1–2.
169 OECD (n 165) 7.
170 OECD (n 165) 7.
171 OECD (n 165) 7.
172 OECD (n 165) 7.
173 OECD (n 165) 7.
174 OECD (n 165) 7.
175 OECD (n 165) 7. For further details and examples of how this works in practice, see OECD (n 165) 8–10.
176 See Samantha Besson, 'Sovereignty in Conflict' (2004) 8 *European Integration online Papers (EIoP)* 1, 22.

6.2 *The Normative Elements of Tax Sovereignty*

The fifth book of Adam Smith's *Wealth of Nations* bears the title 'Of the Revenue of the Sovereign or Commonwealth'.[177] In it, he spelt out what a nation might raise revenue for. In his view, nations should raise revenue for essentially five things: (1) the maintenance of its military;[178] (2) the maintenance of systems for the administration of justice within their own territories;[179] (3) to pay for public infrastructure;[180] (4) to pay for certain public institutions of education;[181] and (5) compensating the sovereign appropriately.[182] The question of what taxes are to be used for is, of course, itself a normative question on which reasonable persons are likely to disagree. Milton Friedman, for example, while generally taking a similar view to that of Smith's, would probably have government spend less revenue in respect of infrastructure and education.[183] Others, such as Anthony Atkinson, argue for spending on comprehensive social security for all citizens who live within a particular state.[184] A list of such positions could go on forever; the debate on the proper functions of government has existed for thousands of years and will likely continue to exist, unsettled, for thousands more.

While this debate is not irrelevant to the present discussion, it is not something which a view needs to be taken on in order for the argument laid out here to hold. In reality, governments act in fulfilment of particular ideas concerning their functions. Within a particular country, it is usually the case that the government takes a view on what its function should be and acts accordingly by altering its budgets and laws. Later in time it may reverse any changes that it has made as the government and/or public perception changes. At a given point in time, however, it can be accepted that a particular stance on what government should do has been or is being enacted and that in putting this stance into effect, the government in question requires a certain amount of revenue. Taking this amount as fixed for a given period of time, the normative questions of interest for the current discussion are simply 'who should contribute

177 See Smith (n 2) 277.
178 See Smith (n 2) 279–97.
179 See Smith (n 2) 297–310.
180 See Smith (n 2) 310–48.
181 See Smith (n 2) 348–404.
182 See Smith (n 2) 404–5.
183 See generally, for example, Milton Friedman, *Capitalism and Freedom* (Chicago University Press, Chicago 1982) 22–36.
184 See generally, for example, Anthony B Atkinson, *Inequality: What can be done?* (HUP, Cambridge, MA 2015) 205–36.

towards the raising of revenue?' and 'to what extent should they contribute to the raising of revenue?'

Any answers to these questions, of course, depend on the answer to the question 'what should government do?' The reason that this question is of little interest here is simple: what the role of government should be is something which states can independently decide on for themselves. Where cooperation may be necessary to ensure distributive justice is attained primarily relates to putting a particular vision of government into place once that vision has been selected; this starts with the two questions identified above: 'who should contribute towards the raising of revenue?' and 'to what extent should they contribute to the raising of revenue?' Here too there are many reasonable perspectives that have been justified over the centuries and continue to be justified today.

Adam Smith, for example, wrote that '[t]he subjects of every state ought to contribute towards the support of the government, as nearly as possible, in proportion to their respective abilities; that is, in proportion to the revenue which they respectively enjoy under the protection of the state. The expense of government to the individuals of a great nation is like the expense of management to the joint tenants of a great estate, who are all obliged to contribute in proportion to their respective interests in the estate'.[185] Smith is accordingly often seen as the original or principal proponent of what is now widely known as the 'ability to pay' theory of taxation,[186] which, having been finessed by John Stuart Mill from equal 'ability' into equal 'sacrifice', has for the most part dominated taxation analysis ever since.[187]

Progressive taxation as it is known today—generally the idea that those receiving higher incomes pay a larger percentage of tax on those incomes combined with the idea that persons equally situated should be taxed equally—is founded on ideas of equal ability to pay and equal sacrifice. Giving meaning to the idea of equal sacrifice naturally entails the making of a normative judgment. This may loosely entail, for example, making the assumption that the marginal value of one unit of additional income diminishes as income increases. This, in turn, assuming horizontal equity, allows for non-proportional taxes to be levied vertically, as is the case when applying a principle of

185 Smith (n 2) 416.

186 See, for example, Jeffrey A Schoenblum, 'Tax Fairness or Unfairness? A Consideration of the Philosophical Bases for Unequal Taxation of Individuals' (1995) 12 *American Journal of Tax Policy* 221, 233–4. For a more nuanced take, see Richard A Musgrave, 'Horizontal Equity, Once More' (1990) 43 *National Tax Journal* 113, 114.

187 Musgrave (n 186) 115.

progressive taxation, without violating the principle of equal sacrifice. When a system of progressive taxation, then, due to unequal enforcement for example, ceases to be progressive, it follows that the taxation system is no longer fair because the equal sacrifice principle is no longer being observed. Similarly, when persons adjudged to be in similar positions are not taxed similarly the principle of equal sacrifice is violated and the tax system in question may be deemed unjust.

Competition implications aside, to the extent that a lack of cooperation in tax matters between states results in situations whereby firms similarly placed for tax purposes pay different amounts of taxes, cooperation would be necessary for attaining distributive justice. Without cooperation, it is not possible for individual states to fully enforce a system of taxation premised on equal sacrifice. Therefore, functional incapacities also result in normative incapacities. In reality, this is exemplified by the profit shifting practices of multinationals whereby they avoid taxes. As noted above, according to Tørsløv, Wier and Zucman, approximately 40 percent of multinational profits are shifted to low tax jurisdictions.[188] This implies by definition that domestic firms and foreign firms in non-haven countries are not subjected to the same tax burden; they do not 'sacrifice equally'.

Moreover, if a particular governmental form is assumed—that is, it is assumed that government takes on a particular set of functions—and the capacity of government to ensure distributive justice depends on the actual realisation of that form, another situation arises where cooperation is necessary for the attainment of distributive justice. For John Rawls, for example, distributive justice predominantly comes down to the choice of a particular social system.[189] The design of a just social system, he argues, necessarily requires that social and economic processes be set 'within the surroundings of suitable political and legal institutions'.[190] This leads Rawls to the assertion that '[w]ithout an appropriate scheme of these background institutions the outcome of the distributive process will not be just'.[191] This would be because '[b]ackground fairness is lacking'.[192] Rawls discusses in turn how this applies to both capitalist, constitutional democracies and socialist regimes, with some appropriate modifications made for each system of government.[193] To make

188 Tørsløv, Wier and Zucman (n 4) 1.
189 Rawls (n 8) 242.
190 Rawls (n 8) 243.
191 Rawls (n 8) 243.
192 Rawls (n 8) 243.
193 See Rawls (n 8) 243–51.

the overarching point of this section, it suffices to describe how Rawls sees distributive justice being attained within a democracy.

Having laid out his assumptions about democracies, including that democratic governments guarantee a social minimum of sorts, Rawls describes four branches of government for the establishment of background institutions, with each branch charged with preserving certain social and economic conditions.[194] The 'allocation branch' exists to ensure that markets remain competitive and to quell the concentration of market power.[195] The 'stabilization branch' is tasked with bringing about full or reasonably full employment.[196] The third branch is the 'transfer branch', responsible for the social minimum.[197] Finally there is the 'distribution branch', the task of which is 'to preserve an approximate justice distributive shares by means of taxation and the necessary adjustments in the rights of property'.[198] For Rawls, '[i]t is clear that the justice of distributive shares depends on the background institutions and how they allocate total income, wages and other income plus transfers'.[199]

The focus presently is on the so-called distribution branch. Further examination reveals that it has two functions. First, it should 'gradually and continually … correct the distribution of wealth and … prevent concentrations of power detrimental to the fair value of political liberty and fair equality of opportunity'.[200] This is done predominantly through the imposition of various types of taxes, but not for the purpose of raising revenue.[201] These taxes are levied purely so as to ensure that wealth does not become too unequally distributed.[202] The second function of the distributive branch is raising the revenue that justice requires.[203] As Rawls puts it, '[s]ocial resources must be released to the government so that it can provide for the public goods and

194 See Rawls (n 8) 243.
195 Rawls (n 8) 244.
196 Rawls (n 8) 244.
197 Rawls (n 8) 244.
198 Rawls (n 8) 245.
199 Rawls (n 8) 244.
200 Rawls (n 8) 245.
201 Rawls (n 8) 245.
202 Rawls (n 8) 246. Rawls draws the line in this regard as follows: 'fair equality of opportunity means a certain set of institutions that assures similar chances of education and culture for persons similarly motivated and keeps positions and offices open to all on the basis of qualities and efforts reasonably related to the relevant duties and tasks. It is these institutions that are put in jeopardy when inequalities of wealth exceed a certain limit; and political liberty likewise tends to lose its value, and representative government to become such in appearance only' (Rawls (n 8) 245–6).
203 Rawls (n 8) 246.

make the transfer payments necessary to satisfy the difference principle'.[204] He accordingly concludes that '[t]his problem belongs to the distribution branch since the burden of taxation is to be justly shared and it aims at establishing just arrangements'.[205]

Distributive justice, then, viewed from a Rawlsian perspective at least, is only fully attainable through cooperation between states. If we accept that some states act based on this or a similar conception of distributive justice—if we accept that some states exercise their tax sovereignty in such a way as to pursue Rawlsian-style distributive justice—then tax sovereignty must of necessity be seen as cooperative sovereignty. To understand tax sovereignty otherwise would be to render it normatively ineffective. Corporate tax rate competition—as a factual given—illustrates this point fairly well: first of all because tax competition impairs, at least to some debatable degree, the capacity of most states to 'gradually and continually correct the distribution of wealth'; and secondly, again as a result of tax competition, because states acting in isolation are constrained in their individual and collective capacity to 'raise the revenue that justice requires'.

At the heart of the Rawlsian argument is social contract theory. Rixen, drawing heavily on Rawls, summarises this as follows:

> [C]itizens negotiate about and define their rights, entitlements, and duties. They determine the different contributions each must make to maintain the common institutional order. The institutional infrastructure also entails the definition of a structure of property rights and a market order, both financed by the taxes that citizens pay. By so doing, individuals determine the distributive principles for their societies. Distributive justice is achieved if all individuals agree consensually on a social contract. Overall, the social contract defines the normative terms (i.e. the moral obligations individuals have toward one another) of the common operative venture that is the nation-state.[206]

It is worth clarifying that the argument presented here is not that states are entirely incapable of delivering distributive justice (or ensuring that everyone keeps acting in accordance with the pre-defined social contract) without

204 Rawls (n 8) 246. On the 'difference principle', see Rawls (n 8) 65–73.

205 Rawls (n 8) 246.

206 Rixen (n 121) 455. For a different take on tax sovereignty and social contract theory, see Allison Christians, 'Sovereignty, Taxation and Social Contract', (2009) 18 *Minnesota Journal of International Law* 99.

cooperating with other states, but rather that their capacity to do so effectively—at least for most states—is enhanced through cooperation. In other words, states are certainly still capable of pursuing distributive justice in isolation and a lack of international cooperation should not be seen as an excuse for not doing so; but cooperation is still a better argument than isolationism if states intend to be effective in their respective pursuits.[207]

7 Recognition of a Distributive Common Concern: Utility and Implications

The common concern of humankind examined here starts from the same general propositions made in Chapter 3 of this monograph.[208] For the sake of clarity, the claim examined here is that the distribution of income and wealth within states has certain adverse effects and that, taken together, changes in economic distributions over time and such adverse effects form the common concern of humankind, referred to here as a 'distributive common concern of humankind' for ease of reference. The adverse effects remain the same as those identified in Chapters 2 and 3.[209] This discussion is different in that it takes a deeper look at one particular cause underlying distributional changes within states: that of corporate taxation. More specifically, it examines the taxation by states of multinationals, which, as argued above, requires certain elements of tax sovereignty to be understood as cooperative sovereignty.

From the outset it should be recalled that a large range of factors affect the distribution of income and wealth within states. The claim made here is not that cooperation with regard to matters of corporate taxation will magically result in the dissipation of distributional concerns within countries. Rather, the claim being made is that the recognition of a distributional common concern of humankind in this particular context is one of many steps that could be taken to restore the distributional autonomy of states; such recognition, in essence, would move in the direction of handing states the requisite tools necessary to ensure that issues of economic distributions within their borders can once again become a function of domestic politics, but in a way that does not do damage to the distributional autonomy of other states or to economic relations between states more generally.

207 See generally Rixen (n 121). As Rixen points out, this argument could also be derived from theories other than social contract theory (see Rixen (n 121) n 32).

208 See Chapter 3 above in this monograph.

209 See Chapter 2 and Chapter 3 above in this monograph.

It should perhaps also be stressed that states still retain a good deal of distributional autonomy at present. There is much that states can do in the absence of cooperation in order to address the trend towards the more unequal distribution of income and wealth over time. It is not uncommon, however, for states to blame their own distributional concerns on the actions of other states. Moreover, while claims blaming other states might be factually baseless, well-reasoned claims can be made that the actions of other states do have significant distributional spill-overs. The above discussions on profit shifting make this fairly clear. These claims are difficult to refute because there is truth to them.

This does not necessarily mean, however, that addressing distributional concerns should be a matter either for the domestic realm *or* for the international realm: it is perfectly consistent for them to be both. Recognising a distributional common concern of humankind would accordingly be part of an effort to minimise the set of claims blaming other states for domestic distributional concerns. It would in essence help root responsibility for distributional concerns in domestic institutions where they are arguably most appropriately addressed. To a large degree, then, the argument for the recognition of a distributional common concern of humankind in certain areas, including multinational taxation, is premised on the idea that matters of economic distributions should be addressed more thoughtfully from a multilevel governance perspective.

Thomas Cottier has addressed the relationship between common concerns of humankind and multilevel governance.[210] He points out that, at least within the field of climate change, the common concern of humankind concept has been developed to the point where it now has implications for multilevel governance.[211] In this context, he further points out that '[t]he emerging doctrines of multilevel governance assist in optimal allocation and assignment of tasks on different layers of governance in the production of public goods relating to the Common Concern at hand'.[212] While acknowledging that plenty of

210 See Thomas Cottier (ed), 'The Principle of Common Concern of Humankind' in *The Prospects of Common Concern of Humankind in International Law* (CUP, Cambridge 2021) 23–6.

211 See Cottier (n 210) 23–4. As evidence for this proposition, Cottier cites the 2017 Declaration of Ethical Principles in relation to Climate Change, where it is recognised that 'climate change is a common concern of all humankind, and convinced that the global and local challenges of climate change cannot be met without the participation of all people at all levels of society including States, international organizations, sub-national entities, local authorities, indigenous peoples, local communities, the private sector, civil society organizations, and individuals' (see Cottier (n 210) 24).

212 Cottier (n 210) 24.

multilevel governance theories exist,[213] he argues in favour of the idea that multilevel governance resembles a five storey house insofar as-

> all levels of governance, from local to global, entail human conduct and behaviour, and share basic traits in terms of legal foundations and sources, albeit in very different constellations and compositions. It no longer makes a fundamental difference between domestic and international law in terms of allocating powers to regulate and enforce. It is similar to the perception of sovereignty-modern developed by the late John H. Jackson. It helps identifying the allocation of common concerns and public goods to different layers of government, and where they best should be addressed.[214]

This in essence accords with instituting a principle of subsidiarity. That is, a power allocation principle—contestable in a similar way that sovereignty is contestable—which 'requires that the entity that can best achieve a task be in charge of it'.[215] As Samantha Besson argues, '[r]ead together with sovereignty *qua* reflexive concept, the principle of subsidiarity implies a *test of efficiency* in power allocation. In each case, the sovereign authority will be that authority which can realize the objective in the most efficient way'.[216] For Besson, it accordingly follows that-

> [the] allocation of competences may be achieved through mutual adjustment and consistency in principle with one authority abiding by the other's past decisions on the issue, but also through actual delegation and transfer of competences; sovereignty may indeed have to be transferred in parts to ensure the best realization of the values it protects. In all cases, this decision is a sovereign one, because it is not pre-decided and sovereignty has not been shared or divided; questioning, emulation and cooperation are part of the regular exercize of sovereignty.[217]

---

213 See Cottier (n 210) 24 where an array of different constitutional theorist are cited.

214 Cottier (n 210) 24–5. Footnotes omitted. On the work of John H Jackson mentioned, see John H Jackson, 'Sovereignty—Modern: A New Approach to an Outdated Concept' (2003) 97 *American Journal of International Law* 782. See also generally John H Jackson, 'Sovereignty: Outdated Concept or New Approaches' in Wenhua Shan, Penelope Simons, and Dalvinder Singh (eds), *Redefining Sovereignty in International Economic Law* (Hart Publishing, Portland OR 2008) 3; John H Jackson, *Sovereignty, the WTO, and the Changing Fundamentals of International Law* (CUP, Cambridge 2006).

215 Besson (n 176) 12.

216 Besson (n 176) 12.

217 Besson (n 176) 12.

In recognising a distributional common concern of humankind in the area of multinational taxation, then, the distribution of income and wealth within states can begin to be properly embedded within a multilevel governance framework with a proper understanding of power and responsibility allocation. In other words, recognition would result in the identification of areas where cooperation is necessary such that the taxation functions of states can be properly allocated in accordance with subsidiarity so as to allow states to pursue distributional goals using tax measures in the most efficient manner possible. It goes without saying, of course, that distributional goals should not be pursued by states in disregard of other goals, such as the pursuit of economic growth or poverty reduction. Distributional goals should be pursued with an appropriate balance being struck between them and these other goals to the extent that they conflict with one another, the upshot being that the nature and extent of cooperation between states in connection to distributional matters should be informed not only by the distributional considerations of, in this case, tax cooperation, but also by the impact of tax cooperation on other goals such as economic growth.[218]

This brings the discussion to causation. Causes are important in giving definitional clarity to a given common concern of humankind. For example, in the context of climate change, the UNFCCC intimates that the parties to that agreement are '[c]oncerned that human activities have been substantially increasing the atmospheric concentrations of greenhouse gases, that these increases enhance the natural greenhouse effect, and that this will result on average in an additional warming of the Earth's surface and atmosphere and may adversely affect natural ecosystems and humankind'.[219] This passage, written in language that clearly denotes a particular causal set of events, clarifies the scope of the concern in question; it clarifies that what is of concern are changes to the climate that are ultimately caused by human activities that increase atmospheric concentration of greenhouse gases.

218 In the context of climate change and its adverse effects, this is essentially reflected, for example, in the preamble to the United Nations Framework Convention on Climate Change (UNFCCC), which affirmed 'that responses to climate change should be coordinated with social and economic development in an integrated manner with a view to avoiding adverse impacts on the latter, taking into full account the legitimate priority needs of developing countries for the achievement of sustained economic growth and the eradication of poverty'. See Preamble, United Nations Framework Convention on Climate Change (UNFCCC) (adopted 9 May 1992, entered into force 21 March 1994) 1771 UNTS 107, 165.

219 Preamble, UNFCCC.

In the context of corporate taxation, as illustrated above in this chapter, tax competition between states leads to increases in the inequality of income and wealth within states in a similar way that human activity increasing atmospheric concentrations of greenhouse gases lead to climate change. In each of these cases, the extent to which the recognition of the common concern of humankind has legal implications is confined to a particular cause or set of causes. For example, to the extent that climate change is caused by the sun's energy output, climate change does not amount to a common concern of humankind in a legal sense. This brings sharply into focus the importance of fact-finding and causal inquiry for the common concern of humankind concept. The more precisely facts and causal connections between facts can be proven, the more precisely a common concern of humankind can be framed.

What makes the distributional common concern of humankind case more difficult is that a predominant cause does not exist. In the context of climate change that predominant cause is the increase in atmospheric concentration of greenhouse gases. If over time, however, this were to change and the amount of energy emitted by the sun were to change to the extent that it, too, has an effect on the degree to which the climate is changing, it is doubtful that such changes in the nature of the sun would be considered a common concern of humankind as framed in the UNFCCC because such changes are unlikely to be driven by human activity and because the UNFCCC also only recognises a common concern of humankind to the extent that climate change is caused by changes in the atmospheric concentration of greenhouse gases.

The drafters of the UNFCCC could, of course, have disaggregated the predominant cause—increasing atmospheric concentration of greenhouse gases—to a far greater degree so as to more precisely frame the common concern of humankind in question. For example, the parties could have acknowledged that carbon dioxide emissions play a greater role in inducing climate change vis-à-vis other greenhouse gases such as methane. The parties could also have noted that greenhouse gas emissions come predominantly from energy production and consumption. The fact that the parties did not do so has important implications for the extent to which states have retained discretion in dealing with the shared problem in question.

In the corporate taxation context, then, it would be important to define 'tax competition' in such a manner that the causal nexus between tax competition and increases in income and wealth inequality is clear. The definition of 'tax competition' would also have to reflect the potential trade-offs between rising economic inequality within states and the efficient allocation of productive capital. It is therefore fairly clear, for example, that the definition of tax competition should incorporate activity which results in base erosion and profit shifting (BEPS) without contributing to the efficient allocation of productive capital. What else the definition might embrace may in turn have to remain an open question because the empirical effects of competition for productive capital cannot be definitively determined as long as BEPS practices persist. With this definition in mind, the potential implications of recognising a distributional common concern of humankind in connection to tax competition can now be properly considered.

The first implication of the recognition of a distributional common concern of humankind in connection to corporate taxation would be that cooperation in the field is of necessity in order to solve the problem at hand. Such recognition would accordingly instil the idea that sovereignty within the realms of corporate taxation is cooperative sovereignty, which would 'trigger[] duties of cooperation on the part of entities which cannot ensure the protection of all the values they should protect, as much as on the part of entities which can help the former protect those values they share'.[220] The 'shared value' in this particular instance is the power to use corporate taxation as a means, amongst other measures, to effectively change the distribution of income and wealth within a particular state in a way that each individual state sees as necessary or just.

The second implication of recognition would be to reconfigure the goal(s) of tax cooperation. As described above, tax cooperation in the area of BEPS starts from the position of guarding against revenue losses under a given set of tax rates. The idea is akin to the now proverbial leaky bucket. While ensuring the bucket does not leak is, of course, an important matter, the size of the bucket may matter just as much depending on the task at hand, especially once the leaks have been fixed. Recognising a distributional common concern of humankind would lead to a situation where states cooperate not only to prevent leaks but also to allow for the bucket to be increased (or indeed decreased) in size should it be necessary for states to attain their distributional goals.

8 Conclusions

This chapter has dealt with three preliminary issues. First, it looked at what multinationals *are*, which is to say powerful, authoritative institutions that are able to doggedly pursue agendas they construct with relative autonomy. Secondly, as presently constituted, multinationals are the *institutional* actors

220 Besson (n 176) 13.

that contribute *most directly* to the distributional common concern that this monograph argues should be recognised. As such, the third and most important issue has been the issue of responsibility, starting from the premise that it is states—and not multinational enterprises or other institutions—that are ultimately responsible, at least *most directly*, for taking steps to address common concerns of humankind. Given that multinational enterprises are the institutional actors that *contribute most directly* to the problems animating common concerns it is implicit that an *effective* Doctrine of Common Concern of Humankind must necessarily entail an understanding of how state responsibility is parsed into helpful actions—whether proactive or reactive—on the part of multinationals. This prompted the development in the latter third of this chapter of a 'responsibility-action' framework for thinking about this process. The conversation then shifted to applying this framework in the remainder of the chapter to the area of law most crucial to reducing economic inequality in a non-violent manner—*taxation*.

In this regard, the chapter started from the premise that tax sovereignty is better viewed from a cooperative viewpoint. In essence, this thesis is premised on the idea that corporate responsibility—including the responsibility to pay an appropriate amount of taxes—must be imposed by states and the only manner in which states can impose such responsibility—factually—is through cooperation with other states. The chapter subsequently proceeded to explain *why* corporate responsibility ought to be imposed. It did so by arguing in favour of the recognition of a distributional common concern in the area of multinational corporate taxation. Once responsibility is taken on by states, responsibility must be parsed into effective action. In other words, states must cooperate in order to ensure that multinationals do not act in a way that contributes to rising economic inequality within states.

This led to three main points of discussion. First, it was pointed out that corporate tax rates around the world have been falling for decades and examined the reasons for this trend. The revenue and distributional impact of this trend were also considered. Secondly, the argument that, insofar as it pertains to multinationals, tax sovereignty is best conceived of as a cooperative enterprise, was expanded on. Finally, the chapter examined the potential implications and utility of recognising a distributional common concern of humankind in the area of multinational taxation, which would ultimately be to improve state-to-state cooperation in respect of corporate taxation of multinationals and to reorient the present international taxation regime to more explicitly address questions of economic distributions within states.

This chapter has made an argument for recognising changes in the distribution of income and wealth within states and the adverse effects flowing therefrom as a common concern of humankind. Central to this argument has been the idea that states increasingly need to cooperate with one another in order to retain their individual distributional autonomy under conditions of contemporary economic globalisation, with the loss of such resulting in deleterious consequences for a substantial majority of humankind. While this point has been made in broad terms during the course of the chapter, it should not be read as an argument that states no longer have *any* distributional autonomy. Rather, the assertion has in essence been that states have lost—and continue to lose—substantial amounts of distributional autonomy to the extent that a principle of subsidiarity in some form or another, whether termed as such or not, is necessary in order to ascertain who is responsible for ensuring economic distributions are appropriately dealt with within states.

This state of affairs has come to be largely as a function of technological change with existing international laws being accepted as part of the pre-existing factual matrix within which these changes have taken—and continue to take—place. In other words, as a combination of factual changes and existing legal arrangements, an existing precept connected to international law—the idea that 'internal' distributive concerns are to be treated as resoluble within a purely domestic framework of laws and regulations—no longer holds. The recognition of a distributive common concern of humankind as conceived of in this chapter is a possible response to this state of affairs that would seek to reconfigure the foundations of international law—mainly through adopting a different understanding of sovereignty—such that distributional matters within states can continue to be dealt with effectively.

CHAPTER 5

Concluding Remarks

> It is, as we assert, necessary in a State which is to avoid that greatest of plagues, which is better termed disruption than dissension [or class discord], that none of its citizens should be in a condition of either painful poverty or wealth, since both these conditions produce both these results; consequently the lawgiver must now declare a limit for both these conditions.
>
> PLATO (428–348 BCE), *Laws*[1]

As we approach the start of decade five of a virtually global trend towards greater inequalities of income and wealth within the world's countries, the main question driving this monograph has been how we can do a better job in respect of handling one of humanity's oldest preoccupations: that of the distribution of economic resources within societies. More specifically, I have been thinking about better ways of addressing long term changes in economic distributions *within* different states, thereby mitigating against or, from an aspirational standpoint, avoiding entirely, the deleterious impacts of such changes; this from the perspective of international law—that is, the rules of engagement as *between* states.

My hope has been to initiate a conversation which apparently seemed unnecessary for international lawyers and other actors to have during the decades immediately following the Second World War, but which I argue should have been taken up to a greater extent; definitely then but especially—and more earnestly—since the mid-1980s. One of the main motivations underpinning this monograph has simply been that, as far as I could tell, this conversation had still not been taken up in any meaningful way when I started my research in the latter half of 2015.

1 Plato, *Laws, Volume I: Books 1–6* (William Heinemann Ltd., London 1926), translated from the original Greek by RG Bury, 378–81. The insertion is Plato's—see 379, note 2.

 | DOI:10.1163/9789004511750_006

While there were myriad ways in which this endeavour might have been undertaken, I initially had trouble finding a home for my proposed research. The success of certain works such as Thomas Piketty's Capital in the Twenty-First Century had begun to mainstream the study of economic inequality to a degree that had not been observed since Simon Kuznets had essentially declared it a non-issue in the 1950s, and economic inequality had begun to pique the interests of scholars outside of the field of economics, including some lawyers. International lawyers, however, appeared to be immune to Professor Piketty's charm.

Professor Cottier founded the project under whose auspices I have written this monograph in order to study in detail the 'Doctrine of Common Concern of Humankind', a theory he had been developing over the course of several years. The Doctrine draws on the recognition of 'common concerns of humankind', particularly in the fields of international climate change and biodiversity law, in order to propose a new framework for international cooperation that is fit for the purpose of solving those contemporary problems shared by all of humankind. With much of the theory and practice surrounding the concept of common concern of humankind having been studied before, the focus of my thesis has been on the recognition of new common concerns of humankind by contemplating the potential form and utility of recognising economic distributions within states and the adverse effects that follow as these distributions change over time as a common concern of humankind. Such recognition would then trigger the application of the Doctrine as proposed by Professor Cottier.

The starting point for this monograph was the central issue when recognising common concerns: the idea of what it means to be a state that has sovereignty. I have argued that the recognition of a particular problem as a common concern of humankind acts as a definitional instantiation of particular aspects of sovereignty such that certain global challenges may be overcome. With respect to the case in point, I have argued that sovereigns can only retain their own distributive autonomy through engaging in collective action together with other sovereigns. Without cooperation between states, the ability of each state to effect distributional change within its sovereign space is severely constrained. The retention of this ability not only does not run contrary to the notion of sovereignty but is manifestly necessary for the continued existence of states properly so called. Seen this way, the need for the legal reconstitution of sovereignty in light of particular factual changes over time is an obvious—and often overlooked—constitutive element of any common concern of humankind.

The set of changed facts contemplated in my thesis are the shifts in economic globalization that began in the late 1980s when the world experienced major advances in information and communications technology (ICT) which are often described as having had—and continuing to have—a 'revolutionary' or 'transformative' impact on the global economy. Most of the states in the world have also seen income and wealth within their respective territories become increasingly unequally distributed. The large majority of this trend has occurred alongside the described shifts in technological change and economic globalization. With this factual context sketched, the main thrust of the arguments presented in my thesis is that sovereignty-based objections to the recognition of the adverse effects stemming from the distribution of income and wealth as a common concern of humankind are premised on an inappropriate understanding of contemporary sovereignty.[2]

Once sovereignty objections are cast aside, the only valid objections that remain to the potential recognition of a distributional common concern of humankind revolve around the perceived severity—or lack thereof—of a substantial loss of distributive autonomy. Objections of this nature, in turn, are becoming increasingly difficult to sustain as our understanding of the empirical effects of distributional changes improve with time. As a result, sovereignty not only does not constitute an impediment to the recognition of a potential distributional common concern of humankind, it becomes one of the chief arguments in favour of its recognition. The utility of recognising a distributional common concern of humankind, at least in large part, would be in its rebalancing of sovereignty—as practiced—in a manner that would place greater emphasis on effectively ensuring the welfare of the human-beings that live within states, something which can be better—or perhaps only—accomplished through international coordination and cooperation, actions which in and of themselves are less likely to occur under conditions of growing economic inequality within states.

Having made the case for the recognition of a distributional common concern as a general matter, I subsequently turned my focus to more specific details of the circumstance under which recognition could be useful. First, I thought about the fact that common concerns as conceptual category, and especially the proposed distributional common concern, do not contemplate issues where states are the most direct contributors to the global problems at hand. Rather, as the most significant direct participants in global commerce, multinational enterprises (multinationals) are the actors that most considerably contribute to the problems the common concern concept seeks

2 I have thus found a potential home for economic distributions within states in international law, something which is clearly necessary given the highly significant implications economic distributions within states have for the future of international law. I return to this issue below.

to address. For example, multinationals are by far the largest contributors to the common concern of climate change. Therefore, while states are the ones that most directly take on obligations in respect of common concerns, obligations undertaken pursuant to the recognition of climate change and its adverse effects as a common concern can only be meaningfully implemented if appropriate mechanisms are devised to parse state obligations into direct actions taken by multinationals. The same is true of the recognition of a distributional common concern. For this reason, the utility of such recognition requires a theory of corporate responsibility in relation to the common concern.

From a conceptual perspective, I understand multinationals in a manner proposed by John Ruggie.[3] The theory of corporate responsibility I thus adopted in relation to the recognition of a distributional common concern is accordingly developed around reconciling the differences between the legal and economic understandings of multinationals so as to enable states, acting in cooperation with one another, to address the shared problem of regulating multinationals in a manner that allows for economic distributions that are viewed as just. Against this backdrop, I proceeded to suggest that recognising a distributional common concern in the area of corporate taxation could be useful for enhancing the sovereignty of individual states through cooperation and for developing a system of law that is actually geared towards reducing economic inequality.

With the work of this monograph done, there remain a large number of questions that I intend on addressing in future. The first set of these, which I hope to turn my attention to in the near future, revolve around democracy. What was clear to scholars at the time of the early democracies millennia ago should not only be instructive in contemporary times but should by now be accepted as obvious: democracies have not been designed to operate under conditions of unacceptable economic inequality.

Instead, they must guard fervently against the concentration of economic resources and power. While exact tipping points are difficult to locate, there exists a level of inequality within each democracy that, if surpassed, has the capacity to render it unworthy of being designated a 'democracy'. Too much economic inequality *breaks* democracies. As such, it is incumbent upon democratic states to fight against highly skewed distributions within their own borders, not only because it is the just thing to do, but also because self-preservation demands it. While I have already quoted him in an earlier

---

3 See John Gerard Ruggie, 'Multinationals as Global Institution: Power, Authority and Relative Autonomy' (2018) 12 *Regulation & Governance* 317.

chapter, the words of Jean-Jacques remain most apposite in this context and worth repeating here. In his book, *The Social Contract*, Rousseau writes as follows:

> [A]s for equality, the word must not be taken to mean that the degrees of power and wealth should be exactly the same, but that, as regards personal power, it should not be so great as to make violence possible, and should be exercised only in accordance with social position and the law; and as regards wealth, that no citizen should be rich enough to be able to buy another, and none so poor that he has to sell himself ... Equality, it is said, is a theorists' vision, which cannot exist in practice. But if an abuse is inevitable, does it follow that it should not at least be controlled? It is precisely because the force of things always tends to destroy equality that the force of law should tend always to conserve it.[4]

The same is true of *international* law.

Beyond threatening their stability and even their existence in extreme cases, the failure of democracies to curb unacceptable distributions from being reached has various consequences worth considering. In a world where rapid technological change is the norm, the agility of a state is one of its most important features. When inequality fractures democracy, other forms of government, which tend to be more agile precisely because they are *not* democratic, become increasingly appealing. There are two immediate reasons for this: first, states that are not currently democracies are far less incentivised to transition, or even to begin to transition, towards democracy. Secondly, democratic states lose legitimacy internally because the will of their people—the *demos*—becomes frustrated.

Non-democratic states arguably function better in times of high inequality, at least in an economic sense. In recent times, the more successful economies—at least from a growth perspective—have tended not to be democratic.[5] This

---

4 Jean-Jacques Rousseau, *The Social Contract* (OUP, New York 1994), translated from the original French by Christopher Betts, 87. Footnote omitted.

5 China (a non-democratic state) to India (a democratic state) serves as a helpful comparison: both have very large populations of a similar size (they are the two largest economies in the world by population), both countries started with economies of a similar size in 1960 and both countries have undergone substantial economic transformations since the 1980s. Since the advent of globalization's second unbundling—a period during which the global economy has not only changed substantially but during which the pace of economic change has arguably been unprecedented—India's economic success, while substantial, has been significantly dwarfed by the success of the Chinese economy. On 'globalization's second

is because non-democratic governance structures are usually at a comparative advantage during such times. This likely comes as a result of democracies not functioning as intended and non-democracies being inherently more agile in the implementation of their objectives. Not only do non-democratic states not have to pay as much attention to high and/or rising inequality within their borders, they are also better equipped to do something about inequality should they elect to do so because internal polarisation, whether political, economic or otherwise, does not hinder the pace or the efficacy of concerted action.

It should be accepted, particularly by believers in the ideal, that democracy does not have a good track record when it comes to peacefully reducing economic inequality. This does not mean that the requisite tools for improvement in this regard do not exist or that the task at hand need be approached with a high level of cynicism. States have many policy options at their disposal which need not be taken in coordination with or impose unnecessary distributional externalities on other states, and which are realistically capable of making a material difference to economic inequality within their own borders. It is, however, incumbent on states, especially democracies, to make use of these options as much as is realistically possible and thereby improve democracy's track record and legitimacy. The argument that democracy is the best form of government cannot rest on the assumption that democracies result in greater equality if that assumption is for the most part a theoretical one.

---

unbundling', see Chapter 3 above in this monograph. On the size of India's economy vis-à-vis China's, see World Bank, 'GDP (constant 2010 $US)', World Bank and OECD national accounts data <https://data.worldbank.org/indicator/NY.GDP.MKTP.KD?locations=CN-IN> accessed 30 September 2021.

Bibliography

Monographs and Books

Agence Française de Développement (Research Department) (ed), *Poverty, Inequality and Growth: Proceedings of the AFD-EUDN Conference*, 2003 (Maggelan, Paris 2004).

Alvaredo, F et al (eds), *World Inequality Report 2018* (HUP, Massachusetts, MA 2018).

Atkinson, AB, *Inequality: What Can Be Done?* (HUP, London 2015).

Atkinson, AB and Harrison, AJ, *Distribution of Personal Wealth in Britain* (CUP, Cambridge 1978).

Auclert, A, *Monetary Policy and the Redistribution Channel* (NBER, Cambridge, MA 2017).

Baldwin, R, *The Great Convergence: Information Technology and the New Globalization* (HUP, Cambridge, MA 2016).

Bhalla, SS, *Imagine There's No Country* (Institute for International Economics, Washington, DC 2002).

Bourguignon, F, *The Globalization of Inequality* (PUP, Princeton 2015).

Brown, HP, *The Inequality of Pay* (OUP, Oxford 1979).

Brownlee, WE, *Federal Taxation in America: A Short History* (CUP, New York 2004).

Chen, J, Stephens, M and Man, Y (eds), *The Future of Public Housing: Ongoing Trends in the East and the West* (Springer, Heidelberg 2013).

Chetty, R et al, *The Opportunity Atlas: Mapping the Childhood Roots of Social Mobility* (NBER, Cambridge, MA 2018).

Collier, P, *The Bottom Billion: Why the Poorest Countries are Failing and What Can be Done About It* (OUP, Oxford 2007).

Cornia, GA (ed), *Inequality, Growth, and Poverty in an Era of Liberalization and Globalization* (OUP, Oxford 2004).

Cottier, T, *Equitable Principles of Maritime Boundary Delimitation* (CUP, Cambridge 2015).

Cottier, T (ed), *The Prospects of Common Concern of Humankind in International Law* (CUP, Cambridge 2021).

Dalton, H, *Some Aspects of the Inequality of Incomes in Modern Communities* (George Routledge & Sons, London 1920).

Davis, GF, *The Vanishing American Corporation: Navigating the Hazards of a New Economy* (Berrett-Kohler Publishers, Oakland 2016).

Dietsch, P, *Catching Capital: The Ethics of Tax Competition* (OUP, Oxford 2015).

Dunning, JH and Lundan, SM, *Multinational Enterprises and the Global Economy* (2ed Edward Elgar, Cheltenham 2008).

Feldman, F, *Distributive Justice: Getting What We Deserve from Our Country* (OUP, Oxford 2016).

Field, CB et al (eds), *Managing the Risks of Extreme Events and Disasters to Advance Climate Change Adaption: Special Report of the Intergovernmental Panel on Climate Change* (CUP, New York 2012).

Findlay, R and O'Rourke, KH, *Power and Plenty: Trade, War, and the World Economy in the Second Millennium* (PUP, Princeton 2008).

Friedman, M, *Capitalism and Freedom* (University of Chicago Press, Chicago 1962).

Gini, C, *Variabilità e Mutabilità* (Tipografia di Cuppini, Bologna 1912).

Goldin, C and Katz, LF, *The Race between Education and Technology* (HUP, Cambridge, MA 2008).

Greengross, P, Grant, K and Collini, E, *Helpdesk Report: The History and Development of the UK National Health Service 1948–1999* (DFID Health Systems Resource Centre, London 1999).

Gurr, TR, *Why Men Rebel* (PUP, Princeton 1970).

Horn, LS, *The Common Concern of Humankind and Legal Protection of the Global Environment* (Unpublished PhD thesis, University of Sydney 2000).

Hornbeck, JF, *Trade Adjustment Assistance (TAA) and Its Role in U.S. Trade Policy* (Congressional Research Service, Washington, DC 2013).

Jackson, JH, *Sovereignty, the WTO, and the Changing Fundamentals of International Law* (CUP, Cambridge 2006).

Krugman, P, *The Conscience of a Liberal* (WW Norton, New York 2009).

Kuznets, S, *Shares of Upper Income Groups in Income and Savings* (NBER, New York 1953).

Larsen, CA *The Rise and Fall of Social Cohesion: The Construction and De-construction of Social Trust in the US, UK, Sweden and Denmark* (OUP, Oxford 2013).

McAfee, A and Brynjolfsson, E, *The Second Machine Age: Work, Progress, and Prosperity in a Time of Brilliant Technologies* (WW Norton, New York 2016).

Milanovic, B, *Global Inequality: A New Approach for the Age of Globalization* (HUP, Cambridge, MA 2016).

Mill, JS, *Principles of Political Economy with Some of Their Applications to Social Philosophy*, abridged, edited, with introduction, by Stephen Nathanson (Hackett, Indianapolis 2004).

National Planning Commission of South Africa, *National Development Plan: Vision for 2030* (Presidency of South Africa, Pretoria 2011).

Olson, M, *The Logic of Collective Action* (HUP, Cambridge, MA 1965).

Pen, J, *The Distribution of Income: Facts, Theories, Policies* (Praeger, New York 1971).

Perrez, FX, *Cooperative Sovereignty: From Independence to Interdependence in the Structure of International Environmental Law* (Kluwer, The Hague 2000).

Pierson, C *Beyond the Welfare State? The New Political Economy of Welfare* (Penn State University Press, University Park, PA 1991).

Piketty, T, *Capital in the Twenty-First Century* (HUP, London 2014).

Plato, *Laws, Volume I: Books 1–6* (William Heinemann, London 1926).

Pope Francis, *The Joy of the Gospel:* Evangelii Gaudiuum (Veritas Publications, Dublin 2013).

Rajan, R, *Fault Lines* (PUP, Princeton 2010).

Rawls, J, *A Theory of Justice* (*Revised Edition*) (HUP, Cambridge, MA 1999).

Ricardo, D, *On the Principles of Political Economy and Taxation* (John Murray, London 1817).

Rodrik, D, *One Economics, Many Recipes: Globalization, Institutions and Economic Growth* (PUP, Princeton 2007).

Roemer, JE, *Theories of Distributive Justice* (HUP, Cambridge, MA 1996).

Rousseau, J-J, *The Social Contract* (OUP, New York 1994).

Sarooshi, D, *International Organizations and Their Exercise of Sovereign Powers* (OUP, New York 2005).

Scheidel, W, *The Great Leveler: Violence and the History of Inequality from the Stone Age to the Twenty-First Century* (PUP, Princeton 2017).

Smith, A, *The Wealth of Nations: Books IVV* (Penguin Books, London 1999).

Stewart, F (ed), *Horizontal Inequalities and Conflict: Understanding Group Violence in Multiethnic Societies* (Palgrave Macmillan, Basingstoke 2008).

Stiglitz, J, *The Price of Inequality: How Today's Divided Society Endangers Our Future* (WW Norton, New York 2012).

Stocker, TF et al (eds), *Climate Change 2013: The Physical Science Basis, Working Group I Contribution to the Fifth Assessment Report of the Intergovernmental Panel on Climate Change* (CUP, New York 2014).

Suttle, O, *Distributive Justice and World Trade Law: A Political Theory of International Trade Regulation* (CUP, Cambridge 2018).

Theil, H, *Economics and Information Theory* (North-Holland, Amsterdam 1967).

Zimmermann, CD, *A Contemporary Concept of Monetary Sovereignty* (OUP, Oxford 2013); and.

Zucman, G, *The Hidden Wealth of Nations: The Scourge of Tax Havens* (University of Chicago Press, Chicago 2015).

Articles, Contributions to Compilations, Working Papers, and Reports (All Online Materials Last Accessed 30 September 2021)

Acemoğlu, D and Robinson, JA 'Why Did the West Extend the Franchise? Democracy, Inequality, and Growth in Historical Perspective' (2002) 115 *Quarterly Journal of Economics* 1167.

Aghion, P, Caroli, E and Garcia-Penalosa, C, 'Inequality and Economic Growth: The Perspective of the New Growth Theories' (1999) 37 *Journal of Economic Literature* 1615.

Ahmad, Z, 'Trade-Related Measures to Spread Low Carbon Technologies: A Common Concern Based Approach' in Cottier, T (ed), *The Prospects of Common Concern of Humankind in International Law* (CUP, Cambridge 2021).

Alesina, A and Rodrik, D, 'Distributive Politics and Economic Growth' (1994) 109 *Quarterly Journal of Economics* 465.

Alstadsæter, A, Johannesen, N and Zucman, G, 'Who Owns the Wealth in Tax Havens? Macro Evidence and Implications for Global Inequality' (2018) 162 *Journal of Public Economics* 89.

Alstadsæter, A, Johannesen, N and Zucman, G, 'Tax Evasion and Inequality' (2019) 109 *American Economic Review* 2073.

Alvaredo, F, Atkinson, AB, Piketty, T and Saez, E, 'The Top 1 Percent in International and Historical Perspective' (2013) 27 *Journal of Economic Perspectives* 3.

Alvaredo, F et al, 'Distributional National Accounts Guidelines: Methods and Concepts Used in WID.world' (WID.world methodological document, 7 September 2020) <https://wid.world/document/distributional-national-accounts-guidelines-2020-concepts-and-methods-used-in-the-world-inequality-database/> accessed 30 September 2021.

Anderson, LR, Mellor, JM and Milyo, J, 'Inequality and Public Good Provision: An Experimental Analysis' (2008) 37 *The Journal of Socio-Economics* 1010.

Arber, S, 'Unequal Partners: Inequality in Earnings and Independent Income within Marriage' in Linda McKie, Sophia Bowlby and Susan Gregory (eds), *Gender, Power and the Household* (Palgrave Macmillan, Basingstoke 1999) 175.

Armour, J et al, 'What is Corporate Law?' in Kraakman, R et al, *The Anatomy of Corporate Law: A Comparative and Functional Approach* (3ed OUP, Oxford 2017).

Assouad, L, Chancel, L, and Morgan, M, 'Extreme Inequality: Evidence from Brazil, India, the Middle East, and South Africa' (2018) 108 *AEA Papers and Proceedings* 119.

Atkinson, AB, 'Bringing Income Distribution in From the Cold' (1997) 107 *Economic Journal* 297.

Atkinson, AB and Lakner, C, 'Wages, Capital and Top Incomes: The Factor Income Composition of Top Incomes in the USA, 1960–2005' (2014), unpublished manuscript <http://www.ecineq.org/ecineq_lux15/FILESx2015/CR2/p196.pdf>.

Avi-Yonah, RS, 'Double Tax Treaties: An Introduction' in Sauvant, KP and Sachs, LE (eds), *The Effects of Treaties on Foreign Direct Investment: Bilateral Investment Treaties, Double Taxation Treaties, and Investment Flows* (OUP, Oxford 2009).

Avi-Yonah, RS, 'International Tax as International Law' (2004) 57 *Tax Law Review* 483.

Avi-Yonah, RS, 'The Deemed Dividend Problem' (2004) 4 *Taxation of Global Transactions* 33.

Babic, M, Fichtner, J and Heemskerk, EM, 'States versus Corporations: Rethinking the Power of Business in International Politics' (2017) 52 *International Spectator* 20.

Baek, J and Gweisah, G, 'Does Income Inequality Harm the Environment?: Empirical Evidence from the United States' (2013) 62 *Energy Policy* 1434.

Bagchi, S and Svejnar, J, 'Does Wealth Inequality Matter for Growth? The Effect of Billionaire Wealth, Income Distribution, and Poverty' (2015) 43 *Journal of Comparative Economics* 505.

Baker, D, Bivens, J and Schieder, J, 'Reining in CEO Compensation and Curbing the Rise of Inequality' (Economic Policy Institute Report, Washington DC, 4 June 2019) <https://www.epi.org/files/pdf/168855.pdf>.

Banerjee, AV and Newman, AF, 'Occupational Choice and the Process of Development' (1993) 101 *Journal of Political Economy* 274.

Baslar, K, *The Concept of the Common Heritage of Mankind in International Law* (Kluwer Law International, The Hague 1998).

Beach, CM, 'Changing Income Inequality: A Distributional Paradigm for Canada' (2016) 49 *Canadian Journal of Economics* 1229.

Bell, A et al, 'Mobility Report Cards: The Role of Colleges in Intergenerational Mobility' (NBER Working Paper 23618, July 2017).

Benhabib, J, 'The Tradeoff between Inequality and Growth' (2003) 4 *Annals of Economics and Finance* 329.

Berg, AG and Ostry, JD, 'Inequality and Unsustainable Growth: Two Sides of the Same Coin?' (2017) 65 *IMF Economic Review* 792.

Berg, AG, Ostry, JD and Zettelmeyer, J, 'What Makes Growth Sustained?' (2012) 98 *Journal of Development Economics* 149.

Besson, S, 'Sovereignty in Conflict' (2004) 8 *European Integration online Papers (EIoP)* 1.

Beyleveld, A, 'Exploring the Recognition of New Common Concerns of Humankind: The Example of the Distribution of Income and Wealth within States' in Cottier, T (ed), *The Prospects of Common Concern of Humankind in International Law* (CUP, Cambridge 2021).

Biermann, F, '"Common Concern of Humankind": The Emergence of a New Concept of International Environmental Law' (1996) 34 *Archiv des Völkerrechts* 426.

Biermann, F, '"Common Concerns of Humankind" and National Sovereignty' in Hiscox, D and Levasseur, J (eds), *Globalism: People, Profits, and Progress: Proceedings of the 30th Annual Conference of the Canadian Council on International Law* (Kluwer, London 2002).

Bodansky, D, 'The United Nations Framework Convention on Climate Change: A Commentary' (1993) 18 *Yale Journal of International Law* 451.

Bodie, MT, 'Income Inequality and Corporate Structure' (2015) 45 *Stetson Law Review* 69.

Boer, B, 'Land Degradation as a Common Concern of Humankind' in Lenzerini, F and Vrdoljak, AF (eds), *International Law for Common Goods: Normative Perspectives on Human Rights, Culture and Nature* (Hart Publishing, Oxford 2014) 289.

Bogdanova, I, 'Reshaping the Law of Economic Sanctions for Human Rights Violations: The Potential of Common Concern of Humankind' in Cottier, T (ed), *The Prospects of Common Concern of Humankind in International Law* (CUP, Cambridge 2021).

Boix, C, 'Economic Roots of Civil Wars and Revolutions in the Contemporary World' (2008) 60 *World Politics* 390.

Bordo, MD and Meissner, CM, 'Does Inequality Lead to a Financial Crisis?' (2012) 31 *Journal of International Money and Finance* 2147.

Borghesi, S, 'Income Inequality and the Environmental Kuznets Curve' in Basilli, M, Francini, M and Vercelli, A (eds), *Environment, Inequality and Collective Action* (Routledge, New York 2006) 32.

Boswell, T and Dixon, WJ, 'Marx's Theory of Rebellion: A Cross-Nation Analysis of Class Exploitation, Economic Development, and Violent Conflict' (1993) 58 *American Sociological Review* 681.

Bourguignon, F, 'The Poverty-Growth-Inequality Triangle?' in Agence Française de Développement (Research Department) (ed), *Poverty, Inequality and Growth: Proceedings of the AFD-EUDN Conference*, 2003 (Maggelan, Paris 2004).

Boyce, JK, 'Inequality as a Cause of Environmental Degradation' (1994) 11 *Ecological Economics* 169.

Boyce, JK, 'Is Inequality Bad for the Environment?' (2008) 15 *Research in Social Problems and Public Policy* 267.

Bradbury, K and Katz, J, 'Trends in U.S. Family Income Mobility, 1967–2004' (Federal Reserve Bank of Boston, working paper 2009) 2 <https://www.bostonfed.org/-/media/Documents/Workingpapers/PDF/wp0907.pdf>.

Brewer, PR, Kimberly Gross and Timothy Vercellotti, 'Trust in International Actors' in Uslaner, EM, (ed), *The Oxford Handbook on Social and Political Trust* (Oxford University Press, Oxford 2018).

Briggs, A, 'The Welfare State in Historical Perspective' (1961) 2 *European Journal of Sociology* 221.

Brown Weiss, E, 'The Coming Water Crisis: A Common Concern of Mankind' 1 (2012) *Transnational Environmental Law* 153.

Brunnée, J, 'Common Areas, Common Heritage, and Common Concern' in Bodansky, D, Brunnée, J and Hey, E (eds), *The Oxford Handbook of International Environmental Law* (OUP, New York 2007).

Brunnée, J and Nollkaemper, A, 'Between the Forests and the Trees—An Emerging International Forest Law' (1996) 23 *Environmental Conservation* 307.

Buhaung, H and Cederman, L-E, 'Square Pegs in Round Holes: Inequalities, Grievances and Civil War' (2014) 58 *International Studies Quarterly* 418.

Calabresi, G, 'About Law and Economics: A Letter to Ronald Dworkin' (1980) 8 *Hofstra Law Review* 553.

Cançado Trindade, AA, *International Law for Humankind: Towards a New* Jus Gentium (Martinus Nijhoff Publishers, Leiden 2010).

Castelló-Climent, A, 'Inequality and Growth in Advanced Economies: an Empirical Investigation' (2010) 8 *Journal of Economic Inequality* 293.

Castillo-Winckels, NS, 'Why "Common Concern of Humankind" Should Return to the Work of the International Law Commission on the Atmosphere' (2016) 29 *Georgetown International Environmental Law Review* 131.

Cederman, L-E, Weidmann, NB and Bormann, NC, 'Triangulating Horizontal Inequality: Toward Improved Conflict Analysis' (2015) 52 *Journal of Peace Research* 806.

Cederman, L-E, Weidmann, NB and Gleditsch, KS, 'Horizontal Inequalities and Ethnonationalist Civil War: A Global Comparison' (2011) 105 *American Political Science Review* 478.

Ceriani, L and Verme, P, 'The origins of the Gini index: extracts from Variabilità e Mutabilità (1912) by Corrado Gini' (2012) 10 *Journal of Economic Inequality* 421.

Chancel, L, and Piketty, T, 'Carbon and Inequality: from Kyoto to Paris, Trends in the Global Inequality of Carbon Emissions (1998–2013) & Prospects for an Equitable Adaptation Fund' (2015) <http://piketty.pse.ens.fr/files/ChancelPiketty2015.pdf>.

Chen, H et al, 'The Global Impacts of US Climate Policy: A Model Simulation Using GCAM-TU and MAGICC' (2018) 18 *Climate Policy* 852.

Chetty, R et al, 'The Association between Income and Life Expectancy in the United States, 2001–2014' (2016) 315 *Journal of the American Medical Association* 1750.

Chetty, R et al, 'The Fading American Dream: Trends in Absolute Income Mobility since 1940' (2017) 356 *Science* 398.

Chetty, R and Hendren, N, 'The Impacts of Neighborhoods on Intergenerational Mobility II: County-Level Estimates' (2018) 133 *Quarterly Journal of Economics* 1163.

Chetty, R and Hendren, N, 'The Effects of Neighborhoods on Intergenerational Mobility I: Childhood Exposure Effects' (2018) 133 *Quarterly Journal of Economics* 1107.

Chiappori, P-A and Meghir, C, 'Intrahousehold Inequality' in Anthony B Atkinson and François Bourguignon (eds), *Handbook of Income Distribution* (*Volume 2B*) (Elsevier, Amsterdam 2015) 1369.

Choi, C, 'Does Foreign Direct Investment Affect Domestic Income Inequality?' (2006) 13 *Applied Economics Letters*, 811.

Christians, A, 'Sovereignty, Taxation and Social Contract' (2009) 18 *Minnesota Journal of International Law* 99.

Cingano, F, 'Trends in Income Inequality and its Impact on Economic Growth' (OECD Social, Employment and Migration Working Papers 163, 2014).

Clotfelter, CT, *Unequal Colleges in the Age of Disparity* (HUP, Cambridge, MA 2017).

Coleman, JL, 'Efficiency, Utility and Wealth Maximization' (1980) 8 *Hofstra Law Review* 509.

Coady, D and Dizioli, A, 'Income Inequality and Education Revisited: Persistence, Endogeneity, and Heterogeneity' (IMF Working Paper WP/17/26, May 2017).

Cobb, JA and Stevens, FG, 'These Unequal States: Corporate Organization and Income Inequality in the United States' (2017) 62 *Administrative Science Quarterly* 304.

Colasante, A and Russo, A, 'Voting for the Distribution Rule in a Public Good Game with Heterogeneous Endowments' (2017) 12 *Journal of Economic Interaction and Coordination* 443.

Collier, P and Hoeffler, A, 'Greed and Grievance in Civil War' (2004) 56 *Oxford Economic Papers* 563.

Corak, M, 'Income Inequality, Equality of Opportunity, and Intergenerational Mobility' (2013) 27 *Journal of Economic Perspectives* 79.

Cottier, T, 'Equity in International Law' in Cottier, T, Lalani, S and Siziba, C, *Intergenerational Equity: Environmental and Cultural Concerns* (Brill | Nijhoff, Leiden 2019).

Cottier, T, 'The Principles of Common Concern of Humankind' in Thomas Cottier (ed), *The Prospects of Common Concern of Humankind in International Law* (CUP, Cambridge 2021).

Cottier, T et al, 'The Principle of Common Concern and Climate Change' (2014) 52 *Archiv des Völkerrechts* 293.

Cottier, T and Losada, RM, 'Migration as a Common Concern of Humankind' in Thomas Cottier (ed), *The Prospects of Common Concern of Humankind in International Law* (CUP, Cambridge 2021).

Cottier, T and Payosova, T, 'Common Concern and the Legitimacy of the WTO in Dealing with Climate Change' in Delimatsis, P (ed), *Research Handbook on Climate Change and Trade Law* (Edward Elgar, Cheltenham 2016).

Credit Suisse Research Institute, 'Global Wealth Report 2017' (November 2017) <https://www.credit-suisse.com/corporate/en/research/research-institute/global-wealth-report.html>.

Dabla-Norris, E et al, 'Causes and Consequences of Income Inequality: A Global Perspective' (IMF Staff Discussion Note SDN/15/13, June 2015).

Dahl, R, 'The Concept of Power' (1956) 2 *Behavioral Science* 201.

Davis, GF and Cobb, JA, 'Corporations and Economic Inequality around the World: The Paradox of Hierarchy' (2010) 30 *Research in Organizational Behaviour* 35.

Deaton, A, 'Health, Inequality, and Economic Development' (2003) 41 *Journal of Economic Literature* 113.

Delbianco, F, Dabús, C and Caraballo, MA, 'Income Inequality and Economic Growth: New Evidence from Latin America' (2014) 33 *Cuadernos de Economía* 381.

Dietsch, P, 'Whose Tax Base? The Ethics of Global Tax Governance' in Dietsch, P and Rixen, T (eds), *Global Tax Governance: What is Wrong with it and How to Fix It* (ECPR Press, Colchester 2016).

Dietsch, P, 'Rethinking Sovereignty in International Fiscal Policy' (2011) 37 *Review of International Studies* 2107.

Dietsch, P and Rixen, T, 'Redistribution, Globalisation and Multi-Level Governance' (2014) 1 *Moral Philosophy and Politics* 61.

Dietsch, P and Rixen, T, 'Tax Competition and Global Background Justice' (2014) 22 *Journal of Political Philosophy* 150.

Dube, A, 'Minimum Wages and the Distribution of Family Incomes' (IZA Institute of Labor Economics Discussion Paper 10572, February 2017) <http://ftp.iza.org/dp10572.pdf>.

Dworkin, RM, 'Is Wealth a Value?' (1980) 9 *Journal of Legal Studies* 119.

Dworkin, RM, 'Why Efficiency?' (1980) 8 *Hofstra Law Review* 563.

Eden, L, 'Taxes, Transfer Pricing, and the Multinational Enterprise' in Rugman, AM and Brewer, TL (eds), *The Oxford Handbook of International Business* (OUP, Oxford 2001) 591.

Eggertsson, GB, Robbins, JA and Wold, EG, 'Kaldor and Piketty's Facts: The Rise of Monopoly Power in the United States' (NBER Working Paper, No 24287, February 2018) <https://www.nber.org/papers/w24287.pdf>.

Ennis, S, Gonzaga, P and Pike, C, 'Inequality: A Hidden Cost of Market Power' (OECD Discussion Paper 2017) <https://www.oecd.org/daf/competition/Inequality-hidden-cost-market-power-2017.pdf>.

Erosa, A and Ventura, G, 'On Inflation as a Regressive Consumption Tax' (2002) 49 *Journal of Monetary Economics* 761.

Ezcurra, R and Palacios, D, 'Terrorism and Spatial Disparities: Does Interregional Inequality Matter?' (2016) 42 *European Journal of Political Economy* 60.

Fajnzyber, P, Lederman, D and Loayza, N, 'Inequality and Violent Crime' (2002) 45 *Journal of Law and Economics* 1.

French, D, 'Common Concern, Common Heritage and Other Global(-ising) Concepts: Rhetorical Devices, Legal Principles or a Fundamental Challenge' in Bowman, M, Davies, P and Goodwin, E (eds), *Research Handbook on Biodiversity and Law* (Edward Elgar Publishing, 2016 Cheltenham).

Fuchs, D, *Business Power in Global Governance* (Lynn Rienner, Boulder, CO 2007).

Furman, J and Orszag, P, 'A Firm-Level Perspective on the Role of Rents in the Rise in Inequality' (Presentation at 'A Just Society' Event in Honor of Joseph Stiglitz, 2016) <https://obamawhitehouse.archives.gov/sites/default/files/page/files/20151016_firm_level_perspective_on_role_of_rents_in_inequality.pdf>.

Fuso, AK, 'Growth, Inequality, and Poverty Reduction in Developing Countries: Recent Global Evidence' (2017) 71 *Research in Economics* 306.

Fuso, AK, 'Inequality and the Impact of Growth on Poverty: Comparative Evidence for Sub-Saharan Africa' (2009) 45 *Journal of Development Studies* 726.

Gallie, WB, 'Essentially Contested Concepts' (1956) 56 *Proceedings of the Aristotelian Society* 167.

Galor, O and Zeira, J 'Income Distribution and Macroeconomics' (1993) 60 *Review of Economic Studies* 35.

Garbarino, C and Garufi, S, 'Transparency and Exchange of Information in International Taxation' in Bianchi, A and Peters, A (eds), *Transparency in International Law* (CUP, Cambridge 2013).

Gassebner, M, Lamla, MJ and Sturm, J-E, 'Determinants of Pollution: What Do We Really Know?' (2011) 63 *Oxford Economics Papers* 568.

Ginzky, H, 'The Sustainable Management of Soils as a Common Concern of Humankind: How to Implement It?' in Ginzky, H et al (eds), *International Yearbook of Soil Law and Policy 2017* (Springer, Cham 2017).

Goldin, C and Margo, RA, 'The Great Compression: The U.S. Wage Structure at Mid-Century' (1992) 107 *Quarterly Journal of Economics* 1.

Golley, J and Meng, X, 'Income Inequality and Carbon Dioxide Emissions: The Case of Chinese Urban Households' (2012) 34 *Energy Economics* 1864.

Grigoli, F, Paredes, E and Di Bella, G, 'Inequality and Growth: A Heterogeneous Approach' (IMF Working Paper WP/16/244, December 2016).

Grigoli, F and Robles, A, 'Inequality Overhang' (IMF Working Paper WP/17/76, 28 March 2017).

Grunewald, N et al, 'The Trade-off between Income Inequality and Carbon Dioxide Emissions' (2017) 142 *Ecological Economics* 249.

Haider, SJ and McGarry, K, 'Postsecondary Schooling and Parental Resources: Evidence from the PSID and HRS' (2018) 13 *Education Finance and Policy* 72.

Halter D, Oechslin, M and Zweimüller, J, 'Inequality and Growth: the Neglected Time Dimension' (2014) 19 *Journal of Economic Growth* 81.

Hao, Y, Chen, H and Zhang, Q, 'Will Income Inequality Affect Environmental Quality? Analysis Based on China's Provincial Panel Data' (2016) 67 *Ecological Indicators* 533.

Hay, J and Mimura, N, 'The Changing Nature of Extreme Weather and Climate Events: Risks to Sustainable Development' (2010) 1 *Geomatics, Natural Hazards and Risk* 3.

Hederos, K et al, 'Trends in Life Expectancy by Income and the Role of Specific Causes of Death' (2018) 85 *Economica* 606.

Heerink, N, Malatu, A and Bulte, E, 'Income Inequality and the Environment: Aggregation Bias in Environmental Kuznets Curves' (2001) 38 *Ecological Economics* 359.

Herzog, L, 'The Normative Stakes of Economic Growth; Or, Why Adam Smith Does Not Rely on "Trickle Down" ' (2015) 78 *Journal of Politics* 50.

Huang, J, 'Income Inequality, Distributive Justice Beliefs, and Happiness in China: Evidence from a Nationwide Survey' (2018) 137 *Social Indicators Research* 1.

Iacoviello, M, 'Household Debt and Income Inequality, 1963–2003' (2008) 40 *Journal of Money, Credit and Banking* 929.

ILC, *Report on the Work of the International Law Commission: Sixty-Seventh Session*, UN Document A/70/10 (2015).

ILO and OECD (with contributions from the IMF and the WBG), 'The Labour Share in G20 Economies' (Report prepared for the G20 Employment Working Group, 26–27 February 2015) <https://www.oecd.org/g20/topics/employment-and-social-policy/The-Labour-Share-in-G20-Economies.pdf>.

Jackson, JH, 'Sovereignty: Outdated Concept or New Approaches' in Shan, W, Simons, P and Singh, D (eds), *Redefining Sovereignty in International Economic Law* (Hart Publishing, Portland OR 2008).

Jackson, JH, 'Sovereignty—Modern: A New Approach to an Outdated Concept' (2003) 97 *American Journal of International Law* 782.

Jaeckel, A, 'Intellectual Property Rights and the Conservation of Plant Biodiversity as a Common Concern of Humankind' (2013) 2 *Transnational Environmental Law* 167.

Jamieson, D, 'The Nature of the Problem' in Dryzek, JS, Norgaard, RB and Schlosberg, D, *Oxford Handbook of Climate Change and Society* (OUP, New York 2011).

Johnson, DB, 'Wealth is Value' (1986) 15 *Journal of Legal Studies* 263).

Jorgenson, AK et al, 'Income Inequality and Residential Carbon Emissions in the United States: A Preliminary Analysis' (2015) 22 *Human Ecology Review* 93.

Jorgenson, AK et al, 'Domestic Inequality and Carbon Emissions in Comparative Perspective' (2016) 31 *Sociological Forum* 770.

Jorgenson, AK, Schor, JB and Huang, X, 'Income Inequality and Carbon Emissions in the United States: A State-level Analysis, 19972012' (2017) 134 *Ecological Economics* 40.

Kahan, DM, 'The Logic of Reciprocity: Trust, Collective Action, and Law' (2003) 102 *Michigan Law Review* 71.

Kaldor, N, 'A Model for Economic Growth' (1957) 67 *Economic Journal* 591.

Kalwij, A and Verschoor, A, 'Not by Growth Alone: The Role of the Distribution of Income in Regional Diversity in Poverty Reduction' (2007) 51 *European Economic Review* 805.

Kapstein, EB, 'Distributive Justice as an International Public Good' in Kaul, I, Grunberg, I and Stern, MA (eds), *Global Public Goods: International Cooperation in the 21st Century* (OUP, New York 1999).

Kaulihowa, T and Adjasi, C, 'FDI and Income Inequality in Africa' (2017) *Oxford Development Studies* (*online*) <10.1080/13600818.2017.1381233>.

Keen, M and Konrad, K, 'The Theory of International Tax Competition and Coordination' in Alan J Auerbach et al (eds), *Handbook of Public Economics* (Vol 5, Elsevier, Amsterdam 2013).

Kennedy, T et al, 'Does Income Inequality Hinder Economic Growth? New Evidence Using Australian Taxation Statistics' (2017) 65 *Economic Modelling* 119.

Kim, D et al, 'Is Inequality at the Heart of It? Cross-country Associations of Income Inequality with Cardiovascular Diseases and Risk Factors' (2008) 66 *Social Sciences & Medicine* 1719.

Korinek, A and Stiglitz, JE, 'Artificial Intelligence and Its Implications for Income Distribution and Unemployment' (NBER Working Paper 24174, December 2017) <https://www.nber.org/papers/w24174>.

Knight, KW, Schor, JB and Jorgenson, AK, 'Wealth Inequality and Carbon Emissions in High Income Countries' (2017) 4 *Social Currents* 403.

Krieger, T and Meierrieks, D, 'Income Inequality, Redistribution and Domestic Terrorism' (2019) 116 *World Development* 125.

Kronman, AT, 'Wealth Maximization as a Normative Principle' (1980) 9 *Journal of Legal Studies* 227.

Kurz, M, 'On the Formation of Capital and Wealth: IT, Monopoly Power and Rising Inequality' (2016) <https://papers.ssrn.com/sol3/papers.cfm?abstract_id=3014361>.

Kuznets, S, 'Economic Growth and Income Inequality' (1955) 45 *American Economic Review* 1.

Lowe, AW, 'Sovereignty and International Economic Law' in Wenhua Shan, Penelope Simons, and Dalvinder Singh (eds), *Redefining Sovereignty in International Economic Law* (Hart Publishing, Portland OR 2008).

Lowe, AW, 'The Problems of Extraterritorial Jurisdiction: Economic Sovereignty and the Search for a Solution' (1985) 34 *International and Comparative Law Quarterly* 724.

Lupo-Pasini, F, 'Financial Stability as a Common Concern of Humankind' in Cottier, T (ed), *The Prospects of Common Concern of Humankind in International Law* (CUP, Cambridge 2021).

Mah, JS, 'Foreign Direct Investment, Labour Unionization and Income Inequality of Korea (2012) 19 *Applied Economics Letters* 1521.

Marshall, A, 'Fragments' in Pigou, AC (ed), *Memorials of Alfred Marshall* (MacMillan, London 1925).

Mason, JW, 'Income Distribution, Household Debt, and Aggregate Demand: A Critical Assessment' (Levy Economics Institute Working Paper 901, March 2018).

McGinnis, JO and Somin, I, 'Should International Law be Part of Our Law?' (2007) 59 *Stanford Law Review* 1175.

Metz, N and Burdina, M, 'Neighbourhood income inequality and property crime' (2018) 55 *Urban Studies* 130.

Milanovic, B, 'Global Income Inequality in Numbers: in History and Now' (2013) 4 *Global Policy* 198.

Muchlinski, PT, 'Corporations in International Law' in *Max Planck Encyclopaedia of International Law* (OUP online, June 2014).

Mueller, HM, Ouimet, PP and Simintzi, E, 'Wage Inequality and Firm Growth' (2017) 107 *American Economic Review* 379.

Murase, S (Special Rapporteur), *Second Report on the Protection of the Atmosphere*, UN Document A/CN.4/681 (2015).

Musgrave, RA, 'Horizontal Equity, Once More' (1990) 43 *National Tax Journal* 113.

National Academies of Sciences, Engineering, and Medicine, *The Growing Gap in Life Expectancy by Income: Implications for Federal Programs and Policy Responses* (National Academies, Washington, DC 2015).

Nicodème, G, 'Corporate Tax Competition and Coordination in the European Union: What Do We Know? Where Do We Stand?' (European Economy, European Commission Directorate-General for Economic and Financial Affairs, No 250, June 2006) <https://ec.europa.eu/economy_finance/publications/pages/publication718_en.pdf>.

Nieuwenhuis, R, van der Kolk, H and Need, A, 'Women's Earnings and Household Inequality in OECD Countries, 1973–2013' (2017) 60 *Acta Sociologica* 3.

Nullmeier, F and Kaufmann, F-X, 'Post-War Welfare State Development' in Castles, FG et al (eds), *The Oxford Handbook of the Welfare State* (OUP, Oxford 2012).

O'Donnell, O, Van Doorslaer, E and Van Ourti, T, 'Health and Inequality' in Atkinson, AB and Bourguignon, F (eds), *Handbook of Income Distribution* (*Volume 2B*) (Elsevier, Amsterdam 2015).

OECD, 'Hybrid Mismatch Arrangements: Tax Policy and Compliance Issues' (Report published under the auspices of the Secretary-General of the OECD, March 2012).

Østby, G, 'Polarization, Horizontal Inequalities and Violent Civil Conflict' (2008) 45 *Journal of Peace Research* 123.

Ostry, JD, Berg, AG and Tsangarides, CG, 'Redistribución, Desigualdad y Crecimiento' (2014) 16 *Revista de Economía Institucional* 30.

Padhan, H et al, 'What Matters for Environmental Quality in the Next-11 Countries: Economic Growth or Income Inequality?' (IZA Institute of Labor Economics Working Paper 11407, March 2018).

Palma, JG, 'Homogeneous Middles vs. Heterogeneous Tails, and the End of the "Inverted-U": It's All About the Share of the Rich' (2011) 42 *Development and Change* 87.

Palma, JG, 'Has the Income Share of the Middle and Upper-middle Been Stable around the "50/50 Rule", or Has it Converged towards that Level? The "Palma Ratio" Revisited' (2014) 45 *Development and Change* 1416.

Patel, V et al, 'Income Inequality and Depression: A Systematic Review and Meta-analysis of the Association and a Scoping Review of Mechanisms' (2018) 17 *World Psychiatry* 76.

Persson, T and Tabellini, G, 'Is Inequality Harmful for Growth?' (1994) 84 *American Economic Review* 600.

Pickett, KE and Wilkinson, RG, 'Income Inequality and Health: A Causal Review' (2015) 128 *Social Science & Medicine* 316.

Piketty, T and Saez, E, 'Income Inequality in the United States, 19131918' (2003) 118 *Quarterly Journal of Economics* 1.

Piketty, T, Saez, E and Zucman, G, 'Distributional National Accounts: Methods and Estimates for the United States' (2018) 133 *Quarterly Journal of Economics* 553.

Pleuger, G, 'United Nations, Millennium Declaration' in *Max Planck Encyclopaedia of International Law* (OUP online, March 2007).

Ponthieux, S and Meurs, D, 'Gender Inequality' in Atkinson, AB and Bourguignon, F (eds), *Handbook of Income Distribution (Volume 2A)* (Elsevier, Amsterdam 2015).

Posner, RA, 'Utilitarianism, Economics, and Legal Theory' (1979) 8 *Journal of Legal Studies* 103.

Posner, RA, 'The Value of Wealth: A Comment on Dworkin and Kronman' (1980) 9 *Journal of Legal Studies* 243.

Posner, RA, 'The Ethical and Political Basis of the Efficiency Norm in Common Law Adjudication' (1980) 8 *Hofstra Law Review* 487.

Rao, JM, 'Equity in a Global Public Goods Framework' in Kaul, I, Grunberg, I and Stern, MA (eds), *Global Public Goods: International Cooperation in the 21st Century* (OUP, New York 1999) 68.

Rathbun, BC, 'Trust in International Relations' in Uslaner, EM (ed), *The Oxford Handbook on Social and Political Trust* (Oxford University Press, Oxford 2018).

Ravallion, M, 'Inequality and Globalization: A Review Essay' (2018) 56 *Journal of Economic Literature* 620.

Ravallion, M, 'Why Don't We See Poverty Convergence?' (2012) 102 *American Economic Review* 504.

Ravallion, M, Heil, M and Jalan, J, 'Carbon Emissions and Income Inequality' (2000) 52 *Oxford Economics Papers* 651.

Reardon, SF, 'The Widening Academic Achievement Gap between the Rich and the Poor: New Evidence and Possible Explanations' in Duncan, GJ, and Murnane, RJ (eds), *Whither Opportunity? Rising Inequality, Schools, and Children's Life Chances* (Russell Sage Foundation, New York 2011) 91.

Reyes, G and Gasparini, L, 'Perceptions of Distributive Justice in Latin America during a Period of Falling Inequality' (World Bank Policy Research Working Paper 8072, May 2017).

Ribeiro, WS et al, 'Income Inequality and Mental Illness-related Morbidity and Resilience: A Systematic Review and Meta-analysis' (2017) 4 *Lancet Psychiatry* 554.

Rinz, K and Voorheis, J, 'The Distributional Effects of Minimum Wages: Evidence from Linked Survey and Administrative Data' (Center for Administrative Records Research and Applications (CARRA) Working Paper 2018-02, March 2018) <https://www.census.gov/content/dam/Census/library/workingpapers/2018/adrm/carra-wp-2018-02.pdf>.

Rixen, T, 'Institutional Reform of Global Tax Governance: A Proposal' in Peter Dietsch and Thomas Rixen (eds), *Global Tax Governance: What is Wrong with it and How to Fix It* (ECPR Press, Colchester 2016).

Rixen, T, 'Tax Competition and Inequality: The Case for Global Tax Governance' (2011) 17 *Global Governance* 447.

Rizzo, R, 'The Mirage of Efficiency' (1980) 8 *Hofstra Law Review* 641.

Rodrik, D, 'Is Global Equality the Enemy of National Equality?' (online working paper, January 2017) <https://drodrik.scholar.harvard.edu/files/dani-rodrik/files/is_global_equality_the_enemy_of_national_equality.pdf>.

Rosenbaum, SM et al, 'Income Inequality and Cooperative Propensities in Developing Economies: Summarizing the Preliminary Experimental Evidence' (2016) 43 *International Journal of Social Economics* 1460.

Rousseau, J-J, *The Social Contract* (OUP, New York 1994).

Ruggie, JG, 'Multinationals as Global Institution: Power, Authority and Relative Autonomy' (2018) 12 *Regulation & Governance* 317.

Sacerdoti, G, 'New International Economic Order (NIEO)' in *Max Planck Encyclopaedia of International Law* (OUP online, September 2015.

Saez, E, and Zucman, G, 'Wealth Inequality in the United States since 1913: Evidence from Capitalized Income Tax Data' (2016) 131 *Quarterly Journal of Economics* 519.

Samuelson, PA, 'A Pure Theory of Public Expenditure' (1954) 36 *Review of Economics and Statistics* 387.

Sandmo, A, 'The Principal Problem in Political Economy: Income Distribution in the History of Thought' in Atkinson, AB and Bourguignon, F (eds), *Handbook of Income Distribution (Volume 2A)* (Elsevier, Amsterdam 2015).

Sarooshi, D, 'The Essentially Contested Nature of the Concept of Sovereignty: Implications for the Exercise by International Organizations of Delegated Powers of Government' (2004) 25 *Michigan Journal of International Law* 1107.

Satragno, L, 'International Monetary Stability as a Common Concern of Humankind' in Cottier, T (ed), *The Prospects of Common Concern of Humankind in International Law* (CUP, Cambridge 2021).

Schäli, J, 'Intergenerational Justice and the Concept of Common Concern in Marine Resource Allocation and Ocean Governance' in Cottier, T, Lalani, S and Siziba, C, *Intergenerational Equity: Environmental and Cultural Concerns* (Brill | Nijhoff, Leiden 2019).

Schäli, J, 'Marine Plastic Pollution as a Common Concern of Humankind' in Cottier, T, (ed), *The Prospects of Common Concern of Humankind in International Law* (CUP, Cambridge 2021).

Schoenblum, JA, 'Tax Fairness or Unfairness? A Consideration of the Philosophical Bases for Unequal Taxation of Individuals' (1995) 12 *American Journal of Tax Policy* 221.

Shaffer, G, 'Retooling Trade Agreements for Social Inclusion' (2019) 1 *Illinois Law Review* 1.

Shelton, D, 'Common Concern of Humanity' (2009) 5 Iustum Aequum Salutare 33.

Soltau, F, 'Common Concern of Humankind' in Cinnamon P Carlane, Kevin R Gray and Richard G Tarasofsky (eds), *The Oxford Handbook of International Climate Change Law* (OUP, New York 2016).

Stec, S, 'Humanitarian Limits to Sovereignty: Common Concern and Common Heritage Approaches to Natural Resources and Environment' (2010) 12 *International Community Law Review* 361.

Stewart, F, 'Crisis Prevention: Tackling Horizontal Inequalities' (2000) 23 *Oxford Development Studies* 245.

Stewart, F, 'Horizontal Inequalities and Conflict: An Introduction and Some Hypotheses' in Stewart, F (ed), *Horizontal Inequalities and Conflict: Understanding Group Violence in Multiethnic Societies* (Palgrave Macmillan, Basingstoke 2008).

Stewart, F, Brown, GK and Langer, A, 'Major Findings and Conclusions on the Relationship Between Horizontal Inequalities and Conflict' in Stewart, F (ed), *Horizontal Inequalities and Conflict: Understanding Group Violence in Multiethnic Societies* (Palgrave Macmillan, Basingstoke 2008).

Thurow, LC, 'The Income Distribution as a Pure Public Good' (1971) 85 *Quarterly Journal of Economics* 327.

Tolba, MK, 'The Implications of the "Common Concern of Mankind Concept" on Global Environmental Issues' (1991) 13 *Revista IIDH* 237.

Tørsløv, T, Wier, L and Zucman, G, 'The Missing Profits of Nations' (NBER Working Paper 24701, 2) <http://gabriel-zucman.eu/files/TWZ2018.pdf>.

Votaw, D, 'Genius Becomes Rare: A Comment on the Doctrine of Social Responsibility Pt. 1' (1972) 15 *California Management Review* 25.

Votaw, D, 'The Mythology of Corporations' (1962) 4 *California Management Review* 58.

Levin-Waldman, OM and Lerman, P, 'Is the Minimum Wage an Effective Response to Income Inequality?' (2017) 60 *Challenge* 574.

Weart, S, 'The Development of the Concept of Dangerous Anthropogenic Climate Change' in John S Dryzek, Richard B Norgaard and David Schlosberg, *Oxford Handbook of Climate Change and Society* (OUP, New York 2011).

Wier, L and Reynolds, H, 'Big and "Unprofitable": How 10% of Multinational Firms Do 98% of the Profit Shifting' (WIDER Working Paper 2018/111) <https://sa-tied.wider.unu.edu/sites/default/files/pdf/WP-24-Decmber-2018-WierReynolds.pdf>.

Wolff, EN, 'Household Wealth Trends in The United States, 1962 to 2016: Has Middle Class Wealth Recovered?' (NBER Working Paper, No 24085, November 2017) <https://www.nber.org/papers/w24085>.

Wu, X, 'Foreign Direct Investment and Income Inequality' in Fung, H-G, Changhong, P and Zhang, KH, *China and the Challenge of Economic Globalization: The Impact of WTO Membership* (Routledge, New York 2006) 61.

Yang, Z, Wu, S and Cheung, HY, 'From Income and Housing Wealth Inequalities to Emissions Inequality: Carbon Emissions of Households in China' (2017) 32 *Journal of Housing and the Built Environment* 231.

Yodanis, C, and Lauer, S, 'Economic Inequality in and outside of Marriage: Individual Resources and Institutional Context' (2007) 5 *European Sociological Review* 573; and.

Zucman, G, 'Global Wealth Inequality' (2019) 11 *Annual Review of Economics* 109.

All Other Websites Cited in this Monograph (All Online Materials Last Accessed 30 September 2021)

Airbus SAS, 'Worldwide presence: At home around the world' <https://www.airbus.com/company/worldwide-presence.html>.

The Boeing Company, 'Boeing's U.S. Footprint' (The Boeing Company Website) <https://www.boeing.com/company/general-info/#/global>.

Economic Policy Institute, 'Union Decline and Rising Inequality in Two Charts' (Working Economics Blog) <https://www.epi.org/blog/union-decline-rising-inequality-charts/>.

The Economist, 'Business in America: Too Much of a Good Thing' (26 March 2016) <https://www.economist.com/briefing/2016/03/26/too-much-of-a-good-thing>.

Gates, B, 'Why Inequality Matters' (online blog post, 13 October 2014) <https://www.gatesnotes.com/Books/Why-Inequality-Matters-Capital-in-21st-Century-Review>.

Obama, B, 'Remarks at the Town Hall Education Arts Recreation Campus' (4 December 2013) <http://www.presidency.ucsb.edu/ws/index.php?pid=104522&st=&st1=>.

Piketty, T, 'Clamping down with law and order will not be enough' (*Le Monde* blog, 24 November 2015) <http://piketty.blog.lemonde.fr/2015/11/24/clamping-down-with-law-and-order-will-not-be-enough/>.

President of the United States (2017: Trump), 'Economic Report of the President: Transmitted to the Congress; Together with the Annual Report of the Council of Economic Advisors' (February 2018) <https://www.whitehouse.gov/wp-content/uploads/2018/02/ERP_2018_Final-FINAL.pdf>.

Qureshi, Z, 'Today's Economic Puzzles: A Tale of Weakening Competition' (Brookings Institute, April 2018) <https://www.brookings.edu/blog/up-front/2018/04/05/todays-economic-puzzles-a-tale-of-weakening-competition/>.

SEC, 'EXHIBIT (21)—List of Company Subsidiaries The Boeing Company and Subsidiaries'<https://www.sec.gov/Archives/edgar/data/12927/000119312505038602/dex21.htm>.

Simpson, J (ed), 'Oxford English Dictionary Online' (OUP online).

Statistics Canada, 'The Fall and Rise of Canada's Top Income Earners' (last modified on 17 May 2018) <https://www150.statcan.gc.ca/n1/pub/11-630-x/11-630-x2016009-eng.htm>.

Steinbaum, M, 'Why Are Economists Giving Piketty the Cold Shoulder?' Boston Review (online, 12 May 2017) <https://bostonreview.net/class-inequality/marshall-steinbaum-why-are-economists-giving-piketty-cold-shoulder>.

United Nations Office on Counter-Terrorism, 'International Legal Instruments' <http://www.un.org/en/counterterrorism/legal-instruments.shtml>.

United States Bureau of Economic Analysis, 'Corporate Profits after Tax (without IVA and CCAdj) [CP]' (Figure created by Federal Reserve Bank of St Louis) <https://fred.stlouisfed.org/series/CP, July 18, 2018>.

Table of Materials

Table of Treaties and Related Instruments

Charter of the United Nations (adopted 26 June 1945, entered into force 24 October 1945).

Paris Agreement (adopted 12 December 2015, entered into force 4 November 2016) I54113 UNTC 1.

United Nations Convention to Combat Desertification in those Countries Experiencing Serious Drought and/or Desertification, Particularly in Africa (adopted 14 October 1994, entered into force 26 December 1996) 1954 UNTS 3.

United Nations Framework Convention on Climate Change (adopted 9 May 1992, entered into force 21 March 1994) 1771 UNTS 107.

Table of Other Primary Legal Sources

United Nations General Assembly Resolution A/RES/70/1 (21 October 2015) with the title 'Transforming our World: the 2030 Agenda for Sustainable Development'.

United Nations General Assembly Resolution 43/53 (27 January 1989) with the title 'Protection of Global Climate for Present and Future Generations'.

Index

www.ingramcontent.com/pod-product-compliance
Lightning Source LLC
LaVergne TN
LVHW010545300926
849162LV00002B/237